CULTURE, CIVILIZATION AND HUMANITY

CULTURE, CIVILIZATION
and
HUMANITY

TAREK HEGGY

FRANK CASS
LONDON • PORTLAND, OR

First published in 2003 in Great Britain by
FRANK CASS PUBLISHERS
Crown House, 47 Chase Side, Southgate
London N14 5BP

and in the United States of America by
FRANK CASS PUBLISHERS
c/o ISBS, 920 NE 58th Avenue
Suite 300, Portland, Oregon, 97213-3786

Website: www.frankcass.com

British Library Cataloguing in Publication Data:

Heggy, Tarek
Culture, civilization and humanity
1. Egyptians – Attitudes 2. Socialism 3. Progress 4. Egypt –
Civilization – 20th century 5. Egypt – Social conditions –
1970–1981 6. Egypt – Social conditions – 1981–
I. Title
962'.055

ISBN 0-7146-5554-6 (cloth)
ISSN 0-7146-8434-1 (paper)

Library of Congress Cataloging-in-Publication Data

Hajji, Tariq Ahmad.
   [Selections. English]
   Culture, civilization, and humanity/Tarek Heggy.
     p. cm.
   Selected and translated from the original Arabic by the author.
   Includes bibliographical references and index.
     1. Egypt–Civilization–1798– 2. National characteristics, Egyptian.
   3. Egypt–Cultural policy. 4. Globalization. 5. Communism. I. Title.

DT107.826.H34213 2003
962.05–dc221   2003048960

Typeset in 11/13 pt Sabon by Cambridge Photosetting Services
Printed in Great Britain by MPG Books Ltd, Bodmin, Cornwall

*To Nayera
and to our daughters
Marwa and May*

Contents

Part I

Essays on the Values of Progress

'The wicked walk on every side when the violent men are exalted.'

Psalm 12

'Never have I seen worse human defect
Than that of people who can, but do not, perfect.'

Al-Mutannabi

Introduction: The English Edition

The aim of Part I of this book is to prove the existence of three intellectual horizons: 'the horizon of cultures', above it 'the horizon of civilizations' and above both 'the horizon of humanity'. The last (and highest) comprises the accumulated products of the entire march of mankind on earth. This part endeavours to provide solid evidence that 'progress' is a product of the 'horizon of humanity'. This implies that in any culture and/or civilization progress could be realized if a certain set of values were adopted by the leading echelons of the society. Without the engagement of these leading echelons in a visionary process of seeding these values in the minds and consciences of the society members through every possible mechanism, 'progress' remains far from being achieved.

Tarek Heggy

Prelude

Part I addresses a subject I believe is better suited than any other to launch a constructive intellectual debate in Egypt today, and one that can, moreover, serve as a rallying point for all intellectuals, whatever their ideological formation.

The philosophical premise from which I proceed is that there exist three frames of reference operating at different levels: humanity, civilization and culture. Civilizations occupy a higher plane than cultures, while humanity occupies a higher plane than both. As such, it can transcend any clash of civilizations or cultures.

Although all the ideas contained here are concerned with the wider notion of humanity, they can serve at the same time to steer the relationship between civilizations on the road towards dialogue, rather than allow it to be swept, by a breakdown of communication between them, on to the road of conflict and collision. If, as Sartre said, the future is what we make it in the kitchen of the present, the answer to whether we can expect a dialogue between civilizations or a clash of civilizations in future depends on what we do today. Thus the future pattern of interaction between civilizations can be dialogue if we make an effort in the present to steer matters in that direction. Alternatively, a pattern of clashes between civilizations can well become the norm if relations between them are left to drift by inertia on a collision course without a serious attempt in the present to open up proper channels of communication and dialogue.

Tarek Heggy
December 2001

CHAPTER 1

Some Basic Remarks About the Values of Progress

Towards the end of 2000, the American University in Cairo invited me to speak on the nature of the educational reforms I wanted to see introduced in Egypt. In my lecture, which I delivered in the university's Greek Campus, I spoke extensively about the difference between a 'qualitative' change in an educational system and a 'quantitative' change. I said we had paid scant attention to the former because our educational philosophy continues to be based on the rote system and memory tests rather than on promoting creativity and dialogue (as opposed to monologue). Education is seen not as an interactive process, but as a one-way street in which the teacher is a 'transmitter' of knowledge and the student a passive 'receiver' of that knowledge.

In the first quarter of 2001, I was invited by Princeton and Columbia Universities on the East Coast of the USA and the University of California at Berkeley on the West Coast to deliver a series of lectures to postgraduate students in Middle Eastern studies. In my lectures, I stressed the need for an educational revolution in the region if we want a scenario of peace (real peace based on international legitimacy and the principles of international law) and comprehensive development (economic, cultural and social) to prevail. For all its complexity, such a revolution would be based essentially on a simple philosophy of instilling in students a set of values that I call 'values of progress'.

Since August 2001, I have devoted much of my time to developing this idea further. In a way, my interest in promoting the notion of values of progress provided an outlet for the frustration I felt at the way public debate in our society tends to degenerate into private squabbles. Any topic can spark off a furious controversy: Muhammad Ali, Taha Hussein, Gamal Abdel Nasser, Anwar Sadat, secularism, enlightenment, modernity, globalization or peace in the Middle East are equally divisive, splitting people across seemingly unbridgeable ideological chasms and entrenching them still further in their respective closed systems. The rules of rational and objective debate are spurned in favour of a dialogue of the deaf, in which the protagonists engage in mutual recriminations and insults, heaping abuse and accusations against one another.

When I began looking for a subject that would not polarize society, or at least polarize it less sharply than has been the case with most topics, the only one that seemed to fit the bill was the notion of values of progress, which I had touched upon earlier in several articles and lectures. Not a subject that can split society into opposing camps – Islamists versus non-Islamists, socialists versus capitalists – it is to a large extent non-ideological and, as such, lends itself to an objective and neutral debate that need not descend into the usual pattern of dogmatic intransigence.

Perhaps this was wishful thinking on my part, a scenario that is closer to fantasy than to reality. But rigid patterns can be broken only by those who have the capacity to dream and the gift of imagination. With this in mind, some schools of modern management require senior managers to exhibit two concomitant characteristics that at first glance may seem contradictory: the power of imagination on the one hand and a sense of reality on the other. In actual fact, however, these characteristics are not mutually exclusive and are often present at one and the same time in ordinary people. It is these individuals who make successful senior managers. I hope my dream that intellectuals and public opinion in Egypt today can deal with the subject of values of progress in a manner free of factionalism and preconception will see the light of day. I hope it strikes the proper balance between the power of the imagination and a sense of reality, otherwise it will be nothing more than an exercise in escapism, a mirage to which I turned out of a deep sense of despair at the inhospitable climate for any reasoned and objective debate in our society today, where name-calling and stone-throwing have replaced logical argument.

A discussion of the values of progress must at the outset address a problematic that no intellectual can afford to ignore: will democracy lead to the spread of the values of progress as defined here, or can these values, even in an environment with a modest margin of democracy, create a general climate that could gradually expand this margin and transform it into full-fledged democracy? I asked myself whether it was possible to come forward with such a discussion when some could justifiably question the feasibility of disseminating such values in the context of a margin of democracy that may be growing but is still extremely narrow. These concerns nearly made me discard the manuscript and place it in the file of other writings whose publication is indefinitely postponed. This file is more voluminous than the file of my published works, although the latter comprises thousands of pages. But I decided to push ahead with publication when, purely by chance, I came across a number of studies on the experiences of ten countries in Southeast Asia and Latin America. Although as recently as ten years ago these countries had not made their economic breakthrough, did not enjoy democracy and had not adopted the values of progress, in the last decade they have become relatively rich in all three elements.

Like many others, I was familiar with the amazing progress achieved by all ten countries in a relatively short period, but finding these in-depth studies explaining the process was a timely eye-opener. According to the studies, while certain societies had made their breakthroughs in the context of open democracy, which served as the framework in which their economic, scientific, educational, cultural and social development unfolded, others, like the case models addressed by the study, had made theirs in a different context. Instead of a slow and gradual development achieved over centuries, as with the case of Europe, the countries of Southeast Asia and Latin America took a short cut to development, making their great leap forward on the backs of two engines. The first was a human cadre of executive leaders who both embodied the values of progress and imposed them on society at large. The second was a radical reform of the educational system and the establishment of a new system based on the values of progress. The first engine served the requirements of development in the short and medium terms, the second in the long term. This two-pronged approach, based on leadership, example and creative education, laid the groundwork for the spread of the values of progress and created a general climate conducive to a dynamic and fruitful social mobility, leading to the emergence of a broad-based middle class standing on a solid cultural and economic foundation.

Parallel with this was a determined effort by the thriving countries of Southeast Asia and Latin America to expand the margin of democracy. Their experience stands as an eloquent rebuttal of the argument that democracy takes centuries to develop and that some countries are simply not equipped to live by the rules of real and open democracy. This argument can be accepted only by the advocates – and beneficiaries – of oppression. Those who believe in democracy as the greatest achievement of humanity must constantly strive to find formulas by which it can be established within the shortest possible time-frame, while at the same time laying down frameworks and mechanisms to ensure that the democratic process is not abused by the enemies of democracy and used as a means of acquiring, and hanging indefinitely on to, power. The successful experiments of the ten countries in Southeast Asia and Latin America prove that we must not allow ourselves to be discouraged from planting the values of progress in our soil under the pretext that it is not ready to receive them.

Finally, despite its title, Part I covers not all the values of progress but only those the author believes to be the most important among them. The list is far from exhaustive, and others may wish to add values they consider to have been overlooked. In the final analysis, the purpose of Part I is to open a debate around the values that can bring about development and progress, not to claim that it is the ultimate authority on what those values are.

CHAPTER 2

The Most Important Values of Progress

An issue that has sparked an animated debate in our part of the world is the discrepancy between the value attached to time by citizens of advanced societies and its value for our citizens. Commentators offer different explanations for the phenomenon, the majority attributing the importance of time in advanced societies to the higher levels of discipline and organization displayed by the citizens of those societies. But this superficial view only skims the surface of a much deeper problem. The more discerning and insightful commentators realize that the issue is symptomatic of a more complex problem in which discipline, organization and punctuality are but manifestations of a profound difference in understanding, evaluating and appreciating time itself. In the more advanced societies, time is the framework in which plans are made and executed, projects are designed and launched – in fact, it is the framework for everything: ideas, projects, plans, programmes and reform movements as well as economic, scientific, educational, cultural and social development. Anyone who is not aware of the value of the framework is necessarily unaware of the value of anything that framework can encompass.

Strangely enough, there is a widespread belief in our society that venerating time, meeting deadlines and showing up for meetings at the appointed time is a question of temperament, an innate quality that one is either born with or not. This is a totally erroneous assumption. A well-developed sense that time must be respected, appointments punctiliously observed and deadlines met, that all ideas, projects, plans and programmes must be set within specific time-frames and that a cavalier attitude towards time and appointments detracts from a person's credibility, authority and, ultimately, his effectiveness, has nothing to do with temperament. It is not an individual's genetic makeup that determines his attitude to time, but the general cultural climate prevailing in the society to which he belongs.

Unfortunately, promptness and punctuality are regarded in our society as idiosyncrasies displayed by an eccentric few who just happened to be born with a natural disposition to stick to schedules, in contradistinction to the laid-back attitude displayed by the vast majority of their fellow countrymen.

And here we come to the crux of the matter. The measure of any society's development and progress lies not in the wealth of which it disposes or the natural resources that it harbours but in the value system to which its citizens subscribe, the mores by which the entire community, from the base to the summit, is governed. The most important of these values are a respect for time, a strong work ethic, a belief in the effectiveness of teamwork, an emphasis on developing human resources, the adoption of an educational system based on promoting initiative and creativity rather than on teaching by rote, fostering a spirit of perseverance and encouraging people to strive for excellence, instilling the notion of universality of knowledge in young minds, and, finally, promoting a spirit of healthy competition from the very start of the educational process.

Once this value system is in place, progress can be made. In its absence, or in the context of a value system that runs counter to these basic principles, a society is doomed to remain locked in backwardness. Rather than admit their own responsibility for the rut in which they find themselves, these societies tend to attribute their inability to move forward either to factors beyond their control, such as a lack of resources, or to external factors, such as a conspiracy hatched against them by foreign interests. Such self-delusion only serves to reinforce the negative features of their society, for it is only by admitting to themselves that what holds them back is their own crippling inertia, their own lack of drive, that they can hope to break the vicious cycle of backwardness.

Venerating time and placing all human, institutional and

social activities within its framework is not simply a personal idiosyncrasy or an innate virtue enjoyed by some and not others; it is what distinguishes between two value systems: one that responds to the requirements of the age and another that derives either from the antiquated cultural traditions of a primitive agricultural society or from a Bedouin culture. Students of the development of values in general and the values of progress in particular know that time did not acquire its high value, its status as the dividing line between progress and underdevelopment, until the advent of the Industrial Revolution. It was this watershed event that imposed a new understanding and appreciation of the importance and value of time and the need to observe it rigorously. Nowhere is the respect for time more graphically illustrated than in Switzerland, where trains run on schedules measured not in hours, or even minutes, but in seconds, in what is surely the highest possible expression of industrial values and the values of a service society. The Information Revolution and the requirements of the age of technology have further enhanced the value of time, which has come to be venerated with an almost religious fervour by those who believe it is the key to progress.

The value system of any society can be enriched with progressive values inculcated in the collective conscience by examples set by those at the summit of the societal pyramid. Conversely, if those expected to set an example fail to uphold the required values, including a respect for time, then it is virtually impossible for those at the base of the pyramid to take on such values as part of their cultural baggage. The influence of the upper echelons of society on the behavioural patterns of that society is recognized by the folk wisdom of all cultures. It is a theme that appears in several Arabic proverbs, such as 'people follow the religion of their king', 'a fish begins to putrefy at its head', 'it is the shepherd who guides the flock', and many more. In other words, if the values conducive to progress, including, of course, a well-developed sense of time, are not promoted by those holding positions of authority, such as senior public officials, cabinet ministers and economic and business leaders, they will never become part of the reference system of society. These values can be disseminated only from the top of the societal pyramid to its base and not the other way round, as those at the base have neither the clout nor the channels through which to impose their values as examples to be followed by society at large.

In the decade during which I served as CEO of one of the largest economic corporations in the world, with thousands of highly qualified employees drawn from some 20 countries working under my direction, I was able to ascertain at first hand the existence of a direct link between high levels of performance and a strict observance of time, an almost mystical belief in the importance of punctuality and of completing work assignments within the designated time-frame. Nor did this apply only to staff members. It was also true of the thousands of high-ranking political and economic personalities I met by virtue of my office: the more punctilious they were about keeping appointments and adhering strictly to schedule, the higher their level of competence and performance – and the more intolerant they were of those who did not attach the same high priority to the time factor.

The nature of my job, which entailed doing business with people from different cultural backgrounds, made me realize that the whole concept of time varied from one culture to another. There were occasions, for example, when I had to terminate a contract for hundreds of millions of dollars because the other party had defaulted on its obligation to complete execution within an agreed deadline. If the defaulting party happened to be from the Third World, the decision would be derisively dismissed as an over-reaction to a trivial matter, and accepted with resignation, if not good grace, when the other party happened to be from the West or from Southeast Asia, where termination is seen as the only possible response to a failure to meet agreed deadlines.

The different reactions to the example I have chosen to give reflect the very different appreciations of time between one culture and another. For Third World societies, time is of such little value that taking a person to task for being late for an appointment or penalizing a contractor for failing to deliver works by an agreed date is regarded with genuine surprise. In fact, being late has become a symbol of personal worth, a validation of one's importance in the scheme of things. After all, important people are so busy that they are entitled to be late, and whoever is lucky enough to be granted a slice of their valuable time must understand that waiting is par for the course. This phenomenon is turned on its head in advanced societies, where people running huge enterprises with budgets greater than the combined economies of all the Arab countries pride themselves on never being late for an appointment or running over schedule. In fact, they consider themselves in a constant race against time, often striving not only to meet agreed deadlines, but to beat them.

I have learned from experience that a lack of respect for time, whether it takes the form of showing up late for appointments or not completing assignments and projects within the agreed time-frames, condemns the individual, company or institution displaying this aberrant form of behaviour to failure, not only in the sphere of business but in all aspects of life. Any exception or willingness to condone exceptions is seen as running counter to science, progress and the movement of history in advanced societies. There is a big difference between punctuality motivated by fear, which is sometimes the case in Third World countries, and punctuality as a way of life, the natural expression of an ingrained sense of the importance of time and a recognition that unless schedules are rigorously observed and time-frames respected, there can be no progress, which is the case in advanced societies.

In Third World countries, members of parliament are invariably late for meetings of the legislative assembly, which are usually chaotic affairs with members chatting among themselves, talking on their cellphones, using the time to catch up on their private business or engaging in side conversations with officials. However, when they are invited to a meeting attended by the head of state, these same parliamentarians show up well ahead of time, sit quietly in their seats and refrain from engaging in side conversations. Such uncharacteristic punctuality and discipline are motivated not by a respect for time as such or by a sense of occasion, but by entirely different considerations that will not be lost on the reader. The problem is that obsequiousness and fear cannot drive the wheel of progress and development forward.

A main reason for the lack of respect in Third World societies for the value of time, the failure to recognize its importance as one of the cornerstones of civilized behaviour and progress, is the emergence of a new moneyed class in many of these societies. The members of this class are for the most part poorly educated and largely uncultured, having built up their fortunes through political patronage and cronyism rather than by virtue of any special business, economic or scientific skills.

As their numbers grew and their political and economic clout increased, they became social trend-setters, a new source for the dissemination of negative values in society, including a lack of respect for time. The notion that time is one of the principal values of civilization and progress is totally lost on the members of this new parasitical class, who acquired unimaginable wealth suddenly and in the complete absence of any cultural background. Moreover, the often dubious way in which they made their fortunes hardly qualifies them to serve as examples to be followed or role models to be emulated. How can we ask our young people to follow the example of the leaders of economic life in the country, the so-called businessmen, when they are the living embodiment of negative values in general and a disdain for time in particular? There is also the fact that in a number of Third World countries the class of businessmen and new rich has been infiltrated by the Mafia – how then can we expect them to serve as examples or to uphold positive values, including a respect for time? I have dealt closely with many of those who pass themselves off as business leaders in our society. Unlike their international counterparts, the vast majority are characterized by a complete absence of managerial talent, astounding cultural poverty, blatant political opportunism and a lack of leadership qualities. Most had established their institutions and businesses on a basis of personal relationships rather than on management skills, proper economic use of state-of-the-art technology or ability to administer services. In other words, they are totally unfit to fill the leadership role into which they have been thrust or to serve as role models for new generations of young people.

Of all the points made in this chapter, the one that cannot be repeated often enough is that the top management of any enterprise cannot hope to run a successful and efficient business unless a respect for time is a basic feature of its makeup. That is not to say that it is a sufficient condition for efficient management, but it is certainly a necessary condition. Although a respect for time is perhaps the most important prerequisite for successful management, other features must also be present. As matters now stand, we do not have a cadre of executive managers capable of achieving what to many may appear to be an impossible task but one that I believe is a goal well within our reach, namely, attaining a degree of economic and educational development similar to that of the countries of southern Europe. This should proceed parallel with the development of a rich cultural life and the social peace that can guarantee for all of us the society to which we aspire: a stable, safe and thriving Egypt in which Egyptians will once again come to display the characteristics for which they have been famous throughout history: humanity, tolerance, kindness, patience, geniality and respect for others, far away from the violence, hatred and daily clashes between people, classes and the various component elements of society.

A Culture of Systems, not Individuals

Some time ago, I was reading an article by a well-known writer when I was struck by his remarks about an Egyptian ambassador who had just been recalled from one of our larger embassies abroad. After heaping some probably well-earned praise on the ambassador, he quoted a highly placed personality as saying that if it were up to him, he would have kept the ambassador in question on at the same embassy, regardless of the rotation system in force at the foreign ministry, because it was a shame to let the many contacts he had built up go to waste and have his replacement start from scratch. As a man interested in management and culture at one and the same time, I was shocked at this logic, not because it was wrong – indeed, it made sense from a practical point of view – but because it revealed a dangerous facet of the Egyptian mindset that has been forged over centuries under specific historical and cultural circumstances. The case of the ambassador is far from being an isolated incident. The same logic is invoked whenever a public official shines at his job, the same voices are raised to call for exceptions in the system to accommodate that particular individual. This graphically illustrates the fact that we believe far more profoundly in the role of the individual than we do in the effectiveness of systems in which the individual is only one cog in a complex wheel of interactive and interdependent elements.

Having lived until the age of 25 in a purely Egyptian environment, it was not until I was exposed to different cultures that I realized how vast a difference separated our perception of the respective roles of the individual and the system from that of other societies, most notably those of northern Europe, where the exact opposite logic prevails. While placing a high value on the individual and devoting huge resources to ensuring his formation in the best possible manner, these societies place an even higher value on the system.

It is hard for most people in our society, who tend to attribute success, efficiency and the achievement of goals to the fortuitous presence of an outstanding individual in a specific post, to realize the disastrous consequences that can flow from such a logic. To count on chance is to suspend all the rules of rationality, while to believe that an outstanding individual must remain in his post because his replacement will have to start from scratch is to give in to a problem rather than attempt to resolve it. Our approach to the issue is a reflection of the discontinuity of our organizational structures and the lack of a coherent strategy governing trends and endeavours in our society. It also works against the social mobility that is essential not only for the promotion of the middle class but for the promotion of society as a whole. Moreover, the approach carries within it the seeds of deeper problems, in that it proceeds from the premise that we are ready not only to pay the high price of dealing with the laws of chance, but to accept whatever results come our way. This is in direct opposition to the rationale governing modern management sciences, which, while believing in personal abilities and talents, believes more strongly in systems than in individuals.

The implication of linking achievements to the fortuitous presence of an outstanding individual in a specific post is that we allow the reins of our lives and future to be controlled by random chance, which operates outside the realm of any rational laws. This approach is the exact opposite of that advocated by the French philosopher Jean-Paul Sartre, who believed the future did not exist as such but was the product of our actions in the present. Stressing the importance of existence and the freedom and responsibility of the individual, he believed the future begins in the here and now, or more precisely, that what we do today will determine the features of tomorrow. We, on the contrary, make no attempt to shape the features of our future through planning today. Rather, we count on the laws of chance to occasionally throw a few outstanding individuals our way – laws that are the direct antipode of the notions of system and planning.

This keenness to keep outstanding individuals at their posts indefinitely is a result of one of our main defects, which is the virtual absence of continuity and methodology in our development drive. For development to proceed as a consistent process rather than in fits and starts, mechanisms must be set in place to ensure continuity regardless of changes in names and faces. The argument invoked to justify keeping efficient functionaries at their posts beyond the prescribed period, which is that whoever replaces them will have to begin from square one, is a painful admission of the lack of continuity between generations of individuals. Adding impetus to this argument is the fact that in our society no public official leaving his post will ever praise his successor, unlike his counterparts in the political, economic, cultural, educational and media institutions in advanced societies. Another disadvantage of keeping the same individual at his post indefinitely, however outstanding that individual may be, is that it is not conducive to the social mobility that is the basis for positive interaction in and the progress of any society, as well as a prerequisite for the growth of a strong and broad-based middle class that can lead that society. Moreover, the tendency to believe more in individuals than in the system exposes society to another, even greater, danger. While a culture of systems can keep destructive elements from occupying prominent positions, the same is not true in societies where a culture of individuals prevails. To the same extent that such a culture can promote outstanding individuals to positions of influence, it can also promote destructive and dangerous individuals. In the absence of an effective mechanism to prevent them from reaching a position of influence in time – and time is of the essence here – these negative elements can wreak havoc.

In addition, our infatuation with a culture of individuals is in direct contradiction with the basic premises of modern management sciences which, while drawing on the best qualities of the individual, give precedence to the big picture, that is, to the framework in which the individual operates – in other words, to the system. In advanced societies, the basic building block for progress and success is the system, and not, as in the case of underdeveloped societies, a few, albeit exceptionally talented, individuals.

There is thus a clear dichotomy between the culture of individuals, which has been all too manifest in our society for tens of centuries, and the culture of systems, which developed and put down deep roots in the West before moving on to many other societies that do not belong to Western civilization, such as Japan and other countries in Southeast Asia, as well as to various societies in Central and Latin America. It is pointless at this stage to make value judgements or to address the issue from an accusatory perspective. Rather, it should be placed in a historical perspective, and seen as the natural result of specific historical and cultural conditions. The question is whether a society governed by a culture of individuals can gradually transform itself into a society of systems. Judging from the experience of many societies, the answer is a resounding yes. These societies transformed themselves through a two-pronged approach, one that set its sights on short-term results and another that aimed at effecting a radical long-term transformation. The first can be summed up in one word, 'leadership', or leading by example, which succeeded to a great extent in imposing a culture of systems on society. The greater achievement, however, was to entrench this culture deep into the collective psyche of society, a feat accomplished through the medium of education. Only education is capable of bringing about a real transformation through curricula designed to minimize the dimensions of subjectivity and promote those of objectivity, the basis of any system or systems.

Once a culture of systems takes root in society, the issue of specific individuals staying on at their posts is no longer a do-or-die proposition that takes on the dimensions of a military campaign as careerists scheme and manoeuvre to remain in place. In a culture of individuals, one of the main concerns of public officials is to fight off potential successors, making for an ugly relationship between incumbents and those they fear will replace them. That is the case in a society like ours, where rivalry for a position often degenerates into smear campaigns in which predecessor and successor are intent on blackening each other's reputation and are not above resorting to slander and character assassination to achieve their ends. This pattern of behaviour is symptomatic of a general cultural climate in which each official seeks out those who are qualified to step into his shoes at some point down the road and goes all out to undercut their chances of succeeding.

As a result, we are left with a static situation in which genuine social mobility is replaced by what some call the rotation of elites, a process that is, by definition, opposed to change.

IMPLEMENTING A QUALITY CULTURE

The idea of setting quality standards has become an independent field of study known as Quality Management (QM), introduced over the last four decades into the system of social sciences. Today there are academies offering Quality Management as their only course of study. Although there is a great deal of literature on QM, the most famous being the works of Dr W. Edwards Deming, who is widely regarded as the father of this new discipline, I do not want to go too deeply into the details and definitions of QM and its subject headings, which are quality management and control at the planning stage, quality management and control at the stage of execution, then a careful check of quality at the final stage. The application of the science of Quality Management and the spread of a quality culture are no more than reflections of a more fundamental issue, namely, the presence of an effective process of social mobility that allows the best elements in society to reach the top of the societal pyramid. It is these people who can spread quality consciousness throughout society and, eventually, lead it to adopt a culture of quality.

A society that does not allow for a process of social mobility that favours its best human elements and propels them into prominence will never be governed by a culture of quality. In the absence of such a process, a culture of randomness and slip-shod performance takes over and the fickle hand of chance is left to determine the course of events, usually with disastrous consequences far removed from any notion of quality control.

As I mentioned in an earlier work, entitled *Egyptian Transformation*, untrammelled social mobility and the chain reactions it sets in motion are what allow the most able elements in society to occupy the leading positions in all walks of life. This creates a solid social pyramid that is developed over time by what some social scientists call Social Darwinism and others (particularly those of a socialist formation) attribute to social mobility and the opportunity it provides for the best elements to reach the upper layers of the societal pyramid and contribute effectively to shaping society's present and future. Whatever the mechanism by which such a dynamic social pyramid is built up, it remains the only way to propagate a culture of quality in society.

Conversely, a society whose composition does not allow for free social mobility leaves the door wide open for inept and mediocre people to make their way to top positions in its organizations and institutions, thereby dealing a death blow to any prospect of a culture of quality and creating a totally different cultural environment in which mediocrity holds sway, quality disappears and virulent campaigns are unleashed against talented individuals by those with a vested interest in maintaining the status quo. They know that unless they work relentlessly to keep the rules of the game from changing, they are doomed to topple from the leading positions they occupy to positions more in keeping with their limited talents and abilities.

The question of the culture propagated by mediocre people in high places and the general climate they create should be a matter of grave concern for intellectuals and scholars who, more than anyone, are capable of seeing the big picture and understanding the negative implications of this phenomenon for society at large. There is no question but that our social and political structures suffer from the ascendancy of mediocrity and the mechanisms set in place by its beneficiaries to keep themselves and others of their ilk in influential positions. The fallout from this phenomenon is reflected in the decline of values, ideals and ethics as well as in a shocking drop in our political, economic, cultural and educational standards.

A point worth making in connection with the notion of quality is that it is linked not to technological development, but to an abstract notion that perfection is a goal one strives to attain using whatever resources are available. This was the theme of a lecture I delivered at the Juran Institute for Quality Management in the United States, in which I elaborated further on the idea that quality was a notion in the minds of certain outstanding individuals and not the fruit of technology, itself the fruit of the intellectual prowess of outstanding individuals. To illustrate my point, I reminded my audience that quality control was a feature of the Ancient Egyptians, which found its most salient expression in the Great Pyramid of the Pharaoh Khufu. The amazing precision and unequalled grace of this remarkable monument to human ingenuity graphically illustrate the fact that quality and high standards of performance have nothing to do with the stage of a society's technological development. Commenting on my lecture, the head of the Juran Institute remarked that I had chosen the best possible example to prove my point, as the logo of the Institute depicts an Ancient Egyptian worker chiselling stone! Thus the biggest quality management institute in the world did not link quality to high technology, but chose to depict the notion with the image of an Ancient Egyptian craftsman using the most primitive technology to create perfection that defies time itself. In fact, the history of Ancient Egypt is filled with evidence that quality is a notion rather than anything else. A comparison between the pyramid built by Khufu and the two built by his father, the Pharaoh Snefru, shows how an enormous leap in the level of quality can be achieved in just a few years, which, in the absence of any significant technological breakthrough, can be explained only in terms of a human cadre that took the vigorous pursuit of quality to a higher level.

As to the notion of quality in Egypt today, it is practically non-existent. No one can argue with the fact that standards have dropped alarmingly in this country over the last half century. The only explanation is that it is no longer people of distinction who stand at the top of the societal pyramid but mediocre elements intent on keeping those who can expose their mediocrity as far away as possible from any position of influence. To that end, they work actively to downgrade the notion of quality, a notion that is completely alien to them. The spread of the values, culture and standards of the mediocre elements now holding leading positions in this country makes the words of Psalm 12 come to life before our eyes every day: 'The wicked walk on every side when the violent men are exalted.'

If it is true that democracy is the greatest achievement of the human race since the march of civilization began, it is equally true that one of the wellsprings of democracy is pluralism. When people came to realize that diversity of creeds, opinions, viewpoints and tastes was one of the most important features of humanity, it was natural for political systems to incorporate and respect different trends without allowing any one of them, even if it enjoyed a strong or even absolute majority, to deprive the others of the right to differ from the majority view and to believe in other programmes, ideas, systems and theories.

Indeed, as the march of civilization progressed, the realization that pluralism was a basic feature of humanity evolved into a conviction that pluralism was a source for the enrichment of human life as it expanded the horizons of creativity, innovation and renewal.

Although most members of the community of nations subscribe to the notion of pluralism as a basic component of their political systems, below the surface is a different reality in which the vast majority of people remain at a very primitive stage when it comes to really embracing this notion and fully understanding and appreciating its meaning and benefits. This is as true of the most advanced societies (led by the USA) as it is of the less developed societies, including those of the Third World. There is a mutual lack of understanding and mistrust between different civilizations that render the benefits and potential advantages of pluralism far fewer than they might otherwise have been. Some see the way out of this dilemma as the 'standardization' of the world, that is, the replacement of diversity by a uniform model of civilization. Not only is this an unattainable goal, it is the direct antithesis of the notion of pluralism. Moreover, any attempt to impose a universal norm would lay the ground for the spread of conflicts and clashes between civilizations to the detriment of humanity as a whole.

Evidence of the vast legacy of mutual misunderstanding, mistrust and misconceptions between civilizations can be found in Western civilization's view of most Eastern civilizations, which is often based on fanciful notions totally divorced from reality. It can also be found in the often distorted perceptions ancient civilizations have of the West, which tend to focus on the negative aspects of Western civilization while disregarding its positive aspects, even those that have benefited the whole of humanity.

In recent years, the traditional mistrust between Orient and Occident has been given new impetus with the emergence of a school of thought in the West in general and in the United States in particular that believes future relations between civilizations will be marked by clashes and conflicts, particularly the relationship between the West and Islam. The literature put out by this school of thought reveals a startling lack of understanding. Samuel P. Huntington's seminal book, *The Clash of Civilizations*, and other similar works by authors such as Paul Kennedy and Francis Fukuyama, are closer to journalistic articles than they are to scholarly works based on a sound knowledge of the subject matter. In fact, Huntington's book is an expanded version of an article he wrote originally for the American quarterly *Foreign Affairs*. Moreover, the authors of these works lack the vision that would enable them to see a mechanism that could replace the scenario of inter-civilizational clashes with a scenario of dialogue between civilizations. That is not to say that the scenario of a clash of civilizations can be altogether excluded, only that dialogue is possible if the vision exists and if serious efforts are made to transform it into reality.

Contemporary political discourse is peppered with references to democracy, human rights, general freedoms and pluralism. But raising these slogans is one thing, applying them is another. While nobody denies that these are noble values representing the highest stage yet in the march of civilization, the fact is that the way they are translated into reality leaves much to be desired. This is particularly true of the value of pluralism. For example, the West raises the banner of pluralism while some of its citizens raise the banner of standardization. This confusion leaves a bewildered world convinced that humanity has a long way to go before it can claim to have genuinely adopted these values.

If pluralism means that a diversity of trends, creeds, cultures, tastes, opinions and lifestyles is a basic feature of human life and a source of its enrichment, it follows that we should strive for 'unity through diversity'. This entails expanding a culture of respecting *Otherness*, provided this applies to all parties simultaneously and on a basis of parity. Respecting *Otherness* is in direct contradiction with the idea of standardizing the world. Fortunately, this idea is not advocated by the West as a whole and has not been taken up by Western Europe. It is an exclusively American notion based on nothing but America's cultural poverty.

SELF-CRITICISM AND CONSTANT SELF-IMPROVEMENT

I have long believed Immanuel Kant's famous statement that 'criticism is the most important building tool devised by the human mind' to be the cornerstone of a healthy and dynamic educational/cultural environment. The analogy of the German philosopher's aphorism in Eastern literature is Omar Ibn el-Khattab's statement, 'Blessed is he who shows us our defects', by which he calls on God to bless those who open our eyes to our defects through the medium of criticism.

After I had embraced the notion that a cultural climate that promotes critical faculties and celebrates critical minds is a prerequisite for a society's development and progress, I had the opportunity to work for 20 years in one of the ten largest economic corporations in the world. The experience allowed me to see this notion put into practice every day. With a history going back over a century, the corporation I worked for had its own internal culture, and it never ceased to amaze me that every single meeting, discussion and seminar I participated in during the 20 years of my tenure embodied the axiom that criticism is the most important building tool devised by man. It did not occur to anyone to hold back from criticizing ideas, plans, programmes and projects, not only before, but during and even after their execution, in order to minimize the negative and maximize the positive aspects of performance in future. Nor was the right to criticize vested exclusively in the upper echelons of the organizational structure; it was a right available to and actively exercised by every thinking person in the firm. And it is from the collective efforts of critical minds that success and distinction are achieved.

For criticism to become an effective mechanism deployed in a constant quest for excellence by pinpointing whatever is negative as a prerequisite for minimizing it in future and identifying the positive aspects of any idea, process or performance with a view to maximizing them, it must operate in a general climate in which every member of society is familiar with the notion of objective, and hence constructive, criticism. It is a type of criticism that differs in spirit, motivations and aims from the subjective criticism found in some cultures, where criticism is often used as a weapon of attack, revenge and defamation in order to further personal agendas or settle old scores. The blame for this aberration lies squarely on the shoulders of a general cultural and educational climate that fails to develop the critical faculty in young minds or to promote the notion that criticism should be used as a rational, objective tool to serve the general interest and not private interests.

It is not surprising that societies governed by a general cultural climate in which pluralism is accepted and respected should be better equipped to use objective criticism as a means of optimizing all aspects of life than societies that do not tolerate any dissenting opinion or any departure from the norm. In such a monistic climate there is no room for the sort of constructive and objective criticism that targets subjects and not individuals. Nor is it surprising that societies I have called in a previous chapter societies of systems, not individuals, should also be better equipped to deploy constructive criticism as a weapon against objective shortcomings.

There is a strong link between a culture of constructive criticism on the one hand and social mobility on the other. In a society marked by an active process of social mobility that allows for a dynamic process of job rotation in general and among elites in particular, there is a wider scope for planting the seeds of a culture of constructive criticism. The opposite holds true in a closed society where, in the absence of real social mobility, hanging on to the job becomes a do-or-die proposition. This blurs the distinction between what is objective and what is subjective and creates a climate that is inimical to objective criticism.

I also believe in a strong link between the values of mediocrity referred to above on the one hand and the difficulty of propagating a culture of constructive criticism on the other. People of mediocre abilities are aware that they cannot survive in a climate of constructive criticism that would expose their limited skills and talents, and so they ferociously oppose the introduction of a system of performance evaluation based on objective criteria by working actively against the dissemination of a culture of constructive criticism.

In the final analysis, the diffusion of a general cultural climate that welcomes and encourages constructive criticism and educates people on the merits of developing their critical faculties and the enormous benefits this will bring to society as a whole is one of the most important values of progress. And, like all the other values of progress, it can become generalized throughout society in the immediate term only by a determined effort on the part of those in positions of leadership to set an example and, in the long term, by means of educational curricula designed to inculcate its importance in people's minds.

UNIVERSALITY OF KNOWLEDGE

One of the most salient features of the globalization process has been the unrestricted flow of information between the various sectors of the global community, not least in the domain of science. Even those who reject some of the aspects of globalization cannot deny the positive effect it has had in opening up channels of communication between the many institutions working in every branch of science and scientific research. This is particularly true in the field of applied science and technology, where universality of knowledge has become an established feature. The main reason why this feature has acquired such importance is the strong relationship in advanced societies between scientific research on the one hand and life in general and economic life in particular on the other. It is also the reason why the field of research and development, or R&D as it is known, which is concerned primarily with the practical application of scientific findings, has come to eclipse in importance the field of scientific research proper, which, in the traditional meaning of the word, is almost totally divorced from life functions.

As advanced societies removed science from behind the high enclosures of universities and research centres, and put many of its branches to work in the service of their life/economic/social functions, universality of knowledge in the service of life functions became an inescapable fact of life in the world of applied sciences. The importance of R&D is reflected in the size of the budgets it commands, which far exceed those allocated to pure scientific research. And, while the latter is subsidized for the most part by states and academic institutions, most R&D is funded by private economic institutions driven by the need to stay ahead of the competition. Anyone working in an industrial, commercial or services sector today must seek out the latest technology in that sector, wherever it may have been developed, and put it to use in enhancing performance, expanding activities and maximizing returns. Hence the growing relevance of the notion of universality of knowledge.

It would be no exaggeration to attribute much of the credit for promoting the notion of universality of knowledge to the unique experience of post-war Japan. Like the fabled phoenix, Japan rose from the ashes of its crushing defeat in the Second World War to assert itself as an economic giant on the world stage, largely thanks to its determination to seek out the latest achievements in science and technology in every part of the world, thoroughly assimilate their inner workings and put them to use in remarkable ways. Things are not quite so simple in the field of social science, where outlooks are conditioned by cultural factors and considerations. And yet the notion of universality of knowledge is gaining ground in certain branches of social science, albeit not at the same pace as in the domain of applied science. For example, modern management, human resources and marketing sciences and many other economic disciplines have managed to cross borders and apply the notion of universality of knowledge in practice. This may be due to the fact that they are largely culture-free. But even those branches of social science with a strong cultural dimension are being infiltrated to one degree or another by the notion of universality of knowledge.

Resisting the notion may appear to some, particularly in the Arab world, as a natural feature of ancient civilizations. Not so. Consider the case of China, one of the oldest civilizations in the world. Among the most passionate adherents to the values of progress in general and the notion of universality of knowledge in particular are the Chinese communities of Southeast Asia, and this allowed them to play an instrumental role in the remarkable progress achieved by the region. Then there is the case of Japan, another ancient civilization, which stands as one of the foremost examples of the values of progress in action, most notably the universality of knowledge. There is also India, an ancient civilization that, despite its many social problems, is one of the few Third World countries whose scientific institutions can hold their own with the best in the world. By keeping the bridges of scientific and technological research open between it and the rest of the world, India was able to score impressive achievements in many fields, notably in the arms industry and in computers and information technology. These examples attest to the ability of ancient civilizations to adopt the notion of universality of knowledge without threatening their own cultural specificity.

How then to explain the reluctance of Arab societies to partake of the benefits of universality of knowledge? I believe it is due to the lamentable deterioration of their educational institutions and scientific research centres as a result of the subjugation of education and science in these societies to political life. This has, not surprisingly, cut them off from scientific progress in the rest of the world, smothered the spirit of creativity and turned them into stagnant entities totally severed from scientific research in all branches of applied and social sciences. As a result, there is a near total Arab absence in the domain of scientific achievements and creative research in these fields.

If the previous six values are among the values of progress in general that must be firmly planted in a society's general cultural and educational environment as a prerequisite for that society's development, they are also among the most important values on which modern management concepts are based. Thus the five values addressed here should not be seen in isolation from the values of progress addressed earlier, as the 11 values together constitute the conceptual framework governing work in the modern workplace.

Teamwork

In the course of the many years I spent working in an environment that was international in the real sense of the word, bringing together as it did thousands of people from different countries and with widely divergent cultural backgrounds, I had many occasions to see how the concept of teamwork is totally alien to most Egyptians. Unlike their colleagues from Asia, notably those from Japan or China, where the spirit of teamwork is particularly vibrant, or from other parts of the world, such as Europe, which also has a tradition of teamwork, the majority of Egyptians I worked with found it extremely difficult to subsume their individuality in collective endeavours as members of a team. The ego issue often led to clashes, as each individual sought to ensure that he would get the credit for any success and others the blame for any failure. None was prepared to have his contribution regarded as just one component element in a collective endeavour. In hundreds of cases, this attitude led to crisis situations, with a disgruntled employee demanding that either he be taken off the team or that so and so be dropped – or else! This was in stark contrast to the attitude displayed by others belonging to different cultural backgrounds, such as the British, Asians and Germans with whom I worked, and only served to confirm how hard most Egyptians find it to put their egos aside and accept thanks for a job well done when they are not singled out for praise.

Given that modern management sciences are based on a set of fundamental values, among the most important being teamwork, applying modern management techniques to large numbers of Egyptians is a difficult proposition – unless they happen to be working abroad, in which case they have no choice but to submit docilely to the prevailing system of work or lose their jobs. Many expatriate Egyptians succeed brilliantly in their chosen field of expertise. All too often, however, their individualistic streak takes over, and they attribute their success exclusively to their own innate talents, conveniently forgetting that these talents would not have flourished as they did had it not been for the healthy environment that imposed on them the modern values of work and brought out the best they had to offer.

In this connection, I recall what a professor at the California Institute of Technology said to me at the end of 1999: 'Ahmed Zeweil is, by any standards, a prodigious scientist. But we should remember that 17 people working in the same institute in which he works won Nobel prizes for their contributions to science. The moral to be drawn here is that the "miracle of the system" is not only equal to but surpasses the "miracle of the individual", although both must be present at the same time in order for the required result to be achieved.' This view has been echoed by Ahmed Zeweil himself, who never tires of praising the 'team' without which he could not have achieved what he did. The Nobel laureate has also praised the 'working environment' in his Institute, which he says deserves much of the credit for his 1999 Chemistry Prize. But as members of a culture of individuals we tend to forget all aspects of the story and focus on the individual, because for over fifty centuries, from the time of the Pharaohs on, the Egyptian mindset has been conditioned by the cult of the individual. The system has no place in our scheme of things, even though it is the primary engine for progress and human achievement. The only mechanisms by which this defect in our makeup can be cured are those referred to earlier, namely, leadership (as a tool of development in the short term), and modern education (as a tool of development in the medium and long terms).

The word leadership here is not just a vague and abstract term, but denotes a modern manager formed in accordance with the requirements and culture of modern management sciences, which make every top executive responsible for managing work in his enterprise according to a system that groups employees into harmonious teams whose members complement one another, as opposed to the top executive who promotes individualism and factionalism by requiring each person in the establishment to owe allegiance to him personally. One of the most important tasks of a manager formed and trained according to the spirit, culture, requirements and techniques of modern management sciences is to foster a team spirit in his establishment. Unfortunately, most executives in our part of the world tend to promote a very different spirit, in which employees are islands isolated from one another and in communication only with the employer. This is a source of personal power for the top man, but it comes at the expense of the collective good and does nothing to promote the spirit of teamwork that is one of the fundamental values of modern management science.

The negative culture that prevails in our workplace derives in large part from the virtual absence of management education, in addition to the fact that most businesses are run by 'bosses' rather than by contemporary executive managers. It is further encouraged and conditioned by the culture of the Egyptian village, where for decades the *omda*, or village headman, has maintained his grip over village affairs by ensuring that the only channels of communication are between his constituents and himself. Any other pattern is frowned upon as a violation of the personal loyalty they owe to his person and as a direct challenge to his authority. All these factors conspire against the adoption of the values of modern management, including the important role assigned by contemporary management sciences to the executive manager. Indeed, most people find it difficult to understand just what the function of an executive manager is. On the surface he does not appear to do much, but the truth is very different. An executive manager can be likened to an orchestra conductor who is required to ensure, at one and the same time, the high performance capability of each orchestra member taken separately, and the high quality of their collective performance as one team.

Thus in the ten years I was responsible for projects worth billions of dollars, my days were not crowded with appointments and meetings and my desk was not covered in paperwork, even though I was handling a daily volume of work running into well over a hundred million dollars, while others who were running businesses and projects amounting to less than one per cent of the volume and value of the projects for which I was responsible were drowning in meetings, paperwork and files. I believe this was because they spent much of their time doing work that should have been done by others. Because they believed neither in teamwork nor in delegating authority, they ended up spending three-quarters of their time wading through mountains of unnecessary paperwork. Despite these strenuous efforts, however, the final results they achieved were at best mediocre and, more often than not, disgraceful.

Disseminating a culture that values teamwork begins with the formation of a human cadre of contemporary executive managers who understand what being a boss entails in the modern sense of the word, not in its Pharaonic or medieval sense, when the top man was everything and his assistants nothing. Without an administrative revolution in this field, any attempts to reform the working environment in our country and make it more amenable to the notion of collective work and the spirit of teamwork are doomed to fail, because the heads of administrative organizations have a vested interest in maintaining the status quo so that they can continue to keep all the reins of authority in their hands and take full credit for whatever success is achieved.

If the development of a high-calibre human cadre of executive managers capable of leading by example is an essential condition for development in the short term, what is required in the medium and long term is an educational revolution that will develop a strong work ethic in future generations, educate them in the importance of collective work and promote the spirit of teamwork at every stage of the educational process. Both targets must be achieved if we are ever to move from the culture of individualistic work inherited from Pharaonic times to the work culture prevailing today, in which teamwork is used as a mechanism to maximize output by drawing on the collective minds, abilities and experience of the members making up the team.

Over two decades ago, I went to Switzerland to study the latest modern management techniques at the International Management Institute of Geneva University, the largest specialized institute of its kind in Europe. The experience was a culture shock, as I found myself having to adjust to a system of learning very different from the one I was used to. Indeed, at first I thought I had made a mistake in registering for the course, and that I had been misinformed about how good the Institute was. In the academic environment where I obtained my graduate and postgraduate degrees from an Egyptian university, the professor was the transmitter of knowledge and the students passive receivers. The situation was very different at the Institute, where the professor would begin each class by bringing up a particular theme or problem that was to be addressed by the students. These would then be divided into working groups and each sent off to a separate room. The groups were given a set time to study the problem, use the library for research and come up with a report representing the collective views of their members. All the members of the group contributed equally to the report and then chose one among themselves to present it on their behalf.

It was a technique of teaching that at first filled me with dismay. However, over the following weeks and months I gradually came to realize that it was in fact a highly sophisticated technique designed to develop leadership qualities and produce a human cadre capable of leading the world in every field. Contrary to the educational technique with which we are all too familiar, which produces submissive followers trained to suppress their creative impulses while indulging their streak of destructive individualism, the technique employed at the Institute produced innovators and believers who displayed a highly developed *esprit de corps*. This educational environment is what produces the best elements in any working environment. After all, what is work but a continuation of the early stages of education? The workplace is where the final output of the educational system, the individual, eventually ends up, and his performance in the workplace is as negative or positive as the education he received.

Accordingly, collective work or teamwork is a phenomenon linked to a society's cultural values, and some societies show a greater inclination for teamwork than others. Two of the leading examples are China and Japan. According to management and QM scientists, these societies show a marked propensity for teamwork. However, it is an acquired characteristic, not a natural one, built up through their cumulative cultural experience. A yardstick that can be used to measure the extent to which a society has adopted the value of teamwork is the management techniques followed by that society's governmental and economic institutions. Another is the philosophy and technique of its educational system. The example set by the executive leaders in society can be instrumental in developing the spirit of teamwork. There is also a link between teamwork and the level of democracy in society. The greater the margin of democracy, the better the prospects of making teamwork an essential component of a society's work ethic. In an undemocratic society, the opportunity for advancement is restricted, and upward mobility in an organization is either slow or non-existent. This does not create a favourable climate for the development of a team spirit.

What we have here is a problem with no one single cause and no one cure, a multidimensional problem entailing a multilateral approach. As the German-born American political sociologist Herbert Marcuse pointed out 30 years ago, the theory of the unidimensionality of cause has collapsed in all spheres of human thinking.

Human resources

If management is the nerve centre of success in all the institutions of advanced societies, the optimal use of human resources is the backbone on which the success or failure of management rests. Human resource sciences have branched out to cover many areas, such as employee recruitment, selection and training, performance appraisal, human resources and organization, discovering leadership qualities and other areas related to one of the most important fields of modern management, namely, human resource management.

Modern human resource sciences proceed from a number of fundamental premises, such as the belief that in every person on earth there exists a 'gap' between his actual performance and his potential performance, and that it is one of the main tasks of management to discover that gap and work to overcome it by placing an individual in the position best suited to his abilities, temperament and personality within the organizational structure on the one hand, and through constant training on the other.

Another fundamental premise is that any individual belongs to one of two basic groups made up respectively of *specialists* and *generalists*. Both groups are equally important and both must be present in any successful and thriving organization.

Yet another is the need to make a basic distinction between *potential* and *performance*. While standards and rates of performance can be raised, all that can be done in respect of potential is to discover whether or not it exists. One of the principal tasks of top management in modern organizations is to discover those with a high potential early on in order to elevate them to leading positions and to devise the required training programmes to hone their potential and imbue it with professionalism. Human resource sciences also attach a great deal of importance to the issue of motivation, whether in the material or moral sense.

The role of the 'chief' in a modern establishment differs from his role in a traditional bureaucracy, where he concentrates most of the centralized power in his hands and, over the years, transforms his fellow workers into an army of followers. In enterprises applying the techniques of modern management science, which are based on delegation, he does not involve himself in the day-to-day workings of the enterprise, leaving himself free to focus on strategic planning. In a sense, his role is closer to that of an orchestra conductor than a military leader.

While traditional bureaucracies create followers, modern management seeks to create a cadre of human resources whose members are believers in the mission and aims of the establishment in which they are working. The sense of identification with the work organization is reflected in the quality of the on-the-job performance of the true believer, who sees the job not simply as a duty but as a medium of self-expression and a source of personal gratification. In modern management terminology, this phenomenon is known as 'ownership', that is, ownership of the moral returns of success at work.

In short, modern management does not regard human resources as machines but as the key to success or failure. As such, they are entitled to enjoy the benefits and glory of the success they were instrumental in achieving. According to this view, there is no more effective engine for the advancement and success of an organization than the people working in it. This view is not the prevailing one in underdeveloped societies, where little attention is paid to creating an environment that encourages people to work and give of their best. The opposite holds true in advanced societies, where the importance of the human element in moving the wheel of progress forward is widely recognized. The wealth of nations is measured not in terms of their natural resources or the riches they have amassed in the past but in the quality of their human resources. This asset is built up through a process of planning and meticulous application of systems designed to discover the best in people, develop their potentialities to the full, and provide them with motivation.

Delegation

Modern management science tries to utilize each person in the best possible way. To that end, it attaches great importance to discovering latent abilities, training and motivation, in the belief that enabling each individual to realize his full potential and allowing the free interplay of ideas is a source of enrichment not only for work but for life in general. Advanced societies discarded the model of centralized management applied for long decades in the work establishment, which some believe they imported from the military establishment, when experience proved that it hindered the development of individual potential. That is why delegation has become one of the most important instruments of successful management today. Delegation is a reflection of the values mentioned earlier, which lead to transforming work groups from armies of followers to teams of believers and create an environment conducive to innovation and creativity.

In some modern establishments, the degree of delegation is such that the manager appears to have no work at all. This is, of course, a fallacy, as he is responsible for strategic planning, not for carrying out work that others can do as well as, and usually better than, he can. It would be safe to say that an establishment run according to all the values of modern management except for delegation is doomed to fail, because delegation is the translation of all these values into practice. However, delegation and training must go hand in hand: delegation without training cannot hope to succeed.

Marketing in the driver's seat

The difference between countries that achieved remarkable progress in the economic field (through manufacturing a product or providing a service then, at a later stage, through information technology) and those that spent billions on 'industrial arsenals' at the expense of real economic development is that the activities of the former were focused on the end product, that is on 'marketing', while the latter's activities were focused on the initial process, that is on 'production'. Modern management science recognizes that a production-driven approach can only lead to failure and bankruptcy, while an approach that is marketing-driven is the best guarantee of success and growth. The truth of this axiom is corroborated by the huge discrepancy between the economies of the East European countries (before the collapse of the Eastern bloc in the 1980s), which were production-driven, and those of Western Europe, which are marketing-driven.

If management is the secret for the success (or failure) of societies in general and economies in particular, marketing is the brains of management, in the sense that a successful management is one whose strategic thinking, business philosophy and internal mechanisms are marketing-driven.

While the importance of marketing as an essential value for the successful management of any enterprise cannot be overstated, its own success is contingent on the adoption of other values of progress. One such value is universality of knowledge. There can be no successful marketing in a closed environment shut off from the outside world. How can anyone hope to market anything successfully on a wide scale if he does not know enough about his competitors, international markets, the demands of those markets and the cultures of the prospective buyers of his products or services? Another value that goes hand in hand with marketing is pluralism. How can we have one unique model for everything (the opposite of pluralism) and succeed in marketing, which is based on the highest objective of quality management science, which is to meet the expectations and satisfy the needs of the recipient of a product or service?

Absolute belief in the effectiveness of management

Many are the truthful statements repeated by people without realizing their real meaning and significance. A statement one hears very often these days is that Egypt's main problem today is 'management'. Although this is absolutely true, any attempt to elicit an explanation from people who utter the statement with a great deal of assurance reveals that, more often than not, they have no clear idea what they are talking about and that, moreover, the word management means different things to different people.

Still, even if they are not clear on the details, they are right in their diagnosis: the main problem in our lives in general and our economic life in particular is that the methods and techniques of modern management sciences and modern marketing sciences are virtually absent from government departments, the public sector, the private sector and all the service sectors.

I have no doubt whatsoever that the Eastern bloc, made up of the Soviet Union and its legion of followers, collapsed at the end of the 1980s because of the absence of effective management in all sectors of the socialist world, particularly in the economic sector, where the absence of management led to a state of bankruptcy, which brought the whole temple of socialism crashing down.

If the collapse of the Eastern bloc can be blamed in large part on poor economic management, much of the credit for the flourishing economies of the Western world and the Asian tigers, which led to the growth of a prosperous and dynamic middle class, can be attributed to the application of modern and efficient management and marketing systems. It is worth noting in this connection that efficient management is capable not only of steering a country on the path of economic prosperity and allowing it to reap the positive social benefits that accrue, but also of dealing with crises and reversals. It was thanks only to sound management that the countries of Southeast Asia and, before them, Mexico, succeeded in overcoming their financial crises in record time, confounding the expectations of some of our pundits who were patting themselves on the back for having adopted a more cautious approach. The swift recovery of the Southeast Asian and Mexican economies proves that a country with a clear vision of where it is heading and that proceeds to implement that vision by means of a scientific methodological approach can, when exposed to a crisis situation that causes it to slip backwards on its chosen path, regain its footing as long as the methodology is still in place.

Before going further, it might be useful here to define exactly what success means when applied to an economic venture. This entails first clearing up a certain ambiguity which arises from the absence of any distinction in the Arabic language between the two notions of *administration* and *management*, both of which are translated as *idara* in Arabic. In fact, the two notions are quite distinct in English. While administration means the set of rules governing work in the workplace, such as personnel regulations, working hours, disciplinary measures and the like, the word management denotes something altogether different. In essence, it is the mechanism by which an enterprise achieves its desired goals which are, specifically, realizing given economic returns, parallel with a process of growth, by using the tools of modern marketing sciences.

Thus the economic enterprises established in countries that adopted a system of centralized planning, the so-called command economies, could impress us with their massive size, machinery, equipment and huge workforce only if we look upon them from the perspective of administration. But however impressive these factors may be, they mean absolutely nothing from the viewpoint of modern management, where the only criterion for success is an enterprise's ability to deploy its resources, machinery and workforce efficiently to realize economic returns which must not be less than the interest accruing on bank deposits.

A project that does not yield a return on investment greater than the interest on bank deposits will inevitably reach a state of bankruptcy that renders it incapable of performing its economic and other functions, the most important of which is employment and the creation of new job opportunities.

The pride with which some people continue to regard the huge enterprises which once dominated our economic landscape and which, because of the absence of effective management, failed to realize economic returns greater than the interest on bank deposits, is both strange and misplaced. What they are proud of in the final analysis is the money spent rather than the returns on expenditure, which were in most cases extremely modest and led to the failure of the entire experiment.

Societies that confuse the notion of management in the sense we have explained and that of administration as the system of checks and balances governing the workplace should understand that, for all its importance, administration cannot be a vehicle for economic prosperity. The only way this can be achieved is through the application of the principles, techniques and procedures of modern management and marketing sciences.

Management, like medicine or architecture, is a profession for which special skills and training are required. Like a doctor or architect, the modern manager chooses his career path on the basis of personal inclination and aptitude and then undergoes an extensive course of study and training. Promotion to a higher rung on the administrative ladder does not in and of itself create a modern executive manager capable of leading and planning in order to achieve the desired targets in terms of profitability and growth, while at the same time giving high priority to the development of the most important element in the success of any enterprise, its human resources.

As anyone who has had the nightmarish experience of dealing with Egyptian bureaucracy can testify, the concept of modern management is a totally alien one as far as all government departments are concerned. Unfortunately, this is equally true for the economic units of both the public and private sectors, which are run according to a bazaar mentality having nothing to do with the spirit and mechanisms of private economic institutions operated in accordance with the principles of modern management, human resources and marketing sciences. Scientists in these fields are well aware that the vast majority of private economic establishments in Egypt today are almost totally dependent on public relations rather than on management in the modern sense of the word. Operating as they do in a general climate in which public relations reign supreme, they have spared themselves the trouble of building modern institutional systems and recruiting efficient human elements capable of running them in accordance with the principles of sound management. On the one hand, building such a system is a costly business; on the other, simple minds cannot grasp its merits, especially in the context of a business culture that venerates public relations as a short-cut to power and influence.

Unless we create a general climate that is conducive to the introduction of modern management practices in government departments, public sector units and the manufacturing and service establishments of the private sector, we cannot hope to attract a significant flow of direct foreign investments. Investors are wary of pouring money into an environment that does not allow them to function in accordance with the mechanisms and techniques of modern management, human resources and marketing sciences, and it is precisely the absence of those mechanisms that stands at the root of our deteriorating economic situation. True, we began to address the problem ten years ago, but we need to adopt a far more forceful approach if we are ever to transform the business environment in this country into an investor-friendly environment governed by the principles of modern management in all spheres of life.

Until then, repeating the slogan 'Egypt's main problem is management' without fully understanding the real significance and implications of this diagnosis will remain nothing more than a meaningless mantra.

CHAPTER 3

Source and Identity

A closer look at the values of progress presented in Chapter 2 shows that, despite the different characteristics of human civilizations, ancient and new, they are values that belong to the whole of humanity, to the march of human civilization in general, rather than to any specific civilization. As civilizations rose and fell, humanity was moving steadily ahead on a course that transcended the fortunes of this or that civilization. Thus human history proceeded along two parallel courses simultaneously: the march of civilization and the evolution of humanity, and the values of progress owe their existence more to the latter than to the former. The failure to recognize that humanity is higher and more sublime than any civilization can only lead to racism and fanaticism. There is no disputing the fact that every civilization has drawn on the cumulative experiences of other contemporary or earlier civilizations and woven them into the fabric of its own culture complex.

Given the undeniable existence of a common fund of human experience, a 'cumulative legacy' as it were, built up through the ages in such fields as mathematics and other applied sciences, how is this common legacy assimilated into human consciousness, which is the repository of values? If we admit that much of modern mathematics came from Ancient Greece, that modern music owes much to Aristotle, that the Latin-Germanic lawmakers based their codification on the principles propounded in the Roman Justinian Code, and if a great Egyptologist such as James Henry Breasted found an undeniable link between the highest contemporary value systems and those in force in Ancient Egypt, which he called the 'Dawn of Conscience', we cannot fail to see that as culture ranks below civilization, civilization ranks below humanity.

Students of history will find that all civilizations, whether ancient or modern, were based on the values referred to in Chapter 2. They will also find that when these values move from one civilization to another, they undergo a process of development and refinement which, on the one hand, represents the contribution of the host civilization to humanity and, on the other, way stations on the road to developing these values further by elevating them to a higher plane and opening new vistas before them. This does not negate the fact that the contribution of some civilizations to this refining process has been greater than others. For example, by far the largest contribution to developing the contemporary values of work has been made by Western civilization which, as the birthplace of the Industrial Revolution, provided a favourable climate for the refinement and consecration of these values. Still, the values of progress in general and the values of work (including modern management concepts) in particular have been developed over the ages by humanity at large and not by any specific civilization, even if the ability of the West to put them to optimal use makes them appear to be products of Western civilization.

The 'humanistic' nature of these values is borne out by the fact that in the course of only one century, the twentieth, they passed over from an environment that was purely Western to others which followed altogether different models of civilization, such as Japan and tens of countries in Asia and Latin America, which adopted these values as part of their culture complex and put them to use in fuelling the engine of their remarkable economic growth. This proves that even if at one stage they took root and flourished in a Western environment, they are, in the final analysis, human, not Western values.

CHAPTER 4

Cultural Specificity

In the last 40 years, fears of a cultural invasion have dominated the thinking of many in our part of the world. When the bipolar world order collapsed at the end of the 1980s and the world began to talk of an emerging phenomenon that is now widely known as globalization, the proponents of the cultural invasion theory adapted their language to the new terminology and began to talk of the globalization of cultures as a dangerous development which threatened to erode our cultural specificity.

I have addressed this issue in many of my writings, and came to the conclusion that only those with a meagre fund of cultural specificity have anything to fear from the globalization of culture. Those standing on a solid foundation of cultural identity, with a cultural specificity derived from factors related to history and geography, such as Japan, need not fear the loss of their cultural identity under any circumstances. The examples some people give of the effects the winds of change coming from abroad have had on Japan's cultural construct can all be classified as 'secondary issues', such as eating fast food, wearing American clothes and the like. But when it comes to human relations, the high esteem in which old people are held, family values and other intrinsically Japanese values, such as the Japanese understanding of work, Japan has not surrendered one iota of its cultural specificity despite the fact that for the last 60 years it has been dealing extensively with the outside world.

But while there might be some justification to fear that our cultural specificity will be unable to stand up to the onslaught of cultural globalization, this does not apply in respect of the values of progress, all of which find much to support them in the models of civilization from which we derive our specific cultural traits. There is nothing in any of these models – the Egyptian, Arab, Islamic or Christian – that can be construed as running counter to values like a respect for time, quality, universality of knowledge, teamwork, a culture of systems rather than a culture of individuals, or a belief that management is one of the most important instruments of success. Indeed, I would assert that these values were upheld and applied in our history hundreds of years before another chapter in humanity's civilizing process took them over and used them in creating a better life. There are those who would agree with me save when it comes to the value of pluralism, on the grounds that Islamic religious thinking is based on 'a unique model of righteousness'. This is an erroneous assumption that is belied by numerous Quranic texts, perhaps the most important of which reads as follows: 'And if thy Lord willed, all who are in the earth would have believed together' (Surah of Jonah, Verse 99). There are also many texts in the Sunna (the rules of life according to the *hadith*, or teachings of the Prophet), extolling pluralism as one of the sublime values that all Muslims should strive to uphold.

How then can anyone allege that values of progress such as time, quality, and even pluralism threaten our cultural specificity? And yet that is the theme of an ongoing debate in our society that is both bizarre and humiliating. Those who argue against the adoption of values of progress on the grounds that they run counter to our value system and cultural identity expect us instead to embrace values that can only drag society on the road to backwardness and underdevelopment. This regressive trend is a relatively recent phenomenon in Egypt's modern history. For additional proof that the values of progress are compatible with our cultural specificity we need only look at the last hundred years of our history. These were marked by periods of enlightenment during which most of the values of progress were far more present in our lives than they became after what has been termed by some as a process of 'dismantling' Egyptian society began.

The debate over cultural specificity versus values of progress takes me back to a period I spent in the 1980s working in one of the fastest developing countries in Southeast Asia, where the two largest ethnic communities, and hence the main sources of labour, were the Chinese and the Malays. The prevailing view at the time was that any economic establishment wishing to run an efficient and successful business had to recruit its staff from the Chinese community, whose members were diligent and hard-working and who, moreover, displayed a natural propensity for teamwork, as opposed to the Malays, who were generally regarded as lazy, slipshod and highly individualistic. This negative image of the Malay worker remained in place until one man came to lead a country 90 per cent of whose inhabitants belong to the ethnic group once maligned in the international labour market – the predominantly Muslim Malays – towards a miraculous recovery. In less than 20 years, Malaysia, whose people were mired in backwardness and stigmatized as lazy and inefficient, broke through the barriers of underdevelopment to gain world-wide recognition for the high quality of its products and services. With one of the fastest growing economies in the world, Malaysia has come to embody all the values of progress, breaking the stereotype of the 'lazy Malay' and opening the eyes of the world to two inescapable truths:

- First, that backwardness is the result not of a biological fatality but of circumstances, and that, to the same extent that circumstances can change, backwardness can be overcome.
- Second, that the values of progress can take root and flourish in any environment, Christian, Buddhist, Islamic or otherwise, and that they are by no means exclusive to any specific environment.

The Malaysian experience can also be used to illustrate another truth, namely, that progress can go hand-in-hand with cultural specificity. Malaysia's strong cultural traditions relating to human relations, family relations and religious values have remained as constant since its economic takeoff as they were when it was a struggling underdeveloped country. The credit for Malaysia's economic miracle is sometimes attributed to its Chinese minority. Even if this were true, it means that progress can come about by 'contagion', which is not a bad thing. But this is an overly simplistic explanation for the Malaysian miracle. After all, the Chinese minority has always been around. The only new factor is the emergence of Mahathir bin Mohamed, the man who wrought this amazing change in Malaysia's fortunes through visionary and efficient leadership.

CHAPTER 5

Building a Strong Society

Every political thinker has a list of priorities which he tries to serve through his writings. My main priority is building an internally strong Egypt, that is, a healthy society characterized by a broad-based and dynamic middle class, economic stability, modern education and a general cultural climate in sync with the age. Of course, moving with the times should never be at the expense of an awareness of and pride in our history, but a sense of history must not be allowed to degenerate into a love affair with the past. Those who have different priorities on their list, be they pan-Arab or otherwise, should realize that none of their priorities stands a chance except in the context of an internally strong, stable and flourishing Egypt. This applies just as much to those who dream of a successful pan-Arab project as it does to those who aspire to see Egypt play a prominent role on the regional or international stage. These are dreams that can come true only if Egypt is stable and strong on the domestic front. In fact, building a strong and stable society is a prerequisite for the attainment of any of Egypt's aspirations and ambitions, whatever they may be.

Despite my boundless admiration for Muhammad Ali, who is generally recognized by scholars and historians to be the founder of modern Egypt, I have no doubt that his preoccupation with matters that distracted him from his main project, which was to build a strong Egypt, led to a series of disastrous setbacks that were to have long-term ramifications. Had Muhammad Ali focused his main efforts on building a strong and stable society, Egypt would have been in a position to play the pivotal role for which it is uniquely qualified by the factors of history and geography. Unfortunately, the pattern of squandering our efforts in other than what should be our main priority, which is to deploy all our resources to build the strong foundations of a modern society, has been repeated in Egypt's recent history with equally disastrous consequences.

Many factors tempt Egypt to play a role beyond its own borders. The real problem is not that it succumbs to the temptation but that it does so before completing its sacred mission to build itself up as a strong, stable and thriving society. It is not by casting its eyes outside its borders that Egypt, or any country for that matter, can hope to take a short cut to development. External ventures undertaken in the absence of a solid internal structure can only result first, in the failure of such ventures and, second, in slowing down the process of building a strong and stable internal front.

My view has always been that our primary mission and the main task confronting us is to mobilize all our resources and focus all our efforts in the direction of building a country that is internally strong, modern, successful, thriving and stable, and that is, furthermore, at peace with its past and its present. The only way this can be done is through a campaign to instil, cultivate, diffuse and propagate the values of progress in society, at the level of the leadership and by means of an educational institution whose primary task will be to instil those values in the minds and consciences of our young people. Parallel with this, there must be a radical change in the religious discourse of this country, whether Muslim or Christian, which is one of the two main elements by which public opinion in Egypt is formed, the other being the mass media.

In the meantime, many of us are wallowing in nostalgia. Some dream of pre-1952 Egypt as an ideal to strive for, others of Egypt as it was under Nasser, and others still of what it was in the days of Sadat. But while we certainly want a middle class of the quality that existed in pre-revolutionary Egypt, we certainly do not want it to be the same in terms of quantity. Before 1952, only a tiny minority of Egyptians belonged to the middle class; the vast majority belonged to a downtrodden lower class that lived in conditions of abject poverty and squalor. From Egypt of the 1950s and 1960s we want to recapture the 'big dream', which saw the emergence of a broad middle class – but we want a middle class standing on solid economic and cultural foundations. From the Sadat years, we want to recapture a climate in which rationality and debate prevailed most, if not all, of the time. I write these words in the conviction that condemning others is an extremely negative process that can only further polarize society rather than bring about the desired reconciliation between the different trends which make it up. Such a reconciliation can be effected only through a comprehensive project to propagate the values of progress in society. This is the only way we can look objectively at the era of Muhammad Ali and see its positive and negative aspects. It is also the only way we can objectively assess the eras which followed it, without downplaying or exaggerating their negative or positive aspects to serve whatever viewpoint we wish to advocate. Only in a cultural and educational climate that succeeds in planting the values of progress can this be possible.

The biggest challenge facing Egypt is its middle class, which is undergoing such structural economic, educational and cultural changes as to make it difficult for anyone to define what the middle class means in Egypt today. The progress of any society depends not on the existence of an upper class but on the quality, type, size and level of its middle class, which depend in turn on the extent to which that class subscribes to the values of progress.

In short, Egypt's economic and social problems can be solved only in a general climate governed by the values of progress. Then and only then can Egypt embark on a role beyond its borders, a role no one can stop it from playing because all the givens of history, geography and culture attest that Egypt is the only Arab and Middle Eastern country that is qualified for the role of 'regional leader'. But before aspiring to any such role, Egypt must first put its own house in order.

Part II

Essays on Egypt's Cultural Dilemma

Introduction

In 1978 my first book was published in Fes-Morocco. In December 2001 my twelfth book was published. My first three books comprised a comprehensive critique of so-called 'Scientific Socialism', both the theory and the practice. Another six books were published between 1986 and 1995 aiming at diagnosing the causes of the current political and socio-economic problems of Egypt and endeavouring to present what I believe to be the remedies to these problems. As of 1997 I started to address 'the mind' that is behind the ill situation that has prevailed in Egypt over the past half century and led to numerous conditions of deterioration in several arenas. My last three books, published in 1998, 2000 and 2001, dealt with the mind behind the problems and a number of culture- and education-related aspects.

This part comprises selected chapters from my two books *Critique of the Arab Mind* and *Culture First and Foremost*. It endeavours to characterize the main features of current Egyptian misconceptions, all related to the educational, cultural and media systems that are also a reflection of the political scene in this country over the past five decades.

Tarek Heggy

CHAPTER 1

Why Do I Write?[1]

In the 1970s, I wrote my first three books (published successively in 1978, 1980 and 1983), which together form a comprehensive critique of Marxism in theory and in its practical application. Although they were written more than ten years before the sudden and devastating collapse of the socialist temple, my books not only predicted the collapse but also described the mechanism by which it would come about (the political and social erosion of socialist regimes as an inevitable result of their economic failure).

From 1986 to 1995, I published six books giving a detailed diagnosis of Egypt's political, economic and social problems, most of which I attributed to the way the country was administered during the 1950s and 1960s.

Since 1997, I have been writing about the imperative need for a complete overhaul of Egypt's educational and cultural systems as a prerequisite for the country's link-up with the modern age, with scientific progress and with the march of humanity.

Why do I write? The reasons are many:

1. I write to urge Egyptians to accept criticism and to engage in self-criticism because, unless they are willing to do so, they will not discover the root causes of the ills they complain of today.
2. I write in defence of the values of knowledge and imaginative thinking, of linking up with the collective human civilizing experience, of accepting the Other and of opening wide the doors that were kept tightly shut throughout the 1950s and 1960s.

3. I write to warn against the debilitating disease of self-aggrandizement that has come to afflict us. Its most obvious symptoms, vainglorious posturing and a tendency to regard ourselves as distinct from and superior to everybody else, are manifested constantly in our written and spoken words. This overweening self-satisfaction is not only unhealthy but totally unjustified, based as it is on an inability to distinguish between the glories of our past and the realities of our present. Moreover, it is to be questioned whether it is truly indicative of a sense of superiority or of something altogether different. And what is the role of the Goebbels-style information media in engendering and fostering this negative phenomenon?

4. I write to promote my basic idea that Egypt must concentrate on putting its own house in order by building a strong, successful, socially stable and modern educational and cultural infrastructure, instead of continuing to give priority, as it has been doing since the 1950s, to its external role. For no country can play an effective external role in the absence of a strong and stable internal structure.

5. I write in defence of freedom of belief, but not in the context of a theocratic culture that places our destinies in the hands of men of religion. No society should allow its affairs to be run by clerics who are, by their nature and regardless of the religion to which they belong, opposed to progress.

6. I write to advocate a new culture of peace, one in which the countries of the region will learn to live together and Israel and its neighbours can work out settlements along the lines of what the French and Germans succeeded in doing less than 50 years after the end of the Second World War. In promoting the notion of peace, I point out that it is only when the region moves from a dynamic of conflict to one of peace that real democracy will spread throughout the Middle East.

7. I write to promote the idea that knowledge and culture are universal, the common heritage of all humankind, and that opening the door to both is a prerequisite for reform and progression.

8. I write to call for an end to the Goebbels-style propaganda machines operating in Egypt and the Arab world and their dangerous manipulation of public opinion.

9. I write to drive home the point that only market economics can bring about the economic takeoff to which Egypt aspires, and that the main players in the world of market economics are huge private corporations based on institutional structures and run according to the latest techniques of modern management, human resource and marketing sciences, not privately held organizations whose familiarity with the tools of business is limited to public relations, specifically, to the cultivation of close relations with decision-making circles.

In a word, I write for the sake of a modern, thriving and stable Egypt, at peace with itself and with the outside world, integrated into the mainstream of science, innovation, humanity and the civilizing process.

CHAPTER 2

The 'Big-Talk' Syndrome[2]

In our tongues so glib
Our very deaths reside
We have paid dearly for our gift of the gab.

Nizar Qabbani

No wonder the war ended in defeat, not victory,
For we waged it with all the Orient's gift for oratory,
With quixotic hyperbole that never killed a fly,
Fighting in the logic of fiddle and drum.

Nizar Qabbani

In the 1960s, we claimed to be the stronger military power in the Middle East, a claim that was revealed to be nothing more than an empty boast on the morning of 5 June 1967. To the same extent that we overrated our own abilities, we underestimated those of our historical enemy, which we dismissed as 'a bunch of Jewish gangs'. Events were to prove that the enemy was far more dangerous than we had talked ourselves into believing. Nor were these the only instances of 'big-talk' during the 1960s, a decade that has become synonymous with hyperbole. A number of notorious examples come to mind, as when we described the British prime minister as an effete sissy – a particularly offensive characterization in the Arabic language – or when we taunted the United States of America by inviting its president to 'go drink from the sea, first from the Red Sea and, after it is dry, from the Mediterranean', or when we spoke of the Qaher and its sister missile the Zaher as the ultimate weapons.

When we listen to the rousing national songs composed in the 1960s, we find that, despite their high artistic standard and the beauty of the national and pan-Arab dream they celebrated, their lyrics are replete with big-talk. The tendency to indulge in bombastic and high-flown language continued and, in fact, grew, throughout the 1970s, 1980s and 1990s, and is now such an integral part of our public life that anyone using a different language today strikes a discordant note.

Thus when we talk of our history, we do not use scientific and objective language but invariably sink into grandiloquent rhetoric that drowns the truth in a welter of words. The same pattern applies in our approach to the here and now. Even a victory by the national football team provides an excuse for a veritable word *fest*. Although our standard in the game ranks somewhere between 'average' and 'poor' at the international level, on the rare occasions our players score a victory on the football field we are not in the least embarrassed to hail them as 'conquering Pharaohs' or to use similarly overblown language to describe what, after all, nothing more than the outcome of a match.

The use of superlatives is rampant in our media where, as a look at the front page of any newspaper will show, big-talk is the order of the day. Thus any meeting is a 'summit' meeting, any decision a 'historic' decision.

It must be said in all fairness that our propensity to use big-talk is in no way contrived: we are only doing what comes naturally. High-flown language has become part and parcel of our code of communication, both oral and written. It is not associated in our minds with obsequiousness or fawning; we do not use it in order to curry favour or to ingratiate ourselves with the object of our flattery but as a spontaneous form of expression. Sadly, this reflects a serious flaw in our mental makeup that has become deeply entrenched in our culture.

Even the few who are conscious of the problem are themselves not above succumbing to the big-talk syndrome on occasion, proving that the problem has pervaded our cultural climate to the point where no one is immune to its effects.

An example that graphically illustrates how this feature has come to dominate the cultural landscape in the country is the coverage by Egyptian television of the marathon that took place around the pyramids shortly after the Luxor massacre in the autumn of 1997. Viewers were treated to the amazing spectacle of about ten foreigners, interviewed separately and supposedly at random, who all said the same thing in virtually the same words, as though reading from a prepared script: 'Egypt is a safe country in which we feel secure ... terrorism does not exist only in Egypt but in all parts of the world ... everyone wants to visit Egypt and see its wonderful antiquities'.

The 20 years I spent in one of the largest industrial establishments in the world gave me the opportunity to discover that this feature is unique to our culture, a mark of dubious distinction that sets us apart from other members of the community of nations, whether Western or Eastern.

Cultural evolution in the countries belonging to Western civilization, including North America, has proceeded along a course that equates big-talk with ignorance. Human knowledge is a complex web of interconnected strands in which there is no room for big-talk, only for moderate language that tries as far as possible to reflect the unembellished realities of science and culture.

As to Eastern civilizations, the reserve that has always been and continues to be one of their most prominent characteristics shields them from any temptation to indulge in big-talk.

The picture is very different in the Arab world, where the temptation is indulged to the full. Indeed, the big-talk syndrome is endemic to our culture, which has a long tradition of declamatory rhetoric that places more value on the beauty of the words used than on their accurate reflection of reality. Nowhere is this more evident than in the rich body of Arabic poetry, which is full of poems eulogizing or vilifying this or that ruler for reasons known only to the poet and often having nothing to do with reality. The dichotomy between language and truth is not only acceptable in our culture, it is actually honoured in a famous saying 'The most beautiful poetry is the least truthful' (*athab al sher ... akthabo*).

No less authoritative a source than the Quran itself addresses the issue when it denounces poets as 'drifters in all directions' and of not practising what they preach.

The writer of these lines believes it is incumbent on all those who are aware of this distortion in the Egyptian mindset to raise national awareness of the dangers inherent in using big-talk that is totally divorced from reality. To that end, they must expose the negative effects of a phenomenon that has led some to describe us a 'culture of words' or, with scientific progress, 'of microphones'.

Educational curricula must be designed to alert our youth to the highly detrimental effects of this phenomenon, which not only distorts our image in the eyes of the outside world but keeps us imprisoned in a fantasy world that we have created for ourselves with no basis in reality. It also holds us hostage to a past we evoke in such glowing terms that it becomes more attractive than any present. There is no doubt that the big-talk syndrome is linked to a number of other negative features, such as lack of objectivity, escaping into the past, excessive self-praise and inability to accept criticism. Indeed, it would be no exaggeration to say that it is the bridge that links all these negative features together.

It is also important to emphasize the link between the big-talk syndrome and the narrow margin of democracy. In a cultural climate dominated by hyperbole, it is as difficult to expand the margin of democracy as it is easy for political forces to win adherents through the use of demagogy. Those who claim that their political project represents 'the solution' to all of Egypt's ills are merely serving up another course in an interminable and indigestible meal of big-talk. Economic and social problems today are far too complex to be cured by a slogan rooted in the big-talk syndrome.

As I listen to our public discourse drowning in a sea of hyperbole, I turn to the words of Nizar Qabbani, who eloquently sums up the situation in these words:

> 'We have donned a thin veneer of civilization
> While our soul remains mired in the Dark Ages.'

CHAPTER 3

Singing Our Own Praises[3]

The wise man's mind will even in bliss cause him
*   misery,*
While the fool in abject misery will a happy man be.
It is futile to separate from his ignorance
He who does not repent,
Or to address him who lacks sagacity.

Al-Mutannabi

This chapter will address another defect of the Arab mindset, one that has come to manifest itself conspicuously in the discourse of the majority of our compatriots. I am talking of the tendency to indulge in excessive self-praise and the aberrant social values this defect has spawned in our everyday lives. Nowhere is this tendency to sing our own praises more evident than in the mass media which, day in, day out, feed our self-infatuation by tirelessly extolling our virtues and glorifying our achievements. The same pattern is repeated at the individual level, where boastfulness and self-promotion are fast becoming the norm.

This has not always been the case. If we compare our mass media today with the newspapers and magazines that appeared in Egypt half a century ago, we find that this feature, so much a part of our lives at present, is a recent phenomenon. And if we compare our mass media with those in other parts of the world, more particularly in the developed countries, we find that we are unique when it comes to an overweening sense of self-satisfaction expressed in a constant torrent of self-praise.

In an effort to trace the origins of this phenomenon, I went through hundreds of back issues of Egyptian newspapers and magazines that appeared in the 1940s and found them to be completely devoid of the least hint of empty self-praise. The phenomenon only began to appear, in a diffident sort of way, some 25 years ago, reaching its present brazen proportions in the last 20 years, with a noticeable leap in the last decade.

It is virtually impossible to read a newspaper or magazine today without coming across one or more articles and/or news items lauding our achievements, superiority and virtues. Often these paeans of praise are attributed to a foreign source, as though this imbues them with greater value.

Although much of the material published in this respect inspires more incredulity than credibility, the phenomenon shows no signs of abating, and we continue to indulge an apparently insatiable need for self-aggrandizement by loudly and incessantly proclaiming how wonderful we are.

For example, not a day goes by without one of the following or similar statements appearing in our papers:

1. The international community praises Egypt's economic reforms.
2. The World Bank praises the Egyptian model of economic development.
3. According to this or that university, the Egyptian economy is strong and stands on solid grounds.
4. According to such and such a centre for economic studies, the Egyptian economy will never be exposed to an economic crisis like the one that shook the Asian tigers.
5. UNESCO decides to implement the Egyptian experiment in this or that area at the global level.

What does this mean? And why do we not read similar statements in any French, German, English, Japanese or American newspaper? How to explain our constant harping on the same theme? The explanation lies, to my mind, in a desire to escape from a harsh reality into a fantasy world we have created to fulfil a psychological need for a reality more to our liking. Escapism is by definition a negative reaction, a passive acceptance of the status quo and a tacit admission of our inability to change it.

The only way we can change the present position and overcome our many problems is to adopt a more positive and constructive approach to the reality we are living. This entails admitting that we are beset by huge economic and social problems, that we are, unfortunately (and, it must be said, unnecessarily) a Third World country, and that these problems are a direct result of the way public life in Egypt was administered in the century and a half since the death of Muhammad Ali in 1849.

Of course, stemming the torrent of self-praise in which we are now drowning and diverting it in the opposite direction of constructive self-criticism is a far from easy undertaking. Its success depends on our ability to sow the seeds of positive values in young minds through educational curricula. But these will yield fruit only in the long term. In the short term we must begin from the top of the pyramid, not its base. Once we admit to ourselves how bad the situation really is, the next logical step is to ask why we have reached such a sorry state of affairs.

The answer lies in the ineptitude of some of the leaderships which ran our public affairs in the middle of the previous century. It is important here to emphasize that evaluating the performance of public officials in today's world is not based on their adoption of specific ideologies. Efficient administration depends, rather, on the availability of an 'executive cadre' at the summit of society with a pragmatic approach to problem solving, more concerned with implementing the results of experiments that proved to be successful than in getting bogged down in futile ideological debates that only hamper progress and perpetuate the status quo.

The phenomenon of excessive self-praise is organically linked to another set of negative values that have pervaded our lives in the last few decades. There are many reasons for this, but perhaps the traumatic events of 5 June 1967 have had the greatest impact. The most important of these negative values are:

- A discrepancy between words and deeds has gradually transformed us from a society attuned to reality to one more comfortable with empty rhetoric. This phenomenon is generalized in a very prominent way throughout the region to which we belong. It goes back to distant dates and deeply entrenched cultural factors. Of all the nations of the world, we sing more loudly and frequently of our history, our past glories and our superiority to others. If we compare our attitude with that of a society like Japan, for example, we find that although the Japanese are extremely proud of their nation and heritage, they do not constantly express their pride in grandiloquent language, oratory and slogans.

• Judgements are formed in the logic of love or hate. This leads to the prevalence of subjectivity rather than objectivity and ultimately to the formation of judgements from a purely personal perspective.

CHAPTER 4

Between a Culture of Peace and a Culture of War[4]

More than 20 years ago Egypt decided to abandon the option of war and pursue the path to peace. Although the decision was met at the time with hostility from its erstwhile comrades-in-arms, peace has since become the declared strategic option of all the front-line Arab states. And yet, two decades after Egypt officially adopted the peace line, a culture of war or, at best, of a temporary truce, continues to dominate the thinking of certain circles. Meanwhile, the information media and cultural organs of the state, which are supposed to serve official state policy, are dragging their feet in actively promoting a culture of peace. This has allowed our official media to be used in the recent period as a forum for angry voices talking of enmity to the United States and of the Arab–Israeli conflict in terms clearly inspired by a culture of war and designed to fan the flames of public sentiment.

The effects of allowing this trend to grow unchecked will be ruinous for Egypt and condemn it to a bleak and desolate future. The best description I read of the phenomenon was an article by Salah Eid published in *Al-Akhbar* (25 October 1999) under the title 'Is There Hope?' In the article the writer soberly warns of what he calls 'a growing cultural trend that is inviting us openly to pursue the path of war, revenge and conflict, and that uses the mass media ... to incite the feelings of Egyptians and push them to direct their efforts at revenge and conflict once again'.

That this trend should manifest itself in a number of opposition papers is not unduly worrying in itself. After all, it is normal in a wide society like ours to find different viewpoints, including some marked by excess and others completely out of touch with the realities of the age. The members of the latter group are calling for a return to the past, some to a recent past that dates back only 40-odd years, others to a remote past going back 14 centuries. What does worry me, as it does Salah Eid, is that a trend so at odds with what has been the basic orientation of the state for the last two decades should be given free rein in the official state media.

In providing a forum for the advocates of a return to Egypt's pre-peace line, the mass media have lost sight of the fact that the choice of material they disseminate should be determined by the cultural climate in which they operate. Thus, the material suitable for a culture of peace is not suitable for a culture of war, and vice versa. The state-owned media have a duty to promote and expand a peace culture knowing that a war culture or even, to a lesser extent, a truce culture, will divert our energies from what should be our main target at this juncture: building up a strong society capable of facing external challenges effectively by using the same tools as those used by advanced, successful societies, not those of a Bedouin mentality used by people addicted to failure who want us to remain locked in what Amin al-Mahdi, in his profound book on the Arab–Israeli conflict, calls 'a duality of war and defeat'.

It is certainly more difficult to focus energy on building up a culture of peace in harmony with the spirit of the age and capable of coping with external challenges effectively than it is to allow ourselves to be passively sucked into the slipstream of a war culture. The former requires planning and concerted scientific and cultural efforts, while the latter requires little more than strong vocal cords. Clearly it is easier to rant and rave, to cast ourselves as victims of a vast conspiracy, than to play by the rules of a civilized game compatible with the requirements of the age, that is, one in which scientific planning and educational curricula are geared towards promoting a culture of peace.

A state which in its wisdom chose and remains committed to peace as a strategic option would serve society best by calling its wisdom into play once again and firmly upholding the culture of peace. To begin with, it must not allow the advocates of hate to spew their poison through the mass media in open contradiction with the line it adopted when it made peace its strategic option. We must recognize here that nations, like individuals, go through different stages of development. When an adult displays the behavioural patterns of a child, whose effervescent nature, limited knowledge, immature thinking and paucity of culture and experience may lead him or her to behave impulsively, the adult is accused of arrested development. So too with nations: a mature nation cannot continue to act against its own best interests by allowing a culture of war to take hold.

The period during which we allowed ourselves to be manipulated by bombastic slogans has had a disastrous effect on the economic, political and cultural life of the country, and opened the door to sterile schools of thought holding themselves up as 'the solution' to our myriad problems. Every effort must be made to show up the huge difference between the 'rhetorical' achievements of the 1960s and the real achievements today, to underscore the fact that we managed to build up the country's infrastructure and successfully implement a policy of structural economic reform by turning our backs on a culture of war that required us to direct all our resources towards a futile undertaking at the expense of social and economic progress. The Egyptian people should be reminded that while they were held hostage by the emotional rhetoric of the culture of war, political life was devoid of freedom and democracy, economic life was in ruins and the social climate allowed the forces of darkness to flourish and drag us further away from stability and prosperity.

The price of allowing the dichotomy we are now living to continue will be exorbitant. On the one hand, there is the official line of the state, which is peace, with all this entails in the way of setting in place the mechanisms that can foster and nurture a culture of peace, much as France and Germany succeeded in doing after 1945; on the other hand, there is a trend that is actively fostering a culture of war through the state-owned media. Like a horse being pulled in two directions at the same time, the Egyptian people have no clear idea where they are being led. While anyone has the right to believe in a culture of war, just as anyone has the right to believe in a culture of peace, no one has the right to defend the present disparity between the official line of the state, which makes peace a strategic option, and a media blitz, conducted through institutions belonging to that very same state, that is promoting a culture of war.

CHAPTER 5

Egyptian Identity and Globalization[5]

With the collapse of the Eastern bloc and the end of the Cold War, only one superpower remained on the world stage. It was a development that opened new vistas before capitalist producers, who saw the opportunity to conquer markets previously inaccessible to them. But first, new rules had to be set in place, rules that would reduce protectionism and open the field wide to competition, the mechanisms of which the capitalist producers were better equipped to deal with. It is from this reality that globalization was born. Although essentially an economic phenomenon, globalization could only be envisaged in the context of wider interaction between different cultures, and it is this aspect of globalization, its cultural over-spill, as it were, that many see as a greater threat than its purely economic aspect. Voices came to be raised against the globalization process and the danger it represents for specific cultural identities that, according to the anti-globalization lobby, are at risk of being altogether lost or, at best, greatly diluted, in the context of globalization.

How true is this in regard to our Egyptian identity? Egyptians are unquestionably Arab – but not in absolute terms. They are also eastern Mediterranean – but again not in absolute terms. And, although they are part of the Islamic civilization, this is not their unique identity. Then too there are important Ancient Egyptian and Coptic components in their makeup. For example, although there is a great resemblance between Egyptian cultural mores and those of the Arabian Peninsula, they are not identical. The same can be said with regard to

Egypt's Islamic and Mediterranean dimensions. For, despite the importance of the Islamic dimension, it has not turned Egyptians into exact replicas of Indians or Indonesians.

In other words, the Egyptian identity is a compound one, a multi-layered tapestry woven of a rich diversity of strands that are rooted in history and geography. Because the Egyptian identity is not the product of transient factors but has distant roots in the time and space dimensions, its specificity cannot be obliterated by new phenomena that are characteristic of the times. To understand the role of history and geography in forming the multi-layered Egyptian identity is to realize the complexity of that identity and the depth of the overlapping layers of which it is constituted. Once this realization sets in, the dire predictions we are now hearing about the adverse impact globalization will have on our cultural specificity, about how the new openness to the outside world threatens the integrity of the Egyptian identity, will appear to be totally unfounded and illogical.

It would be wrong to suppose, however, that because an identity is complex it remains static. The main components of identity are history and geography. The first is in perpetual motion; the latter, though apparently motionless, is in a state of suspended animation. The inevitable conclusion to be drawn from this is that the traits of any specific cultural profile are in a state of constant, albeit slow, change, like time itself, which is a dynamic process in a state of continuous flux. Thus the cultural specifics of an Egyptian living at the dawn of the twenty-first century are different from those displayed by his ancestors at the turn of the nineteenth century, which were in turn different from those displayed by our forefathers at the dawn of the sixteenth century. All of that means that cultural specifics are in a state of suspended animation or apparent immobility at the same time that they are undergoing a process of slow quantitative change that leads cumulatively to a slow qualitative change.

If it is illogical to claim that our distinctive cultural profile has remained unchanged throughout the ages, it is equally illogical to claim that the traits of which it is composed are all positive. The best proof that negative strands are interwoven with the positive strands making up the tapestry of our cultural identity can be found in our popular sayings, which celebrate the positive and decry the negative traits of the Egyptian character. Those who fear that our cultural specificity will be crushed under the weight of others coming our way from more powerful and advanced parts of the world would do well to study the case of Japan and other east Asian nations. Although these have dealt extensively with Western civilization, emulating many of its patterns of work and study, their cultural specificity has remained intact. Indeed, some of the more positive cultural patterns they assimilated from Western civilization and adapted to suit their own realities, like teamwork, have given them an edge in their dealings with the West. A short train journey from Tokyo to any other town in Japan attests to the undiminished vigour of Japan's cultural specificity, despite its extensive dealings with and opening up to a world having its own distinct and very different cultural heritage.

A number of questions need to be put to those who dread the loss of Egyptian cultural identity. Is American culture really capable of uprooting Egyptian cultural specificity and replacing it with its own? And, if American culture can obliterate the Egyptian identity, why couldn't British culture (which is deeper and richer than the American) obliterate India's cultural specificity over four centuries of British occupation? Why does the hamburger and Coca-Cola culture strike such terror in their hearts? Finally, if it is impossible for America to assimilate us culturally, how can some people believe that Jewish culture can subsume our cultural specificity under its own? Egyptian cultural specificity is the result of a historical and cultural continuum stretching over 50 centuries, while Jewish culture has been exposed to many disruptions through the ages. Moreover, it is extremely limited in scope because of the limited number of Jews in the world. If anything, it is the Jews who should – and probably do – fear that once peace is achieved in the region, their specificity will be exposed to a cultural onslaught from the surrounding cultures, especially that much of their cultural specificity stems from a ghetto mentality. Peace will mean the end of the ghetto and, with it, of fully one half of Jewish cultural specificity.

The lessons of history prove that societies which opt for opening on to the outside world, which interact with other cultures, help keep their own cultural specificity intact while promoting its development. There is also ample historical evidence that the total or partial isolation which some believe can protect their cultural specificity from erosion is likely to do just the opposite. Throughout the first half of the twentieth century, thousands of Egyptians were open to Western life and culture without giving up any of their own cultural specificity. In fact, their interaction with another culture enriched them by adding to their own cultural specificity new elements that boosted its positive attributes and helped correct some of its negative aspects. Moreover, it is materially impossible for any society today to lock itself into total or even partial isolation. The globalization of science and technology and the information and communication revolution are not only a bar to economic protectionism, but render dreams of isolation both impracticable and unattainable.

Finally, the axiom that man is afraid of what he does not know is applicable to those who fear that our cultural specificity will disappear if we engage in extensive dealings with the outside world. If these proponents of isolationism had a better understanding of the multifarious strands that have converged to produce our specific cultural identity as well as a wider knowledge of other cultures, they would not have the feeling of inferiority that makes them fear the loss of their identity. Ignorance breeds a sense of inferiority, which in turn leads to a paranoid fear that the Other is intent on destroying our identity. There can be no greater feeling of inferiority, compounded by a superficial and simplistic understanding of reality, than that manifested in the fear that exposure to other cultures will lead to the erosion of our own. To believe that our cultural identity will collapse when exposed to other cultures is an insult to our culture and civilization. For the underlying assumption is that our cultural specificity is so weak that it cannot stand up to the challenge of other cultures if we open up to the outside world, and that it can survive only behind high walls separating our culture from others.

CHAPTER 6

Humanity, America and Civilization[6]

In a lecture I delivered a few weeks ago at Princeton University, I pointed out that what some call 'Western civilization' is not purely Western but the culmination of a number of civilizations that flourished at different historical moments. Like tributaries feeding a river, these civilizations – Egyptian, Chinese, Sumerian, Phoenician, Greek, Roman and Arab – merged together to form the mighty river of human civilization. At the same time, I conceded that the present stretch of the river, in which the civilizing process has attained its highest level ever, owes many of its features to its geographical location, which is the West. Thus it is a product of human endeavour through the ages in some respects while in others it is purely Western, although its greatest achievements in the areas of artistic, literary and intellectual creativity owe more to the collective human experience than they do to its purely Western dimension.

To study ancient Egyptian civilization in depth, especially the aspect dealing with conscience and ethics (which inspired the famed Egyptologist and orientalist James Henry Breasted to call Egypt not only the cradle of civilization but the 'Dawn of Conscience'), or the role of Sumerian civilization in laying down legal and legislative frameworks and developing humankind's idea of God (first propounded by the Chaldaean prophet Abraham), or the aspect of Chinese civilization dealing with values, or the rich contributions made by the philosophers of Ancient Greece and, before them, of Hellenistic Egypt, or the work of Averroes and the early Renaissance philosophers, is to realize that human civilization is an integral whole, a continuum of human endeavour that has flowed in an unbroken stream through the ages. To my mind, human civilization has more to do with ethics and values than with monuments and scientific achievements, its greatest accomplishments represented not in the awesome scientific and technological advances made in the fields of medicine, space and the information revolution but in the following:

1. Democracy
2. General freedoms
3. Human rights
4. Respect for 'Otherness'
5. The expanding frontiers of communication and linkage between people at all levels through a process that some call globalization which, in its present unbridled form, appears to be driven by purely economic considerations without sufficient regard to the humanitarian dimension. I believe this is bound to change and that globalization with a more human face is not far off.
6. The development of education in line with the requirements of the age so that in many societies it has come to serve wide segments of the population and not only a limited elite.

Which is not to say, however, that these six great achievements of human civilization have come to full fruition or even that they are anywhere near maturity. Unfortunately, they are still only localized (that is, present in some places and not others), characterized by duality (that is, double standards) or regarded by some as applicable only to them and not to others. This state of affairs reflects a certain uncivilized, not to say barbaric, way of thinking that is based on reasons rooted in history and known to any student of Western civilization, particularly one familiar with the effect the Anglo-Saxon (Viking) component has had on its development. The legacy of this component takes its most extreme form in what I call the 'cowboy culture', a phenomenon that will be addressed more fully later in this chapter. But this in and of itself does not explain why the six values have not yet come into their own at the global level. Other factors, some internal, some external, conspired to impede their development during the last hundred years and make them accessible to some and not to others.

The most important external factor was the scourge of Marxism, which originated in the West but spread out to afflict many societies in different parts of the world. Without exception, these found themselves sidelined in the march of human civilization as a result of their failure to promote and develop the six notions. Moreover, the collapse of Marxism shifted the leadership of Western civilization away from where a certain balance existed between power and culture (or power and knowledge) to a new focal point where information took precedence over knowledge (the acquisition of information and the acquisition of knowledge being two entirely different things).

For someone who, like myself, followed Marxist literature and experience closely for many years, and has written three critical books on the subject (which were described in a review that appeared in a famous American newspaper as a critique of Marxism using Marxist philosophical tools), it is clear that Marxism is a purely European product born in a purely European environment. European conditions in the nineteenth century are what produced Marxism, and any attempt to depict it as a super-structural theory of history is not only completely off the mark but also in open contradiction of the fundamental Hegelian laws on the basis of which the edifice of Marxism was constructed. This view of Marxism as the product of a specific time and place is shared by numerous scholars who have proved the existence of an organic link between nineteenth-century Europe and Marxist thinking. Given that the soil in which it took root has changed virtually beyond recognition, the demise of Marxism 107 years after the death of its brilliant founder (Karl Marx died in 1883, Marxism in 1990), should have come as no surprise.

There is a great deal of evidence establishing the link between conditions in nineteenth-century Europe on the one hand and Marxism on the other, but I will cite only one here, namely, Friedrich Engels' ground-breaking book *The Conditions of the Working Class in England* (1845), arguably the most influential text in the development of Marxist thinking. Not only does this stand as proof positive that the conditions that prevailed in Europe during the nineteenth century are what spawned Marxism, it also helps explain why, with the disappearance of the specific features which led to its emergence, the scourge of Marxism that had for long afflicted Western civilization was bound to disappear too. It must be said, however, that it has disappeared more completely from the countries of Europe than it has from those of the Third World. There are objective reasons for this, reasons that must be understood and respected, if not necessarily condoned.

In short, it can be said that in its search for social justice Marxism rode roughshod over the six values I consider the greatest achievements of human civilization (in its Western moment), rather than, as should have been the case of a theory of social and economic organization designed to further the welfare of people, consecrating and reinforcing those values.

The second serious obstacle standing in the way of the six values is the fact that global leadership today has devolved to the United States of America, which is culturally the weakest link in the Western chain. Despite its awesome material power, superior scientific prowess and undeniable accomplishments in the field of communications and information technology, it remains the poorest member of the club of Western civilization in terms of culture and knowledge, its elites easily distinguishable from their counterparts in other Western societies by the shallowness of their cultural formation, the paucity of their knowledge and a tendency to confuse information with knowledge. I believe it is this that makes millions of intellectuals in the Third World sceptical of the United States' calls for democracy and human rights. In addition to the cultural poverty of the American government and people, the United States displays a degree of raw pragmatism that would put Machiavelli to shame.

Defined as a doctrine that both truth and conduct are to be judged by practical consequences, pragmatism places interests before moral considerations. America's pragmatic worldview is the result of the supremacy of might in the absence of culture, in addition to the Viking ingredient in its makeup. Although it attempts to sugarcoat the realities of naked power by invoking moral considerations to explain its actions, its blatant use of double standards disqualifies it from its self-appointed role as the moral policeman of the world.

No one can dispute the importance of democracy, general freedoms, human rights, respect for 'Otherness', the removal of barriers between nations and societies and education based on promoting initiative and creativity rather than on teaching by rote. Sadly, there is a huge gap between the words of the main proponent of these values and its deeds, which are marked by double standards and determined solely by immediate economic interests, even if the fulfilment of those interests entails trampling the values underfoot. There is a clear absence of a cultural dimension in most of the United States' orientations and decisions, which display a racism lurking not far beneath its shining surface. Indeed, I believe there is a not inconsiderable theocratic dimension behind the civilized secular façade presented to the world. All of which makes attempts by the United States to market these principles an exceedingly difficult task.

Earlier this year, I spent a month lecturing at some of the most important universities and Middle East research centres in the United States. During my tour, I found an impressive wealth of 'information' on the Middle East but, although my lectures were attended by hundreds of university professors and postgraduate students, I did not come across a single person who could be described as a 'Renaissance man' like those who can be found in the universities of Britain, France, Germany and Italy. What I did find, rather, was researchers drowning in a sea of information but lacking a humanistic cultural formation based on a wide-ranging knowledge of the great classics of human creativity.

Not surprisingly, this lack of cultural depth has caused America to commit monumental blunders, as when it threw all its weight behind the theocratic movement in Iran during the 1960s in a misguided bid to counterbalance the Marxist Toudeh party. When it realized, too late, that its policy had backfired, it switched gears and adopted the exact opposite policy. So too with Afghanistan, where at one time it supported forces that have since brought the country to the brink of ruin. Examples of the USA blithely ignoring the moral imperatives that purportedly shape its foreign policy abound, from Zaire in Africa to the banana republics of Latin America to its backing of medieval regimes in more than one continent (a prime example of the moral ambivalence in which much of the United States' actions are shrouded is the story of its relationship with Omar Abdel Rahman).

Can anything be done to change this bleak picture? The answer lies in one word: dialogue. We have a responsibility to establish an effective presence in the American arena and to use the tools of the age, as others do, to make a sustained and cumulative effort (in concert with Europe, which enjoys a balance between power and culture) aimed at saving the train of civilization from being derailed by a reckless driver blinded by his own power and cultural myopia. But whatever reservations one might have about how the United States has comported itself since it became a great power after 1945 and the sole superpower after 1990, that is no reason to deny that the six values it advocates represent the greatest achievements of human civilization. Those who refuse to recognize this can best be described by the Arabic proverb as 'using truth to conceal a dishonest purpose'.

These 'refuseniks' can be divided into four groups. One group is made up of diehard members of the various socialist camps. The second is made up of so-called Islamic fundamentalists, who are in reality a medieval political party using religion as an attractive shield behind which to hide their real intent, much as Judaism was used by secular Jews to promote the Zionist project. The third is made up of those whose animosity to Western civilization in general and to the United States in particular stems not from a socialist or fundamentalist ideology but from their deep frustration at the failure of both the Arab renaissance movement and the pan-Arab project. The members of this group are firmly convinced that this is a direct result of a Western conspiracy against them rather than of any intrinsic weakness in the structure of their own societies. As to the fourth group, it is made up of the proponents of civil society.

The rejection of the six values by the first three groups attests to a shared fascist dimension that characterizes all those who believe their ideological construct represents a universal truth, a closed system that has attained perfection as opposed to the flawed model of Western civilization. Actually, a perfect model of human civilization has yet to be invented, but at least Western civilization admits that it is flawed and has a long way to go before the six values to which it subscribes are fully developed. The members of the first three groups reject the six values on the grounds that they oppose their main exponents (the West in general and the United States in particular). This only confirms their fascist leanings, in that they do not offer a better alternative to these great human accomplishments, make no distinction between the values themselves and their main advocates and, finally, are not nearly as vociferous in their condemnation of negative features in their own societies as they are when it comes to rejecting the United States' advocacy of these values on the grounds that its policies are marred by double standards, opportunism and the subjugation of principles to self-interest.

Only the members of the fourth group recognize that these values do in fact represent the highest achievements of human civilization, but this does not prevent them from seeing that the negative aspects of the West in general and the United States in particular are reflected in the practical application of those values at the human level. At the same time, however, they see that internal factors in their own societies are also preventing the values from realizing their full potential as a universal frame of reference valid for the whole of humankind. The most important of these internal factors is the absence – or very limited presence – of general freedoms and democracy, the lack of any meaningful social mobility and the political and financial corruption pervading most Third World societies.

I am all for directing the harshest possible criticism at Western civilization, both in its Euro-centrist phase and its current American phase, in order to show up the absence of a humanistic and rational dimension in the West's advocacy of the six principles it considers the cornerstone of its own civilization and the greatest achievements of human civilization as a whole. But I believe the Third World writers and academics who are most sharply critical of Western civilization are motivated not by a desire to expand the scope of application of these values to encompass the whole of humanity but by the determination to maintain a status quo that is totally out of sync with modernity, progress, the onward march of civilization and fundamental human aspirations. The systems they are trying to keep in place are not in the least concerned with promoting these six values into rights to be enjoyed by all the members of the human family rather than exclusively by those belonging to Western civilization. This is borne out most strongly by the fact that on the one hand they do not call for these values, while on the other they turn a blind eye to the countless violations of these principles in their own societies.

It is thus important to make a distinction between those who are critical of the West in general and the United States in particular for not practising what they preach and not extending the application of the noble principles they advocate beyond themselves to encompass the whole of humanity, and those whose criticism is driven by altogether different motives. The latter group is determined to keep conditions as they are in the Third World, that is, totally divorced from the six values that are the proudest achievements of human civilization. Some of the members of this group who are most sharply critical of the model of Western civilization put their criticism to work for the account of alternative models that are inimical to progress, science, civilization and humanity. These alternatives have set their societies on a backward course, either to the Middle Ages or to the totalitarianism that destroyed entire generations in many countries, generations that lived and died without benefiting from these principles in any way. Totalitarian systems worked to the advantage of a handful of despotic tyrants and a circle of close associates who ruled in the name of an abstract entity known as 'the people', an amorphous mass that existed only in the rousing speeches to which such systems are prone, while in reality the people consisted of wretched individuals deprived of the most basic human rights and constantly told how lucky they were to be fed, educated, employed and housed!

If we want to move from generalities to practical mechanisms, we must find an answer to the all-important question of how we can keep our faith in the intrinsic value and majesty of the six principles separate from our view of the West in general, and of the United States in particular, as false prophets of the principles they claim to uphold. To embrace the principles wholeheartedly while condemning the hypocrisy, double standards and Machiavellian self-interest that mark much of the behaviour of their main exponents is not easy, but the distinction must be made. The answer lies in the promotion and greater empower-ment of civil society institutions, not only to guarantee that the distinction continues to be made but to keep our societies from falling into the hands of forces whose leaders claim to be the representatives of absolute Truth. Society can protect itself from the malevolent impact of these forces on the dynamics of public life only by working tirelessly to develop the institutions of civil society. For civil society has an undeniable interest in the propagation of these six principles and in protecting society from the forces of darkness, totalitarianism and backwardness. It also has an undeniable interest in preserving the positive aspects of our cultural specificity and identity, a subject we shall discuss more fully in a coming article.

CHAPTER 7

Reflections on an American Trip[7]

Last January and into part of February, I spent a month in the United States at the invitation of ten of the most famous universities in America as well as of six prestigious research centres specializing in Middle Eastern affairs. The purpose of this article is not to summarize the lectures I delivered at these universities or the long discussions that followed. The full texts of the lectures and transcripts of the discussions will appear in a book currently being prepared for publication by one of the universities I visited. Rather, my purpose is to record some of the impressions I formed during my visit, lessons drawn from a trip on which I was privileged to address over a thousand of the top American academics and experts concerned with the Middle East and with studying its past, present and future from every angle of scientific research, especially in the field of social sciences. The essence of these lessons can be summarized in the following five points.

ON AN ARAB PRESENCE IN INFLUENTIAL INSTITUTIONS

From my visits to more than ten of the Middle East research centres with the greatest impact on what can be called the kitchen of ideas, or think tanks, in which US policies and attitudes are formed, including centres that have for years been supplying the State Department and the White House with Middle East specialists such as Dennis Ross and many others before him, I noticed that despite the presence of sizeable contingents of Arab,

Indian, Turkish and Iranian scholars and top experts in many of these centres, the members of each group do not interact as parts of a whole, but act as individuals, isolated islands scattered in a vast sea.

In stark contrast to the lack of cohesion among the Arabs working in these institutions is an almost palpable sense of community among their Jewish-American colleagues, who have forged strong professional and personal links among themselves as well as with visiting Israeli scholars and pro-Israeli non-Jewish scholars. While the Arabs are fragmented and lack a higher aim transcending their individual personal aims, the members of the latter group operate in tandem as an integrated and synergistic team to attain well-defined short-, medium- and long-term goals. Their mastery of the language and idiom of the age and skilful use of the methodological tools of scientific research to further their common aim, their ability to speak to the world in which they are living in its own language, using its own cultural references and symbols, has enabled them to become an influential force capable of shaping, to a great extent, the basic orientations of the United States in all matters related to the Middle East.

This situation is seen by some as merely confirming the validity of the conspiracy theory to which they subscribe; but that is a simplistic explanation for a phenomenon which is the result, rather, of a well-thought out and diligently applied programme of action, a strategic game plan whose application has met with very little resistance. A counterplan to redress the balance of influence, so to speak, can succeed only through the concerted and sustained efforts of a team using modern research methods and speaking in the language of the age – requirements that are not met by most of the members of the Arab academic community in the United States, with the exception of a small minority made up largely of Israeli Arabs, that is, Palestinians who did not leave their towns after 1948. The other Arabs scattered in these universities and research centres would do well to emulate their example. One of the most prominent Israeli Arabs is Haifa-born Dr Shibley Telhami, who holds the Anwar Sadat Chair for Peace and Development at the University of Maryland and who has successfully mastered the rules of a game he plays with great skill to the advantage of the Arab side. Indeed, he is now a recognized Middle East expert whose opinion is sought by decision makers in the United States. The Arabs need hundreds more of his calibre, but these are unfortunately in short supply.

The majority of Arabs working in these establishments are either concerned only with their own narrow interests, passive spectators of the wider world around them, or demagogues using the fiery language so popular in such throwbacks to the 1960s as the Al-Jazirah TV channel, which is reviving the declamatory style adopted by Arab media during a decade that must assume a large share of responsibility for developing an Arab mindset in which the lines of demarcation between reality and rhetoric are often blurred.

The phenomenon of a substantial yet unfelt – and ineffectual – Arab presence in American universities and research centres needs to be addressed, and who better to do so than the Arab League, which has the resources to study the phenomenon in depth and lay down programmes by which to maximize the strategic potential of that presence. However, it must under no circumstances embark on such a project in what Nizar Qabbani called 'the logic of fiddle and drum', that unnecessarily strident and unconvincing brand of demagogy that has distorted the image of the Arabs in the West and alienated public opinion. Indeed, we can expect no sympathy as long as we continue to conduct our discourse with the outside world in the form of verbal battles fought with the weapon of demagogy which, to quote Nizar Qabbani once again, 'never killed a fly'.

On Education

The discussions I had in more than ten universities with hundreds of faculty members, undergraduates and postgraduate students, many from Third World countries like India and China, confirmed the validity of my views on the subject of education in Egypt. I have long believed that before talking of educational reform in the generally accepted meaning of the term, which is the reform of the four pillars on which the institution of education rests (curricula, teachers, students, schools), we must first lay down the strategic aims of education in a policy paper – which need be no longer than one page – then design detailed programmes translating these aims into concrete procedures in regard to curricula, teachers, students and schools. I have also come to believe in the last three years in the existence of a direct connection between the strategic aims of education and the formation not only of modern citizens endowed with the qualities required to meet the challenges of the age, but also of a cadre of modern management leaderships without which no society can make the required leap forward.

For it is now generally accepted that the driving force for an economic takeoff which realizes social justice, creates new job opportunities, spreads a positive spirit in society in general and among the middle and lower-middle classes in particular and preserves social peace while keeping abreast of the times – but without a loss of identity and cultural specificity – is a cadre of efficient executive managers, not academics or economists, although their expertise in their chosen field of specialization is, of course, indispensable.

As I see it, the institution of education is responsible not only for providing students with a reasonable level of knowledge in applied and social sciences but for instilling in them a set of fundamental values, such as a respect for time, teamwork, perseverance and creativity, as well as the firm conviction that human beings are the most important resource for success and progress, that knowledge is universal and, parallel with this, the importance of respecting their own identity (without falling into the trap of chauvinism), the spirit of competition and a respect for pluralism and the Other.

Until we recognize the importance of making these values part and parcel of the educational process, our students will continue to lag far behind their peers in the advanced countries of the world, not in terms of intelligence, but of acquired skills. In the case of developed societies, these skills evolve as a natural by-product of an educational system based on the set of values mentioned above, while our students are locked behind high walls throughout their school then university years, prisoners of a system based on stuffing their minds with massive amounts of often useless information and teaching them by rote.

A system in which the teacher is relegated to the role of a transmitter and the student to that of a receiver can only instil a spirit of apathy in its recipients, inhibiting any creative impulses they may have, reining in their imagination and stifling their intellectual curiosity and initiative. At best, it is a system capable of churning out traditional civil servants at a time when the demand for their services is on the wane. What is required today is not the public functionaries who were once indispensable cogs in the wheel on which society ran, but creative, competitive citizens who can function within the framework of a team and who, recognizing that knowledge is universal, seek to acquire knowledge from any source that can help them hone their competitive edge.

While there is a pressing need for a complete overhaul of the educational system to bring it in line with the requirements of the age, it is imperative to embark on any process of reform in the order outlined above, that is, by first defining the long-term goals of the educational process in Egypt in a strategic paper, then designing the programmes by which these goals can be reached at the level of curricula, teachers, students and schools. This is the only way not only to ensure the formation of modern citizens who are creative, committed and competitive, but also to solve a long list of problems which, though apparently unrelated to the issue of education, are in fact organically linked to it. These include:

- The formation of a cadre of modern executive managers to lead economic life in the context of a new world order based on competition, whether globalization remains as ferocious as it now is or becomes a tamer process, which I believe is more likely.
- The formation of dynamic citizens eager to participate in public life and to expand the margin of democracy.
- The formation of citizens at peace with themselves and with others, both within their own communities and in other communities, instead of the disgruntled citizens who are becoming all too common in our society, who try to solve their problems with the sword of Jihad rather than with the weapons of the age, through competition, hard work, creativity and keeping pace with the scientific and cultural achievements of human civilization.

On Economic Conditions in Egypt

In some 20 meetings, lectures, round-table discussions and television interviews, I was asked about the economic situation in Egypt, and my reply went something like this:

- Before 1952, there was a thriving middle class in Egypt which somehow managed to be both Egyptian and cosmopolitan, traditional and modern, at one and the same time. But it was limited in size, which meant that it was unable to sustain Egypt's liberal experiment in the political, economic and social spheres.

- The public sector experiment failed in Egypt for the same reason it failed in every single country that adopted it, which is because the public sector produces administrators as opposed to managers. The difference between the two is the difference between administrative affairs and economic management. The establishment of a giant factory is not an aim in itself; the aim is that it should be economically successful. The public sector experiment proved that expressions like 'political viability' and 'social viability' are misleading and that any project, however politically and socially viable it may purport to be, will collapse if it does not meet the criteria of economic feasibility.

- The transition from a socialist-inspired command economy to a free market economy was carried out rather haphazardly in the 1970s. The groundwork for a smooth transition was not properly laid, and the task was not entrusted to those best equipped to perform it, namely, a cadre of efficient modern managers.

- The years between 1981 and 1991 were given over to infra-structural projects whose execution required massive outlays of money, time and energy without this being reflected in economic indicators.

- The years 1991 to 1997 saw the introduction of extensive fiscal reforms which, together with a moderate degree of economic reform, made for a relative improvement in the investment climate which was reflected in positive economic indicators.

- The following years, 1997 to 2000, saw the emergence of problems and difficulties whose significance must neither be downplayed nor overstated. One such problem was that the process of economic reform was not accompanied by a process of reform in the management structure based on a methodological plan designed to reduce the role of the state in size while expanding it in importance. The role of the state should focus on laying down policies and following up their implementation in a spirit compatible with the ideal role of the state as envisaged by German Chancellor Konrad Adenauer in the early 1950s, which is to serve as a social compass for society.

There was also the problem of poor credit lending, a problem which cannot be solved through launching defamatory campaigns against suspected malefactors or throwing them in prison – unless of course there is clear evidence that a crime was in fact committed. Problems of this kind are not unique to Egypt, but have plagued many other countries, including some of the most advanced in the world, although they have managed to solve them through banking procedures rather than media blitzes and police arrests.

It also became obvious during the same period that the regulatory framework governing the investment climate needed to be further streamlined with a view to ultimately creating an investor-friendly climate akin to the Dubai model. Then there was the question of national mega-projects which were exacting such a heavy toll on national resources that there was talk of abandoning them. While these projects do pose a problem, I believe scrapping them altogether would be an unnecessarily extreme measure, and that we should try instead to find a way of pushing ahead with their completion in different forms that can reduce the burden they are placing on the state treasury.

In short, there are problems it would be as much of an exaggeration to liken to a cancer as it would to a slight cold, problems that are an inevitable side product of any economic reform programme. All are curable, even the problem of outstanding debt payments.

I always ended my comments on the economic situation in Egypt with the words of distinguished economics professor and member of the Shura Council Dr Adel Bishai, who believes solutions to current economic problems lie in the field of management, not economics, and recommends that they be inspired by advanced management techniques rather than devised by economics professors.

ON THE ARAB–ISRAELI CONFLICT

I spoke on this issue at such length that I will not even attempt to summarize what I said here. But the main message I tried to get across was a simple one: the sooner the protagonists reach a just and equitable solution which responds to the basic aspirations of the majority of their citizens, the sooner the region can close the page on its turbulent history and concentrate on building strong, flourishing modern communities living in social peace. This applies not only to the Arab side but also to Israel which, though providing its citizens with some kind of democratic mechanism, is far from being a civil society in the real sense of the word. A just peace is the only mechanism that will allow for the emergence of societies which, while retaining their distinctive identity and cultural specificity, can display all the attributes of a modern civil society in the political, economic and social spheres.

I spoke of fundamentalism as one of the main enemies of civil society, noting that Jewish fundamentalism stood as a major obstacle in the way of a comprehensive Middle East peace. This greatly angered my audience, whose sensibilities were offended by an association that is not usually made in the West, where fundamentalism is rarely, if ever, spoken of in its Jewish dimension. The deliberate silence on the dangers of Jewish fundamentalism will remain unbroken as long as there is no one to address the issue in the language of the age and in the right forum, which is not the mosques of New Jersey and Los Angeles, but the main universities and research centres in America.

CLINTON AND THE AMERICAN ECONOMY

Although I am planning to write a separate article on this subject, I decided to devote part of these 'Reflections' to an aspect of the Clinton-era economic boom with which the Egyptian and Arab reader may not be sufficiently familiar. For although much has been written about the greatest economic boom witnessed by the United States in its recent history, not enough light was cast on the real achievement of Clinton's eight years in office, which is not the economic boom *per se*, but the fact that its main beneficiaries are the members of the middle and lower-middle classes. This phenomenon is unlikely to outlive the Clinton administration given that the Republican Party is less concerned with the social dimension than the Democratic Party in general and than former President Clinton in particular. Under the Clinton administration, most of the members of these classes, whether professionals, white-collar or blue-collar workers, saw a twofold increase in their incomes and a rise in their living standards unmatched in the last 50 years. Although fortune did not smile as sweetly on the members of the upper classes during the Clinton years, they can look forward to being better served by the Bush administration. While the Republicans have been busy with the Lewinsky affair, the White House furniture scandal and Clinton's controversial pardon of financier Mark Rich, millions of middle- and lower-middle-class Americans are counting their blessings, grateful for the marked improvement that the Clinton years brought to their lifestyles.

* * *

These are just reflections on a visit to America, notes jotted down to record impressions before they fade with the passage of time. My lectures elicited reactions ranging from enthusiasm to outrage. A particularly heated debate followed a lecture in which I spoke of the fact that the United States was a great power with a remarkably superficial culture, and the dangers this posed for the 'humanization' of such notions as democracy, human rights and accepting the Other. But in all cases, the lectures provided an opportunity for stimulating debates conducted in the right forums. In conclusion, I would just like to add that the happiness I felt lecturing at the biggest univer-sities and research centres in the United States was nothing to compare with the happiness I felt the day I delivered a lecture at the University of Maryland's Department of Middle East Research and Studies which carries the name of the late great president, Anwar Sadat.

Chapter 8

Localized to the Spine[8]

Myriad reasons accumulate to make most of the modern Egyptian citizens heavily dosed up with localism. At the same time, the same reasons gather to make the 'hue' of universality for the same citizens so minimized!

On the one hand, citizens of ancient societies suffered a lot from foundering in localism. The 'World' for them was first and foremost their homeland, hence the saying: 'Egypt is the mother of the World'. On the other hand, throughout the 1960s and 1970s (symbolically 'the jumping-off place' for the external world owing to the eruption of the Communication Revolution, the downfall of separatives to the isolating barriers between nations and people, the starting point of the extension of mass media beyond national borders and economy following the same array) we had been wading in localism, evading further communication with the outside world.

Furthermore, our educational curricula had incessantly concentrated on the interior (local history, civilization and literature) in marked contrast with, for example, education programmes in France where the curricula concern themselves in the history of ancient Egypt, China, and Greco-Roman civilizations ... an interest equal to France's interest in its own history.

In addition, the establishment of the mass media in Egypt as the 'long arm' of the government and similarly the local newspapers had made the message of the Egyptian mass media for many years a 'local message'. The discrepancy between our news bulletins and those in many other countries is enough evidence: local news is preponderant, making a clean sweep, whereas the worldwide news bulletin follows and covers events wherever they are.

The growth of the – relatively backward – ideology in our society had been a grand triumph for 'localism' at the expense of 'universality'. The future of the entire world, most properly, has been witnessing relative shrinkage of 'localism'. This takes place in the economic, cultural, educational and mass media spheres.

Consequently, our negligence of the necessity and significance of assiduous scientific research to effect a balance between 'localism' and 'universality' might make us unable to deal, effectively and positively, with the mechanisms of the new globalized universe.

More than once I have mentioned in my articles and lectures that the 'engine' which the institutes, firms and societies are going to rely on is 'efficient management'. I add, in this respect, that management (in our case 'bureaucracy') foundering in localism is too crippled to play the game of the future success-fully. The basis of this game is twofold:

1. Effective management (that is, profitable leadership).
2. Kaleidoscopic knowledge of the substantial element of the game on the international level.

This is applicable to the economic aspect of society's futurity and the political aspect as well.

CHAPTER 9

The Anatomy of Apathy[9]

The pattern of behaviour displayed by the victims of poverty differs from one culture to another. In some cultures, it takes the form of a defiant refusal to succumb to the grip of poverty and an openly rebellious expression of that refusal; in others it engenders an attitude of resignation marked by a docile acceptance of what fate has decreed. Many factors determine which of the two patterns will prevail. Societies which have been subjected for much of their history to tyranny and oppression and with a tradition of venerating their rulers will tend to exhibit the second pattern, accepting their lot philosophically and expressing their disillusionment by using the weapon of sarcasm against public officials, but only in private conversations conducted behind closed doors. In some countries, this mechanism gives rise to political jokes that reflect what people would have wanted to say openly but which, in the absence of available channels, they are forced to express in epigrammatic form. The ability of some of the political jokes thus spawned to encapsulate prevailing opinions and impressions in terse, witty aphorisms is sometimes nothing short of brilliant.

Despots realize only too well that their people's economic independence and the existence of an economically self-sufficient middle class can have disastrous consequences for them. For it is this which allows a people to move from apathy to action, from a resigned acceptance of whatever the ruler decides at his absolute discretion to active participation in political life. To be answerable to his subjects is the last thing an absolute ruler wants, knowing that his grip on power cannot survive open questions on the source of his legitimacy or on the legitimacy of the privileges he and his cronies enjoy.

APATHY, EDUCATION AND TEAMWORK

Modern educational systems in advanced societies are not based on traditional teaching methods in which the teacher is relegated to the role of a transmitter, so to speak, and the student to that of a receiver. They are based, rather, on a feedback process involving student participation, dialogue and exchanges of view. One of the main features of this process is the division of classes into groups required to seek for themselves answers to given questions by accessing available literature on the subject, whether in libraries or on the Internet, comparing notes, consulting together and finally presenting the conclusions reached in the light of their research. This sort of group endeavour promotes a team spirit among its members, develops a sense of participation and the conviction that every individual is entitled to seek the truth for himself and to express the truth as he sees it openly and fearlessly. It also promotes tolerance and a respect for the right of any member of a group to differ from the majority opinion without this necessarily rupturing the overall cohesion of the group. At the same time, it develops the critical faculties of the students and ensures that they will not elevate anyone to the status of all-knowing oracle, neither teachers, authors nor, by extension, political leaderships.

Students raised under this system, which recognizes and consecrates the value of teamwork, grow into citizens equipped to participate effectively in the life of their community. By the same token, students raised under the system of learning by rote, where the relationship between student and teacher is a one-way street, never develop a team spirit and are content to remain passive recipients of information that will never be translated into active participation in public life. Nor is the material they are spoon-fed by their teachers processed by the students, who merely learn it off by heart and reproduce it word for word in their exam papers.

An educational system based on the quantity of material that can be stuffed into young minds rather than on the quality of the values that should go into their formation, which consecrates the cult of personality and fosters blind obedience to diktats from above rather than the spirit of pluralism that is the driving force of progress and civilization, and which does not teach students how to accept criticism and engage in self-criticism can only produce a breed of passive citizens incapable of rising to the challenges life will throw at them, let alone of participating in the political life of their community. Not only is the inflexibility of the system by which they were governed throughout their formative years capable of killing any initiative, but the fact that it denied them the right to choose, which is the essence of political participation, instils in them a spirit of apathy and a sense that any attempt to change the status quo is an exercise in futility.

APATHY AND THE RULE OF LAW

Most political systems in the Third World claim to uphold the rule of law, but this is usually an empty boast rather than an accurate reflection of reality. The majority of these systems operate according to the absolute will of an absolute ruler who is answerable to no one for the decisions he makes. More often than not, these decisions serve to encourage the spread of corruption and protect the vested interests of the ruling establishment, in the total absence of either democracy or the rule of law to which these political systems pay continuous lip service. It is not surprising that in such a climate apathy should spread. People are motivated to participate in public life only when it is governed by the rule of law. Conversely, when the decision-making process is clearly designed to serve the interests of a select few at the expense of society as a whole, people will retreat into their shells and resign themselves to accepting what they cannot change. There is thus a direct relationship between the absence of the rule of law and the apathy of the citizen.

Apathy of Citizens in an Autocracy

The discourse of most undemocratic systems of government is rife with reverential references to 'the people'. Following a time-honoured tradition which began with Hitler and Mussolini, they glorify the people as an abstract concept but do not display anywhere near as much respect and concern for its constituent elements, namely, the individual citizens. There is a glaring discrepancy between the glorification of the entity known as 'the people' in the official discourse of the state and the abasement of the citizen on a daily basis at the hands of the system, whether in government offices, police stations or hospitals, where no attempt is made to translate the dignity accorded to the people collectively into common courtesy for the individual citizen. In short, undemocratic systems of government pay lip service to an abstract non-existent entity known as 'the people' while treating citizens much as the Mamelukes treated their Egyptian subjects in one of the darkest chapters of our history. The tyranny and oppression to which the Egyptians were subjected by a caste of slaves they themselves had bought and to whom they then inexplicably handed the reins of power have left traces in our general cultural climate. The best description of the long shadow cast by nearly three centuries of Mameluke rule on our present reality can be found in a book entitled *The Serfdom Heritage* by an eminent Egyptian author.

Apathy and the Herd Mentality

I tend to believe that undemocratic systems of government engender a cultural climate that can only be described as a 'herd culture'. Under these systems, the government treats people like cattle, with the result that citizens gradually come to display many of the characteristics of a herd mentality, including a retreat of individualism which, along with democracy, is one of the greatest achievements of human civilization and a prerequisite for the consecration of human rights – in the real sense of the term, not in the sense in which it is bandied about by some of the most despotic systems of government today. Once a herd mentality takes hold in any society, the members of that society will develop a passive attitude incommensurate with the requirements of good citizenship. A positive attitude that leads citizens to involve themselves in the workings of their society requires a perception of self as an individual human being, not as an anonymous member of an abstract and dehumanized group known as 'the people'. A useful device for despots, the term 'the people', which is not necessarily the same thing as 'the citizens', allows them to benefit from the apathy and indifference of their subjects.

This indifference, one of the main symptoms of a herd culture, is most graphically illustrated in the low turnout at the polls by educated voters who simply could not be bothered to participate in the electoral process.

CHAPTER 10

The United States and the World Future[10]

At a symposium held on the Atlantic coast in Abidjan and attended by prominent members of the international political and cultural communities, participants engaged in a lively debate on how US foreign policy is impacting on the rest of the world. The debate centred on trying to find a rational explanation for the support the United States has been extending since the end of World War II up to the present day to a large number of corrupt regimes in the Third World, with often disastrous consequences. Indeed, it was thanks to American backing that many otherwise defunct regimes survived as long as they did, including those of several banana republics in South America, the Shah of Iran and other unpopular rulers. In addition to consistently placing its bets on the losing side, the United States pursued a policy throughout the Cold War of supporting fundamentalist – theocratic – political movements in the belief that they could serve as a bulwark against the spread of communism.

What Washington failed to take into account is that once a genie has been let out of the bottle, there is no way it can be induced into going back in and that, moreover, the impact of its emergence cannot be predicted with any degree of accuracy. Everyone knows that the Iranian revolution, which was to cause the United States a great deal of aggravation, was assiduously courted by Washington in the early days, before Khomeini fled first to Iraq and from there to France, which took him under its wing and away from the American embrace. But far from learning its lesson, the United States continued playing the theocratic card in a number of other cases to counterbalance the communist threat, which it regarded as a greater evil.

Perhaps the most famous illustration of how this irresponsible game can get out of hand is what happened in Egypt in the early 1970s, when the theocratic genie was used to offset the influence of the socialist genie which had been let loose in the 1960s. By the end of the decade, the former had become strong enough to turn on the man who had been instrumental in giving it a new lease of life, Anwar Sadat, who was assassinated by a member of Egypt's fundamentalist movement. Moreover, there is no doubt in my mind that the Palestinian theocratic genie was let out of the bottle in order to clip the wings of the secular Palestinian resistance movement, Fattah – an act of folly its perpetrators will rue for many years to come.

Participants at the Abidjan symposium spent many hours trying to come up with a logical explanation for this bizarre aspect of US foreign policy which, despite an abysmal record of failures, continues to be applied to this day. The theme of the debate was dictated by the venue of the symposium, Africa, where corrupt, despotic rulers kept in power by the United States have wreaked havoc on the peoples of the continent. Examples abound, but perhaps the most notorious was Zaire's Mobutu. My interpretation of the phenomenon differed from that of the other participants, some of whom attributed it to America's inexperience in the field of foreign affairs, others to Jewish domination over the American decision-making process.

My view was, rather, that American foreign policy is influenced by two sets of considerations. One set is related to its long-term interests, which dictate that the political system of the United States support forces capable of moving their societies forward both in terms of democratic development and economic growth; the other, running parallel with the first, is related to the short-term interests of powerful economic institutions, interests which are not necessarily compatible with those of the United States in the long term. The history of the United States since the end of World War II has been shaped by a constant tug of war between the two sets of considerations. Sometimes the decision-making process is more responsive to the short-term interests of economic institutions, leading to the disastrous alliances we spoke of earlier. Much less frequently, it operates to serve America's own long-term interests. When that happens, the United States astounds the world by taking principled stands in defence of legitimate rights, as when President Eisenhower condemned the tripartite aggression against Egypt in 1956.

If scientific socialism died because it carried within it the seeds of its own destruction as represented in its inability to achieve economic success, so too does the so-called 'Free World', which is currently led by the United States, carry the seeds of its own destruction, in the form of the sharp discrepancy between the short-term interests that often determine its political decisions on the one hand and the long-term interests of its own society and those of the world at large on the other.

And yet this bleak picture is not without a glimmer of light. There are grounds for optimism thanks to the technological and information revolution, which could help engender a general climate favourable to the positive development of human rights and environmental protection systems, which are still primitive, uncoordinated and extremely inequitable. In such a climate, long-term considerations that have for long been subsumed into the short-term considerations of special interest groups with an inordinately powerful influence on the political decision-making process will come into their own.

Here a number of key states in the Third World can play an important role in fostering a climate conducive to just such a development. A necessary if not sufficient condition here is to defuse whatever tensions now poison their relations with the United States. Maintaining these tensions will only reinforce the status quo and leave the field open to short-sighted, short-term interests, with all this implies for the prospects of global peace and stability. If these interests are given a free rein, they will eat away at the foundations of world order and pave the way to clashes, bottlenecks and explosions that could destroy the present world order.

Summing up the conclusions reached by the symposium, a noted French professor of political science at Paris I University had this to say: 'In other words, it is only if the United States discards the theory that these strange regimes are the only barrier in the face of global chaos that this worst-case scenario can be averted. By clinging to that theory, the United States is

trying to avoid the breakdown of world order through methods
that will only hasten its coming!'

CHAPTER 11

Egypt's Economic Reform in the Balance[11]

There is no doubt that the massive investments poured into Egypt's public sector during the years of its socialist experiment failed to achieve the desired result, which is an annual return on investment of not less than 15 per cent after the deduction of inflation rates. To those who point with pride to the huge industrial plants and institutions established during that period, we say that modern management sciences have taught us that when it comes to economic performance, pride is not measured in terms of the size of factories and investments, because financial outlays are not an end in themselves. Rather, pride is measured against the economic return on investment. A dictum of modern management sciences is that the greatest disaster which can befall any economic enterprise is when the thinking of its senior management comes to be governed by considerations of scale rather than of return on investment.

As to those who maintain that even if the return on investment was modest the social benefits were enormous, they would do well to remember that there can be no viable societal role in the absence of high economic returns. How is it possible in the context of meagre economic returns to continue guaranteeing high levels of employment for citizens and ensure that they receive decent salaries and humane treatment in the areas of medical insurance, pensions, etc.? In other words, the economic role is the only guarantee for the continuation of the social function of investments, business and projects. The fact that the projects set up during Egypt's socialist phase failed to realize good returns on their investments meant that after a while they were unable to continue performing their important societal role, as represented in providing a large number of citizens with employment and health care.

When the collapse of the socialist world proved beyond the shadow of a doubt that the failure of the socialist model was not confined to Egypt but extended to all the other countries which had applied it, Egypt realized that to continue basing its economic life on a model whose shortcomings were now visible to all was to court disaster, not only in the economic sphere, but also, and in consequence, the social.

This realization brought home the need to embark on a process of fiscal and economic restructuring in the aim of moving Egypt out of the framework of a command economy in which the public sector plays a pivotal role and placing it within the framework of a market economy in which private enterprise is the main driving force behind most economic activities. It was hoped that this would enable private sector enterprises to achieve the positive economic results necessary for economic growth, which is the groundwork for the societal role of economic life, as represented in the creation of real job opportunities, particularly for young people, one of the most important prerequisites for social peace.

There can be no denying the fact that the impressive efforts made during the restructuring programme were extremely important and, indeed, instrumental in sparing Egypt from the fate of other societies whose socialist experiment not only caused them to suffer financial ruin, but exposed them to dangerous social upheavals.

However, that is not to say that Egypt can afford to rest on its laurels or to assume that all is best in the best of all possible worlds. All major human endeavours, including those that are successful, require constant revision, re-evaluation and objective self-criticism. It is on this aspect of Egypt's restructuring endeavour that the present chapter will focus, without in any way belittling the significance and magnitude of the results achieved in this connection or of the efforts made to allow the formation of private sector economic institutions that contribute both to the realization of economic success and to the translation of that success into a societal role.

Any attempt to re-evaluate economic performance entails a

greater degree of self-examination in respect of the public sector experiment, in the sense that every effort should be made to convince society that the public sector, however noble the intention behind it may be, is an institution that is doomed to fail for one specific reason, namely, management. The Egyptian public sector failed to achieve the targeted 15 per cent annual return on investment because its management was incapable of reaching that target. It must be emphasized that management is always the weakest link in the chain of the public sector. Even if there are a few cases where the management of a public sector enterprise is successful, they are merely exceptions that confirm the rule. The public sector experiment in Eastern Europe and in many Asian, African and Latin American countries proved that no public sector enterprise is capable of producing a cadre of executive managers comparable to those who have scored impressive successes in private sector economic enterprises in the West.

The main reason is that a public sector enterprise functions in the absence of a property owner who has a personal stake in the success of his property and hence closely supervises its performance. This is in the natural order of things. On the other hand, those who represent the 'owner' in the public sector are mere employees who do not and, indeed, cannot, fill a role that is not theirs. And so the general meetings of public sector enterprises, which are assumed to represent the owner, in this case 'the people', are transformed into assemblies of employees accountable to no one for their failure to achieve the projected economic returns.

Parallel with this is the fact that the working environment in economic enterprises of the public sector is closer to the culture of a government bureaucracy than it is to an economic management culture. Thus in most cases we find these enterprises run by paper-pushers or glorified foremen rather than managers in the true sense of the word as defined in the lexicon of modern management science. The natural result is that economic enterprises of the public sector give priority to aims other than what should be the main aim of any economic enterprise, which is to realize a return on investment of not less than the interest accruing on bank deposits. Failure to achieve this target ultimately leads to economic bankruptcy, which in turn leads to the suspension of any societal role for the public sector.

At this stage in the process of economic reform, emphasis must be placed on this particular aspect of the public sector. The people should not be led to believe that the public sector is being privatized in order to expand the scope of private ownership; they should be given the real reason for the shift, which is that management in public sector enterprises proved to be a failure and privatization aims at placing projects in the hands of those who can run them according to efficient management techniques capable of achieving the desired return on investment in order to guarantee a vigorous economic climate that will in turn guarantee a societal role.

To recognize the pivotal role of management is to recognize the importance of promoting management education by introducing curricula in various academies and faculties designed to serve this aim, as well as by a massive influx of investment into training academies for middle and senior management teams. For without the formation of a cadre of modern and efficient executive managers who are well versed in contemporary international management sciences, methods and techniques it will be impossible to maximize the impact of the efforts that have been made in the area of fiscal and economic restructuring, because management is what translates sound economic systems into tangible results.

The same degree of concern accorded to management should also be directed to the domain of marketing. For the world is interested not in the production of a given commodity or service but in its marketing. What is the point of any production process, whether of goods or services, that is not crowned by the successful marketing of the product put out by such process? Marketing takes us straight into the heart of the globalization process. When it comes to marketing any product in the world today, no one can afford to ignore globalization and the new dynamics it has generated. It is a fact that people will not buy goods or services unless they conform to the specifications that meet their demand and unless they are more competitively priced than their available alternative. The consumer is not overly concerned with other factors, such as where the goods or services he is buying were produced. Indeed, these factors are expected to play an even smaller role in the world of marketing in future. It is a world in which there will be no room for those unable to speak the language of the age or to understand its realities, those who stand on the sidelines contemplating in bewilderment the rapidly changing landscape in which they find themselves and plaintively questioning the legitimacy and fairness of the new rules of the game. They cannot turn the clock back, and success in the world of marketing will come only to those who ask themselves how they can achieve the best results for their products in the context of a new reality that is here to stay.

It is also necessary to study the real reasons behind the weak flow of direct foreign investments into Egypt, by arming ourselves with the ability to scrutinize our shortcomings objectively and to engage in constructive self-criticism. There are reasons for the phenomenon and they can be overcome, but only if we first overcome our excessive sensitivity to self-criticism. We must recognize that self-criticism is a healthy practice that does not require us to deny the very real achievements already made while at the same time spurring us to ever greater successes.

CHAPTER 12

The Arab Mindset and the Conspiracy Theory[12]

For anyone concerned with the world of ideas, particularly as they pertain to the social sciences and the dynamics governing different societies, some issues acquire greater resonance than others. One issue that has long been at the forefront of my concerns is the prevalence in Arab societies, in general – including Egypt – of the 'conspiracy theory'. In the minds of many millions of Egyptians and Arabs the following propositions have become virtual articles of faith:

- The blueprint for our recent history and present reality was drawn up by the great powers, and what we are now living through is the product of their machinations.
- The powers responsible for this grand design were Britain and France in the past and the United States, aided and abetted by its protégé, Israel, in the recent past and present.
- The plans for 'creating history' were prepared in great detail by those powers, leaving little choice for those down the ladder of power, and for the generations and individuals who followed, but to accept the course of events charted for them – and, thus, for us.
- Accordingly, we bear little responsibility for the past, the present, and indeed, according to some, the future. Rather, reality is the predetermined result of the grand design, and it is beyond our power to change it.

When Israel, as an actor, is factored into this theoretical scenario, the picture becomes even more inflammatory and provocative. Moving from generalities to specifics, it is possible from this perspective to see even the landmark events of our modern history as the consequence of plots hatched by the great powers. These include the 1956 War,[13] Syria's secession from Egypt in 1961,[14] the Yemen War of 1962,[15] the June 1967 disaster,[16] the failure to crown the glorious crossing of the Suez Canal in October 1973[17] with the military liberation of the whole of Sinai, the visit of President Sadat[18] to Jerusalem in 1977, the Camp David accords[19] signed between Egypt and Israel, the demise of the Soviet Union and the structural collapse of socialism everywhere. Also perceived in this light – that is, the realization of a blueprint of plans that are slated to become history – are the emergence of the USA as the sole global superpower, the New World Order, the GATT,[20] and a host of other global developments.

A paradox worth studying is that this view is shared to varying degrees by the following disparate groups:

1. All those who can be classified as 'Islamic' believe profoundly in the truth of the propositions which collectively form the 'conspiracy theory'. This includes groups such as the Muslim Brotherhood,[21] the Gamaat Islamiya,[22] the Jihad[23] and all fundamentalist movements, indeed, even the most moderate of the Islamic trends. It pains me to have to use the epithet 'Islamic' to designate groups that are basically nothing more than political organizations, because this implies that whoever does not belong to those groups could be classified as 'non-' or 'anti-Islamic'. Although I am ready to challenge the validity of this obviously ludicrous implication, I am forced to use what has become the widely accepted terminology to describe these groups. In other words, if we had to identify the most devoted adherents of the conspiracy theory, there is little doubt that this dubious distinction belongs to the Islamists.

2. Those who can be classified under the banner of socialism, from Marxists to socialists and many other leftist subdivisions, including the Nasserites,[24,25] also subscribe to the conspiracy theory, albeit less rigidly than the Islamists. For while they believe in the theory as a whole and, accordingly, in the propositions on which it is based, their belief is not shrouded

in what can be called the spirit of Jihad[26] or militancy, nor grounded in anti-Christian feelings as is the case with the Islamists.

Of course, the difference in the degree of rigidity of the belief and the fervour of the conviction is due to the theocratic ethos of the Islamic groups and the more scientific, progressive and modern spirit of socialist ideas, even if the failure of those ideas to achieve their aims or live up to their slogans proves that they are inherently flawed.

3. The third and final group is made up of ordinary citizens in the Arab world and Egypt, who belong neither to the Islamic school politically nor to the socialist school ideologically. Most of these people are inclined to believe blindly in the conspiracy theory and to accept the validity of the propositions on which it rests.

It is essential to remember, however, that the adherence of each of the three groups to the conspiracy theory is based in a different set of reasons:

1. The Islamists, in all their subdivisions, consider that the history of the region is one of conflict between Islam, on one side, and the Judaeo-Christian world, on the other. As far as they are concerned, the Crusades[27] never ended; they simply moved beyond the traditional battlefield. This group attaches great importance to the Jewish dimension, which it blames for many of the ills besetting the Arab/Islamic world and the disasters that have befallen it.
2. The socialist group, in the broad sense of the word, views matters from the perspective of the struggle between what it calls the forces of imperialism and the oppressed and exploited peoples of the world.
3. Meanwhile, the many ordinary citizens who subscribe to the conspiracy theory reflect public opinion as forged by the media, many of the key constituents of which are controlled in this part of the world either by the socialist camp or the Islamic camp, and which repeatedly tout the conspiracy theory, from its many angles, as though it were gospel truth.

In societies not characterized by a high level of education and culture, the information media (including the *minbar*, or pulpit, of the mosque) can be used to indoctrinate and propagandize, thereby moulding public opinion. Indeed, in some countries the Ministry of Information[28] has been referred to as the 'ministry of guidance', a clear admission of the function it sets itself: to guide and direct.

Actually, the reasons from which the three groups draw their belief in the conspiracy theory are wholly illusory, with no basis in fact, history or logic. The history of the peoples of our region would have been the same, including their subjugation by Western colonialism, even if the Middle East had been part of the Christian world. The West did not colonize us because we were Muslims but for quite different reasons. On the one hand, we were less developed technologically, industrially and otherwise, and hence susceptible to foreign domination – easy pickings, as it were; on the other hand, the whole colonial enterprise was motivated primarily by economic considerations, and, to a lesser degree, by cultural, or 'civilizational', considerations, which constitute a broader framework than religious factors. Although much can be said to refute the naive view that the region's history with Western colonialism can be reduced to a question of religion, it is sufficient here to cite but a few examples attesting to the contrary to realize how widely off the mark this view is.

Those who maintain that we would not have been colonized were it not for our Muslim heritage conveniently forget the dark chapter of our history under the dominion of the Ottoman Empire,[29] when the colonized Arab peoples were subjected to the worst kinds of abuse by their colonial masters, despite the fact that both colonizer and colonized belonged to the Muslim faith. Throughout the eighteenth century our ancestors were in a deplorable state of backwardness, though they were Muslims occupied by Muslims (the Christian West had still not entered the scene).

This situation prevailed when the Zionist movement[30] was launched by its founder Theodor Herzl[31] towards the end of the nineteenth century; indeed, we had remained locked in a state of medieval backwardness for more than six centuries prior the emergence of the Jews as a political force capable of affecting the course of events in any way.

Though in many ways simply wrong, the socialist reading of our history with colonialism is correct in approaching the issue from an economic perspective. Certainly the economic factor was the driving force behind the West's imperialist ambitions in the region over the last two centuries. But this was within a framework quite different from that of the conspiracy theory, as will be explained in later chapters.

As to the ordinary citizens who espouse the conspiracy theory, their logic may be impaired and unable to stand up to serious analysis, yet it is in a way understandable. For even the most outlandish statement, if repeated often enough, can come to be accepted as true, especially in a society in which half the population is illiterate and the other half is exposed to only a very modest standard of education and culture. Put another way, lack of sophistication provides fertile ground for the most untenable and demagogical assertions to take root and flourish.

To my mind, the real issue is that most of those who subscribe to the conspiracy theory know very little about the nature and mechanisms of the capitalist economy – a market, or free, economy. The essence of capitalism is competition, a notion that means many things, some positive and wholesome, others negative and unhealthy.

But given that all the ideological alternatives to the market economy have failed lamentably, wreaking such havoc in the societies which adopted them that they have been relegated to the museum of obsolete ideas, we must not let nostalgia for the past or an emotional reaction to capitalism drive us back into the world of socialist ideas. Those ideas have caused so much loss, damage and human suffering that they have forfeited the right to be given a second chance. Indeed, experience has proved that socialism (both as an ideology and in terms of practical application) is not a viable system of beliefs.

As noted, competition – the backbone of the capitalist economy – is a notion that carries within it not only positive aspects but also highly negative ones.

On the positive side, it works to the benefit of individuals and the enhancement of their quality of life because, by definition, it leads to a process of constant upgrading of type and quality of products and services, which in turn often leads to reducing their cost. On the negative side, it sometimes deteriorates into vicious struggles between the producers of products and services, struggles that can take such diverse forms as driving a rival out of the market, marginalizing the role of others and grabbing the largest share of the market or markets. This feature of the Western capitalist system engenders the belief in countries without a long tradition of industrialization and advanced capitalist services that they are the victims of a well-planned conspiracy.

It is this aspect of competition that I want to address, because unless it is understood well and accepted as an inevitable, if unfortunate, feature of the market economy in the contemporary world we will not attain any of our goals. This competition, which is one of the main cornerstones of economic life based on the dynamics of a market economy, was responsible for the wars that tore Europe apart over the last three centuries, including the two world wars that shook the twentieth century.

Only in the last three decades did the Europeans come to realize that the advantages of ending the strife that had convulsed their continent throughout much of its history greatly outweighed the benefits of allowing a spirit of contentious competition to continue ruling their lives. And so competition in its extreme form was displaced from Europe into other arenas. The rationale now governing competition in Europe, which continues to thrive in many different forms, is mutual coexistence and consensus, based on the framework of checks and balances in which competition is to operate.

To illustrate this point better, I would like to draw attention to a very simple fact: in an economic system based on competition, the strategic interest of the producer, or seller, is to remain a seller while ensuring that the buyer of his products or services remains a buyer as long as possible, preferably for ever. There can be no switching of roles here. This principle is the essence of that aspect of competition which many in our part of the world tend to regard as indicative of a conspiracy. Although in a way it does resemble a conspiracy, it is very different in terms of motivation and the rules that determine its inner workings.

This principle operates within advanced industrial societies. Its application outside those societies can thus be anticipated, and is inevitable.

In other words, the economic system in force in advanced industrial countries (now also advanced technologically and in the services sector) is based on unavoidable conflicts fuelled by competition, which manifest themselves in endless attempts to capture the largest possible share of the market. The big fish are constantly trying to swallow the little fish. This process and its negative, even ferocious, aspects operate both within a given society and beyond (where they are liable to be even more ferocious). The terminology and practices of modern management sciences contain many terms and notions that, in the final analysis, serve competition (positive and negative aspects). While I do not intend to detail this terminology, the analysis here would be incomplete if I did not mention at least some of the principal notions which have become part of the lexicon of modern management sciences in the contemporary world – quality management, global marketing, data confidentiality, environmental considerations – and so on. These and other newly coined terms are tailored essentially to serve the interests of the big fish who, by applying them, can successfully swallow the small fish.

We can now add to the big-fish-eat-small-fish law another, parallel law, which is that the swift and efficient fish will gobble up those less swift and efficient. The huge conglomerates that have emerged on the global stage in the last 20 years in the fields of industry, services, technology and commerce attest to the growing ascendancy of this new law. It is important here to distinguish between what we want to see and what we cannot avoid seeing if we do not want to delude ourselves. These laws exist and are fully operational; there is no hope after the demise of socialism of replacing them with laws that can ensure success, abundance and the avoidance of these aberrations (for those who regard them as such).

It must be said that even the most highly cultured intellectual would be unable to grasp those new realities and laws fully if his cultural formation were based exclusively on familiarity, no matter how extensive, with the human and social sciences but with no knowledge of the modern fields of management, marketing and human resources, and their many spinoffs. In a way, he would be like a physicist who has devoted 50 years of his life to studying physics since the dawn of history – except the last half century. Although that physicist would be an expert on the history of the subject, his knowledge belongs in a museum of the past and is in no way suitable for the modern world.

Unfortunately, a considerable number of Third World intellectuals are like that hypothetical physicist: they know a great deal but their knowledge does not extend to new areas. Moreover, they continue to engage in lengthy debates in which they use obsolete terms of reference which confirm that they are living in the past, and, consequently, are unable to grasp what is happening around them. Indeed, these obsolete frames of reference stand as obstacles in the way of society's ability to take the only means of transportation that can carry it to the desired destination, or, stated otherwise, its ability to play the game according to the new rules, not the utopian rules that exist only in the minds of those who remain locked in the past.

We shall now turn to an issue that is inextricably linked to any discussion on the subject of conspiracies and the conspiracy theory, namely, the Japanese phenomenon. In a lecture delivered in Tokyo in December 1996, I credited Japan with playing a vitally important role in my intellectual formation, explaining that its experience had convinced me that the conspiracy theory, whether imaginary or real, was far less potent than it is made out to be. If one believes in conspiracies, then surely there could be none more heinous than the two atomic bombs dropped on Hiroshima and Nagasaki in 1945. For, by definition, a conspiracy seeks to inflict injury on the party against whom it is aimed, and there can be no greater injury than the devastation rained on Japan at that time.

Japan's refusal to remain locked in the spiral of defeat proves that, even assuming a conspiracy does exist, and that, moreover, it attains its full scope, which is the infliction of maximum damage on the target, the conspirators cannot achieve their ultimate aim unless the targeted victim accepts to be crushed. Japan has risen like a phoenix from the atomic ashes to become the main rival of the very powers that, in 1945, appeared to have succeeded in bringing it to its knees.

The most important thing left to say about the unshakable belief in the conspiracy theory that seems to have taken hold of the Arab mindset is that it denotes a complete denial of a number of fundamental principles of which we must never lose sight:

- It proceeds from the assumption that while the conspirators enjoy absolute freedom of action when it comes to exercising their will, the parties conspired against are totally devoid of that prerogative. This endows the former with the attributes of motivation, determination, will and the ability to make things happen while stripping the targeted parties of all these attributes, reducing them to objects rather than subjects, inanimate pawns moved across the chessboard of history according to the whims of others.
- It denies the parties conspired against the quality of nationalism while attributing it exclusively to the conspirators.
- It makes the conspirators legendary figures in the minds of those who consider themselves victims of conspiracies.
- It assumes that there is no way the parties conspired against can foil the stratagems of the conspirators, making for a defeatist and passive attitude that runs counter to pride and self-dignity and to the notion that nations, like men, can shape their own destiny.

My views on the conspiracy theory would be incomplete – as well as contrary to my beliefs – if the reader were left with the impression that I believe that conspiracy and conflict are one and the same thing and that, accordingly, I do not believe that conflict has been a constant feature of human history, or that I am denying that conspiracies have always been a part of that history.

In fact, I am convinced that human history is made up of a series of conflicts and that the world stage today is the setting for numerous bitter and major conflicts. But conflict and conspiracy are two different notions.

Conflict means persistent efforts by given parties to maintain the edge they enjoy over others, or even to expand that edge and the privileges that go with it. But conflict also means that contradictions are played out in a game that proceeds according to certain rules, which differ from one era to the next, so that whoever wants to attain prominence must wage the conflict using the tools and the rules that will guarantee the optimal results. Here the Japanese model emerges again as the most salient example of this characterization. It goes without saying that conflict is a relatively more open game than conspiracy, and that the degree of ambiguity in which the game of conflict is shrouded (even those features that are so ambiguous as to appear closer to magic than anything else) is relatively less than that necessarily surrounding the conspiracy game. Placing matters in the context of a conflict game rather than within the parameters of a tight conspiracy that determines the course of history encourages people to draw on their inner resources of pride, dignity and determination to enter the game as active participants bent on affecting its outcome to their advantage.

This is very different from the mindset created by a widespread belief in the conspiracy theory as the driving force of history, which encourages people to adopt a passive attitude, albeit with much wringing of hands and loud complaints at the often disastrous results coming their way, rather than rise to the challenge by becoming active, motivated players in the game, even if the cards are stacked against them. The experience of the Japanese, who have waged one of the most ferocious conflicts in human history throughout the last half century, stands as a testimonial to the triumph of the human spirit in the face of great adversity. That is not to imply that history is devoid of conspiracies; indeed, the annals of human history are rife with examples of plots and counterplots. However, history itself is not a general conspiracy but rather the stage for a fierce and relentless struggle on which those who quietly acquiesce to stronger powers are relegated to the sidelines.

Finally, it is necessary to highlight another disastrous aspect of the rampant belief in the general conspiracy theory, which is related to undemocratic rulers like some of those now in power in the Third World. The undemocratic ruler canonizes with his ideas and statements, and through the available information media, belief in the conspiracy theory, which is a useful fig leaf behind which he can hide his own shortcomings: this allows him to blame the problems and hardships faced by his people, and his inability to respond to their aspirations, on outside elements, i.e. a conspiracy, rather than acknowledging the real reason, which is the absence of democracy and the existence of rulers like himself, who are usually not the most efficient, capable, honest or cultured members of the society they represent.

The real challenge as I see it is not a global conspiracy but a global conflict, one that is ferocious, violent and dangerous, which nations can wage successfully only if they are properly equipped for it. And they can be equipped only if their leaders are men of vision operating in a climate of democracy through cadres who demonstrate efficiency, ability, honesty and culture. It is impossible to overrate the importance of this last attribute – for without culture there can be no vision.

In conclusion, it must be said that though the logic of the proponents of the conspiracy theory is based on their patriotic love of country, and though I have no doubt that they are nationalists who want only the best for their country and people, the sad fact is that, in the final analysis, their absolute belief in the conspiracy theory renders them defeatists and advocates of the line of least resistance, which is to bemoan their lot as parties conspired against without making a serious effort to do anything about it.

CHAPTER 13

Complacency: 'Enough is Enough'[32]

In a discussion after one of my recent public lectures I was asked by a young student to name 'one single' dimension in the contemporary Egyptian thinking that requires a full-scale change. My immediate answer was: 'Complacency'. In my elaboration I highlighted the following relevant aspects:

- Any fair outsider cannot deny that Egypt made, throughout the past decade, excellent moves towards a much better economic life. Nevertheless, the inability to admit the gigantic mistakes of the 1950s and 1960s continue to impede the introduction of new systems that would undeniably make the past decade's achievements much greater. We simply need to say, clearly, that the way our economy was structured and managed since the mid-1950s was a complete mess. Most of the systems engineered during this era ought to be replaced by systems that proved to be successful in the advanced economies.
- Our well-deserved pride in our history must not leave us in the currently prevailing 'complacency phenomenon'. On the contrary, we must admit that many features of our contemporary life ought to be changed.
- The advocates of the 'medieval fundamentalism' and equally the old guards of the 'totalitarian era of the 1960s' are the true enemies of the great efforts to build a modern, stable and flourishing Egypt. The first group advocates an illusion that could only throw us back into the Middle Ages. The second group has taken us through a long journey of

failures. Both of them would cut our ties with the world in an age of 'no isolation'.

I remember that I ended my talk about these contradicting notions, i.e. 'Self-criticism' and 'Complacency', by expounding the opinion that I never stop expressing: 'Self-criticism is like all advancement values ... they need to be demonstrated by each leadership in its domain.'

'Self-criticism' does undeniably generate positive (non-passive) citizens, i.e. members of society who profoundly believe that they can make 'a difference'. With such a belief we gain more believers and fewer followers.

With decreasing complacency and a growing ability to practise self-criticism, we shall not disregard 'conspiracy' as an undenied phenomenon, but we shall certainly relate more of our major problems to 'The way things were/have been managed within our borders'. For instance, we shall thence accept that the catastrophic living conditions in many areas such as 'Imbaba' are not the result of an imperialist (or Israeli) plot!

CHAPTER 14

Civilized Debate versus Fascist Intimidation[33]

Foreign students of contemporary Egyptian affairs believe there has been a marked decline in the civility of public discourse in recent years, particularly when two opposing points of view contend over an issue of public concern. I have given a great deal of thought to this phenomenon, which I tried to place in a historical perspective by comparing the language of debate in use today with that used earlier this century. My research centred on the now-defunct review *Al-Kashkool*, and specifically on the issues that appeared in the period between 1923 and 1927. To my surprise, I discovered that the scurrilous language I thought was the product of the last few decades was already in use in the 1920s. But further readings of the political and cultural writings of the period revealed that, side by side with the unfortunate tendency to resort to name-calling and slander, a tendency we suffer from to this day, was a sophisticated debating style that resembled that of the West. When Taha Hussein published his controversial book on pre-Islamic poetry, he came under attack from many critics. Some argued their case soberly, using civilized language and confining themselves to an objective critique of the book, but others stooped to unacceptable depths of calumny and personal attacks. One such was Mustapha Sadeq al-Rafei, whose book *On the Grill* overstepped the bounds of decency in the virulent personal attack he directed at Abbas al-Aqqad.

In other words, public discourse in Egypt was conducted along two tracks simultaneously: one track observed the rules of civility and objectivity, shunning the use of insulting language and personal attacks, the other belonged to the no-holds-barred school of writing, which had no compunction about resorting to vilification and mudslinging to discredit the opposing party.

During the last 50 years, the objective school of public debate has gradually lost ground to a defamatory style based on hurling insults at the opponent, in which polemicists find it easier to demonize the proponents of the opposing point of view than to argue their own case on its merits. Numerous examples attest to the prevalence of this phenomenon in our cultural life today, where differences of opinion over a specific issue are often expressed in the form of vituperative exchanges of accusations and personal insults.

Take the strident campaigns launched on a periodic basis by some opposition papers over one issue or another. All too often, these campaigns degenerate from an objective discussion of the issue over which they were launched in the first place into an all-out war against the person holding the opposing viewpoint, whose personal integrity and morality are called into question and who is accused of all kinds of private and public wrong-doing. At first, I thought this was because a public debate offers an ideal opportunity to give vent to the pent-up feelings of anger and frustration some of us harbour because of the many problems we face in our day-to-day life. I have since come to believe that, although this is certainly one of the factors behind the phenomenon, the real reason is a fascist trend that has marked public discourse in this country for close on half a century.

In the last five decades, public life in Egypt was strongly influenced by two main realities. The first is that the regime that came to power in 1952 was extremely intolerant of any opposition, indeed, even of the mildest criticism. I am not making a value judgement here, merely stating a fact. From the start, the regime brooked no opposition, using all the apparatus of state to crush dissidents, including the media, which launched devastating campaigns against anyone who dared raise a voice against the regime. The other reality is that the strongest under-ground opposition movement in the country was the Moslem Brothers, a party that was and still is notoriously averse to the least hint of criticism, dealing with whoever refuses to toe the party line either with an iron fist or with floods of speeches and writings that are no less fascist. Thus we were caught between a ruling establishment that crushed its opponents with all the means at its disposal and an underground opposition movement that destroyed its opponents both materially and morally.

In the context of a fascist climate where any divergent opinion was ruthlessly crushed, whole generations grew up with no knowledge of the rules of civilized debate, generations raised to believe that opponents and critics were fair game for the most ferocious attacks on their probity and honour, and that personal insults and abusive language were par for the course.

Such a climate is not conducive to the promotion of such values as tolerance of the Other, accepting criticism, engaging in self-criticism, expanding the objective margin in thinking and debate or genuinely embracing pluralism. There have been a number of notable exceptions to this general rule, but these are unfortunately far outnumbered by the examples of oral and written debates conducted along fascist lines, which represent the dominant trend in our public discourse at this time. It is a trend that is likely to remain dominant for some years to come, until the process of economic reform now underway has been successfully completed. The fundamental changes this is expected to introduce to the components of public life will make of those who now feed the fascist trend relics of a bygone time, products of a stage which left its mark on the attitudes of some members of our society until the new global changes divested them of their very *raison d'être*. However, this is still several years down the road and, in the meantime, we will continue to suffer from the fascist trend that dominates public debate in Egypt today.

CHAPTER 15

Technological Advancement Prerequisites: Wealth or Management?[34]

To the same extent that it inspired a great surge of national pride and joy, the Nobel Prize for Chemistry awarded to Ahmed Zeweil raised many questions about the state of scientific research and technological progress in Egypt. Although much has been said on the subject, I had the opportunity to hear two points of view on the same day which I believe encapsulate all that can possibly be said in this connection.

With all due respect to the proponents of the two viewpoints expressed on the day in question, I believe one was completely off the mark and the other absolutely correct. According to the first view, the only thing preventing us from being among the advanced nations of the world in the field of scientific research and its technological applications is a lack of resources. The other view holds that the problem lies in the climate of scientific research, which lacks the spirit of teamwork and the institutional framework which can serve and support the role of the researcher.

From my long experience in the world of management, I believe the people who rely on the lack-of-resources argument are motivated by an understandable, if misplaced, belief that this excuse absolves us of responsibility for the present state of affairs in the fields of theoretical and applied sciences.

There are tens of countries with a lower per capita income than ours and with huge economic problems that have surpassed us in these fields, but I will cite just one example here, namely, India, whose performance in these fields, particularly in the areas of atomic research and computer technology, is impressive by any standards. Thanks to its scientific and technological achievements, India is now a nuclear power. It is also the third largest exporter of software programs in the world and is expected to move up to second place, right behind the United States, by the end of this year [2000].

The massive economic and social problems plaguing India, including a severe shortage of financial resources, have not prevented it from achieving remarkable results in these areas, both of which are based on advanced scientific research. While there are many other similar examples, this example alone is sufficient to rebut the argument that what prevents us from building an advanced and efficient scientific infrastructure is nothing but a lack of resources.

To attribute our inability to develop an advanced scientific infrastructure to a lack of resources is wrong not only because it is based on faulty reasoning but because it allows us to indulge ourselves in a rationale of justification that prevents us from exercising the required degree of self-criticism. What we really lack is modern working methods in the field of scientific research, governed by up-to-date management systems that can provide the necessary elements of success by nurturing people of superior ability, developing the spirit of teamwork, putting an end to the practice of fighting talented people and removing from the world of scientific research the values of careerism and political ambition that have pervaded it over the last few decades.

The problem is thus one of management rather than resources. Overcoming it entails removing from the management process the elements that have led to our present state of backwardness in the domain of scientific research. We must have the courage to admit that unless we diagnose the ills and change the general climate prevailing in that domain we will never be able to overcome the present state of affairs. It is necessary here to entrust Egyptian scientists living abroad with the task of diagnosing the ills and prescribing the means of treating them, as the members of the local scientific community are often too close to the trees to see the forest. Moreover, they could find it embarrassing to direct any criticism at their administrative superiors.

That is not to say that our scientists are unable to diagnose the problem, define its reasons and propose the mode of treatment, only that what might be embarrassing for them would be less so for Egyptian scientists living abroad. Such hierarchical constraints can be a real obstacle on the way to reforming the scientific climate in Egypt.

CHAPTER 16

Does 'Intellectuality' Have a 'Nationality'?[35]

Between 1960 and 1970, more than at other times, I had the opportunity to indulge my passion for reading. During that period, I read the Russian classics, masterpieces of German literature, Italy's sublime works, as well as prose and poetry penned in English, French, Spanish, Norwegian, and other languages.

The 1960s were formative years, when the prevailing cultural climate allowed unfettered access to world literature. Two factors were instrumental in creating this climate: the existence of a strong school of literary criticism and an equally strong translation movement, with its fountainhead in Lebanon. From the former we learned which classics of world literature we should read, while the latter made those works available to us in our mother tongue when our mastery of European languages was inadequate to capture the richness of this human legacy.

The leading critics of the 1960s, such as Mohamed Mandur[36] and Louis Awad,[37] Abd al-Qadir al-Qutt[38] and Raja al-Naqqash, served as our navigators through the uncharted waters of European culture, guiding us in our choice of reading material not only in the field of literature but also in Western philosophy, history, political economy, psychology, sociology, and so on. Other luminaries included the philosophers and intellectuals Abdel Rahman Badawy, Youssef Mourad, Zaki Naguib Mahmoud and Mourad Wahba.

During those years I had no inkling of the dichotomous course my life would later take, as my interests proceeded along two divergent paths: my career (in the economic sphere of petroleum, specifically, as a senior executive in the oil industry) and my vocation (an insatiable appetite for literature, philosophy, music and art).

It never occurred to me then, or to others of my generation who loved knowledge and culture, to question the nationality of what we read. We devoured the works of Naguib Mahfouz, Youssef Idriss, Badr Shaker el-Seab, Nizar Qabbani, Ahmed Abdel Moaty Hegazy, Salah Abdel Sabour, Soheil Idriss, Mohamed Deeb and Yehia Hakki as fervently as we did those of the countless foreign authors, poets and playwrights. It was never relevant to us that Youssef Idriss was Egyptian, Soheil Idriss Lebanese, Mohamed Deeb Algerian, Eugene Ionesco Romanian, Graham Greene English, that Albert Camus was French, Alberto Moravia Italian, Henrik Ibsen Norwegian or Eugene O'Neill American. The issue simply did not arise because we had been raised in a cultural climate in which creativity was presented to us as the ultimate expression of human genius, its fruits part of the common legacy of humanity taken as a whole. Egypt was still unsullied by chauvinism or a fear of the jingoistic expression, 'cultural invasion', that was beginning to rear its ugly head in the late 1960s.

Unfortunately, the irresponsible use by some of this distasteful expression fell on willing ears, coinciding with the emergence of a regressive trend that did not affect intellectuals in the 1960s: the new theory of cultural invasion began to take hold as Egypt fell prey to regressive ideas which were totally incompatible with the age and which rejected the notion that human civilization is an amalgam of many different civilizations and cultures. The numbers of those who subscribed to the cultural invasion theory continued to swell.

Then came the tremendous decline in educational and cultural standards in the latter half of the 1970s, which further promulgated the idea that we were the targets of a cultural invasion. In a misguided attempt to resist the 'invasion' without forgoing any of the benefits of Western civilization, some of the theory's proponents came forward with the absurd idea that Western civilization could be broken down into two distinct components: a material component, represented in the applied sciences, technology, machinery and equipment, and a moral component – culture, art and ideas. They proposed that we adopt from the West only the material component and discard the rest. However, they overlooked two important issues:

1. The material component of Western civilization is the natural result of its non-material, i.e. cultural, component. 'Western civilization' began with ideas, art and literature, and it was only after these had created a climate in which creativity could flourish that the applied sciences could produce their successive inventions and discoveries.
2. 'Western civilization' is not exclusively Western, but is made up of two elements, one derived from the cumulative experience of other civilizations and cultures, the other from the experience built up in a purely Western context. In other words, it has a dimension attributable to humanity in general (being the end-product of the civilization process experienced by all humankind) as well as a Western dimension (linked to the history of Western Europe from the late Middle Ages and the onset of the Renaissance).

Every effort must now be made to ensure that this and future generations understand that the fruits of human creativity and endeavour are *humanity's* public domain and that partaking of those fruits in no way represents a surrender of our specificity. They must be encouraged to emulate the example of a whole generation of Egyptians – Loutfy el-Sayed, Taha Hussein, Ahmed Amin, Abbas el-Aqqad, Tawfik el-Hakim, Naguib Mahfouz – who remained ardently Egyptian despite their extensive forays into world culture and their profound appreciation of its masterpieces. Mahfouz, widely considered the father of the modern Arabic novel and the only Arab Nobel Prize Laureate, does not hesitate to criticize aspects of Egyptian society or to adopt unpopular or defiant stands, such as his support for Salman Rushdie's *The Satanic Verses* or his objection to the Muslim fundamentalists in Egypt, which caused an attempt on his life. All the while, like his peers, his passion for Arabic literature and culture remains resolute.

Standing on the threshold of the twenty-first century, then, Egypt needs to generate a cultural reconciliation between what is 'human', in the broad sense of the word, and what is 'specific'. If the will is there, such a reconciliation is not only feasible but perhaps even easily attained, and this will provide a better and more effective stage from which to deal with the requirements and challenges of the age, locally and globally.

CHAPTER 17

Imperative Management Reform[39]

Experiments in economic reform have been seen in a number of countries over the last 25 years. In some cases the experiments achieved impressive results, while in many others they failed. Somewhere in between lies a third group of countries, those that made significant headway at first only to suffer setbacks further down the road.

In my opinion the experiments that succeeded – and sustained their momentum – were those that did not address the process of reform from a purely economic perspective. After all, economic ideas, systems, structures and mechanisms (usually the creation of economists, who are usually academicians) cannot in and of themselves guarantee consistent and sustained success. Certainly the economists play a vital role, for without them the process of economic reform cannot be initiated in the first place: it is they who determine the framework for monetary reform followed by economic reform. But this represents only the first stage.

To illustrate this point better, let us draw a parallel here between the first stage of economic reform and the construction of a state-of-the-art sports complex. Once the sports complex has been built and fitted out in accordance with the required specifications, the role of the architect and contractor ends and that of the managers, administrators and players begins. However well designed such a complex may be, it cannot in itself guarantee a brilliant record of achievement. So, too, with the planning of monetary and economic reform. Though a vital and indispensable element of any reform programme, the planning (admittedly a difficult and complex task) is merely the first stage in a longer process. In the next stage the economists must stand back to allow the managers, administrators – and players – to take over.

In fact, the reason behind the failure of some economic reform programmes is that they remained under the control of the economists-academicians longer than they should have done. Conversely, the experiments that enjoyed the highest and most consistent rate of success are those in which the planners handed over the reins of control at the right time to a cadre of dynamic, talented and qualified management executives who then implemented the reforms.

As to the countries whose economic reform programmes got off to a good start but faltered later, I believe this was due to the absence of clear lines of demarcation between the role of the economists as planners and that of the cadre of top management executives who are required to put the programme into effect. The overlapping of the two roles beyond the takeoff stage caused some economic reform programmes to suffer the setbacks and reversals that they did, though in some cases these have been depicted as far worse than they really were. For example, the setback faced by the Asian Tigers[40] after the initial brilliant success of their economic reform programmes, though serious, was not devastating. In fact, many of them were expected to overcome the crisis before the millennium. They can draw on the inspiring experience of Mexico, which made a complete recovery from its economic crisis thanks to its excellent cadre of administrators and management executives.

My view then is that prolonging the stage of monetary and economic reform in which academe-oriented economists are in the driver's seat can lead to many problems and reversals. Once the initial phase has begun, the focus must shift from the structural aspect of monetary and economic reform to the practical aspects of administration, modern management systems, marketing strategies and human resources, with particular emphasis on the cadre of leaders in the field of executive management, including the field of marketing, arguably the most important area of modern economic life.

Shifting the focus from the planning stage to the execution stage is extremely difficult and usually involves a power struggle, possibly an all-out showdown, between the adherents of different schools of thought: one whose experience lies in the past and the other which has its eye on the future. There is no doubt that a speedy resolution of the conflict in favour of the modern school is one of the keys to sustainable economic success that is less susceptible to setbacks and regressions.

Let us try to assess where Egypt's experiment with monetary and economic reform stands in relation to this theoretical buildup. Certain developments are worth noting here:

- Since the early 1990s tremendous progress has been achieved in Egypt in the field of monetary reform. Many of the targeted objectives have been reached and, in general, things are moving in the right direction.
- The same period witnessed concerted efforts in the direction of economic reform, but much remains to be done. Of particular importance in this respect is the need for a reassessment of the role of the state in economic life: the state necessarily plays a role when it comes to vision and policies but should be far less assertive in most areas of economic activity. Equally important is the need to dismantle the grossly inflated and ponderous Egyptian bureaucracy that continues to choke most government departments and is a major disincentive for international investments and capital to flow into Egypt in the required volume.
- It has become imperative to focus on three priorities in the area of economic reform: (a) modern management systems, including the selection of executive leaders; (b) human resources, training and the transfer of technology and skills; and (c) the marketing sciences and the executive leaders in those areas, without whom all the efforts in the industrial and services sectors would be wasted. This entails a transition from the stage of the academic economists (the planners) to that of the modern management executives, for it is they who will turn all the great efforts at monetary and economic reform into concrete results – i.e. increased production – in both the manufacturing and services sectors.

Finally, the long-term sustainability of reform programmes can be guaranteed only if a number of basic principles are observed. The economic reform experiments that achieved the highest rate of sustained success are those that believed the private sector should play a pivotal role in economic life and that the views of the business sector should be taken into account without, however, allowing that sector to participate actively in the policy-making process. For here arises the danger of conflict of interests: business people by their very nature have only short-term or, at best, medium-term interests, while those concerning society must be long-term. This makes it imperative to have another level, a contemporary political cadre, which might comprise top management executives but certainly not businessmen, that can strike a balance between the short- and long-term interests.

CHAPTER 18

Fateful Transformation[41]

THE NEED FOR CHANGE

Most Egyptians today agree that there is an urgent need to bring about fundamental changes in public life, and that this is a prerequisite for raising standards of living. This is the theme of an ongoing national dialogue, about which there is a general consensus. It develops into a debate when people – those in public life and private citizens alike – suggest how best to achieve this.

It should be noted, however, that the nature of this 'consensus' has changed in recent years. Thirty years ago, it was still generally believed that the country had to overcome the disastrous defeat it suffered in the 1967 War against Israel, and to regain the territories seized by Israel at that time. Even ten years ago, the national mood was still strongly marked by the trauma of 1967, holding us hostage to the past. Moreover, the then-prevailing world order also helped keep the national debate mired in the rhetoric of the past, specifically, in the time-worn and cliché-ridden slogans of the 1950s and 1960s.

Today our inner maturity and the new conditions in the world have liberated our thinking somewhat. Most of us now realize that those old slogans were not matched in reality and that neither the Egypt of the 1960s nor that of the 1970s responded to the aspirations of its citizens. In addition, the collapse of the citadels of socialism revealed the utter failure of that movement, whether in its political, economic or social form, to bring affluence and social justice for any of the societies that espoused it. These factors led us to break out of our stereotyped thinking of the past, and the collective will for change has come to be informed by the following considerations:

- Change must come about through a process of gradual reform, not in revolutionary upheavals. The experience of many countries over the last 50 years has convinced wide sections of the Egyptian population that the 'revolutionary' path invariably fails to attain the desired goals, not least because power usually ends up in the hands of people who lack leadership qualities and who have neither the experience nor the vision required to lead their countries to a better future.
- Change should not be instituted according to an ideological agenda. Ideology, which dominated the world for a century and a half, was discredited in the last decade of the twentieth century, and promises to remain so for a long time to come.
- Change should be directed in the first instance at achieving economic growth by providing a climate in which the tools and mechanisms of the economy can operate effectively.

Thus, the consensus for change extends also to an agreement over the modalities of how to achieve it. With the exception of a few fringe, albeit dangerous, groups, most Egyptians believe change can best come about through reform, not revolution, and that reform should be instituted according to pragmatic, not ideological, considerations. This is particularly true for economic reforms, which will in turn entail reforms in the political system.

THE GLOBAL SCENE

To probe further whether Egyptians agree on the nature and direction of the required changes, we must first cast a look at today's world and how it has changed since World War II:

- Since the demise of the Soviet Union, we now have the group of advanced Western nations, led by the United States, as the sole superpower at the summit of the world community.

- The economic bankruptcy of the Eastern bloc brought with it the complete collapse of the ideology to which this bloc subscribed.
- The Cold War is well and truly over and, thus, so is the need for a bloc calling itself the 'non-aligned movement'.
- The world now recognizes that a society's progress and its ability to overcome economic crises is contingent on its ability to diffuse the spirit and dynamics of private enterprise among its citizens – that this is the only path to economic success, prosperity and progress.

And so humankind bade farewell to the twentieth century with a global rationale that had nothing to do with that which prevailed for the two decades following World War II, and even less to do with that found in the early 1900s. In the new rationale, the choices are simple. Socialism in all its forms has been relegated to the realm of history; it is no longer a viable option for the future. Only two options remain: either to lurch along without a clear sense of direction or to address the world's problems purposefully through the mechanisms of the new rationale, which are linked to the dynamics of market economy, to democracy and to human rights.

Experts on Third World issues believe developing countries' prospects for socio-economic growth will improve in direct proportion to the rate at which they proceed to apply these mechanisms. The enormous problems facing most Third World countries are time bombs waiting to go off, and any hesitation could prove fatal. At best, countries that procrastinate will lag further and further behind in the race for progress; at worst, they will implode, with dire consequences for their own peoples and for the world at large.

In addition to embarking on the process of reform, some countries can capitalize on their geopolitical importance to speed it up. Egypt is a good example. In the new global rationale, it can invest its unique geopolitical status in promoting internal development and thus defuse what is rapidly becoming a crisis situation.

WHAT MUST BE CHANGED – THE INDIVIDUAL OR SOCIETY?

People whose intellectual and social outlook were shaped by the ideas of Karl Marx view the 'individual' and 'society' very differently from those whose perceptions were shaped by the value systems in Western democracies. Whereas Marxists and, indeed, all socialists play down the role and importance of the individual and magnify the role and importance of society, in Western democracies the reverse is usually the case. Without delving into details, it is clear that developments on the world stage over the last 25 years have vindicated the exponents of the latter school of thought.

Socialists believe in society with a capital 'S', predicating all their systems on the assumption that a transcendental entity called society exists of and by itself, and that the primary function of government and the economic system is to serve it. Liberals, on the other hand, do not believe in society as a mutually exclusive entity but in a community of individual citizens who are collectively known as society. The individual is a tangible entity, society is not. Thus, a prosperous and successful society is nothing more than an aggregate of prosperous, successful citizens. By the same token, a society plagued with problems is also the sum total of its parts: unsuccessful citizens combating a range of problems and deprived of the ability to work create the manner in which public life is conducted.

In Western democracies such basic concepts as human rights, the principle of legitimacy, freedom of thought and speech, and so on all aim at serving the individual citizen.

An obvious conclusion to be drawn from this simplified analysis is that Egypt can propel itself forward on the road to development and progress only by adopting the fundamentals of democratic states focusing on changing individual citizens. This is the key to transforming society. I would go as far as to maintain that society is merely a term coined to refer to average individuals and the common values, trends, attitudes and circumstances they share. To my mind, bringing about a positive change in individuals is the task of those holding the keys to the political, economic, cultural and social machinery of society – in other words, of government, in the broad sense of the word.

While it may be true that modern management sciences did not exist when Karl Marx formulated his all-encompassing theoretical manifesto, today these sciences have become the main driving force of contemporary developed societies. They are the locomotive which allows developed societies to forge far ahead of their underdeveloped counterparts, leaving them to limp along, or, in some cases, to grind to a complete standstill. Among the main principles of modern management sciences are those pertaining to human resources and quality management, which are based on the assumption that human beings are the most valuable resource for production, progress and prosperity. Indeed, human resources management is the determining factor in the progress or decline of any given organization, company, institution or people.

WHAT CREATES PROGRESS – PEOPLE OR IDEAS?

A characteristic shared by many of the countries facing breakdowns in the machinery of public life, and which are now seeking the road to a better future, is the conviction that their hopes could be fulfilled and their goals achieved if only they had 'good' ideas. But it is a dangerous fallacy to think that ideas might be a panacea for all ills. As we in Egypt stand poised to shift from a present fraught with problems to a future filled with hope, we must realize that we will need more than ideas to navigate the choppy waters separating the two safely. It is not ideas alone that can improve our reality or create a better future. Herein lies the difference between intellectuals and philosophers, most of whom are incapable of managing a small business or reforming even a tiny village, and top management and business leaders, who have the necessary skills to transform reality through actions, not words.

Moreover, the search for good ideas is both a lengthy process and one that creates a divisive and polemical climate, as the proponents of any given idea debate ideological differences. What we really need is people who epitomize the ideas that can serve as a *bridge* towards a better future. It should be remembered that great civilizations were built less on abstract ideas than by actions – drive, spirit and imagination, yes, but by individuals with the will and skill to turn dreams into reality. And if it is axiomatic that a man and his ideas constitute an integral whole, it follows that the ideas needed to reform the present and pave the way to a better future will not come from men whose ideas are based less on principles than on expediency.

The real crisis lies not in a lack of qualified people but, rather, in the absence of those people from the public arena over the last 40 years, while others who were not necessarily the most efficient, experienced, honest, intelligent or successful Egyptians dominated. Egypt is one of the rare Third World countries blessed with a huge pool of talented people who are more than capable of efficiently and loyally running its public life. However, most are excluded from this arena because they display characteristics that are out of tune with the system in force, which is based on loyalty to a select group of individuals, the same people who have the monopoly on public posts in the state bureaucracy. Any talk of reform as meaning the implementation of better ideas – not the use of better people to achieve that – will remain no more than talk until the system wakes up and allows new ideas to pervade it.

CIVILIZATION – THE PRODUCT OF HUMAN VALUES

Although the term 'civilization' crops up frequently in public discourse, not much effort is expended on trying to define what the term really means. It is often used as a byword for the model of the developed Western lifestyle which some of us seek to emulate. In fact, any civilization is in its essence nothing more than a collection of values. How a society regards its citizenry, the value it places on the individual and on personal freedom, the way in which it determines his relative position *vis-à-vis* the executive branch of government; whether it casts its rulers in the role of masters over or servants of the citizenry; the status and rights enjoyed by women, and by children; the value it places on time, on work, on the quality of work; its attitude to its minorities; the right of others to differ in beliefs, doctrines, opinions and behaviour – these are the values that form the fabric of civilization.

Some may be sublime and exalted, others degenerate and ignoble. But it is extremely important when looking at other civilizations to distinguish between two levels. At the local level, each civilization has features that are characteristic of it alone. But there is also a dimension of every civilization that is not exclusive to it but belongs to the mainstream of human civilization. For example, much of what constitutes 'Western civilization', in fact, is the product of the accumulated experience of human civilization, whether in the fields of applied sciences or human and social sciences. The most striking example of a civilization where the two levels have merged in close-to-perfect harmony is Japan.

Here we must rethink the enmity and hatred that some of us harbour for Western civilization, on the grounds that it is an alien civilization. Actually, many of its most exalted values are the fruit of mainstream human civilization. Blind enmity to developed civilizations is a rejection of the essence, lessons, wisdom and accomplishments of the collective human experience, not to mention a reflection of ignorance, narrow-mindedness and fanaticism.

There are none more misguided than those who call for the adoption of the applied scientific and technological achievements of the West and the rejection of all other aspects of Western civilization. The essence of human civilization extends beyond the fields of applied science and technology to philosophy, art, literature, human rights and other fields.

Some of us reject Western civilization without realizing that we are rejecting elements of human civilization, to which we, like others, have made many contributions. This enmity stems from a deep ignorance of the fact that Islam extols most of the fundamental principles on which developed civilizations are based. Likewise, much of what we believe to be the basic principles of our civilization are no more than adaptations and embodiments of regressive and degenerate values that first emerged in the Dark Ages, in the years of tyranny, repression and ignorance. Indeed, many did not emanate from our religion but from cultures in the context of which Islamic history unfolded and from which it acquired inferior values.

The phenomenal economic success of Asia's newly industrialized countries (NIC) only confirms how important it is to distinguish between noble cultural values, on the one hand – many of which we should adopt from the West – and aberrant, regressive values (wrongly ascribed by some to our cultural heritage), on the other – which we should discard.

The Ideal Pyramidal Structure of Prosperous Societies

One of the biggest blunders committed by tens of Third World countries with social structures similar to Egypt's is to have turned the social pyramid upside down, thereby creating a new pyramid which allows the least qualified members of society to occupy the top positions. In developed countries, on the other hand, the societal pyramid is constructed so that only the best, in terms of ability, intelligence, culture, ethics and motivation, can rise to the top. These elites command the decision-making process, guiding their countries along what they claim to be the best course. Third World countries where, because of historical conditions, state power is usually seized through coups, are subject to a different system based on personal loyalty and trust, in which men are chosen for their allegiance to the ruler rather than on merit. As a result, the top five per cent of positions are occupied not by society's best but by elements which disseminate the most inferior and abject of values throughout society as a whole.

In developed societies Social Darwinism (the law of natural selection) prevails, based on the selection by society of its best citizens for the highest posts, and this is a dynamic process. In the often regressive societies of the Third World, Social Darwinism is not allowed to operate. Rather, public life is based on loyalty and allegiance, cronyism and, at a later stage, corruption. While corruption is part and parcel of the human condition, it proliferates only in an atmosphere of inferior values where incompetent bureaucrats hold the top positions; in countries where the societal pyramid is based on the principles of Social Darwinism, it can be checked and ferreted out before harming infrastructure.

THE MECHANISMS OF CHANGE

At this stage in its history, Egypt stands at the crossroads of three paths. One will lead to the perpetuation of the status quo, the second to still further decline, and the third to a solution of its problems, to progress and prosperity in the context of social peace and political stability. Access to the third path is contingent on devising a mechanism by which to effect the desired changes.

Certainly the manner in which our affairs have been conducted over the last four decades will not take us along the third path. If that were possible, it would have happened long ago. It is high time we recognized that to make it possible, we need entirely new mechanisms.

To begin with, the political leadership must act decisively to remove from the arena of public life those officials who are evidently unable to perform at the required standard of excellence. According to scholars of constitutional law in Western societies, democracy can be built only by democrats. By the same token, a better future for Egypt can be built only by those of its citizens who have proved their competence and dedication to the governing principles of the new era, namely, the importance of human resources and a belief in the efficiency of a market economy, the merits of modern management and marketing sciences. Public life should be administered by people who have actually succeeded in the context of these objectives, not by functionaries whose ideas, brains and objectives have been atrophied through long years of state hegemony over economic life.

The mechanism that can achieve the desired change lies in using talents similar to those that led the NIC countries of Asia from underdevelopment to remarkable economic vigour and success. The importance of this mechanism cannot be overrated: once it is set in motion, the desired reforms and eventual transformation are simply a matter of time.

To bring about change from the bottom up is virtually impossible in the current setup. Perhaps the main factor working against it is the time needed for the values of change to flow from the base of society to its summit. This could take decades, even centuries. The change that could be achieved in a generation is dependent on competent individuals who are ready to act in accordance with the new values and criteria and apply the successful experiment of the NIC of Asia. The problem in Egypt is that we continue to insist on using the wrong sort of people.

SETTING NEW EXAMPLES

Very few of the players on the stage of Egyptian public life can be held up as examples of exceptional competence or as paragons of intelligence, knowledge and culture. Indeed, many display only modest abilities, mediocre intelligence and little culture. Worse, they often blatantly lack the qualities and moral virtue associated with leadership. Needless to say, the absence of these elements in so many of our public personalities does not bode well for the prospects of change.

The roots of the problem go back to the political climate which prevailed in Egypt in the 1950s and 1960s, when individual freedom and independent thought were suppressed, ostensibly in the name of social cohesion but in actual fact as a means of controlling society. At every level in the chain of command, superiors were obeyed without question, and obsequiousness and sycophancy were *de rigueur*. This is the school from which many of our functionaries graduated. Today's requirements make it imperative to hand the reins of public life over to people who derive their value systems from different sources.

Our young people cannot be blamed for losing faith in a value system that allows inept and second-rate people to attain leading positions, and where success is more often than not due less to competency than to shameful practices or personal relations. The years-long absence of good examples was not the result of a divine curse or historical accident but stemmed from a deliberate attempt to eliminate independent thinkers and people of integrity from the public arena. The suppression and control characteristic of the last 40 years, in which most officials surrounded themselves exclusively with 'yes men', sadly explains the disappearance of good examples and the propagation of the mediocrity we know so well. We cannot ask our young people to believe in or to accept this any longer.

EGYPT'S NEED TO RECONCILE ITS PAST, PRESENT – AND FUTURE

Throughout most of its modern history, which began with Muhammad Ali's[42] accession to power in 1805, Egypt has suffered from a kind of split personality. To my mind, this stems from the educational and cultural poverty that has marked our lives over the last two centuries. This has left some of us unable to come to terms with the challenges of the present and preferring to seek refuge in the past, while others turn to the Western model of civilization, adopting its cultural mores and lifestyles. It seems the most difficult option is the one many of us have abandoned, which is simply to be ourselves, here and now. This entails sifting through our cultural heritage and discarding those elements that were merely the product of a specific time and circumstances, as well as adopting from the Western model elements that are the fruits of the collective human experience. The most important of these are not, contrary to conventional wisdom, science and technology, but the values of progress, creativity, work and innovation.

The lack of a common framework of identity has led to acute tensions between past, present and future. For some, the only acceptable framework is the past, whether the distant past, as in the case of the fundamentalists, or the recent past, such as the Nasserites. Others reject the past in favour of a future whose features and identity are still far from clear. An initiative should be launched to bring about a reconciliation between past, present and future, based on the general consensus that Egypt deserves a future better than its present or its past.

Although Muhammad Ali was a great man, his model was not an unqualified success, as borne out by what happened after his reign. The same applies to Saad Zaghlul,[43] Gamal Abdel Nasser, Anwar Sadat, and the other leaders of our national struggle for independence. Now, however, we need to impose fundamental reforms that properly address the *present* if there is to be a better future for the sons and daughters of this nation.

The dichotomy that exists in the Egyptian psyche is not new. Reading the now-declassified dispatches sent home by Britain's representatives in Egypt between 1882 and 1952,[44] I was struck – and pained – by how often they reported on 'deep divisions among the Egyptians'. It was particularly galling to read Sir Evelyn Baring's account of his farewell party. Sir Evelyn, the Earl of Cromer, was British consul-general and *de facto* governor of Egypt. His farewell party was attended by Egypt's political leaders, each of whom took him aside to complain of the others and seek his support against them.

The deep divisions among Egyptians are symptomatic of an inability on the part of many to distinguish between past, present and future. But for this confusion, there would have been minimum agreement between them. However, because of a severe decline in education and culture, exacerbated by a sequence of leaders who, for over a century following Ali's abdication, were not the most intelligent, cultured or honest individuals, nor necessarily among the most able and talented, this trait became so imbued it seemed to be part of our genetic makeup.

One can only admire the Chinese for avoiding this pitfall and for their accomplishments in recent years. When the leaders of the People's Republic realized that socialist ideas had become obsolete, they decided to open the economy to market forces, thereby giving an enormous boost to China's gross national product. However, they did not open the door to ideological debate because they understood that this would only sharpen differences and bring about a damaging schism between past, present and future.

CHOOSING BETWEEN REALITY AND ILLUSION

There is no doubt that the historical and cultural conditions in which Arab civilization evolved have affected the way Arabs and, by extension, Egyptians, think. One of the most important specifics of Arab thinking is a tendency to confuse the possible with the impossible, a certain romanticism which often blurs the fine distinctions between what should be, what could be and what will be. Because of this tendency, the Arabs have allowed many historical opportunities to slip through their fingers, rejecting offers that they often later realize would have been to their advantage. It is thus vital that those who mould our options, whether in foreign or domestic policy, should be able to distinguish between reality and wishful thinking. To be fair, the decision-making process under Presidents Sadat and Mubarak[45] has been characterized by a high degree of pragmatism in the field of foreign policy. On the domestic front, however, things are different. Although decisions here too are formed in large measure by practical considerations, many of our public personalities still tend to confuse reality with hopes. It is important to understand that domestic issues need people of a different calibre than those for foreign policy matters. At the same time, internal options are closely linked to ideologies. This leaves the field open to beliefs, views and solutions stemming from a past which, though totally discredited, still has representatives in key posts. It is obvious to any observer of the Egyptian scene that men and ideas of the past are obstructing those of the present and future. It is also obvious that their motives are not purely ideological, but linked to personal interests and careerism.

Egypt must base its economic and social options on a realistic appraisal of where things stand. In this it should be guided by the example of the Asian countries which are now prospering, thanks, in large part, to the contribution of efficient, highly qualified people motivated by the ideals of the age: political liberalism, market economy, and modern management systems capable of compressing the time-frame required for change and development.

The temple of socialism has come crashing down, and socialist ideology and experience are buried in the rubble. Standing on the ruins will only perpetuate failure and establish a pattern of crises and disasters. The ability to differentiate between the ideas stemming from the barren wasteland of socialism and those beckoning to the fertile gardens of success, production and prosperity is the key to differentiating between illusion and reality when it comes to choosing the right options.

It is worth noting that some people, despite their professional ability and competence, who should have been among the first to embrace the cardinal principles of the new age, continue to cling to principles and value systems that have no place in today's world. The only explanation for this blind loyalty to socialist ideals (or, in some cases, to the notion of state capitalism) by people who should know better is that it reflects a certain nostalgia for their youth in the 1950s or 1960s.

THE LEADERS OF THE FUTURE: WHO ARE THEY?

Two main features characterize the world of today and promise to become even more prominent in future:

- The world is and will become ever more 'internationalist' in nature, as old frontiers break down and markets and communities are open to all. Thanks to recent developments on the political font, as well as to the information revolution, the world has been transformed into a global village displaying very different characteristics from any we have known in the past.
- In this new world of accelerated change and greater interdependence, decision makers will have to involve themselves intimately with the specifics of economic and social life in their countries – that is, they will have to focus on the trees rather than maintain an overall view of the forest, as they have done in the past.

These two features will lead to the emergence of a new breed of politicians. The challenges posed by an open world in which trade competition will become ever more intense call for leaders who are in effect executive managers, not politicians in the traditional sense of the word. A politician will need more than judiciousness and level-headedness in the new setup. To be successful and effective, he will need to have a broad grasp of many areas of public life, paralleling the managerial talents of top chief executive officers.

Singapore's prime minister who, in just under 30 years, transformed his country from a stereotypically poor and under-developed Southeast Asian state into an outstanding success story, should serve as an example for leaders hoping to give their countries an edge in a fiercely competitive world.

THE CONSPIRACY THEORY

There is a pervasive belief among many Third World peoples that certain forces, including some Western intelligence agencies, are involved in a conspiracy aimed at achieving global domination and grinding the poor countries underfoot. The conspiracy theory is often tinged with an ideological hue, either by diehard socialists or by others obsessed with the idea that they are the main targets of a conspiracy, which of course exists only in their minds.

Another mechanism that fuels the belief in the conspiracy theory among millions of people is the Western economic system, which is based on competition both inside and outside the advanced capitalist societies. If one face of competition is that various economic units vie for a bigger share of the market by enhancing their products and services, expanding operations and maximizing profits, the other is that a bigger share for some means a smaller share for others. The spirit of competition is the cornerstone of Western liberal democracy and it is normal that it should govern the relations between the economic units, governments and companies of the outside world. In other words, if it is logical that those who compete among themselves should also compete with others, then the same logic dictates that they should seek to maintain their edge as seller to the others' buyers, producers to their consumers and exporters to their importers.

Thus, when the proponents of the conspiracy theory accuse the West of wanting Third World countries to remain at their present level of development, they are at the same time quite right and completely wrong. They are right because the laws of the market impose their own logic, and within that logic the West would not like its domination of world markets challenged. They are wrong because *there is no conspiracy*, only the natural workings of the machinery of the capitalist economic (and, hence, political) system. We should seek to understand the inner workings of the system and use them to our advantage if we hope to have a place in a world governed by the law of survival of the fittest. We should also remember that the activities of institutions in countries with a market economy, including the government, proceed in accordance with corporate law mechanisms.

WHO ARE WE TODAY?

If our hopes of bringing about the fateful transformation that can lead us towards a brighter future are ever to materialize, we must overcome the identity crisis that has held us in its grip for so many years. It is high time we come to terms with the fact that we are, before all else, Egyptians. That is not to say our identity does not include an Arab component, only that it is not the primary component. For example, our literature is essentially Arab, including works by Christian Arabs, but that is not enough to stamp us with an all-Arab identity. As to Islam, while there is no doubt that it is one of the most basic elements in our civilizational makeup, clearly Egyptians, Nigerians, Pakistanis and Malaysians are not one and the same thing. We are Muslims in the Egyptian manner: Egypt's Islam has been imbued with the country's historical characteristics of tolerance and coexistence between different faiths.

ETHICS

It is common in Egypt today to hear people from different walks of life bemoaning the 'death' of ethics, the erosion of the country's moral fibre and the proliferation of many ignoble values, such as envy. Unfortunately, they are right. But it is necessary to question why this state of affairs has come about. I believe the collapse of moral principles and the spread of envy, not only between people but also between classes, can be traced to a specific mechanism.

In societies where people know the background of wealth, fame and success, and where this background is based on hard work, struggle and ability, then and only then will people and society accept wealth, fame and success as the natural result of visible processes. More often than not, success stories of this kind are the object of admiration and respect.

When people realize how much effort and will went into achieving success, whether in building up a huge fortune or attaining a high position, they will accept it. But when personal relations, abuse of power, opportunism, corruption and darkness are the main elements behind many examples of fortune and fame, two phenomena are bound to emerge:

- The first is the lack of respect with which people come to regard examples of fortune and fame, and the widespread feeling that these are the fruits of dishonourable and manipulative practices conducted outside the channels of accountability.
- The second is a refusal to admit the right of the rich and famous to enjoy their 'ill-gotten' gains, claiming their success was attained more by chance and opportunity than by hard work or exceptional abilities. This naturally creates an atmosphere of envy and frustration.

By allowing mediocre people to rise to the pinnacles of wealth and success, the system itself breeds envy and hatred in society, devalues the virtues of excellence and hard work and encourages young people to seek short-cuts to success. After all, why should they strive for excellence in a society where success stories based on true talent and ability are few while those based on chance, nepotism and the exchange of favours abound?

CHAPTER 19

The Tragedy of Education and Culture in Egypt[46]

In an article published in *October* magazine, titled 'Those Who Have Withdrawn from the Age ... and Those Who are Up to Its Challenge', my friend the author and historian Dr Abdel Azim Ramadan touched a nerve as he discussed Egyptian postgraduate students abroad. Ramadan's article centred on the tendency of this expatriate community of future university professors to escape into the past and on their inability to face the challenges of civilization and culture in the advanced countries where they spend a good number of years. I have met many graduate students in various countries of Europe and North America and can concur that they are indeed, as Ramadan described them, 'fugitives from our age'. For the most part, they avoid the challenge of adapting to and absorbing these cultures and, instead, opt for the easy path of retreating into themselves.

In the UK, most Egyptian postgraduate students live in Egyptian 'cloisters', quite detached from the golden opportunities available to them at the expense of the Egyptian taxpayer. In all probability, not one of the hundreds of Egyptians who obtained their doctorates from British universities bothered to read such basic literary works as those of Shakespeare, Chaucer, Byron, Wordsworth or Dickens. It is also a safe bet that none of them became anywhere near as familiar with the treasures of museums as they did with the layout of department stores. University professors who lived in Britain for years have admitted to me that they never bothered to follow the political, literary or cultural events in that country throughout their stay.

In the USA, I met several Egyptians preparing their doctorates in various branches of learning. Most had never really experienced American life, preferring to spend their years there in self-imposed isolation because of their inability to face the challenge of civilization and culture. Before meeting with a number of doctoral graduate students at one of the largest universities in the USA, I had hoped to spend a few stimulating hours discussing American political history, cultural life and literature. But that was not to be. Instead, I was subjected to a series of monologues which reflected the speakers' total detachment and withdrawal from their environment and their retreat into the distant past – and to the most fanatical and extremist trends of that past.

The reason for the cultural introversion of our graduate students abroad is, I believe, the poor educational and cultural baggage they bring with them. Forced to retreat into complete isolation, they seek refuge in exaggerated conservatism and extremism as an easy way out of their dilemma. Indeed, with their poor educational, linguistic and cultural assets, how could they accomplish what generations of their forebears had achieved? The generation of Taha Hussein, Tawfiq el-Hakim, the scientist and artist Hussein Fawzi and the two generations that followed travelled to the West armed with a solid educational and cultural background, and at least one or two foreign languages. They then acquired the best that Western civilization had to offer without losing their faith in the greatness of their religion and the glory of their past. Today's students come back to Egypt no richer than when they left, having concentrated on the study of one exclusive subject for the most part. As for the host society, its civilization and achievements in the areas of public freedom and democracy, the rich diversity of its literature and culture, its vibrant political life – these are of no interest to our MA and PhD candidates, who are completely wrapped up in themselves and their own narrow vision, isolated and brewing ideas that belong to the age of darkness and obscurity.

In Paris once I sat in on a heated discussion among a group of graduate students, all of whom have since joined the faculties of Egyptian universities. The discussion was about painting and sculpture, and all those present pronounced both art forms to be works of the devil! Ironically, we were at that time only a few steps away from the city's Latin Quarter, a district alive with art, literature and culture, and just a stone's throw from the Louvre, where hundreds of the world's greatest paintings and sculptures stood in mute reproach to the astounding views put forward by people who had turned their backs on the age.

EDUCATION FOR ALL

The above is by way of an introduction to the subject of education in Egypt today and the sorry state it is in. Egyptian education is a closed system, detached from contemporary realities and isolated from the common cultural heritage of mankind, without which no educational system can hope to produce individuals capable of enriching their nations. But where and when did this tragedy start, and who is responsible?

To answer this, we must go back to the time when Muhammad Ali made education available to all Egyptians. Ali had always dreamed of making Egypt strong and great among the nations of the world, and he believed that this could not be achieved without an appreciation of modern science and contemporary culture. In that belief, Ali was ahead of another great nation, Japan, which discovered the same key to progress a few years later and which has since been using it boldly and effectively. In 1826 Ali sent the first of a series of delegations to France. It is thanks to those delegations that Egypt became so much more advanced than other Arab and African nations by the end of the nineteenth century.

These missions returned from Europe carrying the torch of knowledge and gave Egypt its first modern educational system – the system which formed Egypt's greatest minds at the end of the nineteenth century and in the first three decades of the twentieth. Egypt produced more outstanding figures in that time than any other nation comparable in size or stage of development has in such a short period. Such figures as politicians Mustapha Kamel, Mohamed Farid, Saad Zaghlul and Abdel Aziz Fahmy, artists, writers and poets Hafez Ibrahim, Zaki Mubarak, Sayed Darwish, Aziz Abaza, Al Sanhouri, and the renowned singer Um Kulthum and many more were products of the solid educational system and culture sparked by the first Egyptian mission sent to Western Europe by Ali in 1826.

Tracing the roots of the 'enlightenment' which enriched our scientific and cultural life then is necessary to help us unearth the roots of the present sterility of our educational system and the level to which it has sunk. The virtual collapse of education in our country has gone hand-in-hand with a breakdown in the values system by which society is governed. The moral and cultural decline is painfully obvious. The situation calls for drastic action. Like a surgeon who would not hesitate to amputate rotting limbs so that the patient may live, we too must ruthlessly remove these festering wounds from the suffering body of Egypt.

THE POLITICIZATION OF EDUCATION

What I said about the self-imposed isolation of Egyptian post-graduate students studying abroad and their refusal to taste the host country's opportunities is all the more true of their counterparts in Egypt. The latter have not even been exposed to other civilizations, nor to the challenge of new ideas that shock Egyptian expatriates in the West and cause them to retreat into themselves in what Arnold Toynbee called a 'negative reaction'. In fact, their introversion is a defence mechanism against the challenges posed by the alien culture, and they nurture it with a misplaced belief in their cultural superiority and the sense that they can do without 'Western' ideas.

Now I will examine the causes behind the deterioration of education and culture in Egypt and, later, will propose some concrete remedies.

I believe the main reason education fell from its promising heights to the depths of stagnation in which it is now mired is that the education system, both at school and, more particularly, university levels, was subjected to political currents. The subjugation of education by politics did not begin, as some might believe, in the Nasser era, but in 1925, when the old National University was transformed into a state institution and renamed the Egyptian University.[47] The controversy over Taha Hussein's book on pre-Islamic poetry in the mid-1920s is a striking example of the attempts made by successive governments to subject the university to political orientations. The government of Ismail Sidqi (1930–33) was perhaps the most flagrant at that destructive trend. In the seven years preceding the 1952 Revolution, attempts to politicize the university were further stepped up, culminating in 1953–54 in what came to be known as 'the purge', when the post-revolution regime fired scores of university professors who, it suspected, were not in accord with its policies.

Thus it was that although the process of politicizing education was not introduced into Egypt by the 1952 Revolution, it was the years that followed that saw the most blatant and painful examples of politics ruling academic life and trampling it underfoot. Despite the fact that violent repression disappeared by the 1970s, the harm had already been done. The Egyptian University, the pinnacle of the educational edifice, had become an inanimate corpse, trampled into subservience by politics. My purpose here is neither to insult nor to champion any one group against another because the magnitude of the calamity is such that it no longer matters which leader, regime or era is to blame. A small consolation here is that if power had fallen into the hands of the Muslim Brotherhood or the communists – who, it will be recalled, were a force to be reckoned with in the Egypt of the 1940s – education would have suffered twice as much as it did at the hands of the new regime in Egypt in 1953–54 and beyond.

A second reason for the education problem is the decline in the level of Egyptian school teachers and university professors since they have become state employees. Once a member of an elite corps of scientists and learned men, a professor today is just one of thousands of government employees. The drop in teaching standards parallels the general decline in the level of public services in Egypt, a phenomenon that has grown out of the frightful imbalance between people's growing sense of rights and their diminishing sense of duties. This phenomenon is common in socialist countries. Things cannot be otherwise in an environment where workers are cushioned by a plethora of promises and freed from the constraints of such basic economic laws as that linking salary to production and the law of rewarding excellence and punishing error, and where labour laws encourage slothfulness and idleness while discouraging initiative, creativity, competition and motivation.

I am confident that if we were to liberate teachers and university professors from the fetters of the civil service, we would break the heavy bonds that tie them to the present situation of education in our country and allow them to concentrate on improving the quality of their work rather than their chances for promotion.

A third reason for the situation is the alarming decline in our cultural life since it came under the thumb of politics. Education and culture are two sides of the same coin: if one declines, the other will follow. To understand what politics has done to culture in Egypt, it is enough to see the works of artists and writers in the 1960s, or radio and television programmes of the time, when politicization was at its peak.

The fourth reason is the indiscriminate expansion of the system. Education in Egypt is like a train: once a child reaches the age of six he or she can hop on board and remain there until the very last stop – the university degree. Not one country, either in the socialist or the capitalist worlds, provides education free of charge to every citizen wishing to benefit from that constitutional right. The fact is that no state, whatever its political orientation, can afford to provide free education from primary school through university. The only difference between socialist and capitalist countries in this respect is that while outstanding students enjoy this right in both cases, in the latter students who can afford to pay are allowed to continue studying even when they are not exceptional.

With such an indiscriminate expansion of education as that which took place in Egypt, it becomes impossible to maintain a balance between quality and quantity. Education is, after all, a service like any other, and the largesse of the Egyptian state in extending this service unreservedly to its citizens was, inevitably, at the expense of quality. The damage could have been minimized with proper planning. However, the state did not prepare for increasing the number of public, technical and commercial schools, nor for the necessary boost in the number of teachers needed, nor for ways to generate productive and useful employment for the flood of future graduates. In fact, the expansion of education, like so many other things in Egypt, was a haphazard process born of a vague slogan about education being 'the right of every citizen'. But noble slogans and good intentions never have and never will achieve success at any level.

To make matters worse, several factors combined to make Egyptians come to regard university degrees, and the government jobs that could be secured with them, with excessive respect, even reverence. At the same time, people began looking with disdain at the technical and specialized vocational degree, which limits the social standing of its bearer. In addition to a shrinking private sector and the fact that most citizens are civil servants, and since all high public positions are held by university graduates, not to obtain a degree puts one in a category of social inferiority.

THE DETERIORATION OF THE PRIVATE SECTOR

The decision to nationalize industrial and commercial enterprises in the late 1950s and to limit the role of the private sector to basic commercial activities – a limitation that lasted until the mid-1970s – led to a dampening of individual initiative, the only wellspring from which progress and achievement can flow. This too has an impact on the education system.

Some may argue that the spirit of free enterprise was eliminated from countries that opted for a socialist system – the Soviet Union, the People's Republic of China, Eastern European states – yet education in those countries did not reach the dangerously low level it has in Egypt. Still, it did fall well behind that in Western democracies, which supported a system of free economy and political liberalism. The disparity manifests itself most dramatically in the fields of technology, particularly computer science. It is no secret that since the computer revolution exploded in the 1970s the socialist world became totally dependent on the advances made by the West in this area. I recall a conversation I had with the Yugoslav economist and politician, Jan Stanovinc, a former minister and adviser to President Tito, who said that the fact that the socialist world exports raw materials such as petroleum and natural gas to the West in exchange for computers and industrial and agricultural machinery sums up the real situation: that scientific and educational advancement in socialist countries is at least half a century behind that of market economies.

Others could argue that this state of affairs reflects a temporary historical phase. This argument might have been valid if the gap were diminishing; however, experts agree that the gap has been growing steadily wider since the mid-1960s. This is what lies behind the practical measures recently taken by the socialist world under the leadership of the Soviet Union, measures which tacitly recognize the existence of that ever-widening gap. What actually saved education in socialist countries from plunging to the depths it has done in Egypt is that those countries dispose of reserves of culture, progress and industry which place them in a far better position than Third World nations. Moreover, their acute conflict with the West bred the need to develop scientific research in military fields, in which they were indisputably competitive. But beyond the military-related industries, science in the socialist countries lags at least 50 years behind Western science, according to the most conservative estimates.

Intellectual oppression and the absence of freedom also played a role in the depressed education system before the present democratic experience was introduced. Although still in the embryonic stage, it is the only experience of its kind to have lasted for several years in Egypt without reversal. While sceptics point out that democracy as it is being applied is far from complete, the fact is that the freedom to express political opinions and to oppose the regime's policies is unprecedented in the country's history, with the exception of the 10 months of Saad Zaghlul's government in 1924. The vendettas aimed by political parties at one another prior to 1952 created an unhealthy climate which adversely affected the institution of education. Then came totalitarian rule, the one-party system and the single-imposed view, with all the accompanying, unforgivable violations of human rights. Intellectual oppression prevailed, stifling all possibilities of freedom of research, particularly in the field of humanities – the very sciences that create the necessary framework and climate for progress, contrary to what some Egyptians, particularly technocrats, may believe. The great Arab Renaissance of the Middle Ages started as an intellectual, literary and cultural renaissance in the eighth to ninth centuries, expanding to embrace science only in the tenth to twelfth centuries with great minds such as Gaber Ibn Hayyan, al-Hassan Ibn al-Haitham, Avicenna, al-Razi and Ishaq Ibn Henein. The same is true of the Hellenic renaissance, which was led by such giants as Homer, Socrates, Plato and the Stoics, and followed by the scientific renaissance with Archimedes, Galen, Hippocrates and others. And the pattern did not change for the European Renaissance: first came the giants of art and literature in Italy during the fourteenth to fifteenth centuries and in other European countries in the sixteenth to seventeenth centuries, paving the way for the scientific renaissance which lit up Europe in the eighteenth century and reached full maturity in the twentieth. The reverse is also true: intellectual oppression and the absence of freedom breed intellectual obscurantism that kills creativity in the field of humanities, without which the seeds of a scientific renaissance cannot grow.

The final cause for the deterioration of education in Egypt is the erosion of the scholarly tradition and the demotion in the status of the professor under pressure of the economic privation and social chaos that have prevailed in Egypt during the last 40 years.

There was a time when a professor was the symbol of society's respect for itself. Venerated for his wisdom and his mission to society, a professor was someone who dedicated his life to teaching and educating the young. In return, society gave him the appropriate material and moral appreciation to enable him to pursue his mission. When the university and academic life in general were made subservient to political considerations, the professor's chair became just another form of government employment. The vocation of professor lost its essence and mystique. The situation was even worse for school teachers, who were tossed around by the storms of political expediency, on the one hand, and those of economic need, on the other, since the state could not afford to pay them salaries that met the increasingly heavy burdens of daily life. Teachers also suffered from the intellectual vacuum that affected their profession, as it did all other aspects of life in Egypt. It was no longer possible to expect a teacher to be a symbol of self-respect and knowledge, and to be a conduit for knowledge. The values and the status of the professor and teacher had been shaken, and with them the very foundations of education in Egypt.

IS THERE A CURE?

Such is the description and diagnosis of the disease. What of the cure? Before probing ways and means of reforming education in Egypt, we should be aware that the success of any attempts at reform hinges on the readiness of Egyptians in general and the authorities in particular to admit that the problem of education has reached crisis proportions and that radical reform is a must.

If we can bring ourselves to face this unpleasant truth, we will be taking a step in the right direction. On the other hand, if we persist, as many of us tend to do, in maintaining that education in Egypt has advanced and that it is only a matter of a few reforms here and there, in the curricula, say, or in the methods of teaching, attempting reform would be an exercise in futility. To recognize the existence of a disease is the *sine qua non* for its treatment. Unfortunately, one of the more serious defects we have to contend with – encouraged by some of the media – is a tendency to blur the lines of demarcation between our 'glorious past' and our 'dismal present'! Some art forms, notably national songs, display an obvious narcissistic trend, glorifying Egypt and Egyptians, past and present. This helps blind us to the shortcomings in our present reality and makes us incapable of honestly facing ourselves. For how can someone who believes that he is the worthy son of the best of nations, with the greatest past and the noblest present, concede that some basic aspects of his life are rotting and sorely in need of a radical cure?

A realistic assessment of the educational system in Egypt is the cornerstone on which reform can be founded. Without a national consensus on this question, almost a national front as advocated by the writer Abdel Rahman al-Sharqawi, reforms are doomed to failure.

Let us move now from the general to the particular. It is a fact, for example, that our educational institutions are producing generations devoid of the values and ideals that our nation would have wanted to instil in its sons. Moreover, negative and corrupt values have taken root in the minds of thousands of our young: fatalism, nepotism, loss of faith in work as one of the greatest human and civilizational values, opportunism, a belief that the end justifies the means, and an exaggerated sense of individualism at the expense of the group are the values our young are breathing in the educational institutions in Egypt today.

If we leave values and ideals aside and focus on the actual process of teaching and the imparting of culture, we would find the educational and cultural level of our school and university graduates to be among the lowest in the world. Indeed, they are at best cultural, if not functional, illiterates. Exceptions of course do exist, but these require a special family background which provides its members with a better harvest of knowledge and culture than the norm.

It is in nobody's interest to allow the national debate over education in Egypt today to degenerate into a mudslinging match between political movements. That would not only pull the discussion down to a level we should seek to avoid, but would also be a waste of energy that can be put to better use. I wish to reiterate here what I noted earlier: that we cannot lay the entire blame for the tragedy of education in Egypt on any single period of history.

Instead, let us honestly admit that education in our country has sunk to its lowest level ever and concentrate on finding how this process can be reversed. If we succeed in breaking the present deadlock, the formula could become the source of new solutions to other of Egypt's serious problems and the spring-board for progress and prosperity. Any reform programme will need to be both global and radical.

'Global' reform should apply to the system as a whole, not try to address individual issues pertaining to programmes and curricula, the relationship between the educational institution and other institutions, particularly the government, and so on. 'Radical' reform means it should go all the way – not offer partial change. Once we accept that the situation calls for such drastic action, and if we agree to set aside the acrimony that has governed our political and intellectual discussions to date, we can move on to identify four fronts of action:

1. The education system must be liberated from its subservience to politics in general and to the executive branch in particular.
2. The social context in which the institution of education functions must be upgraded through the implementation of

a national project to eradicate, or at least reduce, illiteracy.
3. The status of Egyptian school teachers and university professors must be promoted.
4. The misguided policy of 'free education', which is in fact anything but free and which has nothing to do with real education, must be rationalized, otherwise it will succeed only in achieving universal ignorance.

Those, in my opinion, are the main fronts on which the battle to save education in Egypt must be waged today, the areas where efforts at reform should focus. Many smaller fronts can be addressed later.

The first practical step, then, is to detach the institution of education from the overwhelming domination of politics. Culture, education and scientific research cannot flourish as long as they are held hostage to politics. This can be achieved only by establishing autonomous agencies to set the general policies for school and university education and to guide education in Egypt without manipulation by successive governments. Such agencies should be made up, particularly at the outset, of an elite of scientists, intellectuals, authors and artists. Their doors should be closed to the civil servants now responsible for education who would have nothing to contribute anyway.

The relationship between these agencies and the Ministry of Education should be organized in such a way as to prevent the ministry from dictating decisions and policies at the whim of the incumbent minister. An example worth emulating here is the relationship between the British government and the British Broadcasting Corporation (BBC), which is run by a council of the best intellectuals and scientists in the country, without any government interference. This formula would guarantee that educational policies in Egypt are not subject to the authority of members of the executive who may, at times, be lovers of freedom and progress, and, at others, enemies of freedom and champions of intellectual oppression.

The second major step is to eradicate illiteracy, or at least to reduce it drastically. It is nonsensical to talk of developing the institution of education in a country where two-thirds of the population is illiterate. Any attempts at reform in such a context would be like trying to plough the waters of the sea.

The greatest proof that successive regimes, from the monarchy to the different forms of republican rule, have been sadly remiss in serving our people is that the illiteracy rate has remained unchanged for the past 50 years. It would be one of the greatest achievements in our contemporary history if the government, in collaboration with different sectors of the population, set the eradication of illiteracy as one of its main targets. It is a target that can be reached in one decade or even less, provided the will is there. The eradication of illiteracy will change the overall social climate in which the institution of education functions. It will also lead to a rise in the standard of the people at the grassroots level, bringing them forward from total ignorance to the world of knowledge.

Third, the tragedy of education will not improve unless the situation of school teachers and university professors is completely reformed. Had successive governments not acted with criminal neglect, both administratively and financially, towards this group of professionals, they would not have had to supplement their incomes by resorting to such practices as working abroad, private tutorship, the sale of books and notes and more demeaning activities.

Obviously, reforming the working and living conditions of teachers and professors involves more than simply raising their salaries and functional status. It means, first of all, that teachers should no longer be chosen from among the lowest ranks of school certificate holders, those who had no choice but to enrol in teachers' training colleges that accepted the lowest percentages. A radical change must be brought to the whole concept, so that it is the best school graduates who will become the teachers of the future.

The last and most important step to be taken is a fundamental revision of the policy of providing 'free' education to all citizens, which, as noted, is neither free nor particularly educational. When, centuries ago, Imam Ali Ibn Abi Taleb (considered the second most important person after the Prophet Muhammad, and Muhammad's cousin) heard the soldiers of his rival Mu'ayiwa shout, 'There is no ruler but God!' he described their slogan as 'a word of truth used to convey a falsehood'. The same is true of the slogan 'free education'. However, before addressing this issue, I would like to draw attention to a number of issues which may seem, at first glance, to be unrelated to the main subject.

One such issue is that the name given to any system often conveys something totally different from the actual reality of such a system. This is particularly true in Third World countries, where the general standard of education and culture is low and terms used are often in contradiction with the substance. In this kind of climate, there is a lot of talk of 'social justice', 'free education', 'workers' rights' and 'equality between social classes', yet these terms are devoid of any real substance and often mean the opposite of the reality they are used to designate.

The same phenomenon often prevails in socialist societies based on a centralized economy and political totalitarianism – Eastern Europe is rife with them. This is the spirit which has prevailed in Egypt since the late 1950s; big slogans have been bandied about, but no one dared to question or examine them closely to see if they reflected the truth.

Another point we should keep in mind is that certain slogans have an in-built mass appeal, particularly in societies where the level of education and culture is not high. The attraction to the ideas embodied in these slogans is often not based on an intellectual conviction stemming from close and scientific scrutiny but is more of an emotional attraction, understandable in an environment where the intellect has ceded its place to emotion. Moreover, circumstances in Egypt are such that the majority prefers the line of least resistance. People shun total and radical change for fear of social and political repercussions, hoping that if the ship is allowed to sail smoothly on course, it will not be overturned by raging winds and storms.

It is obviously difficult to argue against people's emotions. But since when has a true intellectual been content to say what the majority wishes to hear, to accept *a priori* assumptions without careful examination? How can those brought up in the tradition of Western philosophy and its great role models agree to go along with ideas that failed dismally in their application?

While the above may seem a digression from the subject, it was necessary to establish a philosophical framework for our assessment of the 'system of free education' in Egypt – a misnomer if ever there was one. It should have been called the 'system of haphazard and totally unsystematic education'. Most of those who oppose the present system are not opposed to its 'free of charge' aspect (for those who deserve it) but to the haphazard expansion of the institution of education to include well-to-do and bad students, regardless of social class.

If societies far wealthier than ours cannot afford to provide education free of charge for all, how can we, with our scant economic resources, hope to do so? I believe that the vast expansion of general education is the main reason for the tragedy, and that the defects and shortcomings of the educational system in Egypt today all stem, in one way or another, from that expansion, the likes of which has not been seen in any country before. The wisest words on this topic appeared in a recent article by the writer Adel al-Boloq. He said: 'Education is a right for those who are capable ... capable either intellectually or financially.'

Doubtless, many will be outraged at the proposition that education should be made available to the intellectually or financially capable on the grounds that the two forms of capability cannot be equated. However, as a society, we believe in private property, hence in the right to obtain better housing, medical treatment and a better standard of living for those who can afford it. How can we accept such logic in all areas yet reject it when it comes to education – unless we admit that the influence of a leftist ideology in our lives is still greater than most people believe?

The link between quality and quantity is organic, and if the present expansion of free education continues unabated, the 'quantity' uncontrolled, it is impossible to imagine any substantial reform at the level of 'quality'.

It is surprising to see that the project to establish a private university in Egypt, which would be open to those who can afford the real cost of education while not in any way affecting those who cannot, remains unimplemented. The fact is that those who support and propagate leftist ideas do not want the experiment to work simply because it would prove that the haphazard quantitative expansion of education is the reason for its qualitative failure.

Part III

Essays on Contemporary Egyptian Problems

Introduction

This part comprises selected chapters from the six books I published between 1986 and 1995 in an endeavour to diagnose the illnesses of contemporary Egypt and prescribe what I thought to be the solutions that all fall under two big headings: a liberal political system and a modern market economy driven by an advanced human cadre that represents the best of modern management techniques.

Tarek Heggy

CHAPTER 1

The Tragedy of Subsidies[48]

FROM THE 1960s TO THE PRESENT: NEEDS HAVE CHANGED

A state that subscribes to socialist principles is obviously unwilling to admit that prices obey the law of supply and demand, and chooses instead to fix prices, at least of some commodities. But because supply and demand is an infallible economic law, prices fixed by decisions of the state are bound to become, in time, lower than the real prices of these commodities. It follows that in order to maintain the prices at predesignated levels, the state must carry the difference between the sale prices and the real prices. Hence the need for subsidies.

But with the index of state-fixed prices held constant, on the one hand, and real prices steadily rising, on the other, clearly the cost of covering the ever-growing gap between the two becomes progressively heavier. One has only to look at those countries which adopted the system of subsidies to see that the payments they made to finance their commitment in the early years were marginal compared to the cost of maintaining such programmes. Eventually the cost of financing subsidies spiralled out of control, leaving these countries with no funds to spare for any significant investment.

Subsidies were introduced in Egypt in the 1960s when the state was controlling wages. This, in turn, entailed state control over prices, especially of basic commodities for which demand is, in economic terms, non-elastic. Since then, and especially in recent years, debate has been ongoing – and often acrimonious – over subsidies. There are three main schools of thought, all of them, it should be noted, sharing a very narrow perspective on the system as it is applied in Egypt. They are:

1. The so-called 'right' calls for the removal of subsidies due to their heavy burden on the economy. They note that the sum spent by the government to finance its subsidies programme in 1989 alone – just over 10 billion pounds – causes deteriorating economic and social conditions, and with the social injustice and class chaos now prevailing in Egypt, subsidies represent partial compensation for the destitute classes, a lifeline, as it were, that can save them from drowning under the wave of soaring prices.
2. The remnants of the Nasserite movement and the standard-bearers of socialism and communism regard subsidies as an inalienable right of the lowest social classes. Conveniently overlooking the heavy toll exacted on the economy by the subsidies policy, they vociferously support it as an obligation on the part of the government towards the suffering masses. In fact, their real – Machiavellian – concern is the destabilizing effect which the removal of subsidies could have on the Egyptian street.
3. The third group is made up of an eclectic mix of public figures and opinion leaders exactly the size of the Egyptian budget deficit. So the primary justification for subsidies is that they provide economic support to the middle and lower classes, helping them meet their basic needs. But at what cost? Has the state revealed the real cost of the subsidies policy to Egypt? Have political and popular institutions explained the range of effects – positive and adverse – of this policy? Do the mass media project a true picture of the situation?

An outside observer might assume that the views on subsidies held by the various players on the Egyptian political stage are consonant with their general line of thinking. However, he would be mistaken. To explain this inconsistency, we must look at Egypt's recent past which for the most part was devoid of a free political life in which divergent views could be aired. This period also saw the emergence of amorphous 'groupings' of individuals, in contradistinction to Western democracies where like-minded people come together on such clearly defined common ground as unity of thought, ideological consensus, orientations and strategic goals.

Thus we find a party like the Socialist Labour Party,[49] which is actually an offshoot of the now-defunct fascist party, Misr al-Fatat[50] or Young Egypt, using similar arguments to the leftists to defend the subsidies policy. This is less of a paradox than may at first appear if we remember that fascists are among the most ardent believers in the supremacy of the state and its patriarchal role. But while there might be a certain logic in this meeting of fascists and leftists, it is totally illogical for a party like the Wafd,[51] whose whole philosophy is based on liberalism as the mainstay of economic life, to support the subsidies policy and to castigate the government whenever it tries to cut down on its expenditures in that direction.

In fact, both proponents and critics of the subsidies policy depart from the wrong premise. It would be wise for them to liberate themselves from the conventional political dogmas in which the debate is mired and ask themselves, rather, who actually benefits from subsidies. More specifically, it is high time for the man in the street to learn that the subsidies which appeared to serve his interest in the short term have become a very real threat to his well-being in the medium and long term. Having determined his income artificially, thereby creating a work climate not conductive to productivity, the state then decided to help him meet his basic needs by setting up another artificial system, the subsidies, which ultimately is detrimental for all concerned – the man in the street and the state.

The funds sunk into the subsidies programme could – and should have been – invested in projects yielding a high rate of return for the state and, ultimately, for its citizens. Thus as a direct consequence of the subsidies policy huge opportunities for investment, production and wealth were lost. Another, less obvious, consequence of the policy is the spread of unemployment: with huge amounts of capital channelled into subsidies rather than into new projects, no new job opportunities were created for the rising generations, and the state found itself in the bizarre situation of feeding the fathers instead of employing the sons. This is an extremely dangerous social trend which helps lay the groundwork for social chaos and turmoil, and could even lead to civil war. For some inexplicable reason, this aspect of subsidies is largely ignored. No one ever suggested that not only were the 10 billion pounds allocated to subsidies in the fiscal budget for 1989/1990 lost at the end of that year, but also millions of job opportunities which could have been created for our youth if that sum, or even part of it, had been spent in setting up new projects.

Indeed, only by offering employment opportunities in real and productive jobs can the need for subsidies be eliminated. Young people who are given the chance to perform real work can dispense with subsidies, unlike the millions now holding down jobs artificially created by the state who cannot make ends meet on their 'salaries' which are, in fact, nothing more than a handout. One has only to compare private sector salaries, which afford a reasonable standard of living, with those in the public sector to understand this.

FAILING PUBLIC COMPANIES: BLAME SUBSIDIES

Among the most insatiable recipients of subsidies, severely depleting the meagre financial resources of a poor country like Egypt, are the public companies which are either operating at a loss, barely breaking even or, at best, showing a narrow profit margin incommensurate with the capital invested in them. Somehow, this wasteful allocation of resources does not win much attention from any side in the subsidies debate.

For example, no one has noted that loss-making public sector units, as well as those realizing net annual returns below a given level (say, 7 per cent in real terms, or constant money value, i.e. after taking inflation into account), are not only allowed to continue through massive injections of financial aid but also receive vast sums of money which are distributed among employees as 'profits'. This prodigal outflow of capital is ultimately financed by the average Egyptian citizen, whose loss takes more than one form:

• He is deprived of the profits which can legitimately be expected from any project and which should be used either in defraying the cost of public services and utilities or in setting up projects that can generate employment.

- He is deprived of the funds actually generated by profitable sectors of the economy which, instead of being deployed to create new jobs and improve public services and utilities, are used to shore up moribund sectors of the economy.

Sound economic thinking equates loss-making concerns with those realizing marginal profits, since both can be replaced by more efficient forms of investment which can, by generating the minimum profits, avoid the losses we have spoken of. This indirect form of subsidies, more than any other, must be confronted head-on; we must not be deterred by the hue and cry anticipated by the agitators who have been spawned by Egypt in the last three decades. We have listened long enough to these demagogues and, as we see the economy deteriorating at an alarming rate year after year, our patience has worn thin. They must be silenced and their subversive acts put down with an iron fist, a course of action the government followed when it stepped in firmly to quell the disturbance at the Hilwan Iron and Steel Works in August 1989.[52]

The time has also come for responsible members of the mass media to bring this sorry state of affairs to light. The public must be made aware that the money used to subsidize floundering public companies and keep them operating at a loss could have been used to generate jobs and finance infrastructure projects. A campaign must also be launched to alert productive members of the labour force that they are being forced to accept a steady decline in salaries – and thus in their living standards – for the sake of the inefficient workers who contribute nothing to the national economy and actually constitute a drain on it. Leaving the field free to the leftists, Nasserites and certain trade unionists with a vested interest in maintaining the status quo would be a major strategic error. Failure to face up to the problem now will only allow it to grow more intractable and make the cost of solving it in the future prohibitive in political, social and economic terms. It is therefore imperative to confront the problem decisively before it is too late, despite the backlash that can be expected.

Needless to say, we must not overlook the security dimensions of the problem. The security apparatus in Egypt is as duty-bound to stand up to the saboteurs of law and order (a duty they carried out in masterly fashion during the Hilwan events in August 1989) as to the fundamentalists who would turn Egypt into a religious theocracy and to the drug dealers who are destroying its youth and, with them, its hopes for the future.

A METHODOLOGICAL APPROACH TO REDUCING – AND CANCELLING – SUBSIDIES

Advocates of political liberalism and a free market economy maintain that only by abandoning the subsidies policy can Egypt hope to climb out of the long slump which has made it one of the world's poorest nations. Indeed, it is among the ten countries with the largest debts in the world. While there can be no question that subsidies are a major cause of Egypt's economic woes, it is equally true that the seeds of the problem were sown by the political choices Egypt made after 1952. After all, economic backwardness, like economic progress, is the fruit of political choice. It follows that no solution can be envisaged, either on the theoretical or practical level, as long as Egypt remains committed to those political choices. At the same time, removing subsidies in one fell swoop will not solve the problem. In order to create a favourable economic climate in which Egypt can move ahead from economic stagnation, subsidies should be phased out according to a comprehensive plan that provides for the reallocation of funds to spheres and projects that will generate high profits and create new job opportunities. It is only through the successful implementation of a rational plan – reducing subsidies while simultaneously increasing investments in productive projects – that the subsidies controversy can be settled in a manner that will maintain social harmony and win over public opinion to the merits of their cancellation.

For, unless tangible benefits accrue from the removal of subsidies, it will be extremely difficult to convince the public of the wisdom and advantage of such a course. On the other hand, if a reduction in subsidies were to be accompanied by, say, an expansion in government spending or bigger budgets for certain ministries, this would alienate public opinion and bring into doubt the government's credibility – an image it would find hard to shake; nor would it represent any real advantage in economic terms. The real measure of success here is not the extent to which the removal of subsidies will lighten the burden on the government but how far the savings generated by their removal can be channelled into investment areas that translate into higher incomes and new jobs.

A prime minister who can satisfy this dialectical equation will be the economic reformer Egypt has long been waiting for – ever since, in fact, ill-advised political and economic choices plunged it into poverty and hardship.

THE DEFENDERS OF SUBSIDIES VERSUS THE SILENT PROPONENTS OF A FREE ECONOMY

To complete the picture of the subsidies tragedy, which is sapping the vitality of the Egyptian economy and taxing it to the limits of endurance, we must take a look at the configuration of the country's political map. While public life in Egypt is teeming with prominent representatives of the left, it is noticeably lacking genuine proponents of a free market system who also believe in the bankruptcy of socialist regimes, in general, and of those applying a command economy, in particular.

Rather, it is a hybrid class of middlemen, brokers, merchants, speculators and other symbols of the 1970s who are – mistakenly – regarded as the custodians of liberalism and a free market economy. This class emerged as a result of the erratic course of government in the 1960s to 1970s and enjoyed its heyday under Anwar Sadat's economic open-door policy. The mercantile mentality of the members of this class, their narrow intellectual horizons and cultural insularity, renders them incapable of grasping the rudiments of liberalism and a free market economy. It is as unimaginable to regard them as upholders of these values as it would be to apply this description to supporters of corruption, illegal currency dealers and drug traffickers. In short, then, while the left can boast thousands of champions in Egyptian public life, the school of thought which believes in liberalism and a free market economy has practically none.

THE MASS MEDIA AND SUBSIDIES

An important responsibility rests on the shoulders of the mass media to explain to the man in the street that the real beneficiaries of subsidies are the moneyed classes, the members of Egypt's new 'upper class', while the working class and the poor can only lose out in the medium and long term. In fact, the continued application of this policy will impoverish them still further and destroy any hope of a better future for themselves and their children. To get this message across, however, is to swim against the tide of public opinion. The official media spent so many years convincing Egyptians of their right to receive government assistance in the form of subsidies that this belief is now firmly entrenched in the public consciousness, making any attempt to debunk it a daunting task. Moreover, any such campaign would bring fierce reaction from the proponents of a command economy and the demagogues who will not allow their vested interests to be swept under the carpet of reform. This is nothing new: the history of humankind is one long struggle between the harbingers of reform and those who will stop at nothing to preserve the status quo and with it their considerable privileges. The mass media must stand up to them.

Few have been the examples of public figures in Egypt who have stood up for a free economy – and they should be lauded. In fact, only those ministers who have not succumbed to pressure and intimidation and who translated their disenchantment with the subsidies policy into concrete action have achieved real success. For example, thanks to one minister of petroleum who remained uncowed by the vilifying campaign launched against him by an opposition party notorious for its foreign affiliations, base tactics and extremism, Egypt succeeded in building up a strategic reserve of gas as a buffer against any potential energy crisis. He boosted Egypt's natural gas reserve from 10 to 30 years by encouraging private investment in this domain, echoing Egypt's success in becoming an oil-producing and -exporting country since the mid-1960s due to private investment. In addition, a minister of tourism braved the loud protests emanating from the left to institute reforms in that sector, also opening it up to local and foreign private investment, and succeeded in multiplying Egypt's revenues from tourism several times over in recent years. But these are isolated incidents. Too few people are willing to brave the wrath of the self-appointed keepers of the faith, who defend subsidies as a sacrosanct right of the people and decry those who call for their reappraisal, labelling them traitors. That is precisely why, despite their negative aspects, subsidies remain a cornerstone of the regime.

THE CRISIS OF CONFIDENCE BETWEEN THE GOVERNMENT AND THE PEOPLE

This chapter would be incomplete if it failed to address the crisis of confidence between the government and the people of Egypt. One government after another has pledged to institute reforms, to rationalize government spending, to improve government performance and to secure a better future for the Egyptian citizen. But the Egyptian citizen, though assured by successive governments that they will rationalize spending, sees them doing just the opposite. Although Egyptians are renowned for their stoicism and forbearance in the face of hardship, their patience is stretched to breaking point by the obvious discrepancy between a government's words and its deeds.

A plan by the government – any government – to rationalize subsidies and divert some of the massive subsidy allocations into investment projects stands no chance of success unless a real attempt is made actually to implement the plan. In other words, it must be carried out in full view of the people, the press and the world. And it is high time this happened.

CHAPTER 2

The Art of Work: An Art We Have Lost[53]

We were out somewhere in the middle of Egypt's sandy Western Desert, south of the Qattara Depression and north of the Great Sea of Sand, when my companion, one of the three top personalities in the international oil industry, said, 'In my view the Egyptian authorities and people are making a mistake when they attribute current economic problems to a lack of potential or natural resources. In fact, Egypt is rich in both; what it lacks is another vital element – work!' He paused for a moment, then added,

> You know how much I love Egypt and how badly I want to see its economy thrive, yet I must tell you that, because of the political situation over the past 30 years you have lost the 'art of work', and without that you cannot hope to make progress. I recently went through some reports by prominent economic and political analysts in the USA and Western Europe. To my surprise, they all reached the same conclusion, namely, that Egypt's income today is derived from five sources (all unrelated to the 'art of work'): remittances from Egyptians working abroad; oil revenues; revenues from the Suez Canal; tourism; and cotton production. Except for cotton, there is virtually no added value on these income sources. The work performed by Egyptians abroad does not count, being part of the production process of one or more of those countries, and regarding oil, the Suez Canal and tourism, your work is only a marginal source of the revenue they generate.

His words only served to reinforce my conviction that the socialist-style economic and political systems applied in many Third World countries, such as Egypt, Algeria, Libya, Cuba, Tanzania and parts of Southeast Asia and Africa, are wholly to blame for the demise of the work ethic and, with it, the spirit of enterprise and diligence. The disappearance of individual initiative and creativity motivated by personal profit and advantage, the abolition of differences among members of society engendered by the rigid socialist interpretation of 'equality' and the absence of the necessary element of risk – all of which are the result of labour laws that stifle competition and drive and make the task of management, in the private and public sectors, well-nigh impossible by disallowing incentives – have created in countries following the 'socialist path to development' wide sectors of citizens unqualified for, incapable of and unwilling to work. With every passing generation, the 'art of work' diminishes, although it is the secret of progress and welfare and the key to stability. One of the worst disasters that can befall a people applying a socialist political and economic model (particularly those of a poor educational and cultural standard, which can be said for most of the Third World) is the development of a 'civil servant' mentality and the erosion of the 'entrepreneurial' spirit. This permeates all levels of employees and may extend to include the managers of public companies and politicians, up to the highest echelons. In all honesty, out of over 30 ministers in the present cabinet, I can think of only one or two who have a well-developed business sense and base their judgements on commercial considerations (commerce and politics being two sides of the same coin), unimpeded by the civil servant mentality.

One need look no further for proof of this argument than to the Egyptian public sector in which, since the 1960s, the state has sunk the phenomenal sum of over 1,000 billion pounds. Its return? Annual output worth 1,500 million pounds – or a paltry 1.5 per cent of the GDP! The public sector is plunged into a state of apathy that has rendered it incapable of responding to Egypt's call for help. The situation is all the more painful if we realize that, in the normal course of events, this sector should have been able to provide Egypt annually with not less than three times the volume of US aid to the country, aid we must try to do without as an essential first step towards extricating ourselves from our sorry predicament. Our heavy reliance on US aid is the inevitable result of injudicious economic and political practices over the years and by successive governments. While the present regime may not be accountable for reaching this situation, it should accept responsibility for finding a radical and speedy solution. The tables must be turned. After years in which the public was encouraged to substitute 'work' with debate and empty slogans ('ensuring the availability of goods ...' 'raising the level of production ...,' etc.) it is time to reclaim the art of work.

It might surprise people to learn that even in this Third World country the 'made in Egypt' label found on our products is a bluff. A closer look at Egyptian goods available on the market will show that they are, in fact, made elsewhere. This is true for more than half our foodstuffs, clothing, machinery and building materials. We are not even self-sufficient in cement! Worse still: the sum spent by Egypt every day to buy the cement required for its construction industry is equal to its net daily income from the Suez Canal. And how could successive governments have failed to solve the agricultural problem in Egypt, when its solution entails nothing more than repealing the laws which produced the present disastrous situation in the first place? In addition, despite a wide consensus on the need to allow supply and demand laws to govern landlord–tenant relations, the housing sector is bogged down by laws that continue to ensure a flood of demand and scant supply.

How can we hope to speak of 'work' and 'production' when the vast majority of public sector managers prove their failure and multiply their losses every day? The difference between us and countries such as Turkey and Greece, whose economies are steadily growing, is spelled in our lack of productivity, efficiency, creativity – and the simple work ethic.

It is the supreme duty of the government and, in particular, the president, as the nation's chief executive, to break the vicious circle of failure that has characterized the last 30 years. It is within that vicious circle that Egyptians mislaid the 'art of work'. This is what all loyal citizens expect from their government, rather than economic policies reducing expenditures in some areas and levying heavier taxes in others. These measures fall under the heading of 'non-work'. They ask a poor man with only a few pounds to his name to redistribute that sum in his pockets, thereby increasing his poverty, since he cannot increase his wealth, cash supply or value in any way – except through efficient, productive and creative work.

CHAPTER 3

Who are the Makers of History: Circumstances or People?[54]

Every writer concerned with history, politics and, especially, philosophy has a topic of particular interest. For example, the eminent historian Arnold Toynbee devoted much of his life to the study of why civilizations rise and fall. An exponent of the theory of cycles, he believed the universal driving force of progress to be the response to challenges. The eleventh-century Islamic theologian, mystic and philosopher Abu Hamid Muhammad al-Ghazali, known as *hujjat al-Islam* (the proof of Islam), journeyed across the Muslim world driven by the desire to find out whether the human senses could attain knowledge of the existence of God. Meanwhile, Nietzsche's world outlook was pervaded by his 'caste of masters' theory, the belief in an ever-progressing elite up to the level of 'superman', and Karl Marx, who was and remains a philosopher before being a theoretician of economics, politics and sociology, had an all-encompassing philosophy based on his view of the dynamics of history, which stemmed from his basic ideas on the relation of matter (the infrastructure) to ideas (the superstructure).

One of the most dominant figures of contemporary Arab thought, Abbas al-Aqad, focused on his fundamental idea that exceptional human beings are the driving force of human civilization, and history in general. Many of Aqad's disciples, and I am among them, have undertaken the arduous task of researching the role of the individual in shaping human history. Anyone pursuing this line of research is bound eventually to find himself at the crossroads of major philosophical and political paths. He must then choose between them, difficult as this may be. Every single philosophical, political, economic and social school of thought has its own views on the matter, based on its carefully predicated tenets. I believe that extensive and careful readings for years can bring the reader to the first step on the path to a clear answer. Philosophical schools of thought, in general, are divided into idealistic, or moralistic, schools on the one hand, and materialistic schools on the other. All the answers to the major questions concerning the role of the individual in shaping history are also divided into two types of answers, one departing from idealistic philosophical premises, the other, in one way or another, from materialistic philosophical premises.

The Dialectical Materialists (the disciples of Karl Marx who, like the German philosopher Ludwig Feuerbach before them, discarded the idealistic content of Hegel's philosophy of idealistic-dialectics) firmly maintain that the role of the individual and of heroes and eminent men in shaping history is a minimal one. They believe that human history is propelled by a purely material driving force, the class struggle, which is the inevitable result of the interplay of the forces and relations of production prevailing at a given time. As for heroes and eminent men, they are like puppets dancing to the tune written by the supreme composer: the class struggle.

All historians who believe in a materialistic interpretation of history hold that it is socio-economic conditions that govern the movement of history and that these purely materialistic considerations also determine the role of the individual. Hence their view, for example, that when the age of slavery came to an end, it was because changes in the forces of production and relations of production tipped in favour of the slaves, bringing slavery to an end and heralding in the age of feudalism. Similarly, purely material factors brought feudalism to an end and introduced capitalism. This third socio-economic formation, according to the materialists, was the result of the development of the forces of production. It was this development, culminating in the invention of the steam engine, that rang the curtain down on one phase of human history and ushered in a new one.

Such momentous events as the French Revolution are also explained in purely materialistic terms by these exponents of the materialist school of thought, who dismiss the role of the individual and the impact of the presence of certain figures on the scene of historic events as being of little relevance. That is also the way they interpret the wars and revolutions of the nineteenth century, as well as the birth of nationalist movements in Europe, under the leadership of Mazzini in Italy and Bismarck in Germany. It is also the principle guiding their interpretation of Europe's colonialist expansion and the major events of the twentieth century, like the Russian Revolution of February 1917, the Bolshevik takeover in October/November that same year under Lenin's leadership, World War I, the rise of the Third Reich, World War II and all the national liberation movements in Africa, Asia and Latin America.

The materialist interpretation of history could appeal to the scientific-minded reader because it is surrounded by an aura of science and because of the rigour of its methodology. Without drawing the reader into the eddies of the philosophical battle between 'matter' and 'thought', I will say only that I for one believe that the history of mankind, indeed, life itself, is governed by an absolute, transcendental Idea, and that to think that matter alone is the mover does not stand to reason. In fact, the changes attributed by materialist determinists to matter alone are in fact changes brought about purely by 'thought'. The invention of the steam engine, for example, was not the result of a materialist evolution, it was the result of intellectual evolution. From the beginning of recorded history up to the present time, certain individuals have played a major role in shaping events. They have left an indelible mark on our world and, had they not existed, events would have taken a different course. A superficial look that does not go beyond major historical events to analyse the personalities, characteristics and motivations of certain historical figures could lead one to deny the role of such individuals in influencing the course of history and to believe that the major waves of history were governed only by materialist factors. Such a view is totally refuted by the weight of such historical figures as Alexander the Great, without whom much of the history of the ancient world would have been different. And, had it not been for the person of Napoleon Bonaparte, the history of France and of Europe would have followed a course different from the one we know in the ten years following the French Revolution (1789–98). That the reins of the Russian Revolution slipped from the hands of the Mensheviks nine months after they had overturned Tsar Nicholas II in February 1917 is due to the determining role of the man whom the Germans helped return to Petrograd, via Zurich, in a special military train, for they believed in his ability to change the situation in Russia. That man was Lenin who, in a matter of months, signed the Brest-Litovsk treaty by virtue of which the Germans obtained what they wanted of him.

Had it not been for the role played by Adolf Hitler, the events of the 1930s and 1940s on the European scene and in the world at large would not have been the same, for they were the result of Hitler's 'actions' and the 'reactions' of his enemies, the allies, led first by Britain and, towards the end, by the United States.

Actually, coincidences also play an important role in major historic events. To give but a few examples. If Corsica had not been annexed by France at a given point in time and had remained a part of Italy, Napoleon would not have been born French and would not have come to play the crucial role he did in the history of France, of Europe and of many other parts of the world ever since his star began to rise during the last five years of the eighteenth century until his ultimate fall in 1815.

The personal role of King Henry VIII drove thousands of Englishmen into Protestantism, a fact which greatly influenced the climate of political and public life in Britain.

Had it not been for the personal role of Gamal Abdel Nasser, internal events in Egypt, relations between Egypt and the Arab world and between the Arab states and Israel would have taken a completely different course.

If it had not been for the role played by a handful of men during the last third of the nineteenth century and the first third of the twentieth, the Zionist movement would not have gone as far as it has done in the last 40 years. It is thanks to the role played by one man, Lee Kuan Yew, prime minister of Singapore since 1965, that such a small country managed to develop so dramatically in just two decades.

All the above does not imply a negation of the role and impact of socio-economic or material factors on history, nor a belief that history is made up of a series of consecutive events which, like soap operas, are not governed by a certain law or system. What it does say is that the two factors combined have a role to play: the material factor as the general trend, and the non-material factor – the role of individuals and coincidences – as an equally important law having the same impact as that of the material factor.

Two references come to mind here: 'The Heroes' by Plutarch and 'Heroes and Hero Worship' by Thomas Carlyle. These brilliant works, together with Toynbee's extensive history, can clearly show the reader who wishes to pursue the subject further the effect of the two factors combined on the course of human history, with the predominance of the moral factor, as represented by the role of particular individuals, ideas and circumstances.

CHAPTER 4

The Difficult Equation of Change versus Stability[55]

There have been many indications of late, particularly during the past year, that the Egyptian administration has come to realize the failure of the policies that have governed our economic and political life since the late 1950s and through the 1960s. Specifically, I am referring to the policies limiting the role of the private sector and reducing areas of cooperation with multinational companies, and to those governing agriculture, industry, housing and education – policies to which all of Egypt's major problems can be traced.

But while recognizing that no cure is possible without radical reform, the administration believes that any change has to consider the requirements of political and social stability. Several serious incidents have made the situation even more sensitive and complex: the 1977 riots,[57] the assassination of President Sadat and the workers' strike at the Hilwan steel mills in 1987. As we consider how to balance the inevitability of change with the imperative need for stability, we would do well to keep a popular Egyptian adage in mind: 'He whose hand is in water is not like he whose hand is in fire'.

While it is natural for all the opposition factions to favour change, it is equally natural for the ruling administration to be more concerned with stability. The focus in the opposition press has always been on the need for change, regardless of how it might affect stability and political and social security. The Tajamu Party[58] calls for changes of a socialist nature, in line with its ideology. The Wafd Party aims at changes of a liberal nature, based on the amendment of the constitution in the direction of political liberalization. The Labour Party is clamouring for changes that remain undefined, even in the minds of its leaders whose orientations have become more obscure than ever following the recent merger between this successor of the old fascist party, Young Egypt, the Liberal Party, the Socialist Party and the Muslim Brotherhood. As fervently as it reiterates the need for change (of whatever nature), the opposition remains curiously silent about the need to effect change in a way that would not jeopardize political and social stability and plunge Egypt into the anarchy raging through the Middle East today. There are, as we all know, a number of regional and global parties with an interest in keeping the political pot on the boil in various parts of the world, and they would not be averse to seeing a similar situation erupt in Egypt.

An observer confronted with the two positions may wonder where the truth lies – in the over-sensitivity to and awareness of security requirements or in the relentless call for change? Actually, both positions contain a modicum of truth. But to date none of the opposition parties has come up with concrete proposals for change. They have stuck to generalities and catchphrases, disregarding the effects of change on stability and forgetting that, as an opposition, they have never been involved in any form of administrative government. With the exception of the Wafd Party, all the factions of the Egyptian opposition share a common past: totalitarianism, fascism or theocracy. With such a legacy, is it any wonder that their strident calls for change should blithely disregard the disastrous consequences of instituting change without careful planning? There was an opposition party that could have formed an objective and balanced counterpoise to the party in power had it not, regrettably, fallen under the influence of one man's overriding ambition, a man whose race against time is doomed to failure.

These reservations on the opposition's attitude to change do not imply unqualified support for the administration's excessively cautious position in this respect. Although it is wise to aim for change without affecting political and social stability, any error in timing could cause the foundations of security to crack and upset stability. Time is not an ally for anyone called upon to tackle the massive problems of contemporary Egypt. On the contrary, it can work against him and hinder the possibility of reaching comprehensive solutions to our chronic problems.

In other words, while it is right to insist on maintaining security and stability when contemplating changes in political and economic orientations in matters as important as education, industry, agriculture and housing, it is equally true that to postpone instituting the necessary changes is to jeopardize stability.

Let us turn to a notorious historical example of the fatal consequences of indecision. Had the French monarchy in 1789 not refused to institute the democratic reforms that the French people aspired to, had Louis XVI sided with the Commons and not with the Nobles during the constitutional crisis, the French Revolution may not have taken place and the monarchy may have survived, as did its counterpart in England. Scores of examples attest to the validity of the dictum that to postpone taking action may itself be twice as dangerous as the immediate tackling of problems, however intractable they seem to be. Yet in Egypt today we are treated to the spectacle of armchair critics loudly denouncing any attempt to change systems which have become enshrined idols protected by a priesthood whose members jealously guard their privileges.

One system that needs to be changed, and without further delay, is that of housing. The most critical aspect of the housing problem in Egypt is the enormous discrepancy between dwindling supply and burgeoning demand. In the late 1950s and through the 1960s, the state enacted laws that served to deter the private sector from investing in the construction of housing units, particularly those for rent. Faced with an alarming drop in the number of rentals, the state was forced to step into the housing market to meet the demand, which was growing as fast as the population.

The state, of course, failed to perform satisfactorily the task it had set itself, not because of any inherent failing but because it is impossible for a state to accomplish such a formidable task. The only practical solution is to repeal the housing laws that created the imbalance between supply and demand in the first place. The problem will not disappear through such palliatives as prohibiting the sale of apartments, key money or rent advances. Moreover, the longer we wait the more acute the disparity will become between the demand for and the supply of housing units. As the disparity grows, so too does the pressure of the housing problem on society's nervous system, which is growing more intolerable. Eventually, the strains and stresses of the situation may cause cracks in the foundations of political and social stability and security.

The agricultural problem is another example. Agriculture is the mode of production most closely associated with the idea of private initiative, in the sense that it epitomizes more clearly than any other the organic link between private initiative, as represented in an individual's direct personal interest in the success of a private venture, and the overall success of this mode of production. In the area of agriculture, the concept of private property is more firmly entrenched than in other spheres of production. That is why agriculture succeeds brilliantly under systems which encourage private ownership and recognize that individual creativity stemming from personal interest fuels productivity and success. Agricultural production in the USA, Canada, Germany and France is a success story. In the socialist countries it suffers greatly from the lack of enthusiasm of farm workers, from low productivity and from visible degradation. If we compare Algeria and Morocco – two adjoining countries with nearly identical geographic and demographic conditions but with different political systems – we see that in the former, a socialist state, agricultural production is a complete failure, whereas in Morocco, with its free system of agricultural production, this sector is highly successful.

In Egypt the system is mixed and highly intricate. The general framework is socialist, based on severe limitations of agricultural land holdings, and a legal system that has transformed the landlord into a hired hand and made the tenant farmer the real owner. Moreover, a large number of agricultural products, some of them strategic, must be sold to the government. The problem, of course, is that any attempt at reform will necessarily entail changes that could affect political and social stability. But failure to act would be even worse. Postponing the necessary decisions could only lead to the further degradation of agricultural productivity and swelled tension between the parties concerned. As agricultural production drops and the demographic explosion continues to send everwidening ripples through society, the state will be subjected to enormous pressure to provide large amounts of foreign currency to import more and more food.

Another example of the importance of timely decisions is the mutiny of the Central Security Forces in February 1986.[56] The spark that ignited the incident was the deplorable living conditions of the soldiers. Had a decision been taken in time to improve their conditions, there would have been no mutiny and the *agents provocateurs* would have remained silent.

Countless examples show that the dangers inherent in delaying the adoption of decisions concerning crucial problems far outweigh any short-lived continuity and stability that ignoring the problems can provide. In conclusion, it can be said that the real difficulty lies not in having to choose between change and stability but in coming to realize that both factors are necessary: change for the better while ensuring stability and fulfilling security needs.

CHAPTER 5

Religious Extremism in Egypt[59]

On 19 February, the *Al-Akhbar* daily ran an article I wrote on
Saad Zaghlul's extraordinary political skills, which enabled
him to gain the full confidence of Egypt's Copts and Muslims
alike. That confidence reached its peak in 1919 when all
Egyptians saw Zaghlul as the symbol of national salvation and
the rallying point for national aspirations, when both Copts
and Muslims forgot their bitter conflicts, for only eight years
had elapsed since that sombre time. The article won praise from
several readers, including two whose opinions I particularly
cherish: the most eminent religious personality in the Muslim
community and his Coptic counterpart.

Most of those with whom I discussed the article, including
the two religious leaders, urged me to write another on the
subject of religious extremism in Egypt. I would have preferred
to tackle that phenomenon in a book, yet the regrettable flare-up
of sectarian violence in the past few days makes it imperative
for all Egyptian writers who support democracy as the supreme
value attained by civilization to address the subject. Another
motivating factor is the appearance of a spate of recent articles
attributing the spread of religious extremism in Egypt today to
external factors, such as foreign incitement and the financing
of extremist movements in general, and of fundamentalist
Islamic groups in particular.

This attribution is extremely dangerous because presenting
the issue of religious extremism as a security problem – to be
dealt with by the police and other security bodies – removes it
from the realm of problems amenable to political solutions.

Those who are quick to point an accusing finger at external forces should realize that if Egypt had been a haven of social tolerance, brotherhood and peace, it would not have been susceptible to interference from abroad and that it is other, local, factors which have created a climate favourable to the success of such attempts.

In fact, the roots of religious extremism in Egypt stem from three sources. The first is the harsh treatment meted out to the Islamic trend in Egypt by Nasser's regime. Ever since the disputes between the regime and the Muslim Brotherhood erupted into serious conflict, the regime resorted to force and torture against the movement. This happened in 1954 and again in 1965 when the confrontation was even more acute. Certainly the methods used by Nasser against the Islamic currents, whose members were persecuted, imprisoned, exiled and tortured, created generations of extremists among those who had suffered at his hands as well as from their progeny. Had they not been crushed by Nasser, the Muslim Brothers would most likely not have produced elements as extremist, as reactionary and as insular as the militant Islamic groups we see today.

Thus, once again we can see that terror breeds terror. The repression of ideas and beliefs produces unexpected forms of extremism, violence, terrorism and even crime. Significantly, the four largest terrorist groups in the world today emerged in countries which were subjected to repressive dictatorships for long enough to produce those forms of organized violence: the Bader Meinhof gang in Germany, the Red Brigades in Italy, the Red Army in Japan and the Basque group ETA in Spain. These organizations emerged in the fascist countries which formed the Axis in World War II, with the exception of Spain which, nevertheless, was also a bastion of fascism under Franco. In Egypt too, the many years of repressive dictatorship generated a climate of extremism where it had never previously existed.

The second source of extremism in Egypt today is the prevailing socio-economic situation. Poverty, the decline in living standards, the appearance of a very wealthy minority noted for its conspicuous consumption, the harrowing problems of daily life and the social anarchy they create, and a breakdown in society's system of values – the cornerstone on which the system is built – combine to create the perfect climate for extremism and the spread of totalitarian tendencies, whether towards the left into Marxist groups or towards the right into sectarianism and religious dogmatism.

Karl Marx's famous appeal to the working class, 'Workers of the world unite! You have nothing to lose but your chains!' well illustrates the link between extremism and depressed socio-economic conditions. Economic crises generate feelings of deep frustration, especially among the young, who despair of obtaining their legitimate right to a decent life. The lack of access to such basic necessities as a home, food and clothes – and education – make them susceptible to hardliners who claim that society is corrupt and doomed and that it should be destroyed to make room for a better society. These disenchanted youngsters were never given the tools to compare their society, whatever its shortcomings, to the insubstantial dream they are offered. Thus the crushing economic crisis and the ensuing breakdown in social values provide an excellent opportunity for advocates of extremism, whether communists or militant religious elements, to peddle their ideas.

Finding radical solutions to the social and economic problems besetting Egypt would certainly help extirpate some of these problems, reducing the appeal of the extremism we are witnessing today.

The third source can be attributed to external factors. Egypt is in the eye of a storm of radicalism blowing from every direction in the Middle East, especially from Iran and Lebanon, and the contagion is helped along with foreign funding and incitement. This unhealthy climate is due to internal as well as external factors, mainly that the region, which did not succeed in producing democratic regimes, has now fallen into the clutches of ruthless forces: Zionism, arms dealers and other parties with a vested interest in keeping the region in ferment.

The protection of Egyptian society from the scourge of foreign intervention and financing is, of course, the task of the security forces. But important as this is, their role in dealing with the phenomenon of religious fanaticism cannot eliminate its causes nor bring it to a halt. The only proper cure is a combination of real democracy (as opposed to window dressing) and firm action by eminent religious figures who should use their moral authority to contain the problem, not fan the flames of extremism as so many do. Last but not least, we need the vigilance of the security forces, particularly in Upper Egypt where traditional tribal values combined with religious fanaticism constitute a highly explosive mixture.

CHAPTER 6

The Egyptian Problem: Origins and Analysis[60]

The biggest mistake an observer of the Egyptian scene today could make is to accept the popular theory that the country is suffering from an array of 'terminal' diseases that are eating away at the very fabric of society. Of course, a perfunctory look would tend to support this fundamentally flawed theory, with countless examples that appear to validate it.

Blatant violations of laws and regulations are rife, aggressive behaviour is the norm, the collapse of principles and values is clear – the syndromes of a society in crisis are too numerous to cite. Add to that the problems of day-to-day living faced by the average citizen – chaotic traffic, deplorable public transport, pock-marked streets that are often awash with sewage, repeated power failures, taps running dry, as well as a plethora of severe housing problems – and the situation looks terminal indeed. Sometimes it does seem that anyone dealing with Egypt comes across a new ailment daily, be it in the government, the judicial system, or local life in general.

But for all that, the theory would not stand up to careful analysis. Instead these are *symptoms* of a limited number of diseases – and symptoms can be kept in check. The situation could be compared to a cardiac patient suffering from many aches and pains. If the patient believes (or imagines) he is suffering from more than one disease, rather than different symptoms of the same one, he will waste time, money and energy trying to pinpoint each one. Treating the symptoms separately will not help cure the original disease, which produced all the symptoms in the first place.

The same is true of the many problems that plague Egypt today. If we examine the basic functions of the state towards its citizens, we will have taken an important step in the direction of achieving our main objective, which is, first, to identify the diseases inherent in contemporary Egyptian reality and their symptoms, and, second, to treat the most debilitating of them.

The history of political thought provides us with a clear model to use as a starting point: the state is a political organization whose traditional basic functions are: (1) defence; (2) security; (3) justice; (4) public services. Members of any given society expect the state, as a political organization, to assume on their behalf the responsibility of *defence* in case of external aggression. This entails the presence of an army capable of warding off threats and dangers from outside to protect the individuals living within the state's borders. The society also expects the state to guarantee the *security* of its members, which requires the existence of a ministry or mechanism whose job is to protect citizens from internal aggression and criminal activity, collective or otherwise, as well as to provide other aspects of security such as road safety, safe housing, etc. At the same time the state is responsible for the maintenance and administration of *justice* in its broadest sense by promulgating and guaranteeing the application of laws. Finally, the state must provide citizens with certain basic *services*, such as electricity, water, road infrastructure, sewers, means of transport and communication. These are the four traditional basic functions of the state, according to lines of political thinking and constitutional jurisprudence. It is worth noting here that socialist philosophy considers the state responsible for many other functions as well.

If we look at the record of the Egyptian state when it comes to performing its basic obligations towards the people, what do we see? Over the last three decades, the state has, while paying lip service to the maxim, 'in the service of society and the citizens', set itself other aims and functions to which it accorded a higher priority than the four basic functions incumbent on it. Between 1952 and 1970 Egypt's main aims were to extend its influence in Africa, the Middle East, the Arab world and the non-aligned movement, in addition to defending the regime inside, ensuring its continuity and striking its opponents locally and abroad. Under President Sadat, the highest priority – at least during the first five years of his rule – was to liberate the Egyptian territories occupied as a result of an unforgivable mistake made in the Nasser era. The following six years witnessed unscientific, unmethodical and often haphazard attempts by the state to perform some of its traditional basic functions.

The present regime, led by President Mubarak, has been characterized by an apparent intention to perform its basic functions towards Egyptian society, deploying the whole state apparatus to this end if need be. In terms of practical application, there have been many positive steps in the services sector, such as the energetic efforts to build new bridges and houses, prod the sagging centres of national industry into increasing productivity and enhanced performance, both qualitatively and quantitatively, and to upgrade public utilities, notably electricity and sewage networks, many of which have not been in any way renovated since they were built by Khedive Ismail,[61] over a century ago. Yet these laudable efforts are offset by other, contradictory, measures which all too often cancel out many of their positive results. A global political and economic vision can easily detect the two causes of this incongruity: the first is an incapacity to differentiate between the disease and the symptom, the second is a lack of consensus within the governing apparatus as to what the state's basic functions really are.

We believe the most important task of the government, headed by the institution of the presidency, is to diagnose the fundamental *diseases* undermining political, economic and social life, as distinct from the myriad *symptoms* they display. In fact, Egypt inherited from the near and distant past only a handful of basic political and social diseases, but it is these that are causing all the pains and problems today. At the political level, the primary disease is the lack of true democracy. At the economic level, we are suffering from the disease of a command economy, whose main symptom is a flaccid public sector which is allowed by the state to exercise hegemony over industry, production and agriculture.

There can be no tangible improvement in Egypt's economic problems unless the private sector is given a free hand, unless individual initiative is unleashed, and unless the state refrains from its unsuccessful interference in the areas of industry and production. Like all other states which have experimented with centralized economic organization, Egypt's performance in industry and production has been consistently poor. Those who call for reducing imports and promoting products 'Made in Egypt' should know that, though sound from the nationalistic point of view, these measures can be realized only by the Egyptian private sector and individual initiative.

The Egyptian public sector has been given more than one chance, yet it has failed abysmally. Thanks to its primary role in the country's economic life, the economy is a shambles. Moreover, the public sector has created a destructive climate for production as well as a hapless breed of workers and managers. Those who still support the Egyptian public sector must be aware that if it were to be auctioned off and the proceeds placed in a bank, the returns for Egypt would be much higher than those it derives today from this sector, which has produced the worst models of labour and management.

If the Egyptian governing apparatus, more particularly the cabinet, does not tackle the many problems of our present political, economic and social life in full awareness that they are only symptoms of two diseases – lack of democracy and the continued reliance on a command economy – its efforts to improve the lot of Egyptians, however sincere, are doomed to failure.

Moreover, a decision by the government to continue in its present patriarchal role as mover and master of all economic life in the country can only make the present problems worse and, inevitably, lead to a further deterioration in living standards. This will in turn create an atmosphere of alienation, unrest and despair favourable to the spread of leftist ideas, even of a communist movement which could eventually seize power.

While recognizing that the present regime is genuinely willing to deal with our many political and economic problems, and that systematic efforts are being made to redress what the last 30 years have destroyed, it seems, nevertheless, that the cabinet continues to grapple with the symptoms, and not the diseases. Fear of public opinion is the main reason for this. To be fair, a notable exception to its sidestepping was the decision to dismiss the scandal-ridden minister of economy (and former foreign affairs minister), Dr Mustafa al-Said, in 1985. But this should have happened sooner: local and foreign investors – and all of Egypt – are still reeling from the adverse effects of his ill-advised policies.

Let us try, for a moment, to apportion responsibility for the present situation. One might ask:

- Is the government alone to blame for today's tragic political, economic and social situation in Egypt? Or should the finger be pointed at both the government and the citizens? Or possibly just the citizens?
- To what extent are the successive governments' errors over the years accountable for the situation, and should individuals also share the blame?
- Should the government alone look for a solution? Or should this task be left to individual Egyptian citizens? Or, should it be the joint responsibility of both?

Such questions – actually one question asked from several perspectives – stand at the very core of an analysis of this issue. Let us examine a slice of the tissue of daily life in Egypt today to help us find a valid answer.

If we take a large street in any of our big cities, what do we see? A chaotic scene teeming with people, cars and other vehicles, all blatantly violating traffic regulations. One driver, busily chatting with his companion, allows his car to slide backwards, heavily damaging the car behind it; the ensuing heated discussion degenerates into a fistfight interspersed with highly colourful insults. Then, along comes a limousine driven by a boy of no more than 17 irresponsibly weaving his way through the choked street, flaunting his family's newly acquired wealth. Elsewhere on the street, a traffic policeman stops a similar young man at the wheel of a similar car, requesting to see his licence; the young man gets out of his expensive car to berate the policeman standing in his shabby uniform. The latter attempts to defend himself and is rewarded with a resounding slap from the wealthy young man who then climbs back into his car and drives proudly off.

On the opposite, slightly less crowded side of the thoroughfare, a bus zooms past its regular stop, barely allowing passengers to board or alight. Among them, a middle-aged man misses the step, falls in the path of the oncoming traffic and is run over by another speeding driver who was unable to brake in time. This scene is played out with monotonous regularity on every street in Cairo today. Who is to blame for the collapse of law and order on the streets of our cities, which have become veritable jungles where only the strong can survive? Is it the citizens, who at first glance seem to be the ones breaking the law and displaying violent patterns of behaviour? Or should we set emotions aside and ask why Egyptians are doing this to themselves and to their countrymen? Clearly they are aware that such conduct is disgraceful – they will all tell you so. And foreigners through the ages have been witness to the fact that Egyptians are kind, peaceful and exceptionally courteous to strangers, more so even than many other peoples.

What is it, then – ignorance?

The answer is simple: the government alone is responsible for the chaos with its accompanying aggressiveness, violation of law and order and uncivilized behaviour. The citizens, as individuals, do not share the blame and cannot, in all fairness, be expected to find a solution to the crisis. In the streets of more advanced societies, the government's presence is felt right down to the strict traffic regulations enforced by a police force conscious of its duties and not swayed by money or power. Their citizens, too, are constantly aware of the state's presence and power, and its strong arm. Such awareness sinks in over the years to become part of the collective consciousness, so that individuals come to realize that they cannot break the law and disturb public order with impunity. In our streets, on the other hand, the presence of the state is hardly felt and individuals are left largely to their own devices, without a central control or standard criteria of right and wrong. Thus full responsibility lies with the government for failing to make its presence felt. The lack of efficient representatives of the state capable of enforcing the law and effectively penalizing those who violate it means that individuals are left to behave in accordance with their own set of rules and to their own personal advantage.

We know that an individual's behaviour is determined by three fundamental factors:

- level of education and culture;
- level of intelligence and conduct; and
- upbringing and social background.

Those factors obviously vary from one person to another, particularly in societies where public education is quite a recent phenomenon, where the general level of culture is below average and where people are relatively unfamiliar with life in big modern cities. We can thus reasonably claim that the absence of a central control, of standard criteria for traffic rules and of a code of ethics from our streets (because the government is not playing an effective role) is the reason why individuals behave according to their own view of how things should be done.

The 'Egyptian street', then, is a projection of the 'Egyptian problem', which is one of government, not of individuals. Some eminent writers claim that Egyptians hold a 'magic solution' to all the problems of their present-day life. They are absolutely wrong. They would probably try to counter our theory by saying that the government is but a part of us, that rulers are but members of the group. This apparent truism can in fact be challenged: the only ruler the Egyptians ever really chose was Saad Zaghlul, more than 60 years ago – significantly, at a time when he was in exile, stripped of power, influence and position. All other rulers elected by the Egyptian people were chosen when they were already incumbents, in control of wealth and power, as well as of the media, and tamer legislators.

Returning to the issue of the government's role, we find that herein lies the explanation for Egypt's most serious 'disease'. The government's top concern for the last 30 years has been how to retain power and ensure its own continuity. It has involved itself in thousands of futile activities which should, rightfully, have been carried out by the private sector, such as producing and selling bread, selling food, controlling agriculture, the press and all areas of trade and industry, while at the same time neglecting the public services which are its *raison d'être*.

Throughout the 1950s–1960s our government applied increasing degrees of tyranny and oppression with the laws it promulgated to ensure 'loyalty' to the regime. Today, as its tattered mechanism confronts the task of providing fundamental public services, its inefficiency and ineptitude have become clear. Moreover, the people responsible for administering public utilities are completely ignorant of the basic principles of management according to which they should be run.

To sum up, then, all of Egypt's problems stem from two main diseases. The first, manifested at the political level, is represented in the total absence of democracy for the 30 years following 1952, and over the last three years in particular, in the emergence of contingent factors which are stunting its revival and growth. The second disease, which affects our economic and social life, is the severe dislocation in the role of the government apparatus. As we have seen, the government involves itself in activities which it does not and never will master, activities which, by their very nature, fall within the purview of private initiative, the private sector and the market laws of supply and demand. At the same time that very same government is shamefully neglecting the areas to which it should be exclusively devoting its capabilities and resources.

CHAPTER 7

What is to be Done?[62]

The previous chapters attempted to trace and analyse the root causes of the 'Egyptian problem' as we see it. Now we shall explore the solutions available in the light of that analysis.

So – what is to be done? Today Egypt finds itself facing one of the most propitious moments for making a choice in its contemporary history. Indeed, with the exception of just such a moment following the success of the 1952 Revolution, proffering a chance the ruling regime failed to seize, the present juncture is the best opportunity Egypt has had in recent times for making a choice. Yet, like all choices, this one is loaded with implications.

The difficulty with choice, as a philosophical concept, lies in its very nature, suggesting as it does a decision to take one of several paths. But recognizing the difficulty inherent in making the choice does not negate the existence of a great historical opportunity for Egypt to choose among the available options. If it so wishes, and provided its decision makers are up to the task, Egypt can rid itself of economic dependence and, consequently, of the two forms of political dependence it has known under Nasser and Sadat. It can harness huge potential and creative powers capable of generating tremendous sources of revenue for its people from agriculture, industry, tourism, mining and oil resources, in addition to tripling or even quadrupling its present income from the remittances of its nationals working abroad. It can streamline the bloated and ruinous bureaucracy engendered by a totalitarian regime and by the absence of freedom and democracy. It can put an end to its tragic and draining involvement in problems outside its own territories, problems which the parties concerned are in no hurry to solve as long as they can continue to feed on the tragedy and make political capital from the wounds of their people.

There is no doubt that the Egyptian public, having learned its lesson from bitter experience, tends not to support Egypt's involvement in such problems. But it is not enough to avoid becoming embroiled in external problems. Egypt should also avoid becoming further entangled in an economic system that has proved to be a total failure and which has led the country to the brink of bankruptcy, a system that has rendered Egypt unable to feed its people without crippling loans which make a mockery of any talk of political and economic independence.

The situation calls for action on two fronts, political and economic, the latter being a function of the former and not the other way round, as Marxists and others – notably military juntas – would have us believe.

A necessary first step towards solving the problems now besetting the Egyptian body politic is to abolish the present system of parliamentary elections and replace it with one that would serve the goal of freedom and democracy to which the majority of Egyptians aspire. Such a step would be difficult in the present circumstances without a positive initiative from the presidency, led by the president of the republic himself. Until that hope materializes, all the forces of freedom and democracy should champion one of the noblest of national causes: electing their leaders. All the millions of eligible voters should register and to go to the polls at the forthcoming elections for the People's Assembly, scheduled for 1989.

This would allow a wise and moderate opposition to increase its seats in parliament, a natural development expected and, indeed, favoured by President Mubarak. That much can be understood from the many speeches in which he has reiterated his faith in the gradual and constant growth of democracy in Egypt, a growth without sudden starts and leaps which may cause imbalance and confusion in Egyptian society. While there is no disputing the validity of this view, it is important to differentiate between the time-frame in which the opposition would like to see this process unfold and that contemplated by the government. The ideal probably lies somewhere in between.

Reform also entails the abolition of such mechanisms as the 'socialist public prosecutor', the 'court of values' and the 'administrative control agency', which were introduced under the totalitarian regime. These mechanisms cannot coexist with the Office of the Public Prosecutor (the only mechanism that in a democracy enjoys jusrisdiction over matters under the purview of those extrajudicial bodies invented by a totalitarian system) in a political system based on legality, on the separation of powers and the sanctity of the judiciary as a power equal to the legislative and the executive. We call upon the presidency to set up a committee of the best legal minds in Egypt, men like Dr Soliman el-Tamawy, Dr Wahid Raafat, Dr Hamed Sultan and others, who have never been subservient to any regime, to explain to the president that all such bodies operating independently from the Office of the Public Prosecutor make a mockery of the principle of an independent judiciary, the backbone of freedom and the rule of law. How can anyone imagine that employees of a body such as the Administrative Control Agency, none of whom belongs to the judiciary, can accomplish what the Office of the Public Prosecutor is supposedly incapable of doing, although the latter is responsible for representing society as a prosecuting power in all matters involving criminal acts against the rights of individuals or society? And how can anyone understand why the office of the Socialist Public Prosecutor – a title totally devoid of any meaning – is not merged in the Office of the Public Prosecutor? Finally, a text should be introduced to the by-laws of the People's Assembly barring access to the chairmanship of that venerable body to anyone who has not been elected by the people as a member of the Assembly. The selection of the Speaker of the People's Assembly must be made by the Assembly itself and not, as was the case in 1957–84, by the executive.

Another major impediment to the instauration of democracy is the close control exercised by the present government over the so-called 'national' press and other mass media, such as radio and television. A model well worth looking into here is the British Broadcasting Corporation, more familiarly known as the BBC. The presidency should place before the president of the republic the example of the BBC, whose organizational structure and method of operation the author had occasion to study at close quarters in the course of several visits to its corporate headquarters. Since its inception, the BBC has been an autonomous body that remains quite independent from successive governments, both as regards its administrative structure and its editorial policy. The Egyptian presidency could draw several important lessons from the experience of the BBC, which is a superb example of a body that, though wholly owned by the state, is totally independent from the government and the party in power. In addition, the BBC is not dependent on the vagaries of the capitalist market for its livelihood. Unlike broadcasting networks in countries such as the USA, BBC radio and television do not broadcast commercials.

As to the press, either we accept the viewpoint of certain members of the present government and the ruling party that the press is an information medium whose function is to support the regime and justify its policies, in which case we must accept the status quo, namely, a press that, though graced with the title 'national', is, in fact, a government organ controlled by the president of the republic, the chairman of the Shura Council (the upper house of parliament) and the Minister of Information, who select and appoint the editors-in-chief, or we recognize that a press which serves as the mouthpiece of the government cannot serve as the watchful eye and critical mind of the nation, in which case we must accept that it has to undergo a basic transformation. Without serious efforts in this direction, the standard of the national press in Egypt will continue to decline, both as regards the editorial content of the newspapers and the calibre of their editors-in-chief, who can be classified only as civil servants or managers, never as intellectuals or political writers. This sorry state of affairs has serious implications touching on the very integrity of the press as an institution whose primary responsibility is to the public, a responsibility our national newspapers can hardly discharge while they remain as dependent on the ruling power as a hired hand is on his boss.

It would not be unduly harsh to say that most of those who write in the national press lack any intellectual or cultural depth. Sadly, the general cultural level of most journalists – with the exception of a few veterans belonging to the pre-totalitarianism generation – is most superficial. A quick comparison between the level of writing that graced the Egyptian press in the 1930s and 1940s and that to which we are exposed in today's national press highlights the horror of the situation and the extent of the tragedy. Without going too deeply into the whys and wherefores of the present crisis of Egyptian journalism, another quick comparison may help cast some light on the issue. That comparison touches on the nature of relations between journalists of the pre-revolution era and public figures of the time and the undue deference shown to their counterparts today by journalists of the national papers, who will queue submissively for hours at the door of this or that public official, forgetting that the pens they wield are far mightier than any powers vested in these officials.

We should also move away from the pattern of technocratic ministers to that of political ones, bearing in mind that ministers in democratic countries are always political figures not technicians, while in totalitarian countries the opposite holds true. The explanation for this phenomenon lies in the fact that in countries under a totalitarian system of government, a minister is merely a senior civil servant entrusted with the technical management of his ministry, while in democracies a minister is a political figure placed at the head of a ministry to make sure that the strategy of the government/party is implemented in that ministry's area of competence, a strategy which, more often than not, that very same minister helped formulate. In Eastern bloc countries, headed by the Soviet Union, ministries are teeming with technicians, particularly engineers, whereas in the democratic world ministers are prominent political figures in the ruling party. It is not unusual in those countries for the minister of health, say, to be drawn from outside the medical profession – however, he will be fully cognizant of and committed to his party's medical policy and deploy all the resources of his ministry to serve the party line in this respect. Similarly, the ministers for industry, power or agriculture will not be former civil servants in those ministries as is the case in totalitarian regimes.

For Egypt to break out of the mould of technocratic ministers in which it is presently mired is easier said than done, however. The totalitarian regime which lasted close on 30 years in Egypt naturally destroyed the conditions favourable to the emergence of political figures who can only be discovered and groomed in a political climate based on a multi-party, not a one-party, system. But, despite the bleakness of the present picture, which led the late political writer, Ihsan Abdel Kuddus, to describe the ministerial changes of 16 July 1984 as 'managerial changes', Egypt remains a huge reservoir of untapped political talents. The presidency should make every effort to seek them out, not through its security apparatus in which the Egyptian people have lost all faith, nor through the civil service hierarchy, but by casting a global and penetrating look at Egypt's public figures who have long been kept away from the channels of higher executive authority by the wall of totalitarianism. It is depressing to see the kind of ministers hatched by the totalitarian regime. In spite of the great strides towards democracy in recent years, the vast majority of ministers who have held office over the past 30 years do not seem to be intellectually or culturally above the level of a high-school graduate in a country with a flourishing cultural life like, say, France.

Among the most pressing tasks of the political leadership in a situation such as that prevailing in Egypt today is to stop misleading the public with honeyed words and rosy dreams having no basis in reality. Unfortunately, the two late presidents, Nasser and Sadat, consistently lulled the public with glowing accounts of a present that existed only in the realm of the imagination and a future that had more to do with wishful thinking than with hard facts. One can hardly forget President Nasser's description of an army which suffered one of the worst defeats in military history as 'the strongest deterrent force in the Middle East', or his euphoric references to the missiles 'Al Qaher' and 'Al Zafer' (the Conqueror and the Victorious) and to Egyptian industry which, he claimed, could now 'manufacture everything', from 'a needle to a missile'. Nor can anyone forget President Sadat's designation of 1980 as 'the year of plenty', when 'every Egyptian would have a home with a large living-room' overlooking a 'beautiful view'! Equally memorable are his sanguine references to Egypt as a 'state of institutions' where 'the reign of democracy holds sway' and 'the sovereignty of the law' is paramount. He went so far as to claim that Egypt had surpassed Britain in establishing the foundations of democracy, noting that the British monarch could order the dissolution of parliament while he could not do so without a public referendum! As it is not our aim here to vilify anyone or to apportion blame but, rather, to draw lessons from the errors of our recent past, we shall content ourselves with these few examples of how the political leadership misled the public.

Another tendency the political leadership should rid itself of is that of glorifying Egypt's history, presumably to instil a sense of pride and to make the dismal reality in which most Egyptians are living more palatable. Rather than feeling that our five-thousand-year history (President Sadat repeated seven thousand so often he nearly convinced everyone it was true!) places us above all other nations, we should feel guilty that we have frittered away the glorious legacy of our ancestors. A history like ours qualifies us for a flourishing present and a promising future. Instead, where our ancestors built beautiful edifices that are still standing after 50 centuries, we build flimsy edifices that crumble into dust after only a few years, not to say months. A nation that gave birth in one single generation to such men of genius as Ahmed Shawki, Hafez Ibrahim, Taha Hussein, Abbas al-Aqad, Tawfiq el-Hakim, El Manfalouty, Mostapha Sadeq el-Rafei, Abdel Rahman el-Rafei, Mostapha Mesharrafa, El Sanhouri, Saad Zaghloul, Abdel Khaleq Sarwat, Mahmoud Said, Mokhtar, Sayed Darwish, Mohamed Abdel Wahab, Ahmed Amin, Zaky Mubarak, El Mazny and scores of others should wonder why it is so barren today and make every effort to get out of the cycle of mediocrity in which it is caught.

It can, of course, be said that honeyed words have not been a hallmark of President Mubarak's regime, which does not go in for falsely reassuring accounts of our present reality or for extravagant promises of a rosy future. However, if it is true that for the past four years the political leadership has displayed a commendable degree of realism and restraint in addressing the public, it is also true that the government in Egypt adopts a defensive posture in the face of any criticism, as though all were well in the best of all possible worlds. And, if any fair-minded observer must admit that official statements in recent years have been free of empty promises, he cannot have failed to notice that they are often made up of a curious blend of facts and hopes. This is particularly evident in the flood of official statements about the high quality of Egyptian goods and about the level of local expertise and know-how being up to the highest international standards. While such positive talk can inspire a spirit of national pride and determination among the masses, which can spur them on to improve performance and increase production, we must not lose sight of the dangers inherent in promoting an attitude of complacency. We believe that the first step towards treatment and reform is to face up to the unvarnished truth, painful though this may be. Unless and until a process of catharsis is instituted – and here President Mubarak's administration has a vital role to play – there is no real hope of reform.

We must recognize that we, as a government and a people, have reached a critical threshold of backwardness and weakness which we can only overcome by radically changing many of our systems and patterns. We need to take decisive action in respect of a losing public sector which stands at the root of all our economic problems; we need to bring radical reforms to the agricultural sector if we are to break the vicious circle that has transformed us, in just 30 years, from a nation that was self-sufficient in food production to one that has to import 60 per cent of its food requirements; we need to change the unhealthy relationship between employers and workers and replace it with a normal and productive situation compatible with a free economy based on the interplay of market forces; we must, while not losing sight of the achievements of advanced Western societies in the areas of social security, pensions, unemployment insurance, health care, etc., break the fetters of the restrictive labour legislations which are largely responsible for our present backwardness and for the bloated and corrupt bureaucracy prevailing in Egyptian government departments. Once again we repeat that unless we admit how appalling our present reality is and how imperative it is to transform it, unless we accept criticism of the fundamental principles by which we are governed and not only of the secondary symptoms, the chances of breaking out of the present bottleneck are bleak.

While all these reforms are essential, the need to enhance freedoms and consolidate democracy should head our list of priorities, coming even before the need for economic reform. For, as the prominent thinker Mr Khaled Mohamed Khaled pointed out, democracy will lead to reform in all areas, including economic reforms, while the opposite is not true: economic reforms will not necessarily lead to democracy. Even though the author has completely given up on the civil servants who are passing themselves off as writers in the national newspapers, he has boundless faith in the ability of a number of independent writers of the pre-totalitarian generation, such as Mostapha Amin, Ahmed Baha El Din, Khaled Mohamed Khaled, Zaky Naguib Mahmoud, Abdel Rahman El Sharkawy, Ihsan Abdel Quddus and Galal Hamamsy to defend freedom and democracy and to stand up to all attempts to curb or violate any public freedoms, in particular, freedom of thought and expression.

Moving now to the economic front, we are faced with a curious situation in which two divergent economic systems are coexisting in an uneasy alliance. On the one hand, we have an entrenched economic system whose cornerstones are rooted in socialism: public sector; limited agricultural holdings; state interference in all aspects of production; labour relations governed by socialist legislations; compulsory delivery of agricultural output to the state, etc. On the other, we have economic systems of a capitalist nature trying to establish themselves in a hostile environment. Obviously this attempt to accommodate two irreconcilable, indeed, mutually exclusive, economic systems is doomed to failure and the sooner we face up to this the better. None of the makeshift repair operations launched by successive Egyptian governments, particularly over the last four years, can succeed unless we candidly acknowledge that the real reason for our economic decline lies in the socialist economic options to which Egypt has for too long subscribed. Blaming Egypt's economic woes on a shortage of financial resources is a feeble excuse that all the opposition parties should reject. The shortage of financial resources is the inevitable result of specific political and economic options. The opposition should point out to the government that the latter's main function is to generate resources, or at least to create the proper climate in which they can grow. At the end of the day, it is the government alone that can be held accountable for the lack of financial resources.

The government should also stop its vain attempts to create an artificial rate of exchange for foreign currencies, particularly the US dollar. The real price of the dollar or of other convertible currencies is their price on what is wrongly termed the black market, which is in fact the only real market. By following the rules of the free market in this regard, Egypt can effectively multiply its revenues from two main sources, namely, tourism and the remittances of expatriate Egyptian workers. It is frustrating to see the present government shy away from taking this essential decision. Many people, myself included, believed the appointment of as able an economist as Dr Aly Lotfy at the head of government would hasten the adoption of such a decision, especially in view of the campaign he launched early in 1985 against the irresponsible economic decisions taken by Dr Mostapha el-Said at the time, decisions from whose repercussions Egypt is still suffering and which, in our opinion, were tantamount to serious crimes against the nation.

Foremost among the problems besetting Egypt today and which successive governments have avoided coming to grips with are those of housing and education. Unless the root causes of these problems are addressed and serious efforts made to solve them, we cannot look forward to a better future.

The housing problem is highly complex, not so much because its causes are hard to understand, but because the many ineffectual attempts to solve it have created such an intricate web of relationships and conflicting interests that any attempt to bring about a radical solution today is bound to create victims. In fact, the problem is closely connected with the two aspects we have been discussing: the political aspect and the economic aspect. An analysis of the problem that does not address its root causes and historical development would fail to achieve our purpose, which is to diagnose the disease and prescribe the effective cure.

The onset of the disease can be traced to the early 1950s, when the government decided to interfere in the contractual relationship between landlords and tenants of housing units, ostensibly to protect tenants from exploitation by landlords. Government interference was directed at two areas: term of lease and value of rent. Until then, lease contracts for residential housing units were based on the classical legal principle of 'sovereign will', as represented essentially in the freedom of the parties to agree on the term of the lease and the rental value payable for the leased premises. However, the July 1952 Revolution, or, more particularly, its leader, Gamal Abdel Nasser, decided to cast the landlord in the role of exploiter and the tenant in the role of the victim of the former's greed. Having thus assigned roles, the revolution sided with the weaker party, i.e., the tenant, whom it decided to release from any commitment as to the agreed term or value of the lease. Obviously the revolution did not look at the issue from an economic point of view, in the sense that it did not take into account the long-term effects of these measures on the construction market, the housing market, urban planning, etc. Rather, it saw it in political, not to say demagogical terms, as borne out by the fact that the regime sought to make as much political capital as possible by having the president himself announce the freezing of rents and all subsequent reductions thereof. It is irrelevant here to discuss the real motives of the revolution and its leader in this matter. We are even willing to concede that they were well-intentioned and that their desire to protect 'the weak' was sincere. All that is water under bridge. Today we must judge the experience in terms of results, not intentions.

What are the results we are reaping today from this misguided policy? The revolution wished to protect the tenant from the landlord – did it actually succeed in doing so? Did it achieve its purpose of making homes available at prices accessible to ordinary people of the middle and working classes and to small farmers and peasants? In fact, a direct result of its decision to release the tenant from his obligation to observe the term of the lease or the rental value agreed upon has been to discourage investment in the area of housing, as prospective investors realized that they could derive higher returns from trade or even from interest accruing on bank deposits than from building and letting housing units. All aspects of the problem stem from that fact. In the context of restrictive legislations, investors were left with one of two options: either to steer clear of the housing market – and the enormous discrepancy between supply and demand in this area attests to the predominance of this option – or to build housing units for sale or rent in exchange for large sums of money paid under the counter as key money or non-refundable 'advance rent'. Thus the three major problems in the housing sector (a severe shortage of supply as compared to the ever increasing demand for units for rent, an abundance of housing units up for sale and a dearth of those available for rent and, finally, the exorbitant sums demanded by landlords outside the contract) all result from the fact that government interference in lease contracts removed the incentive of profit which alone can induce an investor to move into a given area of investment and rendered the construction of housing units for rent a losing proposition yielding a return far below that accruing as interest on money placed in the bank, not to mention the problems of dealing with tenants, whom the new housing laws considered to be victims of greedy and exploitative landlords. To go back to our question: did the housing legislations introduced by the revolution succeed in protecting tenants? There was a time, before the revolution, when an Egyptian citizen could always find a home for a reasonable rent within his means. Today, he wastes years of his life looking for a home, having already spent years saving up for the price or the key money to be paid to the owner, the only one to profit from the new formula. Who, then, is the ultimate beneficiary? Can the 1952 Revolution claim to have achieved its objective of providing reasonably priced housing for the people? Or would it not be fair to say that tenants are the main, indeed, the only, casualties of a misguided housing policy?

So complex has the issue become, so far-reaching its ramifications that, although we are in absolutely no doubt that the disastrous housing situation is the direct result of a blithe disregard of free-market laws, we cannot condone a solution based on deregulating rents and allowing landlords to fix them at their sole discretion. Such a solution would deal a death-blow to the millions of Egyptians whose incomes are not market-compatible: scraping by on their government salaries or pensions, they can certainly not afford free-market prices. No self-respecting regime could ever take such a step.

The only viable solution is to deal separately with two categories of existing housing units: old buildings used for residential purposes on the one hand and old buildings put to commercial use and newly built units, whether put to residential or commercial use on the other. In respect of the first category of old units inhabited by individuals or families, rents could be raised by no more than 5 to 10 per cent, a rate of increase that could definitely be met by the salaried class while giving land-lords, usually belonging to the same class, a slightly better income that may encourage them to undertake some minor repair and maintenance works to prevent the dilapidation of old buildings that we are witnessing.

As for leased premises that are put to commercial use, such as doctors' clinics, lawyers' offices, offices for financial or trading activities and shops, a new system should be devised to double their rent annually. It is absurd to pay a niggardly rent for premises that are put to commercial use and which bring in thousands of pounds every day. It is equally absurd to consider the landlord here to be the exploiting party and the tenant his victim. The rents payable in new buildings should be left entirely to the laws of the free market, with no interference whatsoever from the state to impose indefinite lease contracts or set up committees to determine the rent, which should be exclusively subject to the laws of supply and demand. This is the only way out of the housing tragedy that successive govern-ments have failed to resolve effectively, because they disregarded the true causes and could not, for political reasons, face the painful fact that the government itself had sown the seeds of the housing tragedy in the 1950s.

If the problem of housing casts a long shadow that promises to stretch well into the future, so too does that of education. There can be no hope of a better life for the coming generations of Egyptians unless serious attempts are made today to find a radical solution to this problem. Any such attempts must spring not from doctrinaire political givens but from an in-depth analysis of the crisis and its causes. Like the housing problem, the problem of education needs to be carefully diagnosed so that it may be effectively treated.

The picture was not always so bleak – in fact, quite the contrary. In the 1920s and 1930s, Egyptian education enjoyed its golden age, thanks to a generation of outstanding Egyptians who were pioneers in their respective fields, such as Dr Mesharrafa in mathematics, Dr Hussein Fawzi in the sciences, Dr Aly Ibrahim, Dr Mahmoud Mahfouz and others in medicine and scores of illustrious names in literature and law, as well as many others in all areas of scholarly achievement, all of whom benefited from the best that Western education had to offer.

We might well ask what has befallen education in Egypt since and why it has sunk to its present sorry level. The answer is that education at all levels received a crippling blow when it became subservient to the orientations of Egypt's new rulers following the success of the 1952 Revolution. The seeds of the tragedy were sown when the victorious revolution placed an officer at the head of education in the country, a military man with no experience in this area and whose own educational and cultural background was very modest. The reference for the reader interested in that particular detail is the study published by Dr Anwar Abdel Malek, Research Master at the CNRS, Paris, under the title 'L'Egypte, Société Militaire', in which he analyses the educational and cultural background of the revolutionary council in general, and of the man fully entrusted with the supervision of education in Egypt in particular.

It is from the moment education was placed in the hands of someone who knew nothing of education or culture, from the moment politics became the prime mover of all educational policies and programmes, that education in Egypt began its downward slide. From the peak level it had attained thanks to outstanding Egyptian pioneers in different branches of knowledge, education dropped into an abyss of backwardness thanks to those who should never have been entrusted with its fate in the first place. Nor did the crippling blow strike secular education alone. It also affected the ancient centre of religious learning, Al-Azhar university, subjecting it to political currents and placing it in the hands of men whose mastery of Arabic and of Islamic culture was far inferior to the level of the original Azhar primary school certificate.

The great man of letters, Dr Taha Hussein, left us with a profound and accurate study, *The Future of Culture in Egypt* in two volumes of 550 pages, which he wrote in 1938. Today, the extent of the tragedy which has befallen Egyptian education is such that to try to diagnose it, let alone to propose a remedy, would require many more volumes. All we hope to achieve with the present study is to show that a problem of this magnitude cannot be solved by the haphazard and stop-gap solutions the present government is experimenting with and which have led nowhere.

The problem of education in Egypt today is closely linked

to the basic production process: as long as no radical solution has been found for the agricultural problem, as long as the state continues to play its present patriarchal role in the areas of economics and industry and to pursue its current employment policy, Egyptians will continue to struggle through years of learning, from school to university, only to end up as government employees and petty clerks. The government seems incapable of instituting radical reforms, whether because it lacks vision or because it adopts a politically biased, often demagogical, view of all matters. No doubt it is this which prevents the government from putting an end to free education for all, from limiting the number of students entering universities, from expanding in the area of technical education, from allowing private universities to be set up and from continuing to impose its own views on institutions of learning.

Having said that, we should not overlook the connection between the crisis of education in Egypt and the absence of democracy from our life for a long period of time. A climate of freedom and democracy encourages the growth of culture and intellectual creativity and allows the development of a better and healthier educational system. Conversely, in a climate of totalitarianism culture and intellectual creativity wither and fade, and a backward educational system, subservient to the whims of the regime, imposes itself. In a situation of this kind, we come across such inexplicable phenomena as the political decision to stop the teaching of French in Egyptian schools, in retaliation for France's participation in the tripartite aggression of 1956. This example graphically illustrates how education can suffer when it is used as a political tool by people who epitomize ignorance and backwardness.

Of paramount importance at this juncture is that the people of Egypt should realize that policies can be judged only by their results, not by the intentions behind them. A ruler is like the captain of a ship who is expected to carry his passengers safely from shore to shore. He is responsible for calculating the speed and direction of winds and waves; he cannot claim that unexpected winds or waves caught him by surprise because a ship's captain, by definition, is supposed to know such things. We must not accept excuses about unexpected circumstances and events from the people in charge, whatever their position.

It is precisely to optimize results in unfavourable circumstances that they were placed in positions of responsibility in the first place. If we apply such a criterion in judging policies, we can also judge the success or failure of public figures. In countries where democracy and public freedoms prevail, public figures are judged on the basis of the results they achieve, not of their intentions. Established democracies do not differentiate between good and bad excuses when judging the failure of public figures to do their duty. A case in point is the 1968 crisis in Paris, responsibility for which was laid at the door of no less revered a personage than President Charles de Gaulle. This example should serve as a lesson to us all.

CHAPTER 8

The Four Idols[63]

The last six years have witnessed what can undeniably be termed the most sincere efforts over the last four decades to redress the political and economic situation in Egypt. However, inasmuch as these efforts have hitherto been directed at reforming this or that aspect of the system, and not at the general framework of that system, we believe they have reached a dead end. The time has come for a different kind of approach. Over the past six years we have been dealing with the symptoms, now we have to tackle the very core of the diseases if they are not to become terminal. The situation calls for a frontal attack on the root causes of the problems plaguing us, not for stop-gap solutions to their manifestations. We advocated just such a global approach in a series of articles which ran in the press through 1985 and were published in book form early in 1986 under the title: *What is to be Done? Diagnosing and Analysing the Problems of Contemporary Egypt.*

The present government seems to be headed towards just such a course. The way in which it is handling the problem of subsidies and the question of foreign exchange rates indicates that it is determined to tackle the root cause of the disease rather than to address each symptom separately in a futile attempt to alleviate each and every one of them. The only treatment that can bring about a cure is one that deals with the ailment, not with its symptoms.

Ending the chaos that has dominated our political and economic life for four decades entails a great deal of preparation. A solid groundwork must be laid before we can come to grips with the roots of the problems and their main causes without occasioning political and social 'cracks'. Nor is the task made any easier by the political opposition groups in Egypt today, whose working methods are characterized by intellectual hooliganism, sectarian priorities and barbaric modes of discussion.

With President Hosni Mubarak's re-election to a second term in office, hopes have been raised in anticipation of a change in the manner of confronting problems, moving from a stage of dealing with the multitude of symptoms to that of attacking the causes of the diseases head-on. In fact, there are no more than four main diseases.

The first disease is embodied in the public sector. We believe the bottom line target we must strive to achieve over the next six years is the liquidation of those units in the public sector that are incurring losses. As long as they remain, they will continue to be large gaping wounds needlessly bleeding our economy white, to the benefit of no one except those who derive personal advantage from the empire of a public sector, so detrimental to Egypt, to its people and to its economy. However, if the public sector is put up for sale in its present shape it would find no buyers. No private investor would accept to purchase the loss-making public sector companies under the present labour legislations. That being the case, we must agree on a policy to get rid of the losing sectors and allow the private sector to operate unhampered by legislation which would abort its success.

As for public sector units that do not incur losses, they can be helped to become economically viable if the millstones now hanging round their necks are removed: namely, the fixed prices at which they are now forced to sell their products and the current Marxist-inspired labour legislation under which the hands of management are effectively tied. These laws have created a climate that not only protects lazy workers and offers no incentive to efficient ones to maintain their standard but, by divesting management of its primordial right to reward and sanction, puts paid to any hopes of successful and efficient management.

Any economist worth his salt, indeed, any informed layman, realizes the primacy of management in the economy. Management is the creative factor that can bring into being all the elements of success, just as it can create the elements of failure and sterility. To deliver the public sector from the constraint of inefficient management is extremely difficult, but it is also a condition *sine qua non*. How else can we develop the public sector under legislation that not only hampers management and operation but also burdens the boards of directors of public sector companies with a quota of ignorance by requiring them to incorporate members who know nothing of management or production?

The same problem facing the boards of directors of public sector enterprises exists on a much more dangerous level, that of the highest legislative council in Egypt, the People's Assembly, which is required by law to draw 50 per cent of its members from among those who have proved to be the least efficient, the least knowledgeable, the least cultured and the least experienced. On this point, we can only echo the views of the prominent writer, Mr Tharwat Abaza, who quite justifiably wonders how we could ever have allowed, indeed, how we could still continue to allow, our laws to be passed by a council half of whose members do not meet the minimal requirements of experience, culture, knowledge and intellect. Suffice it to compare the standard of debate in the People's Assembly with that of the Shura Council (the upper house of parliament), where we have recently witnessed a style of debate marked by a sophisticated and constructive exchange of ideas.

Thus the first disease that plagues Egypt, namely, the public sector, can be attributed to a flood of laws that undermine production and successful management, in addition to imposing a quota of ignorance and inefficiency that turns the boards of directors of public sector companies into sinecures for the least experienced and least efficient groups: those who are fully cognizant of their rights and minimally conscious of their obligations.

The second disease, or idol, that needs to be confronted squarely and to be dealt with boldly, openly and directly is the question of education. Our conclusions on the matter are laid out in a series of articles now being published in *Al-Akhbar* daily under the heading: 'The Tragedy of Education and Culture in Egypt'. The very future of Egypt depends on what remedial steps we shall take in the field of education. If those who wish to retain the idols inherited from years of errors and empty slogans win the day, and impede enlightened efforts to reform the institution of education, there is no future for Egypt. How can anyone believe that the present educational system can possibly breed great scientists or learned men in any field, men without whom there can be no kind of progress or development?

The third disease, or idol, to be pulled down during President Mubarak's second term of office is the general agricultural setup in Egypt. We do not in any way propose the restitution of nationalized land to its original owners. No sane man would make such a suggestion which would, anyhow, not solve the crisis of agriculture in our country which we firmly believe was not, is not and never will be due to the nationalization of land. The main cause was and still is the body of laws governing the legal relationship between landowners and tenant farmers. Unless Egyptian agriculture is liberated from those laws that are so nefarious for the entire agricultural sector, the process of deterioration which began 30 years ago when the new laws governing land lease began to poison every possibility of progress, creativity, development and versatility in Egyptian agriculture will continue.

If we do not break the legal barriers that are so harmful for Egyptian agriculture and the Egyptian economy, we will continue to import half of Egypt's food, with all the implications this carries in the way of political constraints. The greatest service anyone can render Egypt in this respect is to achieve the country's self-sufficiency in wheat production. This is possible only if we can bring about radical changes in the main orientations of Egyptian agriculture, thus allowing Egypt to become truly independent and not independent in name only.

The fourth disease, or idol, to be confronted in the coming few years is that of housing. The onset of the disease can be traced to a series of misguided decisions issued in the 1950s and early '60s by which the state hoped to ease the plight of tenants and which led, instead, to their victimization. It is to be hoped that, when dealing with this major problem, the government will not tackle the symptoms and neglect the disease. It is not by prohibiting the practice of 'key money' or discouraging ownership by tenants of residential flats that the problem will be solved. This piecemeal approach is doomed to failure because it addresses the symptoms rather than the disease itself. Key money is a standard symptom of another disease, namely, housing legislation, which governs landlord–tenant relations and which has produced three major results:

- Investors are reluctant to make substantial outlays of capital in the construction of housing units because of the poor return on investment as a result of arbitrarily fixed rents which neither reflect reality nor the normal interaction of supply and demand. Hence the decreasing number of available housing units as compared to increasing demand.
- The market has engendered subsidiary channels, such as key money and the sale of housing units, to circumvent the crippling effects of housing laws.
- The quality of housing has deteriorated, with poor architecture, poor construction techniques and poorer maintenance now the norm.

Hence the hundreds of thousands of very low-grade houses that have sprung up and the appallingly high incidence of buildings collapsing – often on the heads of the tenants – because their owners tried to cut costs without regard to elementary principles of safety in construction, nor, a priori, to considerations of aesthetics. Those who advocate such measures as prohibiting ownership of residential flats or as compelling owners of vacant flats to lease them out are obviously not versed in economic laws. Had they been, they would have known that such measures are useless and impractical, no more, in fact, than a cure for one of the symptoms and not for the disease itself.

Such then are the four major diseases or idols from which Egypt suffers today. A comprehensive cure, one that attacks the very roots and causes of these diseases, is what we expect from President Mubarak's second term in office. The present government's handling of the problems of subsidies and rates of currency exchange is cause for optimism that the cure is a real possibility and not just a dream.

As to why we chose to head this article 'The Four Idols', it is because the condition of these four major areas, the public sector, education, agriculture and housing in Egypt, has become similar to that of idols of ancient times with their high priests who, alone, benefit from their existence. As for the rest of the people, they are the ones who suffer from the perpetuation of such idols and their professional high priests.

CHAPTER 9

Promoting Reading as a Hobby and a Methodology[64]

The question of how to go about developing, promoting and expanding interest in reading in a society such as Egypt can be approached from a number of angles. But for the overall view that can provide an answer to this big question, it might be useful to address it from all of these angles.

One possible angle of approach is from the perspective of the reader, that is, to try to pinpoint the reasons why the medium of reading is more appealing to some people than it is to others. Many theories have been advanced to explain this phenomenon. Perhaps the most convincing is the one put forward by the famous psychologist and psychiatrist Alfred Adler, who ascribed the predisposition for reading displayed by some people to a desire for excellence and distinction. In much the same way that some people strive for recognition in the domains of art or sports, so too others seek to make their mark by expanding the scope of their knowledge through reading.

Over 30 years ago, the famous man of letters, Abbas al-Aqad, one of the most prodigious readers of the twentieth century, was asked to explain how he had become enamoured of reading at a very tender age and how he had sustained this interest throughout his life. His reply echoed Adler's theory. El Aqad admitted that reading was for him a form of escapism, not from life, but from the confines of one life, his own. He had a hunger for more experiences and examples than one life could offer and to read was to gain access to the lessons and experiences of many other lives. In fact, reading was the key to the whole compendium of human history, with all its genius, creativity and uniqueness.

Another angle of approach is to view the spread of reading as the natural result of certain educational systems and programmes. Experience proves that some educational systems have been more successful than others in encouraging and promoting reading. Most educational systems in the Third World are based on teaching students by rote and on cramming their heads with facts. Although they are often also characterized by exceptionally long curricula, their results are disappointing when it comes to developing a love of reading and to instilling a thirst for knowledge in young people.

The courses of study on offer in these countries are not designed to inspire students or to stimulate a love of learning among them. To do so, they would have to place greater emphasis on quality and less on quantity than is presently the case. This entails cutting curricula down in length while enhancing their content. At the same time, teachers should be more concerned with whetting their students' appetite for learning than with stuffing their heads with unnecessarily long curricula. Success in life is a function not of the amount of information stored in a person's head but on the development of that person's personality and faculties. Hence the superiority of educational systems in certain countries, such as Japan, Germany and France, over those of most other advanced countries, let alone of developing countries, whose educational institutions are incapable of producing creative people with the motivation to learn, read and seek knowledge for its own sake.

Reading can be viewed from yet another angle, namely, the connection between the role of the mass media in a given community and the reading habits of the members of that community. It is very important here not to fall into the trap of believing, as many now tend to do, that reading has lost its ascendancy to radio and television as the medium of choice. In fact, mass media, like television, radio and the press, can play a role in promoting reading and in winning over new converts to the delights it offers. Conversely, they can impact negatively on people's reading habits by offering them a steady fare of vacuous entertainment which tends to numb their critical faculties rather than programmes that can stimulate a desire for knowledge and encourage them to read.

In this connection, it is important to rebut the allegation that the decline of reading is a feature of today's world and that the frenetic pace of modern life leaves very little time for reading which was, until as recently as 50 years ago, the main tool by which people acquired knowledge and expanded their mental horizons. This is a complete fallacy which can easily be disproved by pointing out that while modern mass media like radio and television have supplanted reading in many countries, the same mass media have been used in others to promote greater interest in reading: where the function of reading has been taken over by radio and television in the less developed countries, mass media play an effective role in furthering the cause of reading in the advanced countries.

It is also important to note here that the more preponderant the entertainment component of the programmes presented by mass media such as radio and television (soap operas, songs, films, etc.), the greater their role in depreciating reading. By the same token, the greater their educational/cultural component, the greater their role in upgrading reading, education and culture.

A French, German or British programme on World War I or II, or about a historic, literary or artistic figure (the film *Amadeus* is a case in point) can serve as a bridge between the viewer and reading, by stimulating his interest in acquiring more information on the subject. This is in direct opposition to the reaction of viewers in Third World countries, whose cultural aspirations are badly served by the diet of often inane serials they are subjected to by their mass media, which are designed solely to kill time.

If I have dwelt at some length on the mass media connection, it is out of a profound conviction that modern mass media, specifically radio and television, have an unlimited power to shape people's attitudes, that, in fact, they are capable of building or destroying.

As we have seen, then, the question of promoting reading should be approached from the three angles we discussed. Without in any way minimizing their pertinence, I would like to add a new angle that I feel has not been given the attention it deserves, namely, the socio-economic perspective. When a society follows a market economy it is governed by the spirit of competition. This generates a process of selection, that can be described as Social Darwinism. In this context, reading and knowledge acquire enormous importance, with academic qualifications becoming factors in success and advancement and the means by which to differentiate between the average, the better and the best.

Societies governed by the laws of the market and of Social Darwinism are in a continuous quest for the brightest and best of their sons. This invests culture, knowledge and reading with a vital strategic importance going beyond the realm of personal preference and natural predisposition.

CHAPTER 10

Egyptians Between Rights and Duties[65]

A conversation years ago with Desmond Stewart, a British writer known for his love and appreciation of Egypt and the Egyptian people, serves as the inspiration for this chapter. The author of such works as *Cairo* and *The Friday Men* (Heinemann, 1961), Stewart had very definite views on the distinctive traits of the contemporary Egyptian personality. I recall that one of his most perceptive observations was that an enormous discrepancy has grown in the two decades of autocratic rule since 1952 between Egyptians' sense of rights, on the one hand, and their sense of duties, on the other.

Elsewhere in this book it is noted that the blame for Egypt's present situation lies squarely with the government. This does not mean the responsibility of Egyptians, as individuals, should be overlooked, particularly regarding duties and rights. Rather, there is a connection between the government's attitudes and performance level and those of the Egyptian citizen towards his rights and duties.

It should be stressed that it is as a result of the government's shoddy performance and its poor record that most Egyptians have become passive citizens who are unduly conscious of their rights and privileges – not least in the area of pensions – without developing a corresponding sense of obligation. A typical Egyptian citizen is greatly concerned with his right to public employment and its many benefits. Then comes his right to obtain housing, through the government if possible, followed by his right to a job abroad, preferably on secondment from the government, his right to go on pilgrimage to

Mecca, to buy subsidized food and clothing, and so on through an endless list of state-supported privileges. Never will an Egyptian citizen display a sense of obligation similar to that of, say, his German counterpart, who is fully aware that to enjoy the privileges of citizenship he must first perform such basic duties as actively participating in his country's production process, protecting his environment and contributing towards solving society's problems by giving serious thought to their causes and their possible solutions.

The president recently spoke of the need for a 'great awakening' in the life of all Egyptians. This is certainly true. Moreover, unless there is such an awakening, and soon, we are headed towards certain disaster. But the question is, what does the president mean by 'awakening'? Does he mean the government should waken from the deep sleep into which it has been plunged for three decades of totalitarian rule, never guided by the lights of freedom and democracy? Or does he mean the awakening of the people to the duties and obligations incumbent on them, which they neglected for many years while claiming their right to the material advantages provided by the state, never attempting to expand the circle of rights to encompass political issues, such as the right to influence fateful decisions, the right to choose leaders freely or, at the very least, the right to live in a twentieth century environment where roads and basic public services are concerned? Or did the president mean an awakening of both government and citizens?

We believe the call for a 'great awakening' cannot become a reality unless it is directed first at the government and the administration and only then at the citizens of Egypt, to rouse them from a slumber so aptly described half a century ago by the poet who lamented:

The great Pharaohs shuddered and recoiled, aghast
To see such heritage go to waste.
They saw a nation lag behind its age
Which once had always had the lead.
I almost hear the echo of their cry
Across the centuries to be heard:
Sons of Egypt! Hear our voice!

Life or Death, that is the choice
And nothing in between.

The awakening of the government will come about the day it acknowledges that the situation in Egypt has sunk to an all-time low, in all areas and at all levels, because of its own political and economic policies. The government must also admit that the time for stop-gap repairs is long gone, and that nothing short of a radical shift in those policies, as proposed in earlier chapters, can save Egypt.

At the same time the awakening of the Egyptian citizens requires a rekindling of the flame of positive nationalism in their hearts and minds which can transform them from being interested solely in rights and benefits to being mindful of their duties to society and to the nation. A citizen who accepts the state as a father figure, responsible for providing his children with education, employment and all their other needs is a negative citizen, even if he was rendered thus by years of oppression that stripped him of his will and the spirit of endeavour.

There is no doubt that the transformation of Egyptians into 'hirelings' of the regime, wholly dependent on it for their livelihood – and for all aspects of their life – was a deliberate policy of Egypt's rulers in the 1950s and '60s, designed to help them consolidate their grip on power. In this way, they succeeded in suppressing all opposition; an entire people succumbed.

But there is more than one way to rekindle the spirit of nationalism and a sense of civic duty. The first is by setting an example. When people see their leaders not practising what they preach, they become alienated: their values are shaken and their sense of duty to society and to the nation recedes. The double standards to which the Egyptian people have for so long been exposed has quite understandably made them cynical and filled with bitterness. They need to see their rulers set an example, from the president down.

The second way is by eliciting the help of the mass media, but of media that are free, not that cater to the interests of specific persons or tendencies. Egyptians are bitterly resentful of the opportunism that has characterized our mass media for the past 30 years. The newspapers, radio and television have all, under a series of directors who were no more than lackeys of the totalitarian regime and the secret services, become what they are today: repetitive and dull.

The third way is through educational institutions, at both school and university levels, for these can infuse young learners with a true and effective nationalist spirit, based on love of country and a strong sense of civic duty, not a superficial love expressed in the rote chanting of sentimental anthems.

The fourth way is through mosque and church, where religious leaders should understand that their duty, apart from teaching the precepts of the faith, is not to preach hatred of others or incite extremist ideas but, rather, to instil a profound sense of duty to society and teach that work is sacred.

Literature and the arts offer a fifth way to inspire a civic spirit. Literature is the conscience of the nation, and many a nation has risen from ruin thanks to great literature. Voltaire, Rousseau, Montesquieu and Diderot can proudly claim to have inspired public freedom and democracy in the West. Unfortunately, in Egypt 30 years of hypocrisy by a large number of kowtowing intellectuals and writers who turned a blind eye to all forms of oppression have caused our art and literature to lose their credibility among vast sectors of the Egyptian people.

Opposition groups too have an important role to play in this connection. But unless the opposition ceases to incite and insult, its ability to nurture a sense of civic duty in the people will remain very limited. The opposition will lose its credibility as seekers of reform and will be seen, instead, as aiming to settle personal scores or to reach powerful positions. Little has changed since Saad Zaghlul described the opposition thus: 'To them the insults, and to us the seats in parliament'.

The Egyptian opposition, as a whole, is in dire need of objectivity and seriousness. That is particularly true of the Left which, more than other branches, needs to pause and reflect to ensure that it is not held accountable for the demagogical trend prevailing in many ranks of the political opposition in Egypt today.

President Mubarak's administration should make more effort to respond to the wishes of the opposition, especially since everyone admits that it (particularly the Wafd, Labour and Tajamu parties) is far more representative, at the popular level, than the number of seats it holds in the People's Assembly would indicate. The administration is surely aware that those parties have behind them more than 5 per cent of Egyptian public opinion, and that at least half the country's intellectuals and educated people support them. Thus a positive response by the presidency to the opposition's demands would help generate a sense of civic duty on its part. There must be many issues on which Mubarak's administration could see eye to eye with the most cultured and enlightened groups of Egyptians, more than half of whom are represented by the three parties in question. Among such issues is the opposition's desire to amend the system of election to the People's Assembly, as well as its demand that the president should relinquish the chairmanship of his political party. The opposition also believes the regime should abstain from giving unconditional support to some of its public figures and that the head of state should be chosen through direct general elections rather than through a public referendum on a sole candidate nominated by the Assembly. The opposition would also like to see the administration, for example, abandon a sinking public sector in favour of privatization, forgo the destructive policy of subsidies and cease to apply an artificial rate of exchange.

It is worth mentioning that the reaction of the so-called 'national' press to the president's call for a 'great awakening' does not augur well for its chances of successfully drumming up enthusiasm for such a goal. The hypocritical reaction of the state's eminent writers and editors may well have a negative impact on the citizens, who have long lost faith in the sycophantic national press.

Moreover, the media have taken the president's call to mean the awakening of the citizens alone, whereas observers are unanimous in believing that the awakening should be, first and foremost, that of the government, since the present lethargy of the citizens is but a reaction to the failure of successive governments, a form of passive self-defence, as it were. Where are the eminent writers who insist that there can be no great awakening if the president himself does not recognize the sorry state that Egypt has come to? Yet the government and all its men and institutions never publicly admit the dim situation, nor will they admit the grave errors and failed policies committed against the country over decades – in the economy, agriculture, education, the public sector, the military establishment, and on and on.

Real confidence-building measures are required to win the public back, in all spheres. Without the growth and development of a sense of duty towards Egypt in the government and among its citizens, the 'great awakening' which is necessary to pull Egypt out of its present slump will remain no more than a dream.

CHAPTER 11

Saad Zaghlul and the Unity of the Two Elements of the Egyptian Nation[66]

To my mind, one of the most cogent signs of human progress and adherence to humanist values is the way a civilization treats its minorities. To the same extent that the protection of these minorities is a mark of human civilization, their persecution and the violation of their rights, particularly their right to personal security, private property and freedom of worship, is a sign of backwardness and barbarity. Muslims can be justifiably proud that Islam has a noble tradition of treating religious minorities, especially Christians, according to the most advanced norms of civilized behaviour. In more than one passage, the great book of Islam, the Holy Quran, deplores as sinful the coercion of people to embrace a faith other than theirs, even if that faith is Islam. According to the *sura*[67] of al-Baqara (The Cow), 'There is no compulsion in religion. The right direction is henceforth distinct from error.' Other *sura*s are also unequivocal in deploring the use of coercion to convert people to one single religion: 'And if thy Lord willed, all who are on the earth would have believed together. Wouldst thou compel men until they are believers?' (verse 99, *sura* of Yunes [Jonah]); 'If Allah willed, He could have brought them all together to guidance. So be not thou among the foolish ones' (verse 35, *sura* of al-Anaam [The Cattle]); 'Say: (It is) the truth from the Lord of you (all). Then whosoever will, let him believe, and whosoever will, let him disbelieve' (verse 29, *sura* of al-Kahf [The Cave]).

Quranic texts stating that, had it been God's will, He would have united all men in one nation appear in many more *sura*s as well, in almost identical words. All stress the need to preach

Islam with kindness and not with violence and coercion. Other texts forbid war against non-Muslims as long as they do not fight the Muslims.

In authenticated references of the Prophet's sayings – the *hadith*[68] – Muhammad not only forbids oppression of Christians and Jews but considers such oppression to be a great sin. The *hadith* states: 'He who is unjust to a Christian or a Jew, I shall be his antagonist on the Day of Resurrection.' The history of Islam is rich in examples of noble stands. One of the oldest is the refusal of the second caliph, Omar Ibn al-Khattab, to pray in a Jerusalem church during a visit to that city, lest it become a precedent for Muslims to emulate him, thus violating the right of Christians to their own houses of worship. One of the greatest contemporary Arab writers, Abbas al-Aqad, devotes a chapter in his book, *Democracy in Islam*, to the attitude of Islam to other faiths. In the chapter 'With Strangers', he writes: 'Under an Islamic government, non-Muslim people of the Scriptures who are subjects or allies of the State have the same rights and obligations as Muslims. The State will do battle on their behalf as it does on behalf of all its subjects, and will not judge them by the tenets of Islam in matters where their faith rules otherwise. Nor can they be called before the courts on their feast days, for the Prophet, peace be upon him, said: "You are Jews, and you will not be summoned on the Sabbath".' According to al-Aqad, a Muslim ruler is required to go beyond the letter of Islamic law in dealing courteously and fairly with non-Muslims, for the Prophet said: 'He who insults a Christian or a Jew shall feel lashes of fire on the Day of Resurrection'. He also said: 'He who harms a Christian or a Jew harms me', and, on another occasion, 'He who deals unfairly with a Christian or a Jew and lays a heavier burden on him than he can carry shall be my enemy on the Day of Resurrection'. When Amr Ibn al-Aas became Governor of Egypt after the Islamic Conquest, the caliph al-Khattab sent him a missive enjoining him to deal justly with the Copts, the majority of Egypt's population at the time. He wrote: 'You have with you the people of the faith and the covenant ... Beware, Amr, of making an enemy of the Prophet.' In his *History of Islamic Conquests*, al-Balatheri tells of Omar's visit to the Levant, where he ordered alms to be given to needy Christian lepers. It was also Omar Ibn al-Khattab who granted the Christians of the city of Iliah a treaty that stated: 'They shall be secure as to their persons, their churches and their crosses. Their churches are not to be inhabited, destroyed or diminished in any way; nor shall they be coerced as to their faith.'

Al-Aqad also notes that Islam gave Christians every opportunity to build churches, practise their religious rites and engage in trade. What better proof could there be that Muslims protected religious minorities throughout their long history, particularly Christians and Jews, he asks, than the fact that they were never coerced into embracing Islam? Even under the Abbasids, when the might of Islam was at its height, religious tolerance prevailed. It continued under Ottoman rule, which protected Christian and Jewish minorities, as borne out by the fact that these communities continued to thrive in Syria, Lebanon, Palestine and Egypt, all of which were under the complete domination of the Ottoman State at its strongest and greatest.

In short, history abounds with examples attesting to the importance given by Islam to the protection of religious minorities and their right to practise their faith freely. But this situation did not last. When most Islamic countries, particularly the Arab ones, fell into the clutches of European colonialism, they became a perfect ground for the application of one of the major tenets of colonialism in general and of British colonialism in particular: 'Divide and rule'.

That notorious policy was to leave its mark on the modern history of Egypt. Immediately after Egypt was occupied in 1882 the colonialist authorities began to play Muslims against Copts and nationals against aliens. Inspired by the ideas of Ahmed Loutfy el-Sayed, the Umma Party played a commendable role in endeavouring to establish the unity of the two elements of the Egyptian nation, the Muslims and the Copts. But the one Egyptian leader who not only put a stop to all the tensions, grievances and conflicts between Muslims and Copts, but who found a new formula for brotherhood and profound unity between the two was Saad Zaghlul. His achievement in this area was a sign of his political genius and one of the noblest aspects of the 1919 nationalist revolution. No other leader before or since has been as successful in uniting these two elements of the Egyptian nation.

Zaghlul's death tempered the enthusiasm of the Copts for the Wafd Party he had founded and whose appeal was due in large measure to his personal charisma and unique leadership. Indeed, their attitude to all political parties since then, whether they existed before the 1952 Revolution or date from the days of Nasser and Sadat, have wavered between uneasy resignation at best and burning tension at worst. Relations between Nasser and the Copts were characterized by deep mutual mistrust. Sadat's relations with that community were severely strained, particularly following his shocking decision in September 1981 to remove the head of the Coptic Church by annulling the decree crowning him Patriarch of the Copts of Egypt and of the territories under the jurisdiction of the Patriarchate.

What then is the essence of Zaghlul's political genius that led him to find the unique formula that united the two elements of the Egyptian nation in 1919? To answer that question, we must examine the situation in Egypt in the early twentieth century.

Between 1906 and 1910 relations between Muslims and Copts sank to an all-time low. During those years, and as a result of the policies and practices of the representatives of British colonialism in Egypt, Sir John Eldon Gorst and his successor, the Earl of Cromer, relations between the two communities underwent the worst crisis in recent history. British colonialism had sown the seeds of discord and tension through the clever application of their divide-and-rule policy, notably in the area of government jobs where violent competition between the two communities was actively encouraged. The British fanned the flames of fanaticism by leading the Coptic minority to feel that they were not getting their full rights or the same opportunities as those available to the Muslims. Tensions were further exacerbated by newspaper coverage of the conflicting points of view.

The crisis reached a peak after the assassination of the Coptic prime minister, Boutros Pasha Ghali, by a young Muslim, Ibrahim al-Wardani, on 20 February 1910.

Saad Zaghlul served in all the successive governments that ruled Egypt through the years of Muslim–Copt crisis (under Mustafa Pasha Fahmy from 1906 to 1908, under Ghali from 1908 to 1910 and under Mohammad Pasha Said from 1910 to

1912). In 1912 he tendered his resignation, refusing to be a puppet minister and the mere executor of the British Commissioner's orders and those of other representatives of the occupation forces. The fact that Zaghlul was a lawyer, a judge renowned for his integrity and equity and a man imbued with Islamic and French culture, enabled him to understand the true nature of the crisis, its origin, its prime movers and their motives. His insight and years of experience made him realize that an even-handed approach would end the crisis and totally eliminate its causes. Thus, he understood that if the majority were to take the initiative in providing a sense of security for the minority, peace between them would ensue; the Copts would no longer fear for themselves, for their property or for the future of their children and there would be no more cause for fanaticism.

Saad Zaghlul accumulated a vast store of experience from his participation in the Orabi Revolution, from his early imprisonment, his work as a lawyer and judge, as a minister and elected member of the legislative body (1913–14), and from World War I. He drew the necessary useful lessons and, when he became the leader of the 1919 Revolution, he put all his experience to good use to rally the Copts to his cause. Thanks to his moral stature, the two erstwhile antagonists became united under the banner of the revolution, fighting side by side for the cause of the nation. Muslims and Copts forgot their differences when the man whom both sides trusted without reservation was arrested. Describing the massive popular demonstrations that swept the country on 17 March 1919, Ahmed Hussein (*Almanac of Egypt's History*, part IV, page 1,567) writes: 'Perhaps the most magnificent feature that the demonstrations highlighted, a feature which dominated events from the very first moment, was the close unity between Muslims and Copts. To the surprise of the British, who thought they had succeeded in driving a wedge between the two elements of the nation, in that instant the two elements fused together and, Egyptians all, fought under the slogan: "Religion belongs to God, and the Nation to all". The banners raised on 17 March 1919 bore the Cross and the Crescent together.'

Among Saad Zaghlul's closest and most loyal companions during the revolution and throughout the years of nationalist struggle from 1919 to 1924, were eminent Copts like Wassef Ghali, Wisa Wassef, Makram Ebeid and others. It will be remembered that when the British occupation forces arrested Saad Zaghlul and sent him into exile on 22 December 1921, two of the five companions exiled with him were Copts: Senewet Hanna and Makram Ebeid. The following year seven of Zaghlul's companions were arrested by the occupation forces and sentenced to death; of the seven, four were Copts. Following the arrest of this second group of Wafdist leaders, a new group of nine, including two Copts, took over the leadership of the party. These too were arrested and a fourth group was formed, composed of six leaders, two of them Copts. The prominence of Copts in the upper echelons of the Wafd bears witness to the broad national vision of Zaghlul. Under his leadership, the Wafd won a sweeping victory in the first real elections held in Egypt. When he named the first popular cabinet in Egypt's modern history in January 1924 he did not follow the tradition of appointing only one Coptic minister: out of nine ministers, two were Copts.

Zaghlul actively strove to eradicate fanaticism and bias by pursuing a policy based on the spirit of Egyptian nationalism and on respect for the members of the minority who became an integral part of his popular ruling party. A new spirit of brotherhood prevailed between Muslims and Copts, best exemplified in an incident that took place in the late 1930s. When a soldier, using a poisoned lance, tried to kill Mustafa al-Nahas, who succeeded Zaghlul as leader of the Wafd, Coptic party member Senewet Hanna protected him with his own life. His sacrifice was an unforgettable symbol of the unity that bound the two elements of the Egyptian nation together. This degree of unity and brotherhood can be destroyed only when fanaticism invades the ranks in the form of reactionary ideas which are ill-suited to the age in which we live and to a nation such as ours. National peace and harmony promise the only hope of salvation from the abhorrent storm of fundamentalism that has raged for so long in our part of the world.

CHAPTER 12

Management and Society[69]

The concept of management as an economic process in essence and by function is a modern one, dating from the Industrial Revolution, which began in Europe with the invention of the first power loom in the mid-eighteenth century. During the tens of centuries preceding the birth and growth of the industrial system, the only form of management known to humanity was military leadership. It was only in this area that managerial skills were apparent, and where one commander could excel over another by dint of better management.

But with the development of the industrial system, that is, with the shift from an agriculturally based economy to one based on industry, employers in the societies where the system was born discovered that the output of workers varied in terms of both quantity and quality according to the person of the shift foreman. In other words, the same workers who produced a certain volume of a given quality under the supervision of one foreman produced a different volume and quality under the supervision of another. This brought home to employers the importance of super vision, which is essentially a primitive form of management, in the process production. They realized that it was not a marginal factor limited to imposing formalistic discipline on workers, but that it actually added value to the production process.

The Industrial Revolution introduced a whole new set of values, such as the importance of observing schedules and meeting specifications. It also marks the discovery by employers of the first of the modern forms of management. As the production process grew ever more complex, as it expanded into a chain of correlated stages comprising planning, production and marketing, each with its own sub-stages, the value of management as a decisive element in the success of the production process grew.

It is important to emphasize here that the main axis of management in its modern sense has from the start been a commercial and economic one, in the sense that employers discovered that certain supervisors and managers yielded higher output than others and that this translated into a higher commercial return. Thus the concept of management in industrial societies was linked from the start to the idea of profit, which is the basis of what is today termed economic management, or the enhancement of efficient and profitable operation of the production process through sound management.

In fact, the criterion or unit used in industrial societies to measure the success of management is an economic one. This takes the form of specific economic criteria by which the efficiency of management can be measured, i.e. rules now exist to measure the profitability of work as an economic criterion by which to determine the success or failure of management.

THE ELEMENTS OF EFFECTIVE MANAGEMENT

Although management began in the form of supervision, it has since evolved. It would be totally erroneous today to regard supervision and management as being one and the same thing. Supervision is the most elementary form of management, while modern economic management as we know it today is a complex process that can be carried out only by persons displaying specific traits, some innate, others acquired through training and experience. These traits can be defined as follows.

Leadership skills

A study of economic life as it has evolved shows that society can be roughly divided into two categories or groups. The first, and by far the large, group is made up of people who are temperamentally suited to work either as part of a team under the leadership of an individual, or in isolation from others, such as scholars, researchers or laboratory technicians. The productivity of the members of both these sub-groupings – those who are suited to working closely with others in a spirit of cooperative teamwork and those who, being temperamentally unsuited to working with others, prefer to work alone – can be greatly enhanced through sound management. In the case of those who prefer to work as part of a team, this could be achieved through providing them with training, fostering an *esprit de corps* and offering them motivation; and in the case of those who prefer to work alone, through providing them with opportunities to specialize in their chosen field so that they can in time become experts in that field.

The second group is made up of a limited number of individuals blessed with a natural ability to lead others. This quality, however, is a necessary but not sufficient condition for effective leadership. Like any talent, leadership must be nurtured and honed if it is to realize its full potential. In much the same way that musical talent can develop only through study, training and practice, so too a talent for leadership must be cultivated and directed. Indeed, there is a risk that, without proper guidance, a talent for leadership could degenerate into a form of tyranny.

One of the tasks of management in any organization, corporate or otherwise, is constantly to scout out the potential leaders among its pool of employees by closely monitoring employees to discover those among them with leadership qualities. In advanced industrial societies, the right to occupy leading positions is not determined by reference to such factors as age, academic qualifications and seniority but depends, in the first instance, on the candidate's aptitudes and talents, especially on his possession of the rare quality of leadership, plus of course experience and training. The more an organization selects its managers according to their leadership abilities, the more successful will be that organization.

There is a firm belief in the West that the driving force that impels society forward is the spirit of competition among its members. Another firm belief is that something like the theory of natural selection, propounded by the eminent naturalist

Charles Darwin over a hundred years ago, should prevail in society. In this logic, the higher levels of management must constantly be on the lookout for individuals in the organization who exhibit leadership abilities. At the same time, encouraging the spirit of competition makes the process of natural selection much easier.

Vision

The word vision inevitably crops up today in any talk of leaders or managers. As used in this context, it refers to the ability of some individuals to make projections of the future from the facts at hand. This ability is made up of several component elements:

- A comprehensive grasp of the givens of reality, together with the ability to assess what impact prevailing and potential conditions could have on the course of events.
- A flair for making the optimum choices on the basis of this comprehensive grasp of present reality.
- The capacity to rise above the minutiae of day-to-day reality and formulate an overview of the general picture, to ignore the trees and see the forest, as it were. Management experts in giant international corporations have coined the term 'helicopter ability' to describe this capacity.

There is no doubt that vision in this sense is an indispensable prerequisite for both top- and medium-level managers.

Innovation and creativity

Management experts in advanced societies have noticed from their study of thousands of annual reports on large numbers and sectors of employees in various corporations and economic organizations that most people perform their work according to set patterns, without trying to introduce variations from time to time to their techniques of work or to the idea behind these techniques. They also noticed that, in marked contrast to the vast majority, a small percentage of employees constantly re-examine their technique and performance, making for a corresponding renewal in the form and substance of their work. Constantly trying to break out of the mould in which most of their colleagues are content to remain throughout their working life, these employees seek always to renew, create and innovate. Those who reach the pinnacles of power in the biggest corporations come from this small group or innovative and creative people who refuse to be typecast and who are driven by a compulsion to renew and develop themselves continuously.

Business sense

People in public employment, particularly in government departments, often lose sight of the fact that the ultimate goal of any work is the realization of profits. For economic corporations and establishments in advanced industrial societies, on the other hand, the profit-making ethic reigns supreme. As they see it, each and every employee, however humble his position in the organizational structure, should focus his sights on that ultimate goal of realizing profits and economic success.

Business sense is one of those elusive attributes that separate effective managers from less effective ones. As any economic unit in advanced industrial societies is appraised in terms of its commercial success, a manager's business sense is constantly called into play as he strives to expand the horizons of his unit's success. This should become the norm in a country like Egypt today, where business sense is woefully lacking. Managers of companies and establishments and key executives in these units must be called to account for the economic performance of their units according to standardized criteria. Units that fail to meet these criteria should be subject to sanctions, at the very least, and salaries and bonuses should be linked to the degree of economic success achieved by the unit. Moreover, the continued occupation of positions of responsibility should be made conditional on the incumbent's success in achieving targeted commercial results. If a company that is losing annually, or even showing profits below those projected, remains under the same management year after year, this does not make for a healthy climate of work. Quite the contrary, it dampens the enthusiasm and commitment of most, if not all, the members of the company's workforce and strips them of all initiative.

Ability to delegate

Management in underdeveloped societies differs from that in advanced societies in many ways. One of the most important is that in underdeveloped societies management tends to be highly centralized, often authoritarian if not outright autocratic. Power is usually concentrated in the hands of the man at the top of the organizational structure, the 'boss', while subordinates are relegated to carrying out orders without being involved at any stage of the decision-making process. As a result, large numbers of employees become so alienated that they are unfit for any but the most undemanding work.

In advanced societies, on the other hand, the concept of modern management has greatly evolved in the direction of delegating authority to middle-level managers. Today, delegation has become one of the fundamental principles of successful management. It is a principle founded on the belief that delegation is highly beneficial to all parties: manager, subordinates and organization.

The more day-to-day responsibilities a manager can delegate, the more time he has to pursue a strategic role, defined more in terms of planning, visualizing long-term perspectives and following up the attainment of organizational goals than of actual execution. The scope of vision of a manager who applies the principle of delegation in his organization is definitely broader than that of the manager who gets bogged down in details.

The subordinate to whom some of the manager's responsibilities are delegated develops strong loyalty to the organization, becomes more effective and shows greater initiative. An organization run according to the principle of delegation is one in which a harmonious spirit of healthy cooperation, devoid of in-fighting and power struggles, prevails.

Delegation reflects self-confidence on the part of the manager assigning part of his workload to others, as well as his confidence in the ability of others to carry out the tasks delegated to them. By the same token, a manager who does not delegate authority is an insecure man who lacks confidence in his own abilities, let alone in the abilities of subordinates.

Extensive research proves that a manager who does not believe in delegation ends up running an organization that is fraught with internal tensions, between himself and his subordinates on the one hand and among these subordinates on the other.

Ability to motivate employees

An essential qualification of a successful manager or leader is his ability to stimulate enthusiasm and dedication in the people working with him. Employee motivation is of crucial importance to managers, mainly because of the role it plays in performance. Basically, a motivated employee is one who sees organizational goals as part of his own goal sets and works hard to achieve them. Loyal and dedicated, he is eager to rise to the challenges of his job and unstinting in his efforts to maintain a high performance rate. An unmotivated employee, on the other hand, is one who will do only the bare minimum necessary to get by. A manager who demotivates his employees ends up with a demoralized and inefficient staff, unwilling to make any meaningful contribution to the organization. Motivating employees is thus beneficial not only for the workers themselves, but also, and equally, for the organization and the manager.

There are several methods by which employees can be motivated, including financial rewards and other benefits that reflect management's satisfaction with an employee's performance.

However, while the role of material incentives is important, other, motivational factors have proved equally effective:

- *Future prospects, promotion and advancement:* An employee's will to work can be greatly stimulated (especially during the first two-thirds of his working life) if he believes that his efforts will result in his promotion and elevation to a higher level within the organizational hierarchy.
- *Moral appreciation:* Motivation can be greatly enhanced through job satisfaction, which is the employee's feeling that management is satisfied with his performance and appreciates the value of his input.

Ability to create believers, not followers

One of the main ideas put forward in contemporary management perspectives is that an effective manager is one who succeeds in making the people working for him believe in what they are doing rather than follow orders blindly. A subordinate who is convinced of the value of his work and of the aims of the organization by which he is employed will strive to achieve those aims. The reverse is equally true: a subordinate who does not identify with his organization's goals will not perform effectively. In the same way an army that believes in the justness of its cause will fight better than an army whose soldiers are simply following orders, an organization in which there is a high degree of belief and commitment among the staff will operate at high capacity to achieve its goals.

Charisma

The term charisma has come to be widely used over the last two decades to describe an intangible attribute in a person's personality that inspires loyalty and enthusiasm in his peers or subordinates. As applied to leaders or managers, it denotes the ability to influence the behaviour of others. Charisma-based influence can be clearly discerned in the case of orators: the same speech delivered by two different people can elicit very different responses. Where one speaker can sway his audience through sheer force of personality, or charisma, the other might leave them totally unmoved. A necessary attribute in leaders, orators and preachers, a certain measure of charisma is also an asset in organizational leadership or management.

Ability to achieve the difficult equation of horizontal and vertical job enrichment

A significant contribution to management theory and practice came from a noted professor of management at Harvard University, who noticed that most top leadership positions in the United States are not filled by technocrats. For example, the current Defence Secretary, Dick Cheney, is not a military man, the Health Secretary is not a doctor and the Education Secretary was never a pedagogue. After extensive research, the author concluded that all cabinet ministers and top executives of major corporations in the USA (who are even more powerful in American society than cabinet ministers) are drawn from a pool of public figures known in contemporary management terminology as 'generalists'. The survey conducted by the Harvard professor covered the chief executives of such giant corporations as General Motors, Esso, General Electric and Ford as well as hundreds of top public officials.

According to the study, this is in direct contrast to the pattern prevailing in the Soviet Union, Eastern Europe and Third World countries – especially those applying a command economy – where all ministerial and top economic and managerial posts are filled by specialized technocrats. For example, the Minister for Electrical Power in the Soviet Union is an electrical engineer who began his career in a power plant 30 years ago and moved up gradually to his present post. His case is a typical example of how most of the leading administrative and economic posts are filled in these countries.

Analysing this phenomenon, the author notes that only a free and effective management climate such as that prevailing in advanced societies can produce the generalist manager, whose dependence on his field of specialization ends some ten years after graduation. Following that period, he begins to learn new skills – managerial, economic and technical – that broaden his horizons and enhance his job-enrichment potential. It is the experience and skills he acquires at this time that qualify him for leadership.

To illustrate how the concept of management has evolved from that of the specialized manager, or technocrat, to that of the generalist breed of managers, the author points to the field or hospital management in the United States. The exclusive province of doctors in the past, has, over the last 50 years, come to be seen more as a managerial than a medical function and hospitals are now administered by managers drawn from outside the medical profession. The author drives home the point that the responsibilities of running a hospital are more managerial than medical in nature by listing the functions of any hospital administrator. These include, for example:

- the supply and purchase of material and equipment, including furniture, kitchens, generators, computers, etc.;
- personnel affairs: recruiting, hiring and training of hospital staff, as well as dealing with doctors and surgeons; and

- administrative affairs: the organizational structure of the hospital, departmentalization, spans of control, etc.

These functions make it abundantly clear that hospital management is a speciality that is quite separate and distinct from that of the medical profession.

What applies to hospitals applies equally to any organization, where the scope of management, especially at the highest levels, extends far beyond that of narrow specialization. An effective manager must be skilled in administrative, economic and commercial matters, skills that can be acquired only after long years of training and experience outside the area of narrow specialization. It is these general qualifications which, together with predisposition and talent, create the successful manager. Accordingly, one of the most important tasks of management is to strike the appropriate balance between horizontal and vertical job enrichment in order to create a small group of generalists capable of realizing effective, creative, productive and developed management.

Ability to teach others

The ability to teach others is a vital component of the successful leader or manager. It is impossible for a person lacking this aptitude to lead large numbers of employees. The transmission of experience, ideas and acquired skills to others within an organization, and hence the continued development of that organization, can be achieved only through the process of teaching.

MANAGEMENT'S ROLE IN REFORMING SOCIETY

An enormous gap separates the developed industrial countries from those of the Third World, as well as from those of what is known as the Second World, which comprises the Soviet Union and the countries of Eastern Europe. The gap arose as a result of the general and comprehensive development of the former and the backwardness and regression of the latter. Even if the countries of the Third World were to attain the same rates of productivity and progress as those prevailing in the countries of the advanced world, this would not narrow the gap between the two worlds, because the latter will also continue to move forward. The situation lends itself to one of three possibilities:

1. Either the Third World countries continue to move forward at the same sluggish pace, while those of the advanced world maintain their current rates of development.
2. Or they succeed in achieving the same rate of progress as the advanced countries.
3. Or they succeed not only in progressing at the same pace but in actually narrowing the gap separating them from the advanced countries.

In the first case, the gap between the two worlds will widen still further, exposing Third World countries to acute social problems, which could take the form of social upheavals or even civil war.

In the second case, the gap between the two worlds will remain the same, with the result that the Third World will continue to be dependent on the advanced industrial world in the area of science and technology.

Should the third scenario come to pass, then the Third World could approach the Japanese model and, at a later stage, the South Korean model, both examples of countries which, while not belonging to the advanced Western world, have nevertheless caught up with and stand on an equal footing with the countries of that world.

The third scenario can be achieved only through creative and effective management. Inasmuch as the main challenge for Third World countries is to change individual and group behavioural norms and to modify certain sets of values hindering progress, the only tool capable of effecting the desired changes within a reasonable time-frame is sound management. It is impossible to effect changes in societal patterns of behaviour through political and legislative tools, and all attempts to do so in contemporary history have proved singularly unsuccessful.

A country such as Egypt cannot hope to overcome the multitude of problems besetting it without a revolution in management that would replace the civil servants currently occupying top management posts by economic managers in the contemporary sense of the word. The bureaucratic prototype of the manager produced by Third world countries in the 1950s and 1960s under the influence of socialist ideas has become one of the main diseases plaguing these countries. Keeping glorified civil servants in top management posts can only compound the economic problems of Third World countries, which must rid themselves of these poor excuses for managers without further delay.

FACTORS IMPEDING MANAGEMENT IN EGYPT

A *strong sense of rights without a corresponding sense of* obligations

The members of any society that has gone through a period of socialist rule are highly conscious of their rights without developing a sense of duty and obligation. Much of the blame can be traced to labour legislation whose strong bias in favour of employees and hostility to employers is reflected in the respective scope of the rights granted to each. This makes for a sharp discrepancy between the rights of employees on the one hand and those of employers on the other.

In Western societies, on the other hand, where the spirit of competition is pervasive and where an employee knows he will remain in his job only as long as his performance is satisfactory, the sense of obligation employees feel towards their place of work is as well developed as their sense of rights.

Perceiving employment as a social right

In advanced industrial societies, a job is regarded both as a component element of the production process and as the means by which individuals can earn a living through contributing to this process. In societies with a socialist orientation, jobs are widely regarded as one of the rights of citizenship that is the due of any citizen regardless of the value of his work or the manner of its performance.

A *weak commitment to work*

Management experts in advanced industrial societies talk of a special bond that should exist in the relationship between the worker and the place of work, referring to it sometimes as loyalty and sometimes as commitment. Whatever the term used, an employee who is highly committed to his work is a great asset. When this intangible bond is absent, it is not the fault of the employee alone, but the natural result of a disbalance in his relationship with his place of work. Here management's responsibility is undeniable.

Eastern lifestyle hinders adoption of work ethic prevailing in advanced societies

Life in Eastern societies is characterized by a high degree of social intercourse, which represents an important value in people's lives and takes up a great deal of their time. The tempo of life in these societies being what it is, it is difficult for work to be the focal point of people's lives. While nobody wants our society to become a replica of the West, where individualism has taken precedence over the communal spirit and where social and family ties are disintegrating, a middle course can surely be struck between the two lifestyles, one in which social life need not function at the expense of dedication to work.

Misconceptions concerning the prerogatives of management

The citizens of developed societies recognize that one of the prerogatives of managers and employers is the right to decide, at their sole discretion, to terminate an employee who fails to produce the required quantity or quality of work. This is far from axiomatic in our society, where management's dismissal of an employee for poor performance invariably arouses hostility, which is further exacerbated by the absence of a system of unemployment insurance like that available in advanced societies. This immature understanding of the prerogatives of management is yet another constraint on the freedom of managers.

Decline in general and technical education and in standards of crafts

Egypt's introduction to education in its contemporary sense dates back to the era of Muhammad Ali, who sent the first of many missions of Egyptian students to Europe in 1826. By the third decade of this century, general and university education in Egypt was quite advanced. In fact, the Egyptian educational system at the time was on a par with the systems in the most advanced countries. But with the political trend of the 1950s and '60s to expand education quantitatively, that is, to make it available to hundreds of thousands, rather than tens of thousands, came a sharp decline in the quality of education and in the standards of teachers and students.

The decline in the standard of the teaching profession was further exacerbated by the political and economic conditions prevailing in the 1950s and '60s. This was followed by a sharp rise in the demand for teachers, both internally and in the Arab countries, a development that contributed to the deterioration in standards of performance. As the demand for quantity grew, quality declined. and teaching came to be seen more as a craft than a profession. The decline in general and technical education and in standards of crafts is naturally reflected in the quality of the labour pool from which management is forced to recruit staff members.

Absence of a spirit of competition

The continued progress of Western industrial societies can be largely attributed to the spirit of competition that pervades all walks of life. Starting from primary school and on through all stages of education, training and work, the citizens of these societies are spurred on by their competitive drive. It is this mechanism that allows advanced societies constantly to sift through their human resources for the best and most efficient elements who can lead society and push the wheel of progress forward. The spirit of competition is sadly lacking in Third World societies (as well as in those of the Second World), with the result that mediocrity has become the order of the day. Competing for excellence has been replaced by rivalry in forming cliques and power groups and in fomenting intrigues.

Unfamiliarity with the Western model of the executive manager

The idea of the executive manager, or CEO, so firmly established in the West, is unknown in Third World countries. In Western industrial societies, the executive manager is a person who has proved himself a generalist capable of achieving economic success for his organization and possessed of all the attributes of an effective manager.

In Third World societies, on the other hand, those who go by the title of manager are actually civil service staff totally unversed in the science of management in its contemporary sense. Advanced societies have turned their back on this model of the civil servant manager who has proved incapable of achieving economic success.

Weakness of professional training

One of the most effective formulae by which employee productivity can be maximized is the development of work-related skills through training. Most organizations in advanced industrial societies provide regular training programmes for their staff, which are a key element in the progress and development of these societies. The importance of training is poorly understood in Third World countries, where the civil servant mentality has give rise to such adverse side-effects as promotion by seniority regardless of merit. By developing the potentials of employees, training allows employers to pick the best among them for assignment to special tasks. The current state of the Egyptian labour force in general and of the technical labour force in particular makes it imperative to focus on training as the means by which society's potential for development can be unleashed.

Prevalence of the autocratic model of manager

In Third World countries, the autocratic style of management is predominant. Power is concentrated in the hands of the manager, who relegates those immediately below him in the chain of command to the status of lowly soldiers taking orders without question from their general. There are many reasons for the prevalence of this phenomenon, the most important being that in a society dominated by the civil servant mentality, top positions are all too often filled by incompetent people who could never have risen to positions of responsibility if advancement depended on competence. In fact, the refusal of the autocratic manager to delegate any of his powers is more revealing of his lack of confidence in his own abilities than it is of a lack of confidence in the abilities of others.

Tendency to personalize objective factors

In Eastern cultures, the lines of demarcation between the objective and the personal are often blurred. This curious phenomenon can be seen in any debate between people holding different viewpoints. Instead of arguing their case on the basis of its objective merits, we find them launching personal attacks against the proponent of the opposing point of view. Mixing the objective with the personal is a negative characteristic of tribal cultures that can be overcome only through raising the educational and cultural level of society as a whole.

The attitude to promotions

Promotion in our society proceeds according to outdated notions that need to be totally revolutionized. In the advanced world, promotion and leadership are no longer a function of seniority, age or chronological sequence of graduation or employment, but are based on ability and performance. In our society, on the other hand, age is unduly venerated, perhaps because of our long history. This perception of seniority must change if we are to progress.

Failure to differentiate between performance and potential

Research has clearly indicated that most managers in Third World countries do not distinguish between performance and potential. In advanced industrial societies a manager will try to appraise an employee's performance (that is determine how effective he is in attaining the goals of his actual job) separately from his potential (which is the possibilities of future advancement). High performance merits such rewards as raises, bonuses and moral appreciation but on its own is not grounds for promotion. What determines an employee's promotion is management's judgement of his potential. An employee with a high performance rating could lack the attributes necessary for his promotion to a higher level of responsibility.

Weakness of management system

Lack of discipline within an organizational framework is a major defect of Third World societies. It falls to effective management and the educational institution to remedy this defect and thereby remove one of the main obstacles in the way of progress.

Lack of assimilation of values governing industrial societies

The transition of Western countries from an agricultural to an industrial system, a process that began over two centuries ago, wrought radical changes in society, especially in what sociologists call the system of values. The Industrial Revolution brought with it a whole new set of values, headed by an enhanced appreciation of time, precision and productivity, values that today are firmly established in industrial societies.

One of the most pressing tasks of our educational institution is to implant these values in society. The notion of time in an agricultural society, where life revolves around the cycle of the seasons and the vagaries of nature, is much more fluid than it is in Western societies, where time is money and schedules and deadlines must be strictly observed. Until we adopt the values of industrial societies, we cannot effect the required changes in individual and group patterns of behaviour.

CHAPTER 13

Reflections on 'Buffoonery' and 'Failure'[70]

The heinous terrorist massacre that took the lives of a large number of foreigners and Egyptians in Luxor on 17 November 1997 is one of the worst attacks of its kind. Ironically, the mass killing coincided with my authoring of a scholarly work on the deficiencies of contemporary Egyptian thought and behaviour, which most Egyptians have become numb or unconscious to, although they seem obvious to Egypt's external observers.

As expected, the local press provided us with the customary dose of rhetoric and justifications in the aftermath of the attack. A divergent voice was heard, however, on the day after the crime by the Egyptian president during his visit to the scene of the carnage. He described the country's security arrangements with adjectives that were quite unfamiliar to the official vocabulary that often follows any terrorist incident. No sooner had the premier's visit ended, however, than a return to the traditional line of indignant justification swiftly followed.

This typical rhetorical stance sought to explain the attack in a number of ways that included but were not limited to: a Mossad conspiracy; US punishment for Egypt's valiant and nationalistic policies in the region; a reaction to Egypt's refusal to attend the Doha Economic Summit; that Egypt's prosperity is being targeted by its enemies; that terrorism is an international phenomenon: i.e. 'it could happen anywhere'; that Egypt's lucrative tourist industry is the target, and that despite the massacre, Egypt's lure to tourists will never cease. This is more or less the same line of thought that was perpetuated in the aftermath of previous terrorist attacks in Egypt, such as the attack on Greek tourists in 1996, and the murder of the German tourists in front of the Egyptian Museum a number of weeks ago.

Mubarak's approach on 18 November was therefore quite novel for an Egyptian leader, especially his description of Egypt's so-called security system as outright 'buffoonery', and that the officials in charge of its implementation had 'failed'. This was an unprecedented type of official discourse in a society that is not very receptive to self-criticism. That the top executive leader exemplified this level of earnest self-criticism by describing his own security apparatus as farcical and his law enforcement officers as failures is a very serious matter in a culture that does not easily stomach the admission of guilt.

For people like myself who have spent a substantial part of their careers in an international corporation, the president's words were not at all out of the ordinary, as it is the responsibility of any leader in any context not to belittle the seriousness of any crisis, and to be able to probe within himself and accept responsibility. Admitting that something is wrong is the first step towards creating new systems to prevent problems from recurring. This is the norm in advanced societies, and from our track record, it is quite obvious that our political culture has not yet digested this form of public accountability. In its place, convenient justifications are often quite suitable for our mental, cultural and psychological well-being. Egyptians always seek a comfortable justification where the suspect is always an 'external' party, and the internal element is always the victim.

As proof of this, Mubarak's castigation of his own men was not totally comprehended by the media, which hardly focused on this angle of the crisis and chose to highlight the incessant claim that terrorism was an international phenomenon. The implication here is that our society is still far from a cure, because as a patient, we have still not admitted our illness, as evident from the dearth of self-criticism in our public life. Like any such nefarious crime, the 17 November incident horrified all Egyptians, but they only heard the president's self-criticism, they did not understand it, therefore accentuating our traditional mode of rationalizing matters by refusing to accept responsibility. While the sacking of the Minister of the Interior and many of his top men may have been a subtle affirmation of this desperate need for accountability, the painful truth still remains that our political culture in general, and our educational, cultural and media policies in particular have rendered us unable critically to project deep inside ourselves. Unfortunately, the period of extensive public debate that followed the crime of 17 November, which should have focused on the two themes of buffoonery and failure as a premise for self-betterment, was unimaginatively driven in the same redundant vein of delusive justifications.

While the outlandish conspiracy theories that were circulated about the crime may have been true, the fact still remains that our security system was impotent, and had exhibited a large level of buffoonery and failure. Had the security of historical sites been serious and effective – despite the alleged involvement of the Mossad or the CIA – a massacre of this proportion could never have happened.

But perhaps what is more troubling is that this distorted attitude is not only limited to post-crisis situations, but manifests itself in a wide array of spheres where the inability to be self-critical has led us to subscribe to fantastic theories and justifications. Observers of the Egyptian scene are astonished at these mind-frames, especially when these justifications start from an illusory premise and soon develop into near truths. This was best exemplified by the public reaction to the death of the late Diana, Princess of Wales and her Egyptian friend Dodi al-Fayed, as discussed in an excellent analysis by the Egyptian sociologist Saad Eddin Ibrahim in the October 1997 issue of this publication (*Civil Society*).

Instead of looking for an external culprit to blame for our faults, the post-Luxor period should have witnessed a thorough review of where we stand and where to go next. Every terrorist attack, but especially the 1996 massacre mentioned above, is but another missed chance for us to identify the roots of the problem and develop a pre-emptive system that may have prevented this November's abhorrent crime.

While the political leadership must be commended for identifying the two themes of buffoonery and failure as roots of the problem, they are now in the unenviable position of combating this passive cultural trait of construing all of our problems as malicious external conspiracies. One must recall the proverb that says: 'When you point with your finger condemning, you may forget that whilst one finger points out at the condemned, three point at you.'

Part IV

Essays on the Imperative Fall of Socialism: A Critique of Marxism

Introduction

Three of my books have been published in Arabic, comprising a comprehensive exposé and critique of socialist theories and practices. The first was titled *Marxist Ideas in the Balance*, the second *Communism and Religion* and the third *My Experience with Marxism*. Although numerous editions of each of these books have been published during the past 15 years, I thought that I ought to select some of the chapters and translate them into English.

Part IV comprises eight chapters selected from my three books on Marxism with the aim of giving the reader who cannot read my 800-page three volumes on Marxism in Arabic an opportunity to whet his appetite for what could be described as a much larger work.

Tarek Heggy

CHAPTER 1

Marxism: Where To?[71]

Broadly speaking, all the elements in Marx's philosophy which are derived from Hegel are unscientific, in the sense that there is no reason whatever to suppose them true.
(Bertrand Russell, History of Western Philosophy, *George Allen and Unwin, London, 1961 edition, p. 754)*

Basic Marxist writings by Marx, Engels and Lenin, which expound what contemporary specialists refer to as 'orthodox Marxist theory', in fact comprise not one theory but several, which present, or attempt to present, a comprehensive and integrated system of philosophical, economic and socio-political views. This monolithic world outlook is what, in the final analysis, gives Marxist theory its totalitarian nature. Such an interconnection is the direct outcome of Hegel's dialectics, which reached Karl Marx by way of the German philosopher Ludwig Feuerbach, leader of the left-wing Young Hegelians who turned away from Hegel to form the school of dialectical materialism.

This interconnection between all the aspects of Marxist ideology not only gave Marxist intellectuals their totalitarian view, it is also the reason behind the present crisis of Marxism. A large part of the world began to apply a system entirely derived from this totalitarian and many-faceted ideology, which deals not only with the economic aspect of life but with all other aspects as well, soon after the Bolsheviks came to power in Russia some sixty years ago. Practical application proved that some of the fundamental and major aspects of orthodox Marxist theory did not follow the course they were theoretically supposed to.

The failure of socialist experiences to fulfil many expectations at all levels, along with other reasons to be mentioned further, led to the emergence of what has come to be known as Euro-communism. This movement, which started within the communist parties of Western Europe, then moved on to other communist parties in various countries around the world, rejected a number of orthodox Marxist premises and moved away from what had hitherto been the main objective of all communist parties, namely, to follow the Soviet model of building socialism.

Some Marxists are desperately trying to interpret the trend as being a natural evolution of the theory, as adjustments of non-essential aspects of Marxist thought, imposed by reality and experience in different parts of the world. Is it, however, really so? In fact, the adjustments were not limited to secondary concepts but touched on the very essence of Marxist thought. The theories challenged by the Eurocommunists are an integral part of the logical continuum of Marxist thought: a change in any of these theories necessarily calls into question the validity of those on which it is predicated as well as those for which it serves as a basis.

The collapse of those fundamental premises of Marxist ideology caused cracks in the very foundations of the theory and signalled the beginning of its end. Like many other positivist theories in man's history, it would eventually end up on history's shelves and in the museum of ideas,[72] having affected men's lives here and there, without being, in any way, the definitive, comprehensive and exclusive theory for human life!

This chapter presents the Arab reader with a critique of orthodox Marxist ideas which have been proved false both empirically and through critical analysis. The failure of these ideas in application led communist movements in several countries to abandon them, rejecting tenets which for orthodox or traditional Marxists are pillars on which the entire theory rests. This position constitutes a break in the totality of the ideology, whose exponents have always considered a 'package deal', as it were, to be adopted or rejected *in toto*. Events and experience have proved that history does not accept a positivist ideology in its entirety: for those segments of humanity who apply such an ideology, the experience does not last for more than a few years, almost a speck in the archives of man's history.

The present work offers an analytical presentation of the most important ideas and aspects of the Marxist theory that have been relegated, or which are in the process of being relegated, to the museum of human ideas. One of the first signs of its fall, as previously mentioned, was the emergence of Eurocommunism, which is diametrically opposed to the Marxist theory as expounded by the traditional Marxists, headed by Marx, Engels and Lenin.

Communist parties in industrially developed democratic countries have taken several steps towards moderation and, at long last, separation from the orthodox Marxist theory. The French youth who launched the 1968 student revolution in France saw their leaders turn away from Marxism. These leaders had been raised under the wing of dialectical materialist thought, particularly Marxism. After 1968, they gradually distanced themselves from Marxist thought, having acquired some experience and having come to intellectual maturity. Less than one decade after the May 1968 movement, they came to form the anti-Marxist current dubbed by European intellectuals 'the New Philosophers'.

Even though the New Philosophers do not, in fact, represent one single trend but several, they all agree that a totalitarian theory which presents a worldview encompassing all phenomena and all aspects of life, of which Marxism is the most striking example, must be rejected. Their rejection is based on a profound knowledge of Marxism, since it is within its fold that they were formed. The most renowned of the New Philosophers are Bernard Henri Levi, author of *Barbarity with a Human Face*, André Glucksman, author of *The Cook and the Cannibals*[73] and *The Masters of Thought* in which he criticizes the major German philosophers, and Jean-Marie Benoit, author of *Marx is Dead*. The fame of these New Philosophers spread widely in French cultural circles and beyond.

The Italian Communist Party, one of the most active communist parties in Europe and in all non-communist countries, also announced its rejection of some fundamental concepts of Marxism-Leninism. In fact, Lucio Lombardo, one of the outstanding intellectuals and theoreticians of the IPC, openly urged his party totally to abandon its support for Marxism-Leninism. In an interview in *La Stampa*, he says: 'The term "Marxism-Leninism" disappeared naturally from the Party's lexicon without being officially banned; the same is true of the term "dictatorship of the proletariat".'

In 1964, the Japanese Communist Party declared it was severing all ties with the Soviet Communist Party. Three years later, the Central Committee agreed in the course of its annual meeting to delete from the Party's charter the provision ruling that the objective of the Party was to achieve the Soviet model of dictatorship of the proletariat. The term 'Marxism-Leninism' was replaced by 'Scientific Socialism' and the idea of Proletarian Internationalism abandoned.

In Spain, the Secretary-General of the Spanish Communist Party, Santiago Carillo, publicly called for a brand of independent democratic socialism in Europe. The legendary President of the Party, Dolores Ibarruri, better known as La Passionaria, who had spent more than 30 years in the Soviet Union, declared openly that she did not want to see a repetition in her country of the Soviet experience she had come to know so well.

In India, large sections of the Communist Party call for adherence to a socialist policy independent of Moscow, one that would not follow in the footsteps of the Soviet experience.

In France, we are once again witnessing signs of a break in the coalition of the Left between the communists, the socialists and the radicals, which occurred before power became accessible.

In Portugal, the Left is losing power and popularity daily, and the possibility of their participation in a government coalition has become a dream.

In Britain, the Communist Party declared on 14 November 1977 that it had definitely abandoned the idea of 'dictatorship of the proletariat'.

The conclusion to be drawn from all this is that, for the developed countries, Marxist ideology has been stripped of its mystique. Unfortunately, the same cannot be said for Third World countries, where poor economic prospects coupled with low standards of general education provide an ideal breeding ground for ideas that have been discredited in the rest of the world. Those who succumb to the siren song of seasoned Marxist propagandists are usually students and young people and not the workers who are supposed to form the backbone of communist organizations. Because of their lack of experience, their poor cultural and scientific formation and their youth, these converts become mindless mouthpieces for a theory which, as far as the developed world is concerned, is merely a set of ideas put forward in the nineteenth century, no different from the scores of theories and ideas which that century produced, the only difference being that Marxism found a state where it was applied.[74]

The key word here is youth. The generation gap separating the young from their parents and grandparents is a phenomenon that dates back to the dawn of time. However, until recently, the gap took the form of aspirations by the rising generations to liberate themselves from the constraints placed on them by the older generation. In other words, the young rebelled against the way of life of their elders without a definite view of what was to replace it. And, before too long, they came to discover that the rebellion was no more than an expression of the physical and psychological malaise of puberty and adolescence.

That does not mean to say that everything old should be consecrated, but it is a fact that the refusal of the old by the young throughout the ages was a purely emotional refusal, lacking experience and understanding. Never in the history of mankind had the old been changed under the pressure of and in response to the wishes of the young.[75] Change always occurs under the pressure of generations with more knowledge and experience. Such was the situation before the appearance of Marxist ideology. Since that ideology was essentially a revolution against existing conditions, it became, for large numbers of young people, a philosophical framework for the perennial anxiety of the young and their age-old revolt against all that is established.

Thus the balance tipped in favour of Marxism – as a framework for the revolt and rejection of the young – because its call for radical change responded to aspirations held by the young since time immemorial. Moreover, Marxism's undisguised call for sexual freedom and for the abolition of the bourgeois family structure and its promise of sexual communism when the highest stage of communist society would be attained made it even more attractive to young people in all parts of the world.

In fact, the main response to Marxism, which set itself up as the theoretical expression of the fundamental interests of the working class, came not from that class but from educated youth. Clearly, this phenomenon is not a point in its favour. Quite the reverse, for the response was without substance as most of these young people had no real scientific knowledge of

Marxism. Both as a student and, later, as a university lecturer, I had the opportunity to meet many communist youth in several countries and to ascertain at first hand that, for the most part, their knowledge of the scientific bases of Marxism was woefully inadequate and that very few had read the basic literature that is vital to an understanding of this theory. For them, Marxism was no more than an intellectual and philosophical framework for their deep-rooted anti-Establishment feelings, not to mention the fact that it justified much of what it pleased them to see justified.

Thus, most of those who respond to the Marxist call are young people with little knowledge and less experience, whose ideas rapidly change as they mature and learn the realities of life through personal experience. If, for the sake of argument, we apply a Marxist approach, we could say that Marxism in the world spread among groups, mainly student groups, whose future class loyalties would inevitably and gradually draw them away from Marxist ideas. The spread of Marxist ideas within student circles is thus not to the credit of Marxism. For an ideology whose recruits are usually too young to know any better and who will, inevitably, turn away when they have gained some experience from life, cannot claim to be a successful, let alone a universal, ideology. There are, of course, exceptions, but exceptions, as we all know, prove the rule.

An additional factor that helped the spread of Marxist ideas among students was the intellectual stagnation and dogmatism of other ideological systems which could have offered viable alternatives to Marxism. Alienated by reactionary and old-fashioned ideas that could not keep up with the developments of the age, young people turned to Marxism.[76]

But while Marxism has come to be regarded in the developed states as no more than a set of ideas born in the nineteenth century, many of which have been proved wrong by experience, some of these ideas helped arouse interest in specific economic and social aspects and led many of these states to seek, albeit through completely different means, to provide for their needy classes to a degree not found in a single one of the states which have raised the red banner of communism.

Such major upheavals in the foundations of Marxist ideology have also led to the appearance of leftist movements, particularly in European communist parties. These movements too revise the basic postulates of orthodox Marxist theory. Actually, challenges to Marxism are not new. They accompanied and directly followed Marx and Engels, but the Bolshevik takeover in Russia suppressed such opposition from within the communist movement itself, for it seemed to some that the theory was about to become reality. But when time passed and experience proved that many of that theory's fundamental premises were invalid, intellectuals began to defect in droves.

The early revolts against Marxist ideas are well known. One of the most famous came from Eduard Bernstein (1850–1912), the German social democrat who was held in high regard by both Marx and Engels when he was editor of a well-known publication under Bismarck. Later, under the influence of British socialism, Bernstein gradually abandoned most of his Marxist ideas and criticized them sharply in his book, *Theoretical Socialism and Practical Socialism*, where he said that he had set for himself the task of purging Marxism of all ideas based on illusions. On another occasion, Bernstein called upon the party to 'have the courage to rid itself of ideas that have been overtaken by events'.[77]

In these chapters we will be presenting those Marxist ideas as expounded by the fathers of that theory, now bankrupt in our opinion. We will lay them bare of all proof and argument, and show that they cannot survive objective analysis based on logic, nor the practical experience of everyday life.

CHAPTER 2

The Dictatorship of the Proletariat[78]

I

One of the issues most closely associated with the transition to socialism is 'the dictatorship of the proletariat'. In Marxist theory, the transition to socialism is meant to come about through the eruption of the struggle between the bourgeoisie and the working class, or proletariat, whereby state power would pass into the hands of the proletariat. The latter would exercise its dictatorship until it triumphs over all the other classes which remain in society even after the proletariat assumes power as residuals of a long, deep-rooted past. During that phase, all power would be in the hands of the proletariat to enable it to accomplish its historic task, that of eliminating all classes antagonistic to the working class.[79] Once it has accomplished its mission, its dictatorship will come to an end, since no other classes will exist and the state apparatus will fall, along with the entire system of laws, when all men (those who remain!) will have attained the highest stage of communism.

Briefly, that is the idea of the 'dictatorship of the proletariat', its rationale, functions and fate. To show how basic this idea is to the whole structure of Marxist ideology, and to leave no room for the argument that its repudiation is a development within the framework of the Marxist theory itself and not a blatant contradiction of its very foundations, let us turn to the words of Marx himself.

In a letter postmarked London, Karl Marx wrote to Joseph Wiedmeyer in New York on 5 March 1852, affirming that 'The class struggle necessarily leads to the dictatorship of the proletariat.'[80] Twenty-three years later, in his *Critique of the Gotha Programme* published in 1875, he wrote: 'Between capitalist and communist society lies the period of the revolutionary transition of the one into the other. There corresponds to this also a political transition period in which the state can be nothing but the revolutionary dictatorship of the proletariat.'[81] Communist leaders in many parts of the world still declare their total adherence to that belief; some even hold that the dictatorship of the proletariat must continue beyond the transition to socialism, as long as capitalism remains strong in the world.[82]

II

Contemporary socialist experiments are still at the stage of the dictatorship of the proletariat. However, nowhere has the proletariat come to power through a long struggle against capitalism, nor through the eruption of the struggle in the form of a violent workers' revolution. Rather, it has always seized power either through military coups or through takeovers by communist parties supported by Soviet military presence, and then in countries that did not go through the stage of capitalist development in the orthodox Marxist sense of the word.

In other words, the accession to power by these dictatorships did not proceed in the manner envisaged by Marx. Another glaring discrepancy between the theory he expounded and its application in practice is that not one of the dictatorships of the proletariat existing in countries of the socialist bloc can claim to have been established by the working class. In the Soviet Union, for example, the leaders of the Bolshevik Party all came either from the middle or upper-middle class. Trotsky, Zinoviev, Kamenev, Kaganovitch and other Bolshevik leaders who laid the foundations of the dictatorship of the proletariat in the Soviet Union were all middle-class intellectuals, many of them Russian Jews from professional and merchant families. The same applies to those who created dictatorships of the proletariat in the rest of the socialist countries, including those in the Third World. In Cuba, for example, the dictatorship of the proletariat was established by members of the upper-middle class, by the sons of rich families who had been sent to European capitals for their studies, a great luxury in such poor societies.

What does dictatorship of the proletariat really mean? According to Marxists, it is a dictatorship exercised by the majority in the interest of the majority and against all the classes and groups opposed to those interests. If that is so, why is the majority represented at the higher echelons of the Communist Party by only a few who are selected in a particular manner? Why does the majority in its entirety not enter into the Communist Party, especially since Marxists absolutely reject the idea of representational democracy which is the basis of the Western parliamentary system? Why, if not for the fact that their dictatorship is directed against the proletariat itself in the name of the proletariat. Can anyone maintain that Stalin's regime of violent repression was directed only against the non-proletarian classes in the Soviet Union and that it did not affect the entire population? In fact, the leadership of this regime, like that of every other dictatorship of the proletariat, was made up of members of the middle class who took it upon themselves to protect the interests of the working class in the face of all other classes.

An important development in this respect is that communist parties in most of the industrialized countries, the very climate for socialism according to Marxist theory, have, one after the other, abandoned the idea of dictatorship of the proletariat,[83] declaring that the transition to socialism does not have to come about through class struggle and that, if they ever came to power, they would not establish a dictatorship of the proletariat to abolish all other classes.

To destroy the idea of dictatorship of the proletariat is to destroy the backbone of Marxist political thought as elaborated by Marx, Engels, Lenin and all other Marxist theoreticians over a whole century. For without the dictatorship of the proletariat, the other classes will not be abolished and, consequently, humanity will not attain a classless society. As Marx himself had firmly rejected the idea of 'the free people's state' advocated by Ferdinand Lassalle, this meant the collapse of the following basic tenets of Marxist thought:

- The class struggle (given that, after coming to power, the proletariat would coexist peacefully with other social classes).
- The withering away of the state (since the proletariat would not liquidate the other classes, and the class division of society is the basis for the existence of the state).
- The disappearance of laws (the existence of laws, like the existence of the state, is based on the existence of classes).
- Attainment of the supreme communist stage (unimaginable in Marxist thought without the dictatorship of the proletariat and its liquidation of all other classes).

The repudiation of this basic tenet of Marxist thinking by the communist parties of Western Europe and other parts of the developed world is due to several factors.

First, the democratic climate prevailing in Europe. Western Europe is solidly anchored in parliamentary democracy, in freedom of thought and opinion and in all other human rights and hence, by its very nature, cannot subscribe to any theory that would destroy such democracy and freedoms. This climate of freedom and democracy has imposed itself even on the communist parties of Western Europe and on the staunchest supporters of Marxism in Western Europe[84] and in other parts of the world, such as Japan.

It may have been easy for the peoples of Russia, the Ukraine, Georgia, Siberia or the Caucasus to accept a dictatorship of the proletariat 60 years ago, or to accept the crimes of a tyrant like Stalin who liquidated scores of his closest comrades and millions of those who opposed his views.[85] After all, they were peoples who had known nothing but autocratic rulers and slavery through the centuries.[86] The history of tsarist Russia is a chronicle of brutal repression: one example that comes to mind here is the story of Spiratsky, the nineteenth-century Russian minister who tried to introduce French laws into Russia and who was exiled to Siberia for his pains! For a nation whose historical frame of reference is a saga of harsh dictatorships, the dictatorship of the proletariat was no more than a new name for an age-old pattern.

The communist parties of Western Europe are far more aware than leftist movements in the Third World of the negative consequences that will inevitably follow on the establishment of a dictatorship of the proletariat in their countries. They know that they can come to power only through a coalition with other parties and that there can be no question of those parties accepting a dictatorship of the proletariat. Thus they would have nowhere to turn for help but to the Soviets and, given the liberalism of the leaders of communist parties in Western Europe (their birthright as citizens of a democratic civilization), as well as the lessons drawn from the recent past, this is unlikely to be an attractive prospect.

Western Europe has not forgotten the lessons learnt from the Soviet invasion of Hungary and Czechoslovakia, from Soviet exploitation of the economies of Eastern Europe and from Tito's experience with the Soviets when he aspired to a degree of independence for his country. Not only was he expelled from the Cominform, but Yugoslavia was subjected to strong economic pressure from the Soviet Union and other member countries of the Comecon.[87] There are many other examples attesting to the perils of falling out with the Soviets.[88]

Second, the failure of this basic tenet of Marxist ideology to move from the realm of the theoretical to that of the applied. The socialist experience has proved to the communist parties of Western Europe and other parts of the developed world that the elimination by the proletariat of all other classes and its attainment of the highest stage of communism when there will be no antagonistic classes, no state and no law, but one single class living in peace, was no more than wishful thinking, a naive illusion that has not materialized nor shows the slightest indication of ever doing so in any part of the world. Classes still exist in the socialist countries, albeit under new guises, the state has become stronger and more centralized, laws are gradually coming closer to West European legal theories and many other Marxist expectations appear to be as illusory and elusive as the utopian dreams of Thomas More.

One such expectation, confidently predicted by Lenin in 1917, was that World War I would put such unbearable pressure on the industrial capitalist states that the only way out of the crisis would be through the proletarian revolution. Events have since proved the fallacy of that analysis and we have yet to see a proletarian revolution in any large industrial state.[89] Another such expectation, announced by the well-known Bolshevik

Zinoviev in 1918, was that within one year all of Europe would become communist![90] Only one year earlier, Zinoviev, together with Kamenev, considered that the bourgeois Russian Revolution of March 1917 should not transcend its historical limits and become a proletarian revolution too rapidly on the grounds that such a revolution would fail without the support of a general communist revolution in Western Europe!

The expectation that a proletarian revolution would break out in all parts of Europe was not confined to Lenin and Zinoviev; it was shared by all the leaders of the Bolshevik revolution and by all European communists.[91, 92] That preposterous expectation persisted until the early 1930s, when it became clear to the communist movement in Russia and throughout the world that a proletarian revolution in Western Europe or anywhere else in the developed capitalist world was an impossibility. Having come to that conclusion, they had to revise their views on other matters as well. Thus, after holding that the building of socialism in Russia was dependent on the revolutions to be led by Western workers, they now claimed that it was the latter who needed the Russian experience to sustain, assist and support them.

This new rationale marked the beginning of a new relationship between Soviet Russia and the West. The Soviet Union had to ensure its security in a world that did not seem to be moving, as had been expected, towards a proletarian revolution. Stalin signed several treaties with Germany, then with the allies after World War II, in a bid to expand his boundaries and set up a wall of socialist states to serve as a buffer between the Soviet Union and Western Europe. At a later stage, starting in the 1970s, the Soviet Union sought a *modus vivendi* with the West, deferring its old dream to some distant future and resorting to covert methods of operation.

One European Marxist who did not share the belief of Marxist leaders in the Soviet Union and throughout Europe that capitalism was about to collapse, that the proletarian revolution was about to break out and that the dictatorship of the proletariat would be established in capitalist Europe, was Antonio Gramsci, Secretary-General of the Italian Communist Party, who was imprisoned in 1928 and died in prison in 1937. He showed a more realistic grasp of the situation when he said that the path of the Western proletariat towards power and dictatorship was fraught with defeat.

Third, the disappearance from the developed countries of the working class described by Engels in *The Condition of the Working Class in England* and on whom Marx focused all his studies. The proletariat Marx and Engels knew in the nineteenth century was an exploited working class performing hard manual labour in difficult and primitive working conditions, totally devoid of any guarantees or social security. Such a class no longer exists in the industrialized capitalist world[93], as it did in Munich, Lyon, Manchester, Leeds, London and other large industrial cities of the nineteenth century. There is no longer any trace of those workers in today's factories, where there is no proletariat in the technical sense of the term but, rather, employees engaged for the most part in non-manual work.

In conclusion, the proletariat which toiled under such unspeakable conditions in the last century is a class that does not exist in the industrialized capitalist countries of our age, where technological advances are ushering in an age of industry without workers, where mental work will replace the manual work performed by Marx's proletariat.

A visit to any factory in a large industrial city today will corroborate the fact that today's working conditions are nothing like those that prevailed in the nineteenth century, that an entire system of social guarantees and security is provided to the workers of today, one that is certainly not enjoyed by their counterparts in the industrialized socialist countries. Consequently, there is no need for the communist parties of Western Europe to advocate the dictatorship of a class that no longer exists in developed capitalist systems.

Fourth, the disintegration of the idea of dictatorship of the proletariat is also due to an important economic fact, namely, that the economic hopes pinned by the early Marxist theoreticians on the stages during which the proletariat would be in control have failed to materialize. Marxists believe that between capitalism and communism, societies will go through a transitional stage, the post-capitalist socialist stage. During that transitional stage, the workers, through the dictatorship of the proletariat, would control all aspects of life, including the economy. They would strive to achieve greater growth to realize maximum productivity, the material basis for the establishment of the higher stage of communism, for it is through the realization of such maximum productivity that society can move from the socialist principle of 'each according to his work' to the communist principle of each 'according to his need'.

It is a fact that the dictatorship of the proletariat in Soviet Russia has not realized that dream. Even the progress achieved by the Soviet Union today, in comparison with the conditions which obtained in Russia prior to the Bolshevik revolution, cannot be considered an achievement of the dictatorship of the Soviet proletariat.

The capacity of the dictatorship of the Soviet proletariat can be measured only in terms of the level of growth reached by the Soviet economy (i.e. the level of development of productive forces) in the early days of World War II, because it is only up to that point in time that the growth of the Soviet economy can be credited solely to Soviet economic orientations. Whatever progress was achieved after the war is due to other factors we shall come to further on.

In the period between 1917 and 1941, the Soviet economy achieved noticeable growth. Yet the degree of growth cannot be compared to that of the Western world nor even to the present rate of growth achieved by the Soviet Union. It was closer to the present rate of growth in the countries of Eastern Europe. Thus while the dictatorship of the Soviet proletariat did achieve a certain degree of progress because of economic planning and the protection of the new regime, that progress was never up to the level of what the Soviet Union achieved after the war. It had also begun to slow down noticeably just before the war, when Soviet industry began to slacken in the mid-1930s in terms of investments and development rates. Investments which had been growing until 1936 began to decrease systematically, as indicated by the statistics shown in Table 2.1.

TABLE 2.1

Year	Volume of Investments
1933	2,350 million roubles
1934	2,552 " "
1936	4,621 " "
1937	3,621 " "
1938	3,807 " "

Investment in the iron and steel industry alone (by far the most important of the heavy industries) decreased by 35 per cent from 1935 to 1936. This downward trend continued until the late 1930s.[94] Figures definitely point to growth between 1917 and 1936, but to a rate of growth not comparable to that attained by the Soviet Union after the war. Moreover, growth receded from the mid-1930s to the beginning of the war. The decline continued during the war, but that was due to a concentration on the war industries and to the huge losses in factories and agricultural land incurred as a result of the sweeping German invasion.

So much for the economic achievements of the dictatorship of the Soviet proletariat before the World War II. As to the development of the Soviet economy after the war, this was due to several factors:

- the enormous quantities of raw materials obtained at very low prices from the East European countries which had become Soviet satellites;[95]
- the transfer of hundreds of factories from Germany to the Soviet Union;[96]
- the two million qualified Germans who were brought over to work in all areas of Soviet production,[97] particularly in the chemical and military industries;
- the financial aid extended by the West (especially the United States), which also sent great quantities of goods and machinery to the Soviet Union during the last period of the war and immediately after. The assistance was estimated to be worth billions of dollars;[98]
- the great wealth obtained from Manchuria after its evacuation by the Japanese;[99]
- the annexation of neighbouring territories rich in mines and raw materials.

The thirteen European provinces annexed by the Soviet Union immediately after the war covered a total area of more than 270,000 square miles, an area greater than the Iberian Peninsula, while the Asian provinces of Manchuria were extremely rich in mineral wealth and water.[100]

From the above, it is clear that the economic performance

of the dictatorship of the Soviet proletariat can be divided into two distinct stages. A first stage of steady progress was followed by a decline just before World War II. The progress itself was modest and far from what had been expected from the dictatorship of the proletariat. It was noticeable only because Russia was so far behind the countries of Europe. At any rate, it was not an encouraging sign for the European Marxists, who found little in the economic performance of the dictatorship of the proletariat in the Soviet Union or, for that matter, in any country of Eastern Europe, to justify the expectation that this dictatorship could realize the material basis for the establishment of the higher phase of communism.

A second stage of far greater progress was not, however, due to the intrinsic strength of the Soviet system but, rather, to many external factors without which the Soviet economy would have totally collapsed. This is not an idle assertion but one that is substantiated by facts. The first is the enormous difference between the economic performance of the Soviet Union in the period between 1917 and 1941 and its performance in the post-war period up to the present day. Where during the first period progress was slow and nearly ground to a halt as the momentum of the revolution waned, in the second period it surged forward in leaps and bounds. This dramatic upsurge can be explained only by the external factors we have mentioned, whose role in bolstering the Soviet economy cannot be over-emphasized. Second, the countries of Eastern Europe, which did not benefit from the exceptional circumstances available to the Soviet Union after World War II but had to fall back on their own resources, have been able to generate only minimal economic growth, their modest economies able to provide their peoples only with the bare necessities, exactly the same situation that existed in the Soviet Union before the war.

That is not to say that even at the present rate of growth of the Soviet economy the standard of living of a Soviet citizen is not far below that of an ordinary citizen in any advanced industrial country. He is still far from obtaining what a simple worker in those countries has access to in the way of basic necessities, let alone luxuries. It may be useful to give the reader an idea of the standard of living in an advanced industrial country to show that the Soviet experience, at least in its economic aspect, was not an encouraging example to follow for societies which had far surpassed the inferior living standard of the Soviet citizen centuries before.

Between 1950 and 1975, the following developments took place in France:

- pensions were quadrupled;
- 8.5 million new housing units were built;
- the number of families owning a washing machine rose from near 0 per cent to 70 per cent;
- the number of families owning a TV set rose from near 0 per cent to 90 per cent;
- in 1953, only 8 per cent of workers owned a private car; by 1972, the percentage of car-owning working-class families rose to 66 per cent;
- in 1953, 32 per cent of civil servants owned private cars; by 1972, the percentage had risen to 86 per cent;
- in 1953, 56 per cent of senior civil servants owned private cars; by 1972, the percentage had risen to 87 per cent;
- in 1975, there were six times as many high-school graduates as in 1950;
- between 1950 and 1974, France created 5.35 million new jobs in the fields of industry and commerce;
- despite the apparent steep increase in prices between 1956 and 1976, the price of food is considered to have decreased from 100 to 53, while the prices of manufactured goods decreased from 100 to 41.5, bearing in mind the increase in incomes, e.g., equipment that a Frenchman could have obtained in 1956 at the cost of 100 hours, he obtained in 1976 at the cost of only 41.5 hours; and
- in 1975, half of the French people owned their homes.[101]

According to the statistics of the Soviet state itself, the Soviet people do not enjoy 10 per cent of the comforts enjoyed by the French people. While the above statistics speak for themselves, two observations are in order here.

First, the failure of the dictatorship of the proletariat to achieve anywhere near as high a standard of living as that achieved under the capitalist systems of Western Europe led European communists to question the validity of this key section of Marxist-Leninist theory. Second, the French statistics show to what extent social classes are drawing closer together: whereas the percentage of car-owners among senior civil servants rose by 21 per cent between 1953 and 1972, it rose by 55 per cent among the working class during the same period.

These statistics not only indicate a rapprochement between the proletariat and the bourgeoisie, they also disprove one of Marx's pet theories, namely, that industrial societies are divided into only two classes: a poor class which works and does not own (the proletariat) and a rich class which owns and does not work (the capitalist class). All other classes are reduced to the level of the proletariat, which would be getting ever poorer while the capitalist bourgeoisie would become ever richer. The French statistics turn this theory on its head: it seems the proletariat is catching up with the privileges of the upper classes, that it is getting richer, not poorer, and that it is getting richer at a rate that is bringing it ever closer to the bourgeoisie, contrary to Marx's predictions.[102]

Finally, in a shrinking world where the tremendous development of the communications industry makes it impossible to keep any situation secret, the walls with which the Soviet Union surrounded itself for so long have come crashing down. As a result, the working classes in the advanced industrial countries are now well aware that their situation is far better, both economically and politically, than that of their counterparts in the socialist countries.

The shattering of the great economic hopes placed in the dictatorship of the proletariat was the main factor that led to the collapse of the idea itself, as workers in the advanced industrialized countries asked themselves how the deprivation they see their brothers suffering from in the socialist countries can ever become the material basis for the higher stage of communism, when each will get according to his needs.

In addition to all the above, communist parties in several parts of the world rejected the idea of the dictatorship of the proletariat as totally inappropriate for the non-industrial societies of Asia and Africa in which communists did manage to seize power. With peasants and farmers representing the majority of the population, the formula of a dictatorship of the proletariat seemed contrived and essentially flawed. This led several agricultural countries under communist rule, China being the most notable example, to introduce changes into the Marxist theory which, in our opinion, have shaken it to its very foundations. One is entitled to question how there could be a dictatorship of the proletariat in countries where there are no workers in the Marxist sense of industrial workers, and where an entire stage in the socio-economic evolution of society as advocated by Marx has been skipped, namely, the stage of capitalism out of the womb of which socialism is born.[103]

CHAPTER 3

Eurocommunism[104]

In this chapter, I shall try to present the main features of Eurocommunism, which has recently become the dominant trend in the communist parties of developed industrialized countries. The basic tenets forming the body of Marxist doctrine have been subjected to critical review in the preceding chapters of this book.[105] The rise of Eurocommunism confirms the validity of the thesis put forward in these chapters, which is that, one after another, these basic tenets are being abandoned by European communists disenchanted with the performance of communist parties in power in various countries.

The best exposition of the main features and orientations of the Eurocommunist movement was made by Santiago Carillo in *'Eurocommunism' and the State*. The ideas in the book represent not only the author's personal views but also those of the Spanish Communist Party and the other European communist parties, all of which, particularly those in France, Italy, Britain and Japan,[106] have fully supported them. No better proof of the importance of this work exists than that the Soviet Union was concerned enough to publish an official reply to the ideas raised by Carillo.

On a number of specific issues, the Eurocommunist movement has adopted positions very different from, not to say incompatible with, those of orthodox Marxism. It is my purpose here to highlight some of the most prominent of these issues:

1. abandoning the orthodox Marxist vision of the socialist political regime;

2. abandoning the orthodox Marxist view of accession to power;
3. rejecting the Marxist call to abolish private property and advocating the coexistence of public and private property (while recognizing profit not derived from labour);
4. espousing the cause of democracy and human rights, and accepting political pluralism;
5. advocating autonomy for individual parties within world communism and abandoning the idea of emulating the Soviet model for achieving socialism (in fact, criticizing several aspects of the Soviet experience); and
6. no longer adhering strictly to the traditional Marxist conception of the proletariat.

The detailed exposition of these points given below will reveal the gap between the orthodox Marxist thought still prevailing in the countries of the socialist bloc on the one hand and that developed by the Eurocommunists and prevailing in the communist parties of the developed industrialized countries on the other.

First, abandoning the orthodox Marxist vision of the socialist political regime, i.e. abandoning the idea of the dictatorship of the proletariat and all the ideas related thereto, such as the elimination of all the classes standing against it, the withering away of the state, etc. Traditional Marxists believe that when societies reach the stage of capitalism, they become polarized into two classes: an exploiting class made up of capitalist owners, and an exploited class made up of workers. With time, the former class becomes richer through increasing profits while the latter becomes poorer. Gradually, the working class develops an awareness of its strength as it comes to realize how necessary it is to the exploiting class. Workers begin to form unions and to intensify their struggle, and confrontations between the two classes set in. With each confrontation, the proletariat acquires greater gains and becomes stronger. However, there comes a point when the capitalists refuse to grant the demands of the workers and the contradictions between them flare up into violent confrontation. The workers' revolution explodes and the proletariat seizes the reins of power, destroys the bourgeois machinery of state and establishes its dictatorship. The main task of the dictatorship of the proletariat is to eliminate all other classes, particularly those whose interests are antagonistic to its own. Once the proletariat has accomplished its task and society becomes one single class, the old form of the state gradually disappears and the state as such withers away.

That particular Marxist axiom is now totally rejected by the communist parties of the developed industrial states. In fact, the notion of dictatorship of the proletariat was one of the main points of contention between them and what can be termed the official communist parties in the Soviet Union and its satellite countries, which adhere closely to orthodox Marxist views on this and other questions.

Santiago Carillo devoted the longest chapter in '*Eurocommunism*' *and the State* to the concept of dictatorship of the proletariat. As it would be difficult to reproduce everything Carillo said on the subject, we shall content ourselves here with one passage in which he clearly dismisses this formula as a necessary form of government when communists come to power.

Carillo says:

> On the other hand, I am convinced that the dictatorship of the proletariat is not the way to succeed in establishing and consolidating the hegemony of the forces of the working people in the democratic countries of developed capitalism. In the first part of this essay, I have already tried to explain why I am convinced that in these latter countries socialism is not only the decisive broadening and development of democracy, the negation of any totalitarian conception of society, but that the way to reach it is along the democratic road, with all the consequences which this entails. In this sphere, and at the risk of being accused of heresy, I am convinced that Lenin was no more than half right when he said: 'The transition from capitalism to communism, naturally, cannot fail to provide an immense abundance and diversity of political forms, but the essence of all of them will necessarily be a single one: the dictatorship of the proletariat.' He was no more than half right because the essence of all the various political forms of transition to socialism is, as we can judge today, the hegemony of the working people, while the diversity and abundance of political forms likewise entails the possibility of the dictatorship of the proletariat not being necessary.[107]

Carillo mentions that Dimitrov[108] also supported the idea that it is possible to reach socialism without the dictatorship of the proletariat.[109] Elsewhere, Carillo refers to the position adopted by the renowned French Marxist philosopher, Louis Althusser, on the same issue when he described the Marxist theory on the state as misleading.[110]

That same position was expressed by Lucio Lombardo when he declared in the pages of *La Stampa* that the Italian Communist Party no longer raised the slogan of Marxism-Leninism and that it had abandoned the idea of the dictatorship of the proletariat.

In rejecting the idea of the dictatorship of the proletariat, the Eurocommunists obviously reject all the ideas related to it, such as the elimination of the enemies of the working class, which Marxism considers to be the main task of the dictatorship of the proletariat when it assumes power. In fact, European communists criticize the mechanism of repression that continues to dominate everything in the Soviet Union and in the countries of the socialist bloc.[111]

Similarly, European communists refute the idea of the withering away of the state as an outcome, in traditional Marxist theory, of the dictatorship of the proletariat. According to the theory, the dictatorship of the proletariat is established in the period of transition from capitalism (where the state exists) to communism (where it will have ceased to exist). The dictatorship of the proletariat is a necessary condition for the withering away of the state which, as an instrument of political power by which one class dominates another, or others, will have no reason to exist when the dictatorship of the proletariat will have fulfilled its main task of creating a classless society.

The European communists have also abandoned the notion of violent seizure of power, and speak now of socialism coming to power peacefully, within the constitutional framework of democratic life, through the legitimate channels provided by the existing bourgeois state.

With so many of the notions standing at the doctrinal core of Marxism as an omniscient and irreducible world outlook being discarded by the European communists, what remains then of Marxist political thought? The objective answer can only be: nothing!

Second, abandoning the orthodox Marxist view of accession to power. Orthodox Marxists believe they cannot come to power through parliamentary means, since they consider parliamentary life to be a game practised by the economically dominant classes to imbue their political domination with legitimacy. Accession to power, in the view of these orthodox Marxists, can come about only through the organized struggle of the proletariat against the capitalist class. In this long struggle, the proletariat would seize greater and greater gains until matters come to a head with the outbreak of the violent workers' revolution which will break down the bourgeois state machine and instal the dictatorship of the proletariat in its stead. Obviously, then, accession to power in Marxist theory is synonymous with, one, the dictatorship of the proletariat and, two, revolutionary violence.[112]

However, some Marxists claim that the shift by communists in the advanced industrial countries from the idea of the transition to socialism through the revolutionary violence of the proletariat to the idea of a peaceful transition within the framework of parliamentary life is nothing more than a development in Marxist thinking, similar to developments in its other aspects. Anyone with any knowledge of Marxism cannot accept such a claim. It is impossible to reconcile Marxist ideology the idea of a peaceful transition to socialism, because the idea of violent revolution is central to the Marxist theory.

The struggle between the proletariat and the bourgeoisie, culminating in the workers' revolution, will lead to the destruction of the bourgeois machinery of state. There is thus an undeniable link between class struggle and the transition to socialism through violent means. One cannot exist without the other and the removal of either from the structure of Marxist ideology entails the removal of both. And, as class struggle is the cornerstone on which the ideology is built, its removal would bring the whole edifice of Marxism crashing down.

Nor can the idea of transition to socialism through violent means be separated from the idea of dictatorship of the proletariat, inasmuch as such a dictatorship can be established only through violent means. It is difficult to imagine the capitalist class, the dominant class in the stage of capitalism, calmly handing over the reins of power to the working class! And, as the dictatorship of the proletariat is the bridge on which history moves towards the higher stage of communism, without this dictatorship, communism cannot be attained.

To speak now of socialism coming to power within the parliamentary system, i.e. through free elections, is to admit that there will not be a dictatorship of the proletariat, the necessary precondition for the higher stage of communism. Unless, of course, the acceptance of a parliamentary transition to socialism by European communist parties is but a tactical stratagem to enable them to come to power and, once there, to eliminate all other parties and tendencies.

Those Marxists who are trying to reconcile Marxism as a theory with the idea of a peaceful, i.e. parliamentary, transition to socialism, may be communists from the organizational point of view or in terms of their ideological affiliations, but they are far from possessing a comprehensive understanding of Marxism.[113] Otherwise they would know that a peaceful transition to socialism, with all this implies in the way of main-taining other political parties regardless of their tendencies and the class interests they represent, abandoning the idea of dictatorship of the proletariat, etc., is in direct contradiction of the main conclusions drawn by Marx in his study on the Paris Commune, *The Civil War in France*, 1871. According to Marx, the greatest mistake committed by the communards was that, having achieved their revolution through violent action and seized the machinery of the bourgeois state, they then failed to destroy it. Throughout, he stresses how important it is that the machinery of the bourgeois state be destroyed as soon as the proletariat comes to power. The idea of a peaceful transition to socialism also runs counter to the views of Engels, who believed that the state, as an institution, does not disappear immediately following the proletarian revolution; that what is eliminated is the bourgeois state, to be replaced by the socialist state represented by the dictatorship of the proletariat which, in its turn, dissolves of itself and disappears.

Thus the transition to socialism through violent revolutionary action by the proletariat is one of the cornerstones of the Marxist ideological structure, and its rejection represents a definitive crack in that structure, a crack which has become 'official' as the communist parties in all the advanced capitalist countries publicly declare that 'violence' and 'the proletarian revolution' are no longer necessary for the accession by communists to power.

Third, rejecting the Marxist call to abolish private property and advocating long-term coexistence between the two forms of ownership: public and private.[114]

Carillo makes a point of showing that in advocating the above, the European communists are going against traditional Marxist tenets. He says:

> The coexistence of forms of public and private ownership means acceptance of unearned increment and the private appropriation of part of this, i.e. a mixed system.[115, 116]

He goes on to say that taxes are the means by which society can obtain its share of those profits. That is where he comes close to Fabian socialism and the British Labour Party. After warning that those taxes should not be such as to discourage private projects,[117] Carillo notes that the owners of private projects should have the right to organize themselves, not only economically but also in a political party or parties representative of their interests.[118] This, he affirms, would be one of the component parts of the political and ideological pluralism he advocates in contradistinction to the traditional Marxist position on the question of private property and political and ideological pluralism.

These ideas, which Carillo shares with his fellow Eurocommunists, deal a decisive blow to the most important economic theory in Marxism, the theory of labour as value and, hence, to the theory of surplus value based on it. For we know that Marx and all traditional Marxists recognize labour as the sole source of value and profit and consider any other source to be economic and social 'exploitation', whereas Carillo openly advocates the acceptance of value not derived from labour.

Fourth, adopting democratic values and political pluralism and rejecting traditional Marxist perceptions of the Western model of parliamentary democracy. The call by European communists for a socialism to be built within the framework of democracy, with a multi-party system and an alternation of parties in power, represents a clear departure from the classical Marxist line. Not only that, but the communist parties of Europe are openly critical of the Soviet model. Under the heading of 'Soviet Thinking and the Democratic Road', Carillo says:

> I can already hear doctrinaire people crying out that this is sheer reformism. That does not frighten me. Let us take a look at the socialist countries which have carried out the revolution along a classical road. The greater part of them have already experienced whole decades with the new regime, and while the taking of power was carried out at an extremely rapid tempo from the historical point of view, the economic and social transformation is proceeding at a much slower pace. Examples of inequality still continue. There are vital problems, such as the standard of living and the supplying of the population with goods and foodstuffs, which cannot be considered solved. Problems of productivity, of participation, are on the agenda. And there remains the great unsolved question – that of democracy, and social contradictions which a one-sided propaganda hides but does not solve.[119]

The issue of democracy comes in for a great deal of attention on the part of Carillo, who concludes that there is a fundamental contradiction in Marxist thought concerning the idea of democracy. Whereas Engels exalts the wonders of the democracy which existed simply and spontaneously during the stage of primitive communism, we find other leading Marxists, headed by Lenin, affirming that democracy is a form of government linked to the division of society into classes. Lenin considered democracy to be a state system that recognizes the subordination of the minority by the majority, i.e. an organization for the systematic use of force by one class against another.

Carillo considers this characterization of democracy by Lenin to be somewhat obscure,[120] noting that:

> In the argumentation provided by Lenin on this subject in *The Proletarian Revolution and the Renegade Kautsky*, there are aspects which (also) lend themselves to confusion, since it is stated that ... in communist society, democracy will wither away in the process of changing and becoming a habit, but will never be 'pure' democracy.

Commenting on Lenin's words, Carillo says:

> Perhaps democracy will never succeed in becoming pure – it would be necessary to examine closely what pure democracy is – but if it is 'modified' and becomes a habit, it seems contradictory to deduce that because of this it withers away. What is transformed into a habit remains and becomes habitual.

To underline the obscurity of Lenin's ideas on the subject, Carillo mentions that in his book, *The State and the Revolution*, Lenin affirms that complete democracy will be possible only under communism.[121]

In several parts of his book, Carillo proclaims the commitment of the Eurocommunists to democracy and freedoms. One passage is worth quoting here:

> But the roads we propose – the winning of a socialism which would maintain and enrich the democratic political liberties and human rights which are historic achievements of human progress that cannot be surrendered, and the imparting to them, furthermore, of a new economic and social dimension – for the realization of this ideal, it is not enough to rid ourselves of some of the formulas coined by our theorists, such as that of the dictatorship of the proletariat; or that we should affirm our respect for the democratic process …[122]

This public commitment to the cause of democracy, in which Carillo is joined by all the communist parties of Western Europe, underscores the important role played by the historical and cultural frame of reference in which these parties operate. As we pointed out earlier in this book, it is easy for the Soviet people to accept tyranny and the suppression of all public freedoms as just another link in an unbroken chain of suffering under such absolute rulers as Ivan III, Ivan the Terrible, Peter the Great, Anne, Elizabeth and Catherine I.[123] However, that is not the case for the peoples of developed industrial countries in Western Europe and other parts of the world, who have fought long and hard to obtain public freedoms and rights. With democracy being an integral part of their cultural heritage, it is natural that they should be repelled – even the communists among them – by an ideology that proscribes these public freedoms and rights.

The European communists are not only advocating democracy and pluralism as the values that should govern society at large, they are calling for the application of these values to the internal organization of the communist parties themselves, which had been patterned on the Soviet model. They denounce the undemocratic practices inherited from the Leninist-Stalinist party structure, and call for free and democratic party elections and debates.[124]

Fifth, advocating autonomy for individual parties within world communism[125] and abandoning the idea of emulating the Soviet model for achieving socialism[126] (in fact, criticizing several aspects of the Soviet experience). The Eurocommunists believe the socialist states established in the Soviet Union and, later, in the countries of Eastern Europe, to be very different from the socialist state envisaged by the fathers of Marxism.[127] Accordingly, they insist on the right of each communist party to work out its own policies in total independence from Moscow. This is eloquently expressed by Carillo:

> On the other hand, Eurocommunism should demonstrate that the victory of the socialist forces in the countries of Western Europe will not augment Soviet state power in the slightest, nor will it imply the spread of the Soviet model of a single party, but will be an independent experience, with a more evolved socialism that will have a positive influence on the democratic evolution of the kinds of socialism existing today ... In this respect, the independence of the communist parties in relation to the Soviet state and other socialist states is essential.[128]

In fact, Carillo was not the first to challenge the supremacy of the Soviet Communist Party. As early as 1956, the theory of 'polycentrism', which denies the totally predominant role of the Soviet Party, had been developed by Palmiro Togliatti,[129] Secretary-General of the Italian Communist Party until his death in 1964. The present leader of the Italian Party, Enrico Berlinguer, has taken up his predecessor's call for the independence of the

European communist parties from the Soviet Union. The independent stance of the Eurocommunists is most forcefully expressed in their vigorous denunciation of human rights violations inside the Soviet Union. Their support for the human rights movement was in open defiance of the Soviet regime, which had always considered human rights activists[130] to be traitors and agents who had to be placed in mental institutions until they came to their senses and recovered from their reactionary ideas.

The European communist parties not only advocate independence from the Soviet Union and reject it as a model for their own countries, they call the Soviet experience itself into question. This critical revision is clear in the literature put out by this school of thought. If Arab Marxists are unwilling to admit that fact, how then can they explain the following words of the leader of one of the biggest communist parties in Europe?

> If all states are instruments for the domination of one class over another, and if in the USSR there are no antagonistic classes and objectively there is no need to suppress other classes, then over whom does state exercise domination?[131]

> The October Revolution created a state which is obviously not a bourgeois state, nor is it a proletariat organized as a ruling class nor an authentic workers' democracy.[132]

> Within that state there grew up and operated the Stalin phenomenon, with a series of formal characteristics similar to those of the fascist dictatorships![133]

> But the state with which we are dealing (the Soviet Union), has gone further than Lenin foresaw in this sphere. It has kept not only some of the contents of bourgeois law but has also provided examples of distortion and degeneration which at other times could only be imagined in imperialist states.[134]

Carillo also firmly condemns the absence of objective criticism in the socialist states.[135] How can all that be explained if not as a rejection of both the theory and its applications?

Sixth, recognizing that the proletariat, as conceived by Marx and other traditional Marxists, no longer exists in today's

developed industrial states. Carillo has said openly that traditional Marxists 'speak of a proletariat that no longer exists in
reality'.[136] Most European communists share his views on the
matter. In an article published in *Le Monde* following the defeat
of the coalition of the Left in the legislative elections of 1978,
Louis Althusser says: 'Georges Marchais (General-Secretary of
the French Communist Party), talks of the working class as
though we were still living in the nineteenth century!' It should
be noted that Althusser who, in the same article, denies the
poverty of today's workers, is considered by the European
communists to be dogmatic in his adherence to the letter of
Marxist texts.[137]

The views expressed by the Secretary-General of the
Communist Party of Spain, Santiago Carillo, in his book,
'Eurocommunism' and the State, represent more than the essence
of one man's thoughts. In fact, judging from the support the book
received from all the communist parties in Western Europe, as
well as in other countries such as India, Japan and Lebanon,[138]
it amounts to a statement of principles for the entire Eurocommunist movement. This is also borne out by the Soviet reaction
to the book, which took the form of a lengthy and highly
critical review published in the twenty-sixth issue of the Soviet
weekly *New Times* in June 1977. While admitting that the
ideas put forward by Carillo were representative of a current
of thought that was spreading within the European communist
movement, the review accused Carillo and his supporters of
anti-Soviet tendencies and revisionism.

CHAPTER 4

The Revealing Light of Democracy and the Darkness of the Single Opinion[139]

The disastrous defeat of June 1967 played a decisive role in forcing many intellectuals, Arabs in general and Egyptians in particular, to re-examine established concepts and to question their validity. The process did not take a sudden, dramatic turn but evolved gradually, in my case, for instance, over several years. It was helped along by the performance of the government propaganda machine in the days following the disaster. The pitiful attempts by the defeated regime to pass such a cataclysmic event off as no more than a setback, the loss of one battle in a long-term war, rang hollow to the ears of the Egyptian people. Their wounds ran too deep to be assuaged by the lying slogans launched by the regime just hours after news of the disaster broke. Among the more memorable was the use of the word 'setback' to describe the complete destruction of the Egyptian army, while others, such as eliminating the results of the aggression and direct American/British aggression were equally unconvincing.

For Egyptian intellectuals, the blow was even more devastating, as many of them realized that what had happened was, essentially, the defeat of a regime, and that what was being called a military setback was in fact an acute expression of that defeat. After boasting for years that its foundations were firmly set in steel, the regime had revealed its feet of clay on the morning of 5 June 1967, and the myth of its invincibility lay shattered on the sands of Sinai.

Traumatized by this shattering blow to their national pride, indeed, to their very being, an entire generation became dispersed. Some packed up and left for distant lands. Tens of thousands of educated young Egyptians emigrated to Britain, the United States, Canada and Australia, leaving behind them the motherland covered with the ashes of the conflagration. Others remained, there to serve their cause and compensate them for another kind of soldiering that had been crushed by defeat. Minds were numb with shock, their values severely shaken. Still others found relief in throwing in their lot with extremist elements, which would make soldiers of them.

But there were a few who, realizing that the defeat was more political than military, stayed and tried to understand why the regime had collapsed and, with it, the banners it had raised for 15 years. I was one of those who believed that to describe what happened on the morning of 5 June 1967 as a military setback resulting from an American/Israeli conspiracy was to betray the conscience of the nation and to display the most supreme contempt for the intelligence of the people. After all, war is a continuation of politics by other means, and a military defeat is first and foremost a political defeat.

Ironically, that definition of war came to us from Marx and our Marxist mentors. It was Marx who first described war as an extension of politics and a solution to political problems, he who said it could be characterized only in political terms. Five years after the 1967 debacle, the concept had become well established in my mind. Extensive travels, to more than 200 cities in over 20 countries, helped me understand the reasons for the regime's collapse in June 1967. A first-hand look at the experience of regimes modelled along the lines of Nasser's regime, such as those of Libya and Algeria, was instrumental in making me realize that the defeat of the Nasserite regime had been a natural, logical and inevitable result of the absence of light. Darkness can only breed darkness, and without bright and revealing light, no society can avoid slipping into an abyss like the one into which Egypt fell in 1967. The nature of the fall may vary, it could be military, economic or socio-political, but the final outcome is the same: defeat, collapse, loss of pride and a long shadow over the future. By absence of light is meant absence of democracy and the public freedoms that go with it. Democracy is the bright light that shines on the regime in power, its machinery, mechanisms and institutions. It is what protects society from the repetition of mistakes, from the ascendancy of negative aspects and from the dangers of building on brittle foundations. Only democracy can prevent the total collapse of a structure because of an error committed in the dark and only revealed by the final collapse.

Around 1970–71, this conviction had begun to take hold of me. At the time, I was attending gatherings in Marxist circles on an almost daily basis. When I ventured to suggest at one of these gatherings that the real reason for the disaster was the complete absence of democracy in the country, the reaction of those present was extremely hostile and they dismissed my analysis out of hand. I remember this was at a meeting which took place one morning in the summer of 1970, in the office of M.K.,[140] on the sixth floor of the *Al-Ahram* building in Cairo. This particular floor housed the offices of many Egyptian Marxists who had been arrested in 1954 and 1959 and who had remained in prison until 1964. Following their release, which came about as a result of growing Soviet influence in Egypt, they were given leading positions in the mass media.

Among those present that day were F.M. and I.S.A., each of whom had headed an important communist organization in the 1950s and both of whom later became ministers. There was also M.S.A., considered by the Egyptian Marxists to be their main theoretician today. Several journalists from *Al-Taliaa*, all communists, were there, as were a number of communist university professors, like M.A.,[141] H.A.,[142] S.A.A.,[143] etc. In the course of the discussion, I referred to the 'setback' as being the defeat of a political regime. Although my analysis had not yet matured and even though I addressed the issue from a Marxist angle, backing my statement with direct quotes from Marx on war being an extension of politics, M.S.A. took it upon himself to interrupt me and to deliver a sermon, approved by all those present, on the proper interpretation of the 1967 defeat as being due to two factors:

1. The unholy alliance between the imperialist powers and Israel, both of whom had every interest in destroying the progressive socialist regime established by Nasser in Egypt, which had become a beacon of light for the Middle East, the Arab world and the African continent.

2. The mistakes committed by Nasser's regime, which hindered completing socialist construction in Egypt. If Nasser had built socialism on a scientific (i.e. Marxist) basis rather than adopting selected socialist concepts, had he turned Egypt into an authentic socialist state (i.e. like those of Eastern Europe), things would have been different and there would have been no setback.[144]

This categorical reply, designed to deter any tendency to read the military defeat of 1967 as a political defeat for the regime, served only to strengthen my growing belief that the military defeat was just one facet of the political defeat. The other facet was the economic defeat, which drained the treasury for almost five years following the war and turned the Egyptians into the paupers of the region.

My conviction that it was the darkness of Nasser's political regime that had plunged Egypt into military and economic defeat was further sustained over the next few years as we saw the same pattern being repeated, the same mistakes being committed, in Iraq, Syria, Libya and Algeria, where the absence of democracy was leading them in the direction of defeat.

The absence of democracy in socialist societies, where there is no respect for such public freedoms as freedom of thought, of opinion, of expression, of opposition and of criticism, is rooted in Marxist thought. Marx, Engels and, later, Lenin, convinced their followers that the non-Marxist concept of democracy was fake and deceptive and that the freedom which the bourgeoisie claimed was guaranteed by their democracy was no more than the freedom of the exploiting minority to pursue their exploitation of the exploited majority. The disdain for what they pejoratively refer to as 'bourgeois parliamentarism' is deeply ingrained in all Marxists. This disdain was colourfully expressed by Lenin, who called parliamentary democracy a 'pigsty'.[145] It was also Lenin who said:

To decide once every few years which member of the ruling class is to repress and crush the people through parliament – such is the real essence of bourgeois parliamentarism, not only in parliamentary-constitutional monarchies, but also in the most democratic republics.[146]

In the same vein, Lenin described representative institutions as 'talking shops'[147] and social democrats as 'lap dogs'.[148] He said:

> Parliament itself is given up to talk for the special purpose of fooling the 'common people'. This is so true that even in the Russian Republic,[149] a bourgeois-democratic republic, all these sins of parliamentarism were immediately revealed, even before it managed to set up a real parliament. The heroes of rotten philistinism, such as the Skobelevs and Tseretelis, the Chernovs and Avksentyevs, have even succeeded in polluting the Soviets after the fashion of most disgusting bourgeois parliamentarism and to convert them into mere talking shops.[150]

A careful reading of Marx, Engels and Lenin will show that they affirm the impossibility of combining the state and freedom and democracy, since democracy in non-communist societies stands for the state regime and the state stands for exploitation and oppression.[151] In an introduction to a series of articles published just one and a half years before his death and 11 years after the death of Marx, Engels says that the Communist Party can never use the term social/democrat, because it is a party whose ultimate political objective is to transcend the state altogether and, consequently, democracy as well.[152] In 1917, Lenin developed this theme as follows:

> In the usual arguments about the state, the mistake is constantly made against which Engels uttered his warning and which we have in passing indicated above, namely, it is constantly forgotten that the abolition of the state means also the abolition of democracy; that the withering away of the state means the withering away of democracy.
>
> At first sight, this assertion seems exceedingly strange and incomprehensible; indeed, someone may even begin to fear that we are expecting the advent of an order of society in which the principle of the subordination of the minority to the majority will not be observed – for democracy means the recognition of just this principle.
>
> No, democracy is NOT identical with the subordination of the minority to the majority. Democracy is a state which

recognizes the subordination of the minority to the majority, i.e. an organization for the systematic use of violence by one class against the other, by one section of the population against another.[153]

Lenin was also the one to call the democracy of capitalist society 'democracy for an insignificant minority, democracy for the rich ...',[154] noting that Marx had 'grasped the essence of capitalist democracy when, in analysing the experience of the (Paris) Commune, he said that the oppressed are allowed once every few years to decide which particular representatives of the oppressing class shall represent and repress them in parliament!'[155]

In *Imperialism, the Highest Stage of Capitalism*,[156] Lenin wrote: 'Imperialism is the era of financial capital and the monopolies which everywhere tend towards domination not freedom.' He devotes an entire book, *The Proletarian Revolution and the Renegade Kautsky*, written in October/November 1918, to developing the theme of Western democracy being a game used by the dominant class to consolidate its exploitation and privileges. To this end, he invokes Rosa Luxemburg's description of German Social Democracy as 'a stinking corpse'.[157] In a chapter entitled 'Bourgeois and Proletarian Democracy', Lenin says:

If we are not to mock at common sense and history, it is obvious that we cannot speak of 'pure democracy' so long as different classes exist; we can only speak of class democracy. (Be it said in parenthesis that 'pure democracy' is not only an ignorant phrase, revealing a lack of understanding both of the class struggle and of the nature of the state, but also a thrice-empty phrase, since in communist society democracy will wither away in the process of changing and becoming a habit, but will never be 'pure' democracy.)

'Pure democracy' is the mendacious phrase of a liberal who wants to fool the workers. History knows of bourgeois democracy which takes the place of feudalism, and of proletarian democracy which takes the place of bourgeois democracy.[158]

In the same chapter, Lenin launches his most violent diatribe yet against Western democracy, parliaments and the idea of parliamentary representation:

> The learned Mr Kautsky has 'forgotten' – accidentally forgotten, probably ... a 'trifle', namely, that the ruling party in a bourgeois democracy extends the protection of the minority only to another bourgeois party, while on all serious, profound and fundamental issues the proletariat gets martial law or pogroms, instead of the 'protection of the minority'. The more highly developed a democracy is, the more imminent are pogroms or civil war in connection with any profound political divergence which is dangerous to the bourgeoisie.[159]

Tens of similar passages can be found in the works of Trotsky and Mao Tse-tung. According to the former, the problems between the proletariat and others 'can only be resolved by blood and steel'. It was also Trotsky who boasted that the Bolsheviks had never paid heed to Hegel's 'babble about the sanctity of human life'. In fact, it was Marxism's inbuilt propensity for violence that led Kautsky to attack it, thereby incurring Lenin's wrath. Mao Tse-tung is even more blunt: 'Our state is that of the people's democratic dictatorship, led by the working class and based on the alliance of workers and peasants.' Defining the functions of that dictatorship, he says its first task is on the internal front, where it must suppress the reactionary classes, exploiters, all those standing against the socialist revolution and all those working to subvert socialist construction, 'in order to resolve the contradictions between us and our enemies inside the country. Among the functions of the proletariat, for example, is to arrest and sentence anti-revolutionary elements and to deprive landowners and bourgeois bureaucrats of their right to vote and of freedom of speech.'

In an article published on 27 February 1957, under the title 'The Proper Treatment of the Contradictions Between the Rights of the People', Mao reiterates the views he expressed on 23 June 1950, in the closing address he delivered at the Second Consultative Political Congress of the Chinese People, in which he said: 'The people's democratic dictatorship follows two paths: against the enemies, it follows the path of dictatorship, i.e. for a necessary period of time, the enemies are not allowed to participate in political activity ...'[160] Elsewhere, Mao explains the essence of what he calls democratic dictatorship,[161] noting that it is based on:

* subordination of the minority to the majority;
* subordination of the majority to the Party; and
* subordination of the Party to the Central Committee.[162]

The Marxist doctrine requires Marxists to reject parliamentary democracy and to build their proletarian democracy on the elimination of all other classes and, by extension, of their political organizations, i.e. their parties. Thus a Marxist who comes to power cannot allow freedom of political opposition nor freedom to form parties, because all parties other than the Communist Party represent classes at war with the proletariat. As Lenin put it bluntly: 'once the proletariat seizes power, it must impose a series of restrictions on the freedom of the oppressors, the exploiters and the capitalists'.[163] To drive the point home, he points out:

> It is clear (that) when there is suppression, when there is violence (on the part of the proletariat), there is no freedom and no democracy ...[164] Democracy for the vast majority of the people (the proletariat) and suppression by force, i.e. exclusion from democracy, of the exploiters and oppressors of the people – this is the change democracy undergoes during the transition from capitalism to communism.[165]

Under communist rule, therefore, indeed, under any of the regimes which revolve, to varying degrees, in the communist orbit, parliamentary democracy is regarded with deep suspicion. Political opponents are class enemies that the regime should crush, not engage in dialogue with, and who should not be given a forum from which to speak out against the interests of the proletariat. In this logic, all who stand with them are 'comrades', all who do not are 'enemies', towards whom the only possible language is repression. As they see it, freedom of thought cannot be absolute. On the one hand, nothing is absolute from the philosophical point of view and, on the other, thought is subordinate to economic and class interests and any thought that does not express the interests of the working class is a deviation to be suppressed. Thus freedom of expression is viewed through one single political prism: that of the Party, which sets itself up as the sole representative of the proletarian majority. The twin concepts of freedom of thought and freedom of expression, inherited from a long evolutionary process in human thought and culture, have no place in a society ruled by communists.

The same narrow perspective is applied to the press and literature in communist societies. The press must be in the hands of the representatives of the proletariat, not in the hands of its enemies; it must defend only the interests of the workers and make war on their enemies; no party or trend other than the Communist Party can have access to the press ... As to 'human literature', it is a meaningless expression, for literature is one of the components of the superstructure and a reflection of the economic basis of society. In a society ruled by communists, literature should be concerned solely with the problems and interests of the working class. From all these concepts the ideal society is formed: the Soviet Union, with its conception of freedom of the press, of opinion and of political opposition.[166]

It is true that the 1970s and 1980s saw the West European communists, particularly the Italian, French and Spanish communist parties, rejecting the traditional Marxist view of democracy and proclaiming their belief in Western parliamentary democracy and political pluralism as embodied in the multi-party system. But it is also true that they did so only because they knew that unless they affirmed their respect for democratic values, their own societies, where these values were firmly entrenched, would continue to reject them. For the peoples of the Western democracies firmly believe in the importance of public scrutiny – or the light of democracy – in revealing errors and preventing negative trends in good time. But whatever the motivation of the Eurocommunists, their doctrine, officially described by the Soviets in 1972 as 'provocative' (in the review *The Contemporary Nation*), met with implacable opposition from orthodox Marxists.

In short, the lessons drawn from the Nasserite experience in Egypt and similar experiences in other countries, as well as the record of societies ruled by communist parties or pro-communist regimes, prove beyond the shadow of a doubt that the nature of Marxism, as a philosophical and political school of thought, as well as in its practical application to date, is in total contradiction the notion of democracy as it has evolved in Western societies and as it is reflected today in Britain, the United States, France, and other countries. By its very nature, Marxism inevitably leads to the suppression of freedom of thought, of opinion, of political opposition and of the press, and cannot admit of any mechanism that would put political life under the light of democracy and reveal it to the public eye, so that defects do not remain hidden until they erupt in the form of a disaster such as a military, political, economic or social setback.

Anyone who has read Soviet *samizdat* ('underground') literature cannot fail to be struck by the negative aspects of Marxist theory and practice. The list of Soviet dissidents who have written of the brutal repression to which they were subjected, the years they spent in labour camps and psychiatric hospitals, the persecution of their families and friends is an impressive one. Among the names that spring to mind are Alexander Solzhenitsyn, Andrei Sakharov, Roy Medvedev, Mikhail Bulgakov, Anatoly Marchenko, Mikhail Sholokhov, Yuli M. Daniel (alias Nikolai Argak), Andrei Sinyavsky (alias Abraham Tertz), Aleksandr Ginsburg, Larya Gurz, Yury Galanskov, Pavel Leptvinov, Valentin Moroz ...[167]

The long hours spent reading the works of dissident Soviet authors, particularly Alexander Solzhenitsyn and Anatoly Marchenko, helped confirm my belief that the aberrations they describe are all due to what I termed, in a lecture delivered on 29 April 1979, at the University of Asuncion, the darkness resulting from the absence of any mechanisms of illumination in societies subscribing to the Marxist concept of democracy. This concept is closely related to another, that of revolutionary, or socialist, legitimacy. The notion of constitutional legitimacy born of mankind's long struggle to obtain civil liberties and protect human rights by devising a system of checks and balances whereby the political authority is accountable to the people and the powers of the ruler are strictly defined by constitutional and legislative texts, is totally rejected by Marxism, both in theory and in practice. For Marxists, who see everything from the perspective of class struggle, legitimacy means anything that serves that struggle. Indeed, the only constraint on the actions of the proletariat when it is performing its historic mission to propel society forward from capitalism to socialism – while abolishing all other classes in the process – is that these actions must serve the interests of the proletariat. This elastic proposition lends itself easily to abuse: the political authority can justify any excess in the name of the interests of the proletariat. Hence the dismal human rights record of all communist regimes, where purges and brutal repression of any opposition, in flagrant violation of the basic principles of legitimacy as established by centuries of human struggle, are justified as necessary to protect the interests of the working class.

The years 1917 to 1921 witnessed the worst such violations in the Soviet Union, when the entire judicial system was subsumed under the banner of 'revolutionary legitimacy' to serve one man's vision of political expediency. During that black period, Stalin liquidated his opponents, murdered millions of his countrymen and held the infamous Moscow trials.

The same banner was raised by Gamal Abdel Nasser to justify eliminating all his opponents from 1954 onwards. Under that banner, thousands of Muslims were massacred in Syria. Such leaders as Castro, Ben Bella, Boumedienne, Gaddafi, successive rulers in Aden, Agostinho Neto, Miriam Mengistou, Abdel Kerim Kassem and Abdel Fattah Ismail applied what they called revolutionary legitimacy in their respective countries to 'protect the revolution and the interests of the people'.

However, it is not by reading the mass of theoretical works written on the subject that one can judge between the relative merits of the two notions of legitimacy. For oppression, like freedom, can be theoretically justified, and honeyed words on the need to repress injustice, tyranny and exploitation can act like a heady brew, particularly on headstrong young people with a natural enthusiasm for fiery slogans. The real test lies in practical application, and there is no disputing the horrible crimes committed by communist regimes in the area of human rights. Under the banner of revolutionary legitimacy, they have trampled underfoot all public freedoms and silenced all dissent. The picture is very different under a constitutional democracy, which is not, as Lenin called it, a charade, but a system designed to prevent abuses of power and to protect public freedoms.

Democracy is the torch that illuminates the workings of the state and lays them bare for all to see. No one can claim that democracy has created the ideal paradise, only that its revealing light prevents the tyranny and injustice that occur in the darkness of dictatorial rule, whatever its nature: Marxist, Fascist, Nazi, military or theocratic.

The tragedy of the Cultural Revolution launched by Mao Tse-tung in the mid-1960s[168] is a glaring example of where the concepts of revolutionary legitimacy, proletarian democracy, committed communist literature, etc. can lead. But the price of the lesson was exorbitant in terms of human suffering and it was a lesson humanity could have done without. Sadly, many people in the Third World seem to have learned nothing from the Chinese experience.

For some strange reason, none of those who have been seduced by the Marxist concept of democracy ever asks himself why no communist ruler has ever left power except for one of two reasons: death or a coup d'état. Nor do they question why each communist ruler begins his reign by denouncing that of his predecessor. Not one of them wonders how Tsarist Russia, with all its social inequities, produced such towering figures as Pushkin, Gogol, Turgenev, Dostoevsky, Tolstoi, Chekhov, Tchaikovsky, Rimsky-Korsakov, Rachmaninov and scores of others, whereas the dictatorship of the proletariat has produced no creative works other than those of the dissidents who turned against the regime.

This perception of constitutional democracy is dictated by the moral code of Marxism. Morality is determined in Marxist eyes by reference to the proletarian revolution: whatever serves the cause of the revolution is moral, anything else is not. With this in mind, how can we see the behaviour of communists in Western democracies, who have suddenly become apostles of pluralism and constitutional democracy, as anything but inconsistent? While traditional Marxists admit that their ultimate aim in participating in political life in non-proletarian states (i.e. Western democracies) is to promote the proletarian revolution by smashing the machinery of state – political institutions, parliamentary, or bourgeois, democracy, etc., they are the first loudly to condemn any violation of democracy and the staunchest supporters of the freedoms it guarantees, such as freedom of opinion and of expression.

It is hard to reconcile this attitude with what Engels himself said in his address to the First International London Conference on 11 September 1871:

> Political freedoms, such as the right of assembly and freedom to publish and print are our weapon. Can we, then, remain with our hands tied and boycott politics if they try to seize this weapon from us? It is said that any political activity means recognizing the existing system. But as long as that system places in our hands the weapons with which to fight, then using those weapons does not mean recognizing the existing system.[169]

In other words, the communists have no qualms about using the channels and privileges available to them under a system of bourgeois parliamentary democracy to achieve their ultimate aim of destroying that system. For they are aware that under a democracy they cannot come to power as Lenin and his cohorts did in the anarchy that prevailed in Russia in October 1917 or through a military takeover. Their use of democratic channels to preach communist ideas, fan the flames of class struggle and spread rumours against their opponents is a blatant example of the immoral opportunism of communists, which they consider entirely moral from their neo-Machiavellan point of view.

Western democracies seem oblivious to this threat to their very existence. Surely the essential condition for participation in democratic life should be a profound belief in democracy and a desire to protect and maintain it? Anyone who does not satisfy that condition should be barred from exercising the right to participate in political activities in Western democracies. It is absurd for people who have learned from long historical experience that parliamentary democracy is all that stands between them and tyranny and despotism to allow those who call for its destruction to operate under its umbrella. Especially when the traditional Marxists, like those in the Third World, declare their Leninist aim of replacing bourgeois democracy by proletarian democracy.

We are not alone in finding the behaviour of Marxists in Western democracies inconsistent and immoral. The accusation of immorality has been levelled against them by many European intellectuals sympathetic to Marxism, such as Howard Laski, who described the behaviour of communists outside the Soviet Union as 'deceptive, ruthless, iniquitous, willing to resort to lies and treachery to achieve their end and unscrupulously falsifying facts to suit their purpose'. Nor is the immoral behaviour of the communists limited to the period before they seize power. The slogans they raise when they participate in political life under a democracy are soon forgotten when they come to power. In fact, the allies who stand by them in their struggle to attain power are usually their first victims. A notorious example is how the Mensheviks, who had stood by the Bolsheviks in their struggle, were liquidated by Lenin soon after he came to power. The opportunistic communist attitude with regard to parliamentary democracy is best expressed by Lenin himself in *'Left-Wing' Communism, an Infantile Disorder*, published in Russia in June 1920. Among the most explicit Marxist texts upholding the legitimacy of anything that serves the proletarian revolution is Chapter 8 of the said book, in which he bitterly denounces the German 'Left' communists who dared criticize the Bolsheviks for compromising with bourgeois parties, noting that: '... the German Left must know that the whole history of Bolshevism, both before and after the October Revolution, is full of instances of manoeuvring, temporizing and compromising with other parties, bourgeois parties included'. Developing this theme further, he asks:

> To carry on a war for the overthrow of the international bourgeoisie, a war which is a hundred times more difficult, protracted and complicated than the most stubborn of ordinary wars between states, and to refuse beforehand to manoeuvre, to utilize the conflict of interests (even though temporary) among one's enemies, to refuse to temporize and compromise with possible (even though temporary, unstable, vacillating and conditional) allies – is not this ridiculous in the extreme?[170]

During a spell abroad in the first half of the 1970s, I devoted myself to the study of hundreds of volumes written during the early years of the great Islamic civilization, particularly the works of eminent Islamic jurists compiled in a volume entitled *Bab Al Jihad*. I often found myself comparing the immorality of the communists with the chivalry displayed by the early Muslims in all their wars, starting with the Battle of Badr. The history of Islam is rich in examples of noble stands. One example that springs to mind is that of Imam Ali Ibn Abi Taleb, who could have had the whole world at his feet if he had gone against the dictates of his conscience. When he was offered the caliphate after the assassination of Omar on condition that he pledge not to be as strict as Omar, he refused – thereby sacrificing a position that would have brought virtually the whole world at the time under his rule. His words to his opponents at the Battle of Al Gamal are just the opposite of the communist creed that the end – the accession to power, the furthering of the proletarian revolution, etc. – justifies the means. Another case in point is Saladdin, who met every underhanded plot hatched against him by the Crusaders with chivalry and gallantry. In recent times, this noble tradition was upheld by the late King Feisal of Saudi Arabia who, despite the vicious attacks launched against him by the Nasser regime, was the first to rush to Nasser's support at the Khartoum Conference of 1967, following the regime's defeat.[171]

The very narrow Marxist concept of democracy as being proletarian democracy and none other not only shapes the attitude of the communists to other parties and trends, but also their attitude to fellow Communist Party members. Right after the Bolsheviks seized power in Russia and established the dictatorship of the proletariat, the question of whether or not to allow freedom of opinion within the Party was decisively settled. Actually, the question had been raised as early as 1903, when a bitter debate broke out over whether the communist organization should be a tight organization, in the sense of high centralization and iron discipline, or a loose one, encompassing various communist tendencies. The concept of a tight organization, championed by Lenin, won the day. Lenin came under strong attack for his stand from several leaders of the communist movement both inside Russia, like Trotsky, and outside, like Rosa Luxemburg in Germany. In *Our Political Duties*, Trotsky went as far as to compare Lenin to Robespierre. Under the pressure of so many attacks, Lenin published *One Step Forward, Two Steps Back* in 1904, in which he violently attacked the advocates of an open communist society and their description of democracy as being the rule of the people by the people. He declared that the idea of organization, so essential to the communist movement, could not be fulfilled without the total submission of the minority to the majority inside the Party and that anyway he could conceive of no opposition within the Party save from 'opportunistic, non-revolutionary elements'. He reiterated the same views later, when he boasted in *'Left-Wing' Communism, an Infantile Disorder*, published in 1920, that 'the application of the dictatorship of the proletariat would have been impossible without an iron party'.

After Lenin's death, the debate flared up again between Stalin and his bitter enemy, Trotsky. The former adhered strictly to the Lenin line and advocated the idea of a tightly controlled Party in *The Foundations of Leninism* in 1924 and *Problems of Leninism* in 1926. Trotsky, for his part, continued to defend the idea of an open Party – especially when it became apparent that Lenin was closer to power than he was – that would cooperate with the Mencheviks and all the other parties whose support had helped the Bolsheviks come to power and establish the dictatorship of the proletariat. Trotsky's views on the matter are forcefully expressed in *The New Method*, which he wrote in 1923. But, in the event, it was Stalin's theory that ultimately prevailed, and Trotsky's call for an open Party has never been applied in any state ruled by the dictatorship of the proletariat as embodied in a Communist Party. The formula of a narrow Party applied by Lenin and Stalin was also applied by Mao in China, where the Communist Party was quick to eliminate any trend that did not strictly adhere to the path he laid out. Under various banners, the most famous being the Cultural Revolution, the most brutal methods were used to correct any deviation from this path.

Thus the absence of the light of democracy is an inbuilt feature of communist rule that affects not only its enemies but also those of its followers who do not see eye to eye with the ruler. An area that provides ample evidence of this is the literature of Soviet dissidents and their trials and tribulations in defence of human rights. While a full analysis of the issue would go beyond the scope of this essay, the story of one of them can serve as a representative case history for all of them.

The life of the Nobel laureate Alexander Solzhenitsyn, from

the day he was born in 1918 until he was deported from the Soviet Union in 1974, epitomizes the brutal oppression visited by the Soviet Union on its citizens. In this model communist society, which serves as a shining example of the successful implementation of the dictatorship of the proletariat to all the others, fundamental freedoms are conspicuously absent and human rights violations the order of the day.

Alexander Isayevich Solzhenitsyn was born on 11 December 1918 at Kislovodsk. Six years later, his father was killed in an accident, and his mother moved with him to Rostov-on-the-Don, where she worked as a typist. Life was hard in the early days of Stalin's rule, especially for a young widow and her orphaned son. Young Alexander was an outstanding student from primary school and up to Rostov University, where his genius in mathematics and physics won him a scholarship for graduate studies. Throughout those years, Solzhenitsyn remained true to his love for culture in general and literature in particular, and he took a correspondence course in literature at the Moscow Institute of Philosophy, Literature and History. He obtained his diploma from the Institute in 1941, one year following his appointment as teacher of mathematics at a secondary school in Rostov.

During those years, he tried to publish his novels and short stories in the literary review, *Znamya*, but they were all rejected by the editor. When Hitler's invasion of the Soviet Union began, Solzhenitsyn joined the Red Army as an artillery officer on 18 October 1941, and fought at the battles of Kursk and Konigsberg (later Kaliningrad).[172] His heroism earned him several promotions, and by 1945 he was a captain with two decorations for bravery in defence of his country: the Order of the Patriotic War, Class II, and the Order of the Red Star.

In July 1945, he was suddenly arrested by the secret police, the NKVD, and charged with making derogatory remarks about Stalin in private correspondence with a friend and in his personal diary. He was detained without trial in the Lubyanka prison in Moscow pending further investigation of his case by the secret police, then sentenced by a special tribunal of the NKVD to eight years' hard labour as a traitor to Leninist socialism and to the socialist society. Solzhenitsyn served his sentence in a number of Soviet prisons, but instead of releasing him when his term was up in 1953, the secret police arbitrarily decided to exile him to Kok Tern in the Dzhambul region of Kazakhstan, where he remained until 1956. During his exile, it was discovered that he had cancer and he was sent to a hospital in Tashkent to undergo treatment.

For more than eleven years of imprisonment and exile, Solzhenitsyn underwent horrible sufferings which he movingly describes in *One Day in the Life of Ivan Denisovich*. The novel is considered a literary masterpiece in its description of the sufferings of hundreds of thousands of detainees in the Soviet Union, although I, personally, share the opinion of the *Daily Telegraph*'s literary critic who considers *My Testimony* by Anatoly Marchenko to be the best account of life in Russian prisons and labour camps since Dostoevsky's *House of the Dead*. Solzhenitsyn uses the same setting for his play, *The Tender Foot and the Tramp*. His outstanding novel, *Cancer Ward*, recounts his experience with exile and his brush with death from cancer. During his years of imprisonment and exile, his family knew nothing about him. Thinking him dead, his wife remarried but went back to him after his release (1956) and his rehabilitation (1957).

In 1956, his case was reviewed by the Military Section of the Supreme Court of the Soviet Union, which issued the following ruling under No. 4N/083/56:

On 6 February 1956, the Court examined the appeal raised by the Military Prosecutor against the decision passed by the Fifth Tribunal of the NKVD on 7 June 1945, and predicated on paragraphs 10 and 11 of article 58 of the RSFSR Criminal Code, sentencing to eight years' imprisonment in correctional labour camps Alexander Isayevich Solzhenitsyn, born in 1918 in the city of Kislovodsk, holder of the highest scientific awards and commander of an artillery unit before his detention who fought in the war against the Fascist German armies and was awarded the Order of the Patriotic War, Class II, and the Order of the Red Star. Having heard the report of comrade Konev and the statement of Colonel Terkov, Assistant Military Prosecutor, the Court rules as follows: the charges against Solzhenitsyn which are that between 1940 and 1945 he committed acts of anti-Soviet propaganda among his friends and took steps aimed at forming an anti-Soviet organization are declared null and void for absence of proof of the alleged crimes ...

Throughout these years, all Solzhenitsyn's attempts to publish his works were met with adamant refusal. However, in November 1962, Khrushchev himself authorized publication of *One Day in the Life of Ivan Denisovich*, Solzhenitsyn's harrowing novel about life in a Siberian labour camp under Stalin, in the context of Khrushchev's destalinization policy. After Khrushchev's downfall in 1964, Solzhenitsyn again became *persona non grata* and was the target of violent attacks by official Soviet writers. But by then, which is around the time the literary dissidents' movement was born, he had acquired many supporters and admirers. The attacks continued for almost ten years, during which the author was accused of being a traitor to socialism and an agent of American imperialist powers. He was persecuted in his private life and transferred from one place to another. The attacks reached a climax when he was awarded the 1970 Nobel Prize for Literature and continued unabated until he left the Soviet Union in 1974.

Those who have followed the case closely affirm that Solzhenitsyn would have been assassinated or locked up in a psychiatric institution like so many others had it not been for the support of the free world and of the European communist parties, particularly those of Italy, France and Spain, and had his case not become a *cause célèbre* at the centre of world public opinion.

Although the case of Solzhenitsyn provoked a great political furore and much international publicity, the history of communist societies is rife with similar, albeit less sensational, cases. The moral to be drawn from the story of Alexander Solzhenitsyn is that in communist societies, where the rule of law is replaced by 'revolutionary legitimacy', there is no room for divergent views, which are invariably branded as anti-revolutionary and imperialist. In fact, conformity or otherwise to 'revolutionary legitimacy' is determined at the sole discretion of whoever happens to be in power at any given time. The vicissitudes of Solzhenitsyn's fortunes prove just how flexible the concept of revolutionary democracy is:

1. At a first phase, he was a legendary hero who had fought valiantly for the socialist fatherland and had been decorated twice for bravery.
2. At a second phase, he was accused of betraying that same fatherland and sentenced to eleven years' hard labour in the Siberian labour camps.
3. A third phase saw an upward turn in his fortunes. He was absolved by the Supreme Court of the crimes for which he had paid with eleven years of his life and nominated for the Lenin Prize in 1963 for *One Day in the Life of Ivan Denisovich*. Solzhenitsyn's rehabilitation did not mean that the climate of tyranny and oppression had changed, but only that his writings served the interests of the new rulers.
4. With Khrushchev's fall, a new stage in the decline of Solzhenitsyn's official standing began. Once again he was denounced as an agent, a traitor, an enemy of socialism and a mediocre writer.[173]

What emerges from Solzhenitsyn's life and writings, especially in the period between 1967 and 1974, and from all that has been written about him in the Soviet Union and abroad, is that under communist rule, art and literature are tolerated only to the extent that they serve the regime and echo its slogans, regardless of intrinsic value. Since the October Revolution, the Soviet Union has regarded its artists and writers as foot soldiers in its war against the enemy, deploying them to trumpet the victories of the regime and attack its critics. A look at the novels, plays, short stories and literary articles published in the Soviet Union since 1917 will show how the functional role assigned by the political leadership to literature and art has devitalized these traditionally strong forms of expression and rendered them sterile. It is enough to compare the works put out after 1917 by the 'approved' authors, whose names are listed in the *Soviet Encyclopaedia*, with those of the great pre-revolutionary Russian writers, to realize the extent of the tragedy. That the Soviets regard authors as instruments to be used for the furtherance of the regime's interests is clear from many official statements issued by the Soviet Writers' Union and from numerous articles that have appeared in *Pravda*. A statement worth quoting here is that delivered on 5 October 1967, by the editor-in-chief of *Pravda*, M. F. Ziemanin, at the Press House in Leningrad:

> The Western press has recently been full of malicious fabrications, using many of our writers whose works have reached the hands of our enemies. The camp formed by the Western press to defend Tarsis only stopped its activities when Tarsis left for the West, thereby proving that he – Tarsis – was not sound of mind. Nowadays, Solzhenitsyn is at the centre of capitalist propaganda. He too is psychologically unbalanced. He is a schizophrenic, a former prisoner who was subjected to oppression, deservedly or otherwise, and is now seeking revenge against the Soviet government through his literary works. The only topic he seems able to write about is life in the labour camps, it has become a kind of obsession with him. Solzhenitsyn's works are an attack against the Soviet regime in which he sees nothing but bitterness and cancerous growths. He sees nothing positive in our society.
>
> By virtue of my functions, I have access to unpublished works. One of these was Solzhenitsyn's play, *The Feast of the Victors*, which deals with the persecution of those who returned from the front. It is an example of the anti-Soviet literature for which people in the past were imprisoned.
>
> Clearly, we cannot publish his works, that is his one wish that we cannot gratify. However, if he were to write stories that are in keeping with the interest of society, we will publish them. Solzhenitsyn will not want for bread and butter; he is a teacher of physics, let him teach. He likes to make public speeches and to read his works to an audience ... he was given the opportunity to do so ... He considers himself a literary genius.[174]

This text clearly expresses where literature stands in the country that, in a previous age, gave humanity some of its greatest writers and composers. Today, any literary work that does not conform strictly to the general line of the state is considered to be anti-Soviet and serving reactionary imperialist forces. The problem is that the general line of the state differs from one ruler to the next – Lenin to Stalin, the transition to Khrushchev, then to Brezhnev and so on and so forth. How can talents grow and develop when they are circumscribed by the party line? How can literature be expected to fulfil its traditional function of educating, enlightening and correcting society in such circumstances? Literature not only holds up the mirror in which society can see itself reflected, but, as the light which seeks out and reveals all that is negative in that society – in the political, economic and social spheres – is a vital tool for democracy, working relentlessly in the interest of society as a whole.

Repression in socialist societies, headed by the Soviet Union, has not only emptied literature of its essence and transformed it into an organ of state, it has created a new model of morality characterized by social apathy and selfishness. Those who think that the Soviet people are all dissidents, whether overt or covert, are mistaken. Apart from a small group, the Soviet people have been shaped by 60 years of a repressive police state into a unique moral mould.

First of all, the ordinary Soviet citizen has a totally unrealistic picture of the outside world, created by the all-powerful communist media which, as we mentioned in our book, *Communism and Religions*, is the most dangerous weapon in the hands of the communists, whether before they come to power or after. He believes that workers in the United States, France, West Germany, Canada and Britain live lives of poverty, suffering and humiliation. As the Russian writer Lidiya Chukovskaya puts it, a huge wall has been erected between him and the outside world. A good example of the ability of the Soviet media to shape the minds of Soviet citizens according to the party line and in total disregard of accuracy and truth is given by Hedrick Smith in his book, *The Russians*. As the Moscow correspondent of the *New York Times* in the early 1970s, Smith had come to know Andrei Sakharov well. Known as the father of the Soviet H-bomb, a full member of the Soviet Academy of Sciences at the age of 32,[175] Sakharov had donated all his savings, some 140,000 roubles (representing the proceeds of the huge financial privileges he had received as a member of the elite club of Soviet nuclear scientists, which Sakharov says were paid to him secretly in sealed envelopes), to a government fund for a new cancer research centre.

In 1974, Smith met a prominent Soviet medical scientist. The conversation turned to Sakharov, and the scientist, unaware that Smith knew him personally, volunteered the information that

Sakharov was mentally unbalanced. When Smith disclosed that he was personally acquainted with Sakharov, the scientist leant over to whisper in his ear: 'And how was he when you met him? Is he really mad?'

Sakharov himself had a similar experience while on holiday at a Black Sea resort. He became friendly with a group of Soviet intellectuals, to whom he did not disclose his real identity. For days on end they spoke to him of Andrei Sakharov, the father of the Soviet H-bomb who had become a raving madman. In an interview with the Swedish radio correspondent, Olle Stenholm, Sakharov expressed the situation very well:

> I am sceptical about socialism in general. I don't see that socialism offers some kind of new theoretical plan, so to speak, for the better organization of society ... We have the same kind of problems – that is, crime and personal alienation – that are to be found in the capitalist world. But our society represents an extreme case with maximum restraint, maximum ideological restrictions, and so forth ... Moreover, and very characteristically, we are also the most pretentious – that is, although we are not the best society we pretend that we are much more ...

The situation described by Sakharov is the natural outcome of the role assigned by the Party in the Soviet Union to thought, literature and to the mass media, whose discipline to the party line can be likened to that of military troops in battle to their commander: unthinking obedience. If we compare the role of the Soviet mass media to that of the American, which were instrumental in bringing about the downfall of the president because of the Watergate scandal, we would immediately see the difference between what the Soviets denigrate as 'bourgeois democracy' and their brand of revolutionary democracy. Another small example is worth giving here. In the United States, Western democracy has created a new profession in the field of medicine: a representative of the media who is in contact with hospitals and medical centres to track down any cases of malpractice. Any suspicion of malpractice is followed by a thorough investigation and, if it is confirmed, the media launch a strong campaign with serious consequences for the person or persons responsible, including civil liability. This system is just one of many that have emerged in various fields as positive by-products of the democratic process and its integration in all aspects of life in Western societies.[176] An interesting comparison here is the account of Soviet medical facilities given by Solzhenitsyn in *Cancer Ward*. Throughout the 600 pages of the novel, we are given a bitter description of medical services in a state that boasts the best free medical care in the world.

The glaring discrepancy between reality and the image projected by the mass media is not limited to the field of medicine, but is a phenomenon that extends to all aspects of life in the Soviet Union. In fact, it is a natural consequence of the peculiar concept of democracy prevailing in the Soviet Union, where any opinion that does not conform to the official line is regarded as seditious talk by agents in the pay of foreign enemies. According to Sakharov, Soviet citizens have been brainwashed by the Soviet media into believing that no one on the face of the earth tells the truth for the sake of truth. The world is divided into parties and everyone belongs to one or the other of these parties, to which he gives his full loyalty. This belief, nurtured by the Soviet mass media, has allowed the regime to keep the intelligentsia in line and to immunize most of the Soviet people against what they hear from the Western world. Certainly too, the state's monopoly over the job market helps it maintain its grip on people who are totally dependent on it for their livelihood.

Those who do step out of line pay a heavy price. To cite but a few examples: Daniel and Sinyavsky spent more than five years in prison camps for smuggling out of the Soviet Union literary works that the authorities considered slanderous to the Soviet state; the poet Natalya Gorpanyevskaya lost her job and was committed to a mental institution because she took part in a demonstration held in Red Square to protest against the Soviet invasion of Czechoslovakia; the historian Anatoly Petrovesky was dismissed from his job and blacklisted because he signed a statement in support of Daniel and Sinyavsky; the members of Sakharov's immediate family were persecuted simply because of their association with him,[177] and so on and so forth. All this confirms the validity of Harold Laski's proposition that a people who relinquish their political rights in exchange for promises of economic security will soon discover that they struck a losing bargain, for there is nothing they can do if the promises are not kept.

It took me many years of reading, of following up the activities of various communist parties and frequenting their leaderships, especially in Egypt, Algeria and Morocco, to realize just how deeply shrouded in darkness are the societies or groups which fall under the influence of Marxism. When I look back, the evidence was right there before my eyes all through the period I was meeting regularly with veteran Egyptian communists. Those meetings, at which Marxist texts were reverently quoted as though they were holy scriptures, were a microcosm of communist societies, with their intolerance for the other opinion and their use of heavy-handed methods to silence all dissent, not to mention their open advocacy of using all and any means to achieve the desired end. I remember L.K. saying one day in 1972 that the regime would be digging its own grave the day it introduced Western-style representative democracy in the country, which is in fact what the regime tried to do less than three years later. I remember too that they were all for forming an alliance with the Islamic groups whose star was in the ascendancy, especially on university campuses, by building a common ground with what they called leftist Islamic trends.

On the evening of 9 September 1972, I attended what was to be my last meeting with my former comrades. It marked a turning point in my life, a rite of passage, as it were, from darkness into light. Many of the pundits of the Egyptian communist movement were gathered in the office of their mentor, L.K., editor of the monthly magazine that served as a forum for the dissemination of Marxist views among Egyptian and Arab intellectuals at the time. The discussion centred on the fires that had destroyed the Cairo Opera and the Jawhara Palace near the Citadel. L.K. lectured his listeners on the importance of these events as revolutionary moments that, if properly handled, could trigger a revolutionary movement that would hasten the transition to socialism and from there to the higher stage of communism. He spoke with his usual eloquence, and his audience was spellbound by the vision of destruction and revolution he invoked. At that point, I interrupted to say that I rejected this characterization of the two events, which I considered to be crimes against the nation. This undisciplined outburst from a 22-year-old was not to be tolerated. L.K. launched into a personal attack, in which he accused me of being a prisoner of the filthy bourgeois values I had grown up with. He warned that, as the avant-garde of the progressive movement in Egypt, we must not – and I quote – feel any nationalist kinship with the enemies of the people, the bloodsuckers who kept them in humiliating chains. Again I interrupted, pointing out that I had read the same Marxist texts as he and all those present had done, and that I had never been convinced by Marx's theory on nationalism. In fact, nothing that had been written or said on the subject by Marx, by Engels, by Lenin, by Stalin, by him or by any other Marxist had succeeded in changing my mind. All I saw in the burning of the Opera and the Jawhara Palace were acts of sabotage that were in total contradiction with any nationalistic feelings for this country.

Trained to contain such situations, L.K. smoothly changed tack, noting sadly that my class affiliations were responsible for my negative attitude and that, as Lenin had correctly pointed out, genuine commitment to the aims of the proletariat could be found only within the proletariat itself. But I too had been well trained for such discussions and was well versed in Marxist sophistry. You are absolutely right, I said, but then where does all this leave you? You yourself have admitted that your Havana cigars cost you sixty pounds a month, and that your almost daily breakfasts with M.S.A., son of a feudal pasha, cost you twice as much. Your home, which I have visited, is palatial. So while I do agree with everything you say, I would like to add that it disqualifies you from sitting in that chair preaching to comrades who have not been able to afford a decent meal since the last feast ...

Pandemonium broke out and bitter recriminations and personal insults were exchanged, but I had already detached myself from the meeting and taken my first step towards a higher ground from where I could clearly see my former comrades for what they really were. This was my first glimpse of the appalling intellectual darkness of Marxism, which was further revealed to me over the years of extensive reading and study.

CHAPTER 5

Marxist Economics Between Theory and Practice[178]

Although Marxism is above all a philosophy, located slightly to the left of the philosophical ideas of the Young Hegelians such as Feuerbach, Bauer and Strauss, it has always sought to project itself as essentially an economic theory. It was Marx himself who played up the economic dimension of his theory by considering *Capital* to be the cornerstone of his entire ideology.

The secret of this Marxist insistence on characterizing their ideology as an economic theory is easy to understand. For it is Marx's economic theory that proves the validity of his philosophical, political and social theories, all of which depart from the premise that economics is the driving force behind all aspects of social life.

The materialism of Feuerbach took on a purely economic dimension with Karl Marx. In the latter's philosophy, there is no independent or absolute existence for a political system, customs, traditions, ethics, society, art, literature, law or religion; they are all reflections and results of a material/economic reality as embodied in the forces of production prevailing at a given time.

The material foundation of all aspects of human life, according to Marx, is an economic foundation which consists of two main elements: the forces of production and the relations of production, the latter being a direct reflection of the first.

The forces of production, and the relations of production at any given time, give rise to a particular political, social, moral and legal system in which a certain art and religion will exist. Karl Marx refers to all those matters as being the superstructure based on forces and relations of production, which are the infrastructure.

This idea, which has been simplified above and which is the basis of historical materialism, is the foundation of the entire Marxist ideology, from which Karl Marx derived all the other aspects of his ideology.

The idea of class struggle, the fuel which fans the flames of the proletarian revolution that will overthrow capitalism, is based entirely on the theory of historical materialism – which is in turn based on the idea of infrastructure and superstructure. The conflict of interest between the proletariat and the bourgeoisie and the growing enmity between the two classes is due to the production relations prevailing in the stage of capitalist development, in the sense that the exploitation which, in the eyes of Marx, is the basic characteristic of the relationship between the capitalists and the proletariat, is the source of the class struggle.

The theory of violent transition from capitalism to socialism through revolutionary action, strongly endorsed by Engels in *Revolutionary Violence*, and by Mao Tse-tung in *Questions of War and Strategy*, 1938, where he says that armed struggle is the only way not only for the Chinese proletariat but for workers all over the world,[179] is based on historical materialism and the theory of class struggle. The contradictions between capitalists and proletariat, and the tenacious clinging of the former to their privileged position makes a confrontation between them inevitable. As it grows both quantitatively and qualitatively, as its social consciousness matures, the proletariat will come to realize that it is only through violent revolution that it will throw off its chains. Once it has done so, the proletariat will also have brought to an end a complete stage of historical materialism and political economy, namely, the stage of capitalism.

The theory of the dictatorship of the proletariat, which is the backbone of Marxist political theory in the transition stage between capitalism and communism, is based entirely on the ideas of historical materialism, class struggle and revolutionary violence.[180]

In fact, all Marx's theories on private property, the family, the state, society and laws stem from the concept of historical materialism. Yet Marxists refuse to consider their ideology as being a philosophical doctrine first and foremost, and insist on characterizing it as an economic theory. The explanation for this lies in the history of Marx himself, who considered all philosophical systems preceding his own to be unscientific. This appears clearly in his early writings, particularly *The German Ideology*,[181] where he asserts that philosophy from Hellenistic times up to the time of his contemporaries, Max Stirner and David Strauss, was a science which was not scientific. In fact, he considered that, of all the social sciences, only history could be classified as a science, and then only if it were divided into the history of nature and the history of man, which, as he says in *The German Ideology*, are interrelated.

His insistence on stressing the economic dimension of his theory was a desperate attempt to confer a scientific quality on his philosophical world outlook.[182] In 1867, he tried to dedicate *Capital* to Charles Darwin, thinking that this would ensure his entry into the scientific community, but Darwin declined the honour, under the pretext that he had only a perfunctory knowledge of economics. However, this did not deter Frederick Engels, who knew and shared Marx's longing for scientific recognition, from invoking Darwin's name in the eulogy to Karl Marx which he delivered at the latter's grave site at Highgate Cemetery in London on 17 March 1883. Mourning humanity's loss of the 'greatest living thinker', he says:

> Just as Darwin discovered the law of development of organic nature, so Marx discovered the law of development of human history:[183] the simple fact, hitherto concealed by an over-growth of ideology, that mankind must first of all eat, drink, have shelter and clothing, before it can pursue politics, science, art, religion, etc.; that therefore the production of the immediate material means of subsistence and consequently the degree of economic development attained by a given people or during a given epoch form the foundation upon which the state institutions, the legal conceptions, art and even the ideas on religion, of the people concerned have been evolved, and in the light of which they must, therefore, be explained, instead of vice versa, as has hitherto been the case.

But it is obvious for the serious student of Marxism that it is essentially a philosophical doctrine and that the economic part of Marx's theory was just one of the many bricks he laid carefully over the foundation underpinning his entire ideology, namely, historical materialism, in the aim of bolstering that foundation. That Marx's concerns were purely philosophical is clear from his early works, such as *The Difference Between the Philosophy of Nature of Democritus and that of Epicurus*,[184] his articles in *Kolne Zeitung*, the manuscripts he wrote in 1844 which were published posthumously,[185] and other early essays and books, like *Critique of Hegel's Philosophy, of the State* (1842), *Critique of Hegel's Philosophy of Rights* (1844), *The Jewish Question* (1844), *The Holy Family* (1845), *The German Ideology* (1845–46), *The Poverty of Philosophy* (1847) and *The Manifesto of the Communist Party* (1848).

When they are not laying down the philosophical framework of the concept of dialectical materialism, these early works are for the most part violent criticisms of Hegel, Feuerbach, Bauer and Strauss. In other words, they are purely philosophical and/or political in character, without a trace of Marxist economics. The term 'historical materialism' frequently crops up in these early writings, with the same significance it came to have later. An entire chapter of *The German Ideology* is given over to the subject. The terms 'forces of production' and 'relations of production' are also clearly established at this stage.

In fact, a number of pro-Marxist Western scholars also believe that Marx's economic theory was devised only to support his political theory. The British political analyst Harold Laski notes in his book *Communism* that: 'It was imperative for the communist Marx to show that an implacable enmity existed between the masters in general and the proletariat. He was able to do so through the theory of surplus value.'

In the same chapter, Laski quotes a German economist as saying that the theory of surplus value – by far the most important Marxist economic theory as the reader will see in the following pages – derives its importance not from its predication on economic facts but from the political and economic slogans it contains.

Innumerable examples in the early works attest to this. However, we shall content ourselves with quoting a passage from a chapter in Volume I of *The German Ideology*. In a critique of Feuerbach, Marx writes under the sub-heading, 'History':

> The production of life, both of one's own in labour and of fresh life in procreation, now appears as a double relationship: on the one hand as a natural, on the other as a social relationship. By social we understand the co-operation of several individuals, no matter under what conditions, in what manner and to what end. It follows from this that a certain mode of production, or industrial stage, is always combined with a certain mode of co-operation, or social stage, and this mode of co-operation is itself a 'productive force'. Further, that the multitude of productive forces accessible to men determines the nature of society, hence, that the 'history of humanity' must always be studied and treated in relation to the history of industry and exchange.

It is clear from the above passage that the concept of historical materialism, the cornerstone of Marx's entire ideology, had already been fully developed at that early phase. All his writings during this period and until he settled in London were directed at establishing the concept of historical materialism – which Marx and Engels described as a 'discovery' – and at interpreting all human history from this angle.

Marx's economic writings came at a later stage. Between the end of May and 27 June 1865, he wrote his first economic work, in the academic sense of the word, a paper entitled *Wages, Price and Profit*. It was publicly aired first as an address he delivered in June 1865 at two sittings of the General Council of the International Working Men's Association, and was published much later – in 1898 – by his daughter, Eleonor, as a pamphlet entitled *Value, Price and Profit*. The title was later amended by the Central Committee of the Soviet Communist Party to *Wages, Price and Profit*. According to the Institute of Marxism-Leninism, it was in this paper that Marx first presented his theory on surplus value.[186]

Scholars consider this book as the basis for his major work, often called the bible of Marxism,[187] *Capital*, Volume I of which was published by Marx in London in 1867. Several unpublished works were compiled by Engels after Marx's death in 1883 and published in two subsequent volumes, Volume II in 1885 and Volume III in 1894. The chronological order in which these works appeared is no accident, but the natural result of Karl Marx's process of thinking. His youth, early education, schooling and his doctoral thesis (on Epicurus' philosophy of nature), his writings over a span of 20 years (1840/60), his political activities during that period, as well as his articles and speeches, all clearly indicate that historical materialism is the cornerstone of his theory and that Marxism is, first and foremost, a philosophy which Marx sought to render different from other philosophies by calling it scientific and claiming that it was of universal significance. That is why he strove to give his philosophy a political dimension (with his theories of class struggle, revolutionary action, the proletarian revolution and the dictatorship of the proletariat), a social dimension (with his and Engels' theories on the family, on marriage and on private property) and an economic dimension (with theories which were completed only after his death, theories which aimed at constructing a Marxist economic system from the set of theories on labour, value and surplus value and from the side theories stemming from these two basic postulates, like the law of accumulation of capital, the law of concentration of capital, the law of pauperization, etc.).

All these theories – political, social and economic – were devised to buttress the ideological or philosophical essence of Marxism, namely, historical materialism, and to make of Marxism a comprehensive and all-encompassing ideology that could provide a theoretical framework for the entire history of mankind in all its aspects: religion, economy, law, literature, nationalities, systems of rule and social systems. It was meant to provide an answer to every question, a solution for every problem and a framework for all forms of social research. At a later stage, when this Marxist conceit (universality) combined with national pride (Russian), the Soviets and Marxists all over the world extended their claim of universality beyond the field of social sciences to that of applied sciences, referring in their encyclopaedia to 'communist science' in the domains of genetics, psychology, biology, the atom, etc.

What we have sought to demonstrate with all the above is

that Marxism is in essence a philosophical doctrine and not, as Marxists would have us believe, an economic theory. A study of Marx's works shows that he started to lay the foundations of his doctrine in 1840/41 and spent the next 20 years elaborating it as a philosophical-cum-political system.

Only later, when he realized that to make good his claim that his doctrine presented an integrated and all-encompassing worldview, he had to develop the economic aspect of the theory, did he proceed to elaborate Marxian economics.

As for Engels, there is hardly a trace of economics, in the academic sense of the word, in all his writings and speeches, with the possible exception of his rather contrived – and comic – study *The Role of Labour in the Evolution of Ape to Man*,[188] written in 1876 and published for the first time in the 44th issue of the German review *Die Neue Zeit* in 1896. There is also his role in compiling and publishing the second and third volumes of Marx's *Capital*.

In May and June 1865, Marx wrote his famous *Wages, Price and Value*. Two years later, in 1867, he published the first volume of his main work, *Capital*. If we look at these two works, which together with his book, *A Contribution to the Critique of Political Economy*[189] published in 1859, form his economic doctrine, we find that the two most important theories advanced by Marx in these works are those on value and surplus value. His theory on value was formulated in Chapter 6 of *Wages, Price and Profit*.[190] Two years later, he explained it in greater depth in Part I of *Capital* under the heading 'Commodities and Money'. In *Wages, Price and Profit*, Marx explains the main theory in his economic doctrine – which is the theory of value based on labour – in terms similar to those with which he began *Capital*.[191]

We shall give a brief presentation below of the two theories which Marxists believe to be the basis of the only scientific economic system ever devised: value and surplus value. For Marxists, these theories prove the validity of Marx's philosophical and political analysis and of the exploitative essence of capitalism. Our purpose in doing so is twofold: one, to prove our claim that Marxist economics was devised to buttress the political aspect of the system and, two, to show that the system in its entirety collapses when confronted with the reality of economic life in the modern world, specifically the development of the forces of production and their reliance on oil.

MARX'S THEORY OF VALUE

In the opening lines of *Capital*, Marx says:

> The wealth of those societies in which the capitalist mode of production prevails, presents itself as an 'immense accumulation of commodities', its unit being a single commodity. Our investigation must therefore begin with the analysis of a commodity ... The utility of a thing makes it a use-value ... A commodity such as ... iron, corn, or a diamond, is therefore, so far as it is a material thing, a use-value, something useful. ... In the form of society we are about to consider, they are, in addition, the material depositories of exchange-value ... Exchange-value, at first sight, presents itself as a quantitative relation, as the proportion in which values in use in one sort are exchanged for those of another sort, a relation constantly changing with time and place ... A given different commodity is exchanged for other commodities in the most different proportions. Instead of one exchange-value, wheat, for example, has, therefore, a great many ... But since each commodity represents the exchange-value of a given proportion of wheat, they must, as exchange-values, be replaceable by each other or equal to each other ... Therefore, first: the valid exchange-values of a given commodity express something equal; secondly, exchange-value, generally, is only the mode of expression, the phenomenal form, of something contained in it, yet distinguishable from it ... Let us take two commodities, e.g., corn and iron. The proportions in which they are exchangeable, whatever those proportions may be, can always be represented by an equation in which a given quantity of corn is equated to some quantity of iron: ... What does this equation tell us? It tells us that in two different things – in 1 quarter of corn and x cwt. of iron, there exists in equal quantities something common to both. The two things must therefore be equal to a third, which in itself is neither the one nor the other. Each of them, so far as it is exchange-value,

must therefore be reducible to this third ... This common 'something' cannot be either a geometrical, a chemical, or any other natural property of commodities. Such properties claim our attention only in so far as they affect the utility of those commodities, make them use-values. But the exchange of commodities is evidently an act characterized by a total abstraction from use-value. Then one use-value is just as good as another, provided that only it be present in sufficient quantity ... As use values, commodities are, above all, of different qualities, but as exchange-values they are merely different quantities, and consequently do not contain an atom of use-value.

If then we leave out of consideration the use-value of commodities, they have only one common property left, that of being products of labour ... there is nothing left but what is common to them all; all are reduced to one and the same sort of labour, human labour in the abstract ... A use-value, or useful article, therefore, has value only because human labour in the abstract has been embodied or materialized in it.[192]

In an extensive study of Marx, as part of a study of socialist theories,[193] an Egyptian professor of economics sums up the essence of Marx's concept as follows:

1. Commodities comprising labour are the only commodities with value.
2. Those commodities that include labour are the only ones that have an exchange-value.
3. The value of commodities that have an exchange-value is determined and measured by the quantity of labour they contain.

It is worth noting that in the third volume of *Capital*, published by Engels in 1894, 11 years after the death of Marx, the latter states: 'The theory of labour within value does not conform either with factual processes or with the real form of production.'[194]

Of Marx's theory of value, Dr Galal Amin says: 'There is no agreement among interpreters of Marxism, not even among Marxists themselves on the aim of Marx's theory of value'.[195]

What Dr Amin means is that Marx's critics and supporters disagree as to the purpose of the theory of value, whether it is to define 'price' or 'profit'. While Marx's critics, headed by the Austrian professor, Bohm Bawerk, tend to hold that Marx meant to determine 'price', Marx's supporters, headed by the American professor, Paul Sweezy, maintain that Marx established his theory of value to explain capitalist profit.[196]

We do not agree with Dr Amin that the aim of the theory of value is obscure. The only conclusion to be drawn from an extensive study of Marx's work, particularly of the political part of his system, is that, contrary to what may be suggested by such texts as Chapter 6 of *Wages, Price and Profit*, he was less concerned with determining price than with finding an explanation for capitalist profit that would fit in with his political doctrine. The best proof of this is that the only use to which he put the theory of value was in building up his more important theory of surplus value, which he considered to be the 'scientific' bulwark of his political theory.

THE THEORY OF SURPLUS VALUE

Once Marx had established that the value of any commodity can be measured only by the amount of labour expended on it, he moved on to say that the gain of the capitalist or employer is unjustifiable acquisition. If a worker spends a certain number of hours producing a given commodity, then the capitalist employer sells that commodity for a certain price, gives the worker part of that price as wages and retains the balance, that balance represents an unjustified acquisition for the capitalist employer, since the price is the result of the labour put in by the worker. It is this balance that Karl Marx calls surplus value.[197]

Marx first defined surplus value in 1865, in *Wages, Price and Profit*, when he wrote: 'The surplus value, or that part of the total value of the commodity in which the surplus labour or unpaid labour of the working man is realized, I call Profit.' Marx says, furthermore, that:

A rent, Interest, and Industrial Profit are only different names for different parts of the surplus value of the commodity, or the unpaid labour enclosed in it, and they are equally derived from this source, and from this source alone. They are not derived from land as such or from capital as such, but land and capital enable their owners to get their respective shares out of the surplus value extracted by the employing capitalist from the labourer.[198]

With the theory of surplus value, Marx believed that he had presented 'scientific' economic proof of the exploitation of workers by the capitalist employers.

Before we try to evaluate these two basic theories of Marxist economy, it should be made clear that the theory of 'Labour in Value' was not discovered by Karl Marx as is commonly believed. It is to be found in its entirety in the writings of the classic British economist, David Ricardo, specifically in his book *Principles of Political Economy and Taxation* (1817). This may come as a surprise to Marxists, who may also be surprised to know that after presenting his theory on capital in *Wages, Price and Profit* in 1865, and again in Volume I of *Capital* in 1867, Karl Marx then went back on the theory in Volume III of *Capital*. This makes it difficult to continue accepting the economic part of Marx's theory, particularly when one realizes, through observation, that the essence of that theory is false, as we shall explain below.

That is undoubtedly what led Eduard Bernstein, founder of the German Social Democratic Party, to say in his book *Evolutionary Socialism*, written in 1899: 'The theory of surplus value based on Marx's theory of value is itself founded on an assumption that the science of economics has been proved false.'[199] It is also what led the greatest economist of the twentieth century, John Maynard Keynes, to describe *Capital* as being 'a contrived textbook on economics, not only wrong from the scientific point of view, but also of no importance to the modern world and inapplicable in it'.[200]

In his book *Roads to Freedom* (1918), Bertrand Russell, one of the greatest philosophers of the twentieth century, said: 'The theory of surplus value is not so much of a contribution to economic theory as it is hatred expressed in abstract terms and mathematical formulae.'

If Marxists are surprised to learn that it was not Marx but

Ricardo who discovered the theory of the labour element in value, they will be even more surprised to learn that Marx did not discover the theory of surplus value. It was in 1824, when Marx was sixteen, that William Thompson, the Irish intellectual, presented the same theory, with the same purpose and under the same name, 'surplus value'. This led to the assertion by Menger that: 'Those who really discovered the theory of surplus value are Goodwin, Hall and, particularly, Thompson. The whole theory, meaning, name and assessment of the quantity of surplus, is, in fact, borrowed from Thompson's book.' And, centuries before Marx, Ricardo and Thompson, Ibn Khaldoun spoke of labour as the main source of value, yet he avoided Marx's two main errors, that of giving a very narrow sense to labour and that of making the concept an absolute rule on which to build what he had in mind.

Going back to Marx's economic theory, we find his statement about labour being the only source of value to be totally refuted by reality. This forced one of the best-known Marxist Western professors of economics, R. Meek, to admit exceptions to the rule, even though he believed that those exceptions did not affect the validity of the rule in general.[201]

Let us examine a few examples before we accept or oppose Professor Meek's opinion, by looking at both direct labour and indirect or inert labour:[202]

- Two brothers, similar as to age, physical and mental fitness, go out fishing one morning. After spending ten hours each at his work, the first returns with 20 kilograms of fish which he sells for 20 pounds, while the second returns with 20 pounds of shrimps which he sells for 60 pounds.
- Two painters, A and B, spend ten hours each producing a painting; the first is sold for 30 pounds, the second for 10,000 pounds.
- 'A' worked for 20 years in his shop, adjoining the shop of 'B'. Throughout those years, each of them worked ten hours a day, alone and using no machinery (no 'dead labour' according to Marx); they both manufactured wooden chests with mother of pearl inlay, sold in the Cairo souks to tourists. Yet 'A' has always been complaining that tourists prefer the products of his neighbour 'B', because of the latter's innate

talent, even though both have been trained in their craft by their fathers; as a result, 'B''s monthly income is almost four times as high as 'A''s.

- 'A', 'B', 'C' and 'D' have been working for ten years on four identical machines in a factory. They are of the same age, have all had the same training programme. Yet their foreman at the factory says that if 'A''s output is estimated to be 100 units, 'B''s average production would be 90, 'C''s would be 80 and 'D''s would be 70. He attributes the difference to their different levels of intelligence, physical capacity and assimilation of experience.

- What is produced by 1 million Soviet workers in the oil industry in Baku at the rate of 150 million hours of labour per month is estimated at a value equal to 70 times the value of what is produced by 1 million Soviet workers in cotton plantations for the same number of hours, disregarding the role of dead or indirect labour (machines etc.).

- 'A', owner of a well-known fashion designer-house in Paris, spent one thousand hours designing a line of ladies' clothes. 'B', his competitor, spent five hundred hours designing another line. At the beginning of the winter season, when both started actually producing their designs, 'B''s designs swept the market, earning him a hundred times more fame and money than 'A'. The following year 'C' enters the competition with a new set of designs that conquer the market; the demand on the clothes manufactured by 'A' and 'B' falls drastically, and they have to cut their prices.

It is clear from the above examples that there are cases where value resides in elements other than the labour put into the production of goods. In the past, Marxist economists would dismiss this argument out of hand, claiming that it applied only in such rare cases, as the sale of a hair from a prophet's beard, of a letter signed by Napoleon, of a painting by Delacroix or Renoir, of a sculpture by Michelangelo or Rodin or of a manuscript by Dante or Shakespeare.

This specious argument conveniently overlooks the fact that, as we have shown, the cases where a commodity's value does not derive from the labour put into it are too numerous to be dismissed as exceptions. And, even if, for the sake of argument, we accept that they are exceptions that do not change the rule, the basic premises on which the rule itself was predicated have been rendered invalid by a major development of the century, namely, the oil revolution. With the total dependence of the world economy on oil as the main source of energy and the backbone of the forces of production in our age, the Marxist claim that labour is the sole source of value becomes nonsensical. The value of oil cannot be measured in terms of the amount of labour that has gone into extracting it, contrary to what Marx, who totally rejected nature as a source of value, would have said. Marx held that only if the labour of man was added to the work of nature would the latter acquire value. But is such an analysis compatible with the reality of oil? Is the value of oil on the world market determined by the law of supply and demand, i.e. by the indispensable need for oil to keep the wheels of modern civilization rolling, or is it determined by the number of labour hours spent in extracting it? Obviously, the market value of oil far exceeds the value of the direct and indirect labour that has gone into extracting it. Let us look at the following examples:

- The same labour is expended and the same machinery is used to drill two oil wells. Yet one will yield 10,000 barrels a day while the other will yield only 500. Is the effective role in determining value here played by labour or by nature?
- The value of a barrel of North Sea crude is equal to that of a barrel of Gulf crude, despite the fact that the cost of extracting the former from offshore oil wells is five times greater than the cost of extracting Gulf crude from onshore wells. Does the equivalence in value here derive from the fact that there is an equal demand for both on the world market or does it derive from the labour element, which is very different in the two cases?
- In some oil fields in California and the Gulf area, oil is extracted without human intervention. Pumps are placed at the mouth of the wells and the force of pressure in the production pipes can keep the oil gushing out spontaneously for tens of years. Pressure in other geological formations is sometimes so weak that injection operations have to be substituted for the natural pressure (this proved necessary in

some of the oil fields in the Gulf of Suez, like the Morgan and July fields in the Ras Ghareb area). Yet in both cases, the value of the barrel of oil is the same. Does this not prove that value is determined by factors other than labour?

All of the above examples confirm that the growing importance of and demand for oil have eliminated the role of labour in determining value. In many other spheres, such as architecture, interior decoration and industrial design, labour is not the sole, or, indeed, even the main, determinant of value. Other elements, such as talent, predisposition and a better ability to benefit from training[203] are more important in determining value. A striking case in point is tourism. Can the national income from tourism in countries like Spain, Italy, Morocco, Tunisia, Lebanon (before the crises) and Egypt be explained in terms of labour? What labour is involved in Egypt's revenues from tourists visiting Abu Simbel, Luxor and Aswan or the Pyramids and the Sphinx?

Any Marxist justification of value in the last example would be self-defeating for any 'dead labour' inherent in those ancient historical sites which a Marxist economist might claim as a source of their value and the revenues they generate is artistic work to which Marx's theory of value does not apply in the first place, since it is the quality and not the quantity of labour that counts in this case.

So much for the theory of value, the foundation on which Marx built his key theory of surplus value, which he defines as the amount by which the value of a product exceeds the value of its constituent elements. In fact, the reasoning process by which he moved from the theory of value to that of surplus value is far more political than economic.

Herein lies the basic flaw of Marxist economics as a whole. If the main defect of the theory of value lies in its rigid view of labour as the sole source of value and in its dismissal of all other sources such as nature, talent, skill or organization, the main defect of the theory of surplus value lies in its narrow perception of the role of capitalist or employer. Marx departs from an assumption that he considered to be axiomatic, namely, that the capitalist does nothing! Such an assumption is, needless to say, contrary to logic and to reality. The basic postulate on which the theory of surplus value is predicated is that the capitalist always makes a profit. It follows that what he gets, which is always more than what he pays his workers in consideration of their labour, is a surplus value which he obtains by exploiting his workers, who, as Marx repeats twice in Volume I of *Capital*, produce more than they gain and consume. Clearly, this postulate is totally unfounded. As he may make a profit, so too can the capitalist employer incur a loss. How would a Marxist economist explain such a loss? And why should he not put the profit realized by a capitalist employer down to the law of probabilities governing all commercial enterprises? If an employer is as likely to suffer a loss as he is to make a profit, does this not mean that he has a role in the production process greater than that of a mere source of exploitation for his workers? Can his role in bringing together workers on the work premises be dismissed as irrelevant and as not representing a contribution to the production process itself? If labour is defined as direct manual labour only, where does this leave organization, management and mental work? In fact, the theory of surplus value unequivocally denies to organization and management, which are the essence of an employer's role, the quality of labour.[204] And, while Marxists recognize the contribution of dead labour (site and machinery) to the production process, they do not recognize its contribution to surplus value, inasmuch as they perceive it as the result of labour performed by others and transmitted to the capitalist employer only by inheritance, a mechanism that is totally rejected by Marxism.[205]

Can anyone who has ever been involved in the field of trade or industry deny the decisive role of organization, management, marketing and personal capability in determining the success or failure of any enterprise? How would a Marxist who subscribes to the theory of surplus value explain the following phenomenon that is prevalent in Western Europe, particularly Britain, France and Italy?[206] Identical wages are paid to two workers, similar as to age, ability, education, experience and training, one working in a public enterprise, the other in an identical but private enterprise. In fact, the private sector worker could get even more than his public sector counterpart. Is the percentage retained by the public enterprise for organization and management legitimate, while the same percentage retained by the private enterprise is labelled surplus value, the embodiment of an employer's exploitation of his workers?

In a study on the theory of value and exploitation in his book on Marxism,[207] Dr Galal Amin points out that the theory of value does not necessarily prove the existence of exploitation. Even if we accept Marx's claim that the worker has a right to what he produces, that in itself would not prove that the capitalist exploits the workers. This proposition is based on the false assumption that the capitalist does not contribute to the increase in the value of the commodity. In fact that is not so. On the one hand we have the capitalist's role in organization and management, and no one would dare claim, in this day and age, that management and organization are examples of non-productive labour as Engels said one hundred years ago. Reality proves that management and organization are forms of labour in the sense that they are added to the value of a commodity, which explains the fact that thousands of enterprises, both public and private, in countries like England, France, Germany and the USA are willing to pay up to 200,000 dollars a year for a capable and successful manager.

On the other hand, contemporary economic science recognizes the fact that mechanization of industrial or agricultural production raises the price of a commodity; that is what encourages capitalists to invest in machinery.[208]

In her study of Marxist economy published in 1957 in London, the world-renowned professor of economics Joan Robinson described the way Marxists use the theory of surplus value to prove capitalist exploitation of labour as leger-demain.

Once it has been proved that the theory of surplus value, the cornerstone of the Marxist economic doctrine, fails to establish the exploitative role of capitalists in the production process, the whole structure of Marxist economics comes crashing down, and with it the political theories the economic theory was designed to serve: the theory of class struggle, the inevitability of revolution and the ultimate collapse of the capitalist stage of development.

If we turned to other basic theories of Marxist economics, such as the law of the accumulation of capital and the law of pauperization, we would realize that time has proved their lack of validity as well. Marx predicted that as the capitalist system developed it would lead capitalists to depend on machinery and do away with workers. Now, one century later, we note that there is an ever-increasing need for workers in the capitalist systems and more jobs available for them.

As for the phenomenon of unemployment in capitalist societies, it is, in essence, only a candid way of calling a spade a spade, far better than the extensive masked unemployment in all socialist systems where there is a place for everyone in state offices, factories or farms, regardless of the actual work to be done. Moreover, in the capitalist systems the unemployed are provided with legal and social securities to guarantee them a minimum income superior to the income of most workers in the socialist systems.

According to Marx, under the law of accumulation of capital,[209] the number of capitalists will dwindle, whereas the number of wage-earners will increase. In fact, the opposite is true, as the ranks of the capitalist class are systematically swelling in industrialized capitalist countries with the incorporation of former wage-earners.

Actually, the law of accumulation of capital was proved wrong even before the death of Karl Marx in 1883 and that of Friedrich Engels in 1895. In Britain, where Marx made his permanent home, a law was promulgated in 1862 that doubled the number of firms and enterprises by establishing the pattern of shareholder companies. This led to the appearance of a new type of capitalists who did not manage their business themselves but entrusted them to experts. The result was the exact opposite of the law of accumulation of capital.

There is no doubt that the developed capitalized systems have succeeded in transforming the proletariat which existed in the time of Marx, into a Middle/Middle Class in the full sense of the term.

We refer the reader here to the report compiled by former French President Valéry Giscard d'Estaing (excerpts of which are reproduced in Chapter 14 of this book) where he uses statistics to prove the upward social mobility of the working class in the capitalist countries. As to the law of pauperization according to which Marx predicts that, with the exception of a narrow circle of capitalists, most members of society would grow steadily poorer until society becomes sharply polarized into two classes: a shrinking ever-richer capitalist class, and an expanding ever-poorer proletariat, this law, like all other Marxist economic theories, was established to serve Marx's political analysis. This is clear from Engels' statement in 1890 on the acute conflict of interest between capitalism and the proletariat: 'When the capitalist mode of production has transformed the majority of the population into a proletariat, it will have created the force that will either accept to be destroyed or will make the revolution.'

The middle class, like the petty bourgeoisie, civil servants, intellectuals, small businessmen and craftsmen, would be crushed downwards to join the ranks of the proletariat, according to the law of pauperization, one of Marx's main economic laws, as the capitalists systematically lower wages and worsen working conditions.

The years since the death of Karl Marx in 1883 have shown beyond doubt that the law of gradual pauperization is a myth that has been dispelled by steady improvement in the status of the working class.

The worker described by Marx and Engels a century ago did have to work day and night in appalling conditions and without any security: his life was a tale of woe, financially, physically and socially. In fact, the description of that life by Charles Dickens is far more eloquent than the description given by Engels in his famous book on the conditions of the English working class in the mid-nineteenth century. But that worker no longer exists in our time in the industrialized capitalist countries, although something similar still exists in the countries of Eastern Europe and the Soviet Union.

The worker in modern Western societies enjoys high wages, a good life and the latest in material comforts. Scores of reliable sources and references, however, describe the poverty and the difficulty of life in the Soviet Union, particularly for the ordinary citizen who does not have the privileges of the ruling class. Unfortunately, many of those references do not exist in Arabic; the only works we do have in Arabic about life in the USSR and in the societies of the socialist bloc are very superficial (like the book by Musa Sabri, *Communists Everywhere*). Thus we are forced to refer the reader to one of the best books written on the subject, *The Russians* (Sphere Books, London, 1980, seventh edition), for which the author, the noted British journalist Hedrick Smith, was awarded the Pulitzer Prize. The reader will particularly enjoy Chapter Two of Part One of the book, the Art of Queueing.[211]

The book was described by both the *New York Times* and the *Sunday Times* as a brilliant work. The *Observer* wrote: 'If you want to know as much as possible about life in Russia today, the best thing you can do is to go to Hedrick Smith. For years to come, his book will remain the definitive introduction to Russian life.' Yet, surprisingly, Arab publishers have ignored the book.

Facts and practice have proved Marx's economic theories wrong, leading John Maynard Keynes to dismiss *Capital* as having no relevance in the modern world. It has also led the famous French sociologist, George Sorel, to say: 'The experience of Marx's theory of value shows the importance of remaining cryptic so as to confer solidity on an ideology!' All of this goes to show that Marx was in no way an economist. The chronology of his works shows that he turned to economics only to give a scientific dimension to his system so that it would not be looked upon merely as an offshoot of the philosophy of the Left Hegelians. Marx's study of economics did not start, as did those of Adam Smith, Ricardo and John Stuart Mill, by observing economic life in order to draw conclusions and laws; Marx's point of departure was political.

The three volumes of *Capital* indicate that Marx had been searching for proof that capitalists exploit workers by expropriating the surplus value of their labour. This led him to formulate his economic theories of value and surplus value.

Moving now from the theoretical to the practical aspects of Marxist economics, what do we find? Have the regimes subscribing to Marx's theory in the Soviet Union, in the People's Democratic Republic of China, in Cuba and in the countries of Eastern Europe managed to provide the economic wealth which is the material basis for the highest stage of communism, when the state, laws and private property will have disappeared and wealth and women are available to each according to his need? Our readings of serious economic studies on Marxist economics, our own observation of socialist experiences in countries of the Third World, especially in Egypt, Syria, Iraq, Libya and Algeria, and visits to several other countries of different social and economic levels, have all led us to believe that socialist economy can never provide the abundant productivity which is the basis for communism.

In all the socialist countries, whether they are dictatorships of the proletariat according to the Soviet model or countries of the Third World, like Nasserite Egypt and similar countries, the economic situation does not indicate any possibility of achieving the abundance of production that can allow the emergence of a communist society as envisaged by Marx. The poverty of socialist economy augurs no significant improvement for the future.

Undoubtedly too, those who relinquished public freedoms in exchange for better economic conditions have discovered that they have in fact lost both. For years socialists claimed that real freedom is economic and social, not political, yet their regimes clearly show that they have none of those freedoms.

The picture of the economic situation in countries of the socialist bloc that emerged from discussions with such noted experts on the subject as professor Alec Nove and from the accounts of scores of artists and intellectuals who had fled from the USSR and other socialist countries whom I met in Paris was a shocking revelation. For years, Marxist comrades in Egypt had extolled the economic situation under socialism in general and in the Soviet Union in particular. For hours on end, the author of these lines had listened to Soviet statistics read out to young Marxists in the late 1960s by the Egyptian communist leader, F.M., claiming that the citizens of socialist countries enjoyed better food, better clothes and better holidays than those of capitalist societies!

So many fictitious statistics about weekend holidays, education, sports, entertainment and health care in the Soviet Union, the paradise of the proletariat and of all the downtrodden, were repeated to us who had no references then save Soviet magazines and publications, those all-powerful weapons of communist propaganda.

The same pragmatic approach that has shaped our attitude to ideological, economic, political and social issues also shaped our perception of Marxist economics. If the tales of socialist economic successes are true, then the economic and social freedom which Marxists regard as the true essence of freedom must also exist in those societies. So too must the political freedom that ensues from economic and social freedoms. Why then the walls erected by socialist regimes around their peoples? Why the fetters that prevent them from travelling freely to that capitalist world burdened with exploitation and class inequities? How to explain the fact that the 'infernal' capitalist systems allow their proletarian slaves to see the world, to visit the workers' paradise in the socialist states?

We maintain that Nasserite Egypt is the best example in the Third World of the failure of socialist economic systems where the regime controls the people's livelihood, leading to total economic, cultural, social, military and political disaster.

Socialist societies lack the main component or element of progress, the one that has allowed humanity to achieve so much, namely, individual initiative. The failure of socialist systems to realize the productive plenty which is the basis of the higher stage of communism can be put down only to the absence from such systems of this factor, the primary driving force that has propelled humanity forward through its successive stages of development. The incentives which allow the elite to carry their respective societies ever forward disappear under socialist regimes. This task is left to the broad masses who are quite simply not qualified to perform it, as borne out by the total absence of artistic creativity from socialist societies.

Is the literature of Soviet Russia comparable to that of Tsarist Russia? What has the socialist regime anywhere produced in terms of culture, music, opera, drama and cinema? If we look to scientific inventions, we find that those of the socialist states lack innovation. The atom bomb was first invented by the Americans and then produced by the Russians. The same is true of other weapons, missiles and planes, which were all invented by Westerners then reproduced by the Soviets. The pattern is repeated in other fields like medicine, engineering, electronics and other industries.

We believe that without the role of outstanding individuals and personal initiative, mankind would soon regress to Stone Age level. We would go even further to say that the only hope and salvation for the masses resides in the genius of the elite, that it is thanks to the personal initiative of the latter that they obtain much more than they do in a society where the 'ordinary' control power. Let the peoples of our region observe the outstanding figures which Egypt produced in all domains before Nasser's regime stifled all personal initiative.

In the field of medicine, Egypt produced great doctors in all fields of specialization, on a par with the most advanced nations of the world. In the sciences, a generation of Egyptian scientists, headed by Dr Mesharaffa. Egypt produced such men of letters as Al-Aqad, Taha Hussein, Ahmed Amin Al Mazny, Shoukry, Zaky Mubarak, Ahmed Shawqy, Hafez Ibrahim, Al-Rafei, Al-Manfalouty and Naguib Mahfouz. In the fields of law, politics, music, sociology, psychology, architecture, etc., whole generations of great men drove Egypt forward and would, had it not been for the disaster caused by Nasser's regime, have placed Egypt on a par with the greatest nations of the world.

Yet the socialist regime in Egypt crushed personal initiative and brought the country to its present state. Why is contemporary Egypt so barren of great artists and scientists? The answer is simple: personal initiative has been crushed while it alone creates the conditions and framework for real progress.

The greatest proof of the success of demagogically Marxist propaganda is that comparisons are still being made between the economic system of the socialist East and that of the capitalist West. In my opinion, this is like conducting a debate over whether light is stronger in daytime or at night.

CHAPTER 6

The Individual and Society

Marx and his disciples have a special theory concerning the role of the individual in history. The gist of it is that the movement of history is governed by laws of a purely materialistic (economic) nature in which there is no room for man's will. The whole history of the human race, from the time man lived by gathering the berries and roots that grew wild in the forest (before the invention of hunting implements in the Stone Age), moving on to the stages of hunting, animal husbandry, land cultivation and from there to the great stages in the progressive development of mankind, from the primitive communal system through the systems of slavery and of feudalism and serfdom, to the stage of early industry, on to the Industrial Revolution, the stage of capitalism and the socialist and communist stages to come, along with all events, political developments, religious and intellectual movements, etc., all this, according to Marxist theory, is governed by purely materialistic laws.

As the movement of history proceeds according to economic materialistic determinism, or necessity, it follows that the individual plays a very minor role in influencing the course it will take, and even that minor role is a natural and inevitable result of economic materialistic laws. This applies to all the great figures of history; from military commanders like Alexander the Great, Ramses, Mark Antony and Napoleon, to social reformers like Martin Luther, and to prophets like Moses and Jesus. It also applies to Lenin, in the sense that it was not he who brought about a fundamental transformation in contemporary history, but the socio-economic conditions which produced him and determined that he should lead the proletarian revolution. According to Marxism, the same is true of all those who have made their mark on the history of mankind through the ages: they were natural and inevitable products of the socio-economic conditions prevailing in their society at a given time. If not them, then others would have emerged to play the same roles assigned to them by the materialistic laws of history.

This perception of the role of the individual in history is the one Marxist tenet which has never been challenged by any 'deviationist' trend. From Marx to Carillo, through tens of official and unofficial Marxist theoreticians and interpreters, it has remained constant, unlike many of the other orthodox Marxist theories which have fallen by the wayside. The most eloquent description of this theory is to be found in *Theory and Application in Communism*, by Carew Hunt, where he quotes the following words of Trotsky:

Homer sang, Plato philosophized, Jesus and Peter changed man's moral consciousness, and they all did what they had to do without realizing that they were merely tools in an economic process which dictated all their actions. To say that they and others like them have made history is contrary to the principle that history is determined by economic forces and that those forces have led to their emergence.

Carew Hunt adds:

Hence the affirmation by Husson that Newton did not discover the law of gravity because an apple fell on his head, but because the economic requirements of the age made it imperative that the law of gravity be discovered.

This theory is the clearest example of the radical difference between Marx's philosophy of historical materialism and Hegel's philosophy of objective idealism. It was Hegel who said that Napoleon on his horse at Iena represented the spirit of the world and that if there had been no Napoleon, the supreme spirit would have placed someone else astride his horse.[212] Thus the Marxist view is entirely different from the traditional view of heroism and heroes; it maintains that, in fact, there are no heroes, just roles dictated by materialistic, economic inevitable necessity.[213]

Although Marxists cherish the theory of historical materialism as one of Marx's greatest achievements – indeed, Engels considered it to be as important as Darwin's theory of evolution – history itself offers irrefutable proof of its invalidity. For the study of history reveals the importance of the role of the individual. Throughout the ages, certain individuals have been pivotal in determining the course of history, and many events and major historical transformations cannot be explained in isolation from human volition.

The works of Abbas al-Aqad, Arnold Toynbee and Bertrand Russell and my own personal observations in the course of my studies and extensive travels led me to embrace a view of the role of the individual in history that is diametrically opposed to the Marxist view. Their dismissal of the role of great men and of chance in history is refuted by countless examples to the contrary.

Had Adolf Hitler not existed at a given point in time, the political map of our time would have been very different. If it had not been for Kemal Ataturk, the history of modern Turkey would have taken a very different course. Napoleon Bonaparte changed history. So did Gamal Abdel Nasser – for better or for worse – not only in Egypt, but throughout the Middle East and Africa and the Third World.

But for the decisive role played by Lenin, the Bolsheviks would not have succeeded in seizing power from the Mensheviks and we would have seen none of the enormous transformations brought about by the downfall of the bourgeois democratic republic in Russia and the instauration of the dictatorship of the proletariat.[214] Had it not been for Karl Marx, the political landscape of the modern world would not have been the same. The decisive role played by Plekhanov in the dissemination and victory of Marxism in Russia is indisputable. Saudi Arabia as we know it today would not have existed but for the personal role of King Abdul Aziz Al Saud.[215] The outcome of the Crusades would have been very different without the personal role of Saladin and his military genius.

Without Sun Yat-sen and Mao Tse-tung after him, an underdeveloped agricultural society like China would never have adopted and implemented such a revolutionary theory as it did.

If we set aside the role of the individual in history and turn to that played by chance, a role that is entirely denied by Marxists, again we would find a series of events where chance played a decisive role. Bertrand Russell gives several irrefutable examples of this.

If the German government had not allowed Lenin to return to Russia, events would have taken a very different course. If the sovereignty of Corsica had not been sold by Genoa to France in 1768, just one year before Napoleon Bonaparte's birth, he would not have been born French. Had the Tsarist authorities executed Lenin as they did his older brother, instead of exiling him to Siberia, Russia would not have come under communist rule in 1917. Had Hitler reached agreement with Britian on taking joint action against the Soviet Union, the map of the contemporary world would have been different. Had the lords of Quraish assassinated the prophet Muhammad the night he fled to Medina, the entire area would not have stepped from the darkness of the Jahiliyya into the light of Islam.

I remember that during meetings of the Egyptian Komsomol (an appellation which, because of its association with the Soviet youth organization of the same name, was a source of great pride to the young comrades), we were constantly being warned against the works of William Shakespeare, who was described by L.K. as 'the enemy of the people' and by A. Sh., the ideal of young Marxist writers at the time, as 'the poet of the nobility and the exploiters'. While I did not understand what lay behind these violent attacks against the greatest dramatist the world has ever known, I, like all my comrades, blindly accepted every-thing our militant mentors told us as gospel truth.

However, after reading Shakespeare in the original, I came to understand why he aroused such hostile feelings among the communists. Many of his works exalt the role of the individual and revile the morals of the masses, or mob, as he called them. Both points are vigorously made in *Julius Caesar*, where Shakespeare uses Antony's speech following Caesar's assassi-nation to show, one, the importance an individual can have in influencing events and, two, how fickle the masses are and how easily they can be swayed by a skilled orator. The 'official'

Marxist displeasure with this side of Shakespeare is reflected in countless reviews of his works by Soviet literary critics – many of which the author has read in their English translation – as well as in Soviet productions of his plays, particularly *Hamlet*. This greatest of all Shakespeare's tragic heroes is portrayed as a weakling in most Soviet productions.

As I have previously mentioned, the writings of Abbas al-Aqad were instrumental in revealing to me the flaws in the Marxist theory of history, where the role of individuals is seen as marginal and of chance as non-existent. His biographies of the great figures of history in general and of Islamic history in particular prove that just the opposite is true; the role of individuals in history is a central one. In fact, the dismissal of the role of the individual is, like many secondary Marxist theories, a blind application of the philosophical generalities of the ideology. Obviously when an ideology holds that matter is the driving force of all human endeavour, regards ideas as a reflection of objective reality (i.e. of economic relations according to Marx's theory of basis and superstructure), and accuses philosophical schools that put ideas before matter of turning history on its head, it follows that commitment to such an ideology entails denying any role for the individual in history.

Just as Marx and his followers had to concoct tens of theories to substantiate their philosophy, like their shoddy theory on art and literature, so too they had to come up with their own theory on the role of the individual in history, a theory which, as it happened, was very much in keeping with the character of Karl Marx himself. For those who have studied the life of Marx and his psychological makeup, it is easy to understand his loathing of greatness and the great, of heroism and heroes. His was an envious and bitter character, inherited from generations of Jewish ancestors who hated society for treating them like outcasts. The violent and vindictive streak in his character was given full play against those of his contemporaries who dared oppose him in any way. Small wonder then that the great men of history, none of whom shared his views, should have been dismissed by Marx as irrelevent in the scheme of things.

None of his close collaborators or disciples was allowed to share the limelight, and anyone suspected of being a potential rival was exposed to the full brunt of his fury. A case in point is Bakunin, towards whom Marx's attitude has been described as despicable by many authorities. The only exception was Engels, who posed absolutely no threat to Marx. On the contrary, he systematically glorified Marx's role and minimized his own, repeating *ad nauseum* that whatever he had done was nothing compared to Marx's great achievements.[216] Even in such books as *The Condition of the Working Class in England*, *The Origin of the Family, Private Property and the State* (1884), *Dialectics of Nature* (1875–76), *Anti-Duhring* (1880), *Socialism: Utopian and Scientific* (1880), *The Peasant War in Germany* (1874), *Ludwig Feuerbach and the End of Classical German Philosophy* (1886), all of which Engels wrote alone, he made a point of mentioning that the main ideas were those of Marx. Thus Marx knew he had nothing to fear from Engels, who was in no way a competitor but, rather, his most ardent admirer and eulogist. Another factor that certainly figured in Marx's calculations was the fact that Engels was his meal ticket. For over a quarter of a century, Engels paid Marx a regular income, thus allowing him to devote all his time to research and writing.

The Marxist denial of the role of the individual in history finds its greatest challenge in the history of the communist movement itself. Having studied the inner workings of communist organizations, and having been personally involved with those in Egypt (1962–72), Algeria (1973–76) and Morocco (1976–79), I can say that from the days of Karl Marx to the present time, the role of the individual in the communist movement has been a decisive one. Marxists would argue that this is a superficial way of looking at things, since those individuals are no more than the products of given socio-economic conditions, as though this magical incantation will settle the matter once and for all. For the uninitiated, however, this is a far from satisfactory explanation. One might well ask how the disparate socio-economic conditions of countries like Egypt, Algeria, Morocco, South Yemen, Italy, France, Ethiopia, Iran and Cambodia could possibly have spawned communist movements sharing the same ideology. How can anyone claim that the medieval socio-economic structure of South Yemen is conducive to the emergence of a communist avant-garde, exactly as the communist avant-garde in Italy or France were produced by the socio-economic conditions prevailing in those two countries? Indeed, the use of such an argument not only strips the term 'socio-economic conditions' of all significance, it invalidates the twin Marxist theories of socio-economic determinism and historical materialism.

If we were to reverse the concept and say, as the Bolsheviks did following their victory in 1917 (and as Mao Tse-tung did 40 years later), that it was the superstructural formations (revolutionary ideas) of the communist avant-garde that brought about the great upheaval in Russia, would this not be to attribute to non-material factors the decisive role in a major historical event? Let us, for the sake of argument, accept the Marxist proposition that the superstructure (ideas, organizations, institutions) is brought into being by, and is a reflection of, the infrastructure (the production forces and relations that make up the economic basis of society), and that, although the superstructure does affect the infrastructure, the latter remains primordial. This proposition admits, however grudgingly, that a feedback process exists between the two,[217] which brings us to a question that I have often put to experienced communists in Europe and elsewhere: is it the general rule that all changes in the infrastructure are brought about by the superstructure (i.e. revolutionary ideas), or is it that, since the superstructure is no more than a reflection of the infrastructure, no radical changes can be brought in the economic basis of society by superstructural revolutionary ideas? The answer to that question can be only one of two things:

- either to admit that the general rule is that radical changes in the infrastructure are brought about by the superstructure (thereby admitting that ideas can change material things);
- or to hold that the general rule is that the infrastructure leads and directs the superstructure, which is no more than its reflection, while admitting that in certain exceptional cases radical changes may be brought about by the super-structure (again admitting that ideas can change material things).

No Marxist in the world can accept the first formulation, because to admit that ideas shape matter would be to destroy the theory of dialectical materialism on which Marx's whole philosophy is founded. This leaves the second formulation, which is the one to which Marxists subscribe. It was consecrated by Engels himself a few months before his death.[218] In a letter to H. Starkenburg dated 25 January 1884, Engels says:

> ... two points must not be overlooked: (a) Political, juridical, philosophical, religious, literary, artistic, etc., development is based on economic development. But all these react upon one another and also upon the economic basis ... It is not that the economic condition is the cause and alone active, while everything else is only a passive effect ... So it is not, as people try here and there conveniently to imagine, that the economic condition produces an automatic effect. No. Men make their history themselves, only they do so in a given environment which conditions it and on the basis of actual conditions already existing, among which the economic relations ...[219]

What lent this second formulation further credence in communist eyes was the success of the Bolsheviks, under Lenin's leadership, in establishing the first dictatorship of the proletariat in 1917. The Bolshevik experience was a clear example of revolutionary ideas (i.e. the superstructure) bringing about a radical change in the economic basis, or infrastructure, of Russian society. No Marxist can claim otherwise, first, because Lenin, Trotsky, Zinoviev and other Marxist authorities have admitted this openly and, second, because in many of his writings Lenin admitted – particularly after his abortive bid for power in 1905 – that the objective (economic) conditions for revolution were not yet ripe in Russia, which, still at the early stages of capitalist development and industrialization, was a predominantly agricultural, semi-feudalist society.

But if the first formulation carries within it a negation of Marxist ideology in its entirety, so too does the second, albeit in a different form. The second formulation assumes that the general rule is that the economic basis asserts itself on ideas – political, moral, legal, etc. – while admitting the possibility that, by way of exception, ideas can affect and change the economic basis. But how true in fact is this general rule? Judging from practical experience it is totally false. The socialist revolution which Lenin launched in Russia is a typical case of the superstructure transforming the infrastructure. Mao Tse-tung himself admits that the same is true of the Chinese revolution. This was also the case in Bulgaria, Czechoslovakia, Romania, Hungary, East Germany, Cambodia, Mongolia and South Yemen, where the transformation to socialism came about as a result of the role of the communist avant-garde and their revolutionary ideas (components of the superstructure), and not because these societies had reached the highest stages of capitalist development, where the contradictions between the capitalist class and a class-conscious proletariat explode in a bloody confrontation through which the proletariat seizes political power. If all those cases are exceptions to the general rule, where can the Marxists point to the one example that confirms the rule? Does not the fact that socialist transformation has always come about through exceptional means arouse some scepticism as to the validity of that cornerstone of Marxist ideology, socialist transformation through the dictatorship of the proletariat? All the cases cited above attest to the decisive role played by the individuals making up what is dubbed the communist avant-garde in bringing the communists to power.

Actually, the Marxist position in this debate is an untenable one, as I mentioned in *Marxist Ideas in the Balance*. Marxists are caught between the devil and the deep blue sea, as it were: if they concede that the general rule is that socialist transformations take place in non-industrial societies, they come up against Marx's concept of historical stages based on economic divisions; if they admit the role of individuals as embodied in the communist avant-garde in the countries where socialist transformations have taken place, they come up against the theory of historical materialism itself.[220]

We cannot accept the argument that the experience of the European communist parties shows that Marxism has developed itself and changed some of its concepts. This argument is persuasively advanced by Santiago Carillo in *'Eurocommunism' and the State*, and in countless declarations made by Berlinguer, Marchais and Althusser. However, I am one of many who believe that Eurocommunism comes under the banner of Social Democracy, and is closer to Kautsky and Bernstein than it is to the original Marxist ideology. So too, apparently, does Moscow, judging by the accusations of revisionist heresy hurled at the Eurocommunists by the Soviet mass media.[221] Moreover, Marxism is an integrated and comprehensive doctrine that does not allow for selective derivations. Otherwise we would have revolutionary officers in Third World armies, with the usual military mentality[222] and meagre educational and philosophical background, using this as a precedent to select Marxist economic and social concepts while rejecting Marx's views on religion (!!).

We have sought with all the above arguments to disprove not only the Marxist theory of historical materialism, but also one of its main offshoots, namely, the theory of the role of the individual in history. As we have seen, individuals have been of paramount importance in shaping the history of communist movements all through – which makes the denial by Marxists of the role of individuals in history all the more strange. We see in this denial of the greatness of humanity as embodied in the great figures of history a denial of what sets man apart from other animals, as well as ingratitude for the contribution of these figures to our common heritage. It also denotes a curious spiritual blindness that equates the great and constructive roles played by some with the destructive roles played by others.

CHAPTER 7

Marxism Between Protestantism and Catholicism[223]

For all that I had spent years studying Marxism, both in theory and in application, it was not until recently that I was struck by the phenomenon which is the subject of the present chapter. A few months ago, I was invited to deliver a series of lectures on Marxism at a Saudi university. During one of these lectures, a student asked how widespread communism was in Western Europe. It was while I was replying to his question that the first glimmerings of an idea flashed through my mind. Back in my room, I decided to test my idea against a map of Europe. There it was: my theory was confirmed beyond the shadow of a doubt.

The student's question had provided the key: as I visualized the map of Europe in preparation for my reply, it suddenly came to me that in the Catholic, or predominantly Catholic, countries of Western Europe, the communist parties were strong, politically influential and enjoyed broad support at the grass-roots level, while in the Protestant, or predominantly Protestant, countries, they were nowhere near as strong or as popular. A look at the map later confirmed that the four biggest communist parties in Western Europe are to be found in France, Italy, Spain and Portugal, where the Catholic faith is predominant. These parties exert a marked political influence and enjoy undeniable public acceptance. In Protestant countries such as Britain, Sweden, Norway and the Netherlands, on the other hand, communist parties are marginal and political life is dominated by right-wing parties. Even the social-democratic parties in those countries, which are more to the left of the right than to the right of the left, have lost the momentum they had in the 1960s and their fortunes are presently at a low ebb. Today, the Conservatives are in power in Britain, Canada (which is an extension of Western Europe) and Sweden, and are expected to be swept into power in West Germany very shortly. In fact, the case of West Germany offers the best proof of this theory, for, in this predominantly Protestant country, the only communist presence to contend with is found in the Catholic province of Bavaria.

To test my theory further, I made a survey of how the communists had fared at the polls in parliamentary and other elections held in Western Europe over the last few years. Figures indicate that their influence is relatively strong in Catholic countries and practically non-existent in Protestant countries. I say relatively because I am comparing their influence now with what it used to be. In the main Catholic countries of Western Europe, namely, France, Italy, Spain and Portugal, communist influence rose steadily after World War II and peaked in the early 1970s. Since then, it has been on the decline. In Italy, where power seemed to be within the grasp of the Communist Party, the 1979 elections came as a rude shock. They got only 31 per cent of the vote and lost tens of parliamentary seats. In France the communists suffered massive defeats in the latest parliamentary elections (1978) and presidential elections (1981). In Spain, they gained only 10 per cent of the vote in the 1979 elections. In Portugal too the story is the same. But despite this recent drop in their track record, the communists still enjoy a far stronger presence in the Catholic countries of Western Europe than they do in the Protestant.

Having proved the existence of this phenomenon, I now set myself the more difficult task of analysing the reasons behind it. If we look to the history of Western Europe, we find that it suffered for centuries from the tyranny of the Catholic Church and from the unacceptable expansion of its authority, power and privileges in the Middle Ages. The Church imposed a harsh discipline on its followers, going so far as to decide which of them would go to heaven and which to hell! The Catholic Church had become synonymous with feudalism, tyranny and oppression, and it was only a question of time before its stranglehold would be challenged. The first challenge came in the sixteenth century, from Martin Luther, founder of Protestantism. The Reformation split Europe into two: those countries that chose to remain in the fold of the Catholic Church on one side and those that embraced the new, moderate, creed on the other. Luther preached a tolerant religion, in which the Church did not set itself up as a mediator between man and God and where man's salvation depended upon his own actions rather than on the observance of certain rituals. Tolerance breeds tolerance, and so the climate in the countries that embraced Protestantism was not favourable to the emergence of extremism.

By the same token, intolerance breeds intolerance, and those countries that remained within the Catholic fold answered extremism with counter-extremism in the opposite direction. Thus Marx's call fell on deaf ears in his homeland, Germany, the cradle of Protestantism. Where it did find a favourable response was in Catholic France, the fertile soil where the seed of socialist ideas in general, and Marxist ideology in particular, took root and flourished.

Thus Marxism is not, as its founders claimed and its adherents affirm, a comprehensive and integrated scientific theory encompassing all aspects of life, but a direct reaction to a specific feature of Europe's past, namely, the excessive power wielded by the Catholic Church.

This simple truth carries within it the negation of the universal significance of the Marxist world outlook. Marxism is the product of a given age and specific circumstances and when these circumstances disappear, Marxism becomes nothing more than an ideology that should not be given more importance than it deserves.

Al Aqad was right when he affirmed more than once in his book, *Communism and Humanism*, that, had it not been for the nineteenth-century tendency to take any idea seriously, Marxism would not have warranted more than a few, fleeting hours of research as a reaction to particular circumstances which no longer exist. And, had it not been for the organized activities of world communism since the establishment of the first socialist state in 1917, the majority of the inhabitants of our planet today would never have heard of Marx and his doctrine. It is an irony of fate that Marx should have provoked so much more debate than the intellectual giants in comparison with whom he is a dwarf!

CHAPTER 8

Communist Propaganda in the Balance of Truth[224]

My faith in communism is like my faith in religion: it is a promise of salvation for mankind. If I have to lay my life down that it may succeed, I would do so without hesitation.
(André Gide, before his visit to the Soviet Union)

It is impermissible under any circumstances for morals to sink as low as communism has done. No one can begin to imagine the tragedy of humanity, of morality, of religion and of freedoms in the land of communism, where man has been debased beyond belief.
(André Gide, after his return from the Soviet Union)

These two contradictory statements graphically illustrate the enormous gap between the image of Soviet society as projected by communist propaganda and the reality of the situation. I shall try in this chapter to shed some light on the subject of communist propaganda and invite other writers to address it in greater detail. It is by no means an exhaustive study of the issue, which is too vast and intricate to be covered in one or two chapters.

The reason we are drawing attention to this issue is that propaganda is the strongest and most dangerous of the communist weapons. The communists use propaganda like a mine-sweeper that clears the way for the communist hordes to sow their seeds, unhindered, in a soil that has been ploughed for them. The systematic use of propaganda as a weapon dates from the early days of communism. It was Marx himself who initiated this policy and passed it on to his disciples, who have since developed it further. Its two main characteristics are, one, the use of relentless repetition to instil communist slogans in people's minds, and, two, its unscrupulous use of false or incomplete facts and figures, both about itself and about its enemies. Communist propaganda is ruthless when it comes to attacking the enemies of communism, and does not hesitate to twist the facts in order to distort their image, sully their reputations and destroy their lives.

The first characteristic – endless repetition – appears clearly in the flood of Soviet and other communist publications, all containing the same ideas and slogans under various headings, which are printed in tens of millons of copies in all languages. This technique is bound to ensure a high degree of exposure for any ideology. The works and speeches of Lenin have been published in all the languages of the world, in hundreds of editions and millions of copies, and sold for a token price that does not even cover the cost of paper and ink. No other author or philosopher before or since has had access to such a wide audience.

This widespread distribution of Lenin's works can in no way be ascribed to their intrinsic worth. No one can claim that his works are more valuable than those of Aristotle, Jean Jacques Rousseau, Voltaire, Diderot, Kant, Hegel, Shakespeare, Ricardo or John Maynard Keynes. Quite the contrary, in comparison with these intellectual giants, Vladimir Ilich Lenin is a dwarf. He was nothing more than a politician whose stature was blown up out of all proportion by a superpower which has been willing to spend tens of millions of roubles to propagate his works, translating them and distributing them at token prices. And, had it not smacked of party propaganda, they would have been distributed free of charge.

Even the works of Karl Marx himself, for all that they have been widely printed by the Soviet Union, have not had such a high profile as those of Lenin. Does this mean that in Marxist eyes the works of Lenin, who was never more than an interpreter of Marxist dogma, are more important than those of Marx and Engels? Obviously not. The real explanation for this inordinate promotion of Lenin, in terms of the sheer number of volumes of his works printed, lies in his nationality: it is Russian chauvinism which has placed this Russian Marxist way above other, non-Russian, Marxist writers. But what applies to Lenin's works, in terms of countless reprints and extensive dissemination, applies also, on a lesser scale, to the works of Marx, Engels, Stalin, Khrushchev and Brezhnev.

The extremely high turnover of the Soviet publishing industry is one example of the first characteristic of communist propaganda, namely, persuasion through constant repetition. As to its second characteristic, namely, the unabashed use of any facts and figures, regardless of truth or accuracy, to promote communism and project a rosy picture of life in communist countries, numerous examples can be found in any one of the Soviet reviews that are distributed all over the world.

Any issue of the magazine *The Soviet Union* is crammed with facts and figures attesting to the wonderful life of the Soviet citizen, whose government provides him with the highest level of nutrition, clothing, health care and social security of any country in the world. We are told that Soviet children are raised under the best possible living conditions and that Soviet citizens enjoy a life of stability and happiness, free from worry, struggle, injustice and exploitation.

Side by side with the statistics and figures glorifying life in the socialist countries, Soviet magazines publish statistics and figures to prove that the quality of life in non-communist societies, particularly in the developed capitalist countries, is very poor and that the citizens of these societies face severe hardships and endless problems in all spheres of life. The irony reaches a peak when they compare the comfort and security enjoyed by Soviet citizens to the lack of comfort and security suffered by American citizens.

Communist propaganda will stoop to anything to disparage opponents and glorify communism as an ideology and a way of life, including slander and defamation of character. In fact, one of its favourite methods is to launch personal attacks against political opponents, rather than limit itself to an objective criticism of the trends they represent.

This characteristic has been noted by many authorities on communism, including the noted British writer, Carew Hunt, who says in the introduction to his book, *The Theory and*

Practice of Communism, that the flood of communist propaganda is such that a researcher seeking to disprove the false allegations and claims with which it is riddled would not know where to begin. For, he says, communist propaganda, the strongest weapon of communism, will use all means, honourable or otherwise, and say anything, true or false, that will serve the cause of communism in any sphere. Because of the sheer volume of statements, claims, allegations and facts that are constantly spewed out by the communist propaganda machine, it would take specialized research centres years to wade through this vast sea of material and prove that most of the facts and data it contains are pure fiction. Even if such centres were to be set up by individual states, the results of their research would not reach the people to whom this propaganda is addressed. Most of them are disinclined to read serious scientific studies that will make them think, preferring the simplified pamphlets that distort reality and defy logic. How many Marxists in the Arab world or in any Third World country have read even one of the hundreds of serious books published by the various research centres specializing in Marxist and Soviet studies in such leading universities as Manchester University, the University of Paris or Johns Hopkins?

Not surprisingly, communist propaganda is directed mainly at the younger generations, particularly students, whose natural rebelliousness and emotional instability make them particularly vulnerable to the apocalyptic vision of the world served up by the communist propaganda machine with a total disregard for truth.

That is not to say, however, that someone with a sound understanding of communist ideology and practice cannot stand up to the avalanche of communist propaganda and prove that it is a tissue of lies. Any sensible man subjected to the absurd claims of the communists and their denigration of all other systems can only ask:

• If what you say is true, if life in non-socialist countries is indeed unbearable and life in the socialist countries so wonderful, why do you surround your peoples with walls? Why do you prevent them from travelling abroad? If they are so happy under socialism, why do you not let them visit non-socialist countries to see for themselves the misery in which others live and so count their own blessings?

- If what you say is true, why do we hear daily of people defecting from the paradise of socialist countries to the hell of the other side? Since when have people chosen misery and pain over happiness? If, as you say, they are encouraged to defect by bourgeois propaganda, how is it that your own propaganda has failed to convince one person to defect from the non-socialist hell in which he is living to the paradise awaiting him under communism?

Millions of Germans have fled from the socialist East to the capitalist West; not one has fled in the opposite direction. Perhaps it is because they did not hear the eloquent call of the Iraqi communist poet who could not wait to reach the East: 'O, you train of the far North/Hasten our arrival to East Berlin!' How can they explain this one-way exodus from East to West? How can they explain the fact that the citizens of capitalist countries, who are free to travel where they wish when they wish, do not seize the opportunity to escape to the paradise of socialist countries but invariably return to the hell from which they came?

What of the deprived and destitute citizens of the socialist countries, who follow foreign tourists around for scraps of food or a cigarette? We have seen many of them in Egypt, Algeria and Morocco, where their frenzied shopping sprees attest to the privation they suffer at home. Why is it that every time a sports team or artistic troupe travels to the West to represent a socialist state, more often than not one or more of their members choose to stay behind?

It is true that there are enormous class disparities in the capitalist countries, yet the lowest classes enjoy a standard of living undreamed of by any citizen in a socialist country, other than privileged Party members.

Honourable writers in all parts of the world, not least in the Arab Islamic world, who are driven by a love of freedom and a belief in lofty human values, have a sacred duty to stand up to and expose communist propaganda. For, if socialist, then communist, world society ever becomes a reality, these values would be trampled underfoot and a depraved species of humanity, closer to the level of cattle and beasts, would replace humanity as we know it.

Every decent person who is determined to fight the scourge of communism must direct his efforts at breaking the arrows of communist propaganda. This would leave the communists naked, their ugliness revealed for all to see. And then people would realize that the proper place to study communism is not in the institutes where true knowledge is imparted, but in the institutions for the psychologically warped and the mentally sick.

Notes

1. Original appeared in *Pharaohs* Magazine, September 2000.
2. This is the English translation of Chapter III of the author's book *Critique of the Arab Mind*, 1st edn, Cairo, 1998.
3. This is the English translation of Chapter II of the author's book *Critique of the Arab Mind*, 1st edn, Cairo, 1998.
4. This is the English translation of an article that was published in *Al-Ahram* daily, Cairo, 19 November 1999.
5. Original appeared in *Pharaohs* Magazine, June 2000.
6. Original appeared in *Al-Wafd* newspaper on 12 April 2001 and was republished in *Watani* newspaper on 10 June 2001.
7. Original appeared in *Pharaohs* Magazine, May 2001.
8. This is the English translation of Chapter XIII of the author's book *Critique of the Arab Mind*, 1st edn, Cairo, 1998.
9. This is the English translation of an article that was published in *Al-Akhbar Al-Youm* newspaper, Cairo, 23 September 2000.
10. Original appeared in *Pharaohs* Magazine, August 2000.
11. Original appeared in *Pharaohs* Magazine, July 2000.
12. This is the English translation of Chapter IX of the author's book *Critique of the Arab Mind*, 1st edn, Cairo, 1998.
13. The coordinated attack of Egypt by Israel, Britain and France in October–November 1956, in which Israel occupied the Egyptian-controlled Gaza Strip and the Sinai Peninsula and Britain and France landed ground troops in the Suez Canal area. The parties were forced to withdraw and cease all actions because of heavy UN pressure and US and Soviet intervention. The attack followed a period of mounting tension between the parties, during which Egypt's new regime nationalized the Suez Canal Company and was perceived as threatening other interests of the former colonial powers of the region. The tension between Egypt and Israel originated in the 1954 Egyptian imposed blockade on Israeli navigation in the Gulf of Aqaba (Eilat) and the cross-border infiltration and sabotage raids into Israel by Palestinian guerrillas (*fidaiyyin*), for which Israel held Egypt responsible. As a result of the war, Egypt consolidated its control of the Suez Canal, Israel's navigation rights in the Gulf of Aqaba were guaranteed, and a special UN force, the UNEF (United Nations Emergency Force), was created and stationed in the Sinai to patrol the Egyptian–Israeli border.
14. In January 1958, after a long period of internal instability and under the threat of its own army, the Syrian government found itself compelled to request a union with Egypt. On 1 February the United Arab Republic (UAR) was proclaimed. The union did not survive for long due to growing Syrian disillusionment and animosity towards what was perceived as an Egyptian takeover rather than a true union. Syrian antagonism was further fuelled by the Egyptian attempt to impose socialist reforms, effected also in Egypt. On 28 September 1961 the Syrian Army staged a coup and declared the union dissolved. Egypt retained the title UAR until 1971.

15. The struggle between the Saudi-backed royalists and the Egyptian-backed republicans for the control of the Yemeni state. On 26 September 1962 the latter overthrew the royalist Saudi-backed regime. The Egyptian government almost immediately committed troops to protect the fragile new regime. With Saudi support, and using Saudi Arabia as their base, the royalists waged a guerrilla war against the republicans and their Egyptian allies. With no clear winner, after five years of costly and demoralizing involvement, the Egyptians withdrew from Yemen (as agreed in the Khartoum Summit, August 1967). The fighting between the factions in Yemen continued until 1970.

16. The war between Israel and its Arab neighbours – Egypt, Jordan and Syria – waged between 5 and 10 June 1967. As a consequence, the Arab states lost to Israel's control the Sinai Peninsula and the Gaza Strip, the entire West Bank of the Jordan River (including East Jerusalem), and the Golan Heights, respectively. During the period preceding the war the already tense relations between the sides deteriorated over the continuing actions of Palestinian guerrillas against Israel, the strengthening of the Palestinian national movement, and the dispute over utilization of the waters of the Jordan River. The situation was exacerbated by the signing of the Egyptian–Syrian Joint Defence Agreement in November 1967, the Israeli shooting down of a Syrian aircraft (April 1967) and erroneous Soviet reports of an Israeli amassment of troops in the Golan Heights. Friction peaked when, on 18 May, complying with Egyptian demands the UN withdrew its forces from the Sinai Peninsula (see note 13). This was followed by the arrival of large numbers of Egyptian forces in the Peninsula. The Egyptians imposed a blockade over Israeli navigation in the Gulf of Aqaba (21 May) and signed defence agreements with Jordan (30 May) and Iraq (4 June). On the morning of 5 June Israel launched a large-scale air strike, practically destroying the air forces of all Arab countries involved, and thus began the war. Apart from the territorial losses, Egypt saw most of its army destroyed in the fighting and its hegemony in the Arab world greatly weakened. The defeat also affected the regime, causing the resignation of President Jamal Abd al-Nasser (see note 25), which he retracted 24 hours later. Another of its important results was the adoption of Resolution 242 by the UN Security Council, which called for an Israeli withdrawal from occupied lands in return for peace and Arab recognition.

17. The war between Israel and its neighbours, Syria and Egypt, in which the latter attacked Israel. It was waged between 6 and 22 October 1973. After the failure of peace efforts in 1971 and the Israeli refusal to withdraw from the Sinai, President Anwar Al-Sadat (see note 18) was convinced that the only way to regain Egypt's lost territories and to force a breakthrough in the impasse situation was another war. Plans for a joint Egyptian–Syrian attack were drawn up and implemented in a surprise attack on Israel, on 6 October. The Egyptian forces managed to cross the Suez Canal and occupy its west bank but in a counter-offensive Israeli forces crossed the Canal, occupying part of its eastern bank and surrounding the Egyptian Third Army on the Suez western bank. In the Golan, Israel managed to push back the Syrian offensive and reoccupy the heights. The war witnessed also the involvement of the world's two great superpowers of that time, the USSR on the Arab side and the USA on the Israeli side, which manifested itself in massive arms shipments to both sides and rising tension between the powers themselves. The perception of Israeli invincibility was shattered during this war, causing social and political unrest in Israel, which would bring about the fall of the long-ruling Labour Party and a new Likud-led government. The Egyptian leadership had been given, by what was considered a victory, leverage for its future peace negotiations with Israel and it also regained its standing in the Arab world. During the war the UN Security Council adopted Resolution 338, which primarily reiterated Resolution 242 (see note 16).

18. Anwar al-Sadat (1918–81): Egyptian President from 1970–81. Graduated from the Military Academy in 1938. Expelled from the army and imprisoned in 1946 for

subversive political activities and suspicion of participation in plots to assassinate senior political figures. He was released in 1948 and rejoined the armed forces in 1950. He took part in the 1952 Free Officers Revolution and was a close ally of Jamal Abd al-Nasser, who appointed Sadat in 1969 as his vice-president. When Nasser died, in September 1970, Sadat succeeded him as president. During the first years of his presidency Sadat quelled leftist opposition, surprised Israel in what was considered the victory of the 1973 War (see note 17), reoriented Egyptian foreign policy towards the West (especially towards the USA), reversing its long pro-Soviet inclination. He introduced a series of economic and political reforms, promoting liberalization. In 1977, in a dramatic act and as a gesture demonstrating his will for peace, Sadat flew to Jerusalem and addressed the Israeli Knesset (parliament). The culmination of the process initiated by this visit was the signing of an Egyptian–Israeli peace agreement at Camp David (see note 19). In his last years in power Sadat's rule suffered from growing disillusionment and opposition (mainly from Islamic elements), manifested in the popular riots that broke out in 1977 and in his assassination, during a victory parade, on 6 October 1981 by Islamic militants belonging to the Jihad group.

19. The agreements signed between Israel and Egypt with US mediation on 17 September 1978 at Camp David, the official retreat of the US president. The agreements were reached after hard and tense negotiations (5–17 September 1978) between Egyptian President Anwar al-Sadat (see note 18) and Israeli Prime Minister Menachem Begin; President Jimmy Carter acted as intermediary. The accords set up the framework for the Egyptian–Israeli Peace Agreement, which was signed on 26 March 1979, and for the solution of the Palestinian problem. The former called for Israeli withdrawal from the Sinai Peninsula and the establishment of normal and peaceful relations between Israel and Egypt, and the latter for Israeli withdrawal from the West Bank and the Gaza Strip, the establishment of Palestinian self-rule there and recognition of Israel's right to exist within secure and recognized borders.

20. The General Agreement on Tariffs and Trade (GATT), an international agreement created in 1947 which stipulates reductions in tariffs and other measures for trade liberalization between its members. In 1993 the member countries signed the most comprehensive and liberalizing agreement ever, under which a new organization, the World Trade Organization (WTO), was formed whose function is to supervise the implementation of the GATT and mediate in trade disputes among the signatories.

21. The Muslim Brotherhood is a political-religious movement founded by Hasan al-Bana in Ismailia in 1928. The group calls for the reinstitution of Islam and Islamic law as the main pillars upon which the Egyptian – indeed, all Arab and Muslim societies – should be based. The group rejects secular and Western notions of the running of Islamic societies. As part of these Islamic notions the group set up a well-organized network of social independent institutions, such as schools and medical clinics, and gained much influence in Egyptian society. During the 1940s its secret wing was involved in subversive and violent acts against leading political figures and others who were perceived as its enemies. In 1954 Jamal Abd al-Nasser (see note 25) banned the group and suppressed it, executing its leader, Sayyid Qutb. The movement resumed its activities in the 1970s under Sadat's (see note 18) political liberalization, and even published its own journal, though its publication ceased after renewed political suppression in September 1981. Although the movement stresses its peaceful nature and distances itself from more extreme and violent groups, the official ban on it continues. In spite of this, the movement continues to operate and even takes part in Egyptian elections by presenting its candidates as independents or by forging coalitions with legitimate parties.

22. Al-Gamaat, or A-Jjamaat Al-Islamiya, is a general term denoting extreme Islamic groups, first formed under the Sadat regime (see note 18). These include the Takfir wa Al-Hijra, the Jihad (see note 23) and the Jamaa Al-Islamiya (the last

two are the most prominent). Such groups preach extreme Islamic ideology, oppose the regime and use violence and terror to achieve their goals. Generally, they distance themselves from the Muslim Brothers. They were responsible for the assassination of President Sadat in 1981, for the attempted assassination of President Husni Mubarak in Addis Ababa, Ethiopia in 1995, and were also accused of involvement in the New York Trade Center bombing in 1993. In the 1990s they launched a terrorist campaign against tourism and tourists in Egypt, deeming them the corrupting agents of Egyptian society. They realized that this would enable them to hurt the regime economically (tourism is one of Egypt's main sources of income) and to discredit it both internally and internationally. The Luxor terrorist attack of 1997, in which 57 tourists and Egyptians were killed, is the last big example of this campaign. In response to this and other attacks the regime launched a fierce counter-offensive, mainly in Upper Egypt (the southern part of the country), where these groups rallied more support and influence, arresting and executing many of their members. An unofficial truce seemed to have been reached in the last years.

23. The Jihad, or Al-Jihad Al-Jadid, is an extreme Islamic group, part of the Jamaat Al-Islamiya (see note 22), which was behind the Sadat assassination in 1981. Its founder and main ideologue was Abd Al-Salam Faraj. He was executed with Khaled Al-Islambuli, the principal assassin of the president, in 1982. The group and its offshoots are credited with involvement in numerous terrorist acts in Egypt and abroad through the 1990s.

24. The Nasserites are followers and adherents of the political ideology known as Nasserism. This was the term applied to the political philosophy of former Egyptian President Nasser. It included international neutralism, Arab nationalism and socialism. Following Sadat's reforms Nasserism came to represent the views of those opposed to his policy, i.e. political but mainly economic capitalist liberalization. On 19 April 1992 the Nasserite Arab Democratic Party was formally approved and given permission to participate in Egyptian elections.

25. Jamal Abd al-Nasser (1918–70): Egyptian President 1954–70. Graduated from the Military Academy in 1938. Participated as battalion commander in the 1948 War between the Arabs and the fledgling State of Israel. After the war he organized the Free Officers group, which consisted mainly of low-ranking officers, mainly from humble backgrounds, whose objective was to revamp what was believed to be a corrupt system (implying the ousting of the then-ruling royal dynasty). On 23 July 1952 they successfully executed a coup. Initially the officers installed coup leader General Muhhamad Najib as president. After growing dissent and rivalry, Nasser ousted Najib and became the official president in 1954. Under his leadership Egypt underwent a series of economic, social and political reforms. He banned all parties except his own Arab Socialist Union. In the economic sphere he pursued a socialist policy, nationalizing in 1961 all major industries and utilities and adopting an ambitious development plan, with the project of the Great Dam of Aswan being one of his main achievements. His regime also carried out agrarian reform, redistributing agrarian lands in Egypt. In the international and inter-Arab sphere he adopted a nationalistic revolutionary Arab policy and was one of the co-founders of the non-alignment bloc in 1955. During his time in office Egypt's foreign policy tilted towards the Soviet Union and the Eastern bloc. Some of his most salient actions in the international arena were the nationalization of the Suez Canal in 1956, the union with Syria, the Egyptian involvement in Yemen and the 1967 War, after which he resigned for 24 hours only to be reinstated following popular clamour. After his death, Nasser was succeeded by Anwar al-Sadat.

26. Jihad is the struggle or holy war in the defence of Islam against its attackers. It has come to mean the holy war of Islam against all non-Muslims or unbelievers so as to spread the rule of Islam and the word of God and his prophet Muhammad. In modern times it has also taken on some new meanings. The Islamic extreme groups

advocate Jihad against Arab regimes that do not comply with Islam as they perceive it. Some Islamic modernists and other moderates advocate Jihad in a peaceful manner. In other circles, mainly official, it refers to a major effort towards advancement, in general or in a specific field (e.g. the economy).

27. The Crusades were the Christian-driven military campaigns that originated in Europe against the Muslim-dominated territories of the Near East, especially Palestine (the Holy Land). The campaigns and invasions took part between the end of the eleventh century to the thirteenth. Their main objective was to save those territories from what was perceived as a Muslim desecration and to restore Christian control there. In modern times the Crusades have come to symbolize in some Muslim/Arab circles Western aggression, colonialism and imperialism in the area, of which the State of Israel is considered to be the gravest manifestation.

28. The Ministry of Information is found in many Arab countries. Among its responsibilities are the regulation and control of state and non-governmental media. In many cases the ministry also acts as the government's main official mouthpiece.

29. The Ottoman Empire was founded by Turkish-origin tribes in Anatolia at the end of the thirteenth century. At its peak it comprised most of southwestern Asia, the Balkans, Egypt and large portions of the North African coast. The capital of the empire during most of its existence was Istanbul (Constantinople). The Ottoman Empire was a multinational Islamic state dominated by elements of Turkish descent or affiliation. It ceased to exist in 1919. Egypt was ruled by the Empire between 1517 and 1798 or 1517 and 1882 (differences originated in historic exegesis). During the nineteenth century the Ottomans granted much of their power to their governor Muhammad Ali and his dynasty, which became the Egyptian royal family, who ruled the country until overthrown by the Free Officers revolution in 1952 (see note 25).

30. Zionism was the movement seeking the creation of an independent national Jewish home in Palestine or Israel. The movement originated in the late nineteenth century among Eastern European Jewry. From 1896 the term was adopted by Theodor Herzl (see note 31) for the political movement founded by him and which eventually led to the formation of the State of Israel.

31. Theodor Herzl (1860–1904). The founder of the political worldwide Zionist movement. An assimilated Jew, Herzl became aware of the Jewish problem during his work in Paris for a Viennese newspaper (1891–95) and his coverage of the trial of the Jewish army officer Alfred Dreyfus, falsely accused of treason. The anti-Semitic atmosphere surrounding the trial, and prevalent in France in general, led him to write and publish *The Jewish State* (1896), in which, after an assessment of the Jewish situation, he proposed a plan for the establishment of a Jewish state. Herzl began to travel to publicize his ideas and try to gain support for them. On 23 August 1897 in Basel, Switzerland, the first Zionist Congress was convened, in which Herzl and Jewish representatives from the world over laid the foundations of the World Zionist Organization, which became the main organ of the newly established Jewish national movement.

32. Original appeared in *Pharaohs* Magazine, February 2000.

33. Arabic version appeared in *Al-Akhbar* daily newspaper on 12 January 2000.

34. Arabic version appeared in *Al-Ahram* daily newspaper at 11 January 2000.

35. Arabic version appeared in *Al-Ahram* daily newspaper on 18 October 1999.

36. Mandur (1907–65) was an influential literary critic and translator before becoming a member of the Egyptian Parliament in 1944. In 1956 he visited Romania and the USSR and was impressed by their socialist systems. His commitment to change in Arab society characterized his cultural and political career.

37. Louis Awad (1915–90), literary critic, writer and poet, was one of the most influential Arab cultural figures of the second half of the twentieth century.

38. In addition to serving as a critic and poet, al-Qutt (b. 1916) held cultural and teaching positions in Egypt and Lebanon. One of al-Qutt's most recent books is *Conversations with the Writer Najib Mahfuz.*

39. Arabic version appeared in *Al-Ahram* daily newspaper on 29 September 1999.
40. The economic 'Tigers' are Singapore, Hong Kong, South Korea and Taiwan. Due to their economic boom and rapid development in the 1990s, some observers include also Thailand and Malaysia.
41. This chapter first appeared as four articles in a Cairo daily newspaper and later in a book of essays, under the same title. This essay could be described as the 'core' of my writings on Egypt's socio-economic problems and the 'chart' of a project to make the near future of this country as prosperous as desired by its citizens.
42. Muhammad Ali (1769–1849), Egypt's Ottoman viceroy and founder of its royal dynasty. In 1801 he was sent to Egypt as second in command of an Albanian contingent to help drive out the French (who arrived with Napoleon in 1798). With the help of the local elite classes, he won appointment as the Ottoman governor in 1805. In 1811 he massacred the Mamluks – the most powerful of the elites. Under his rule Egypt underwent a series of reforms: he initiated irrigation projects on the Nile, intoduced new agricultural crops (mainly cash crops) and imposed state monopoly over agricultural land and output. He also tried to create modern industry (munitions and textiles) but this failed due to mismanagement and later trade agreements. His government encouraged education (he himself learned to read at the age of 45), sending students abroad and importing foreign experts, mainly to benefit the army. Ali's military campaigns included the conquest of Hijaz (part of the Arabian Peninsula) and in 1821 of eastern Sudan; his forces also took part in the Ottoman effort to quash the Greek rebellion, but were ultimately defeated. When the Ottomans refused to award him Crete as promised, he sent his son Ibrahim to invade Syria in 1831. Ibrahim conquered Palestine, Syria and advanced through Anatolia towards the Ottoman capital, when he was stopped by Britain and Austria. In the ensuing agreement Muhammad Ali was awarded by sultanic decree the right to the hereditary governorship of Egypt, thus establishing his dynasty as the effective ruler of Egypt (his last descendant to rule Egypt was King Farouk, ousted by the military revolution of 1952).
43. Saad Zaghlul (1859/60–1927) is considered one of the founding fathers of Egypt's independence movement. Served as a minister between 1906 and 1912; elected to the Legislative Assembly in 1913, where he eventually became vice-president and, soon after, leader of opposition. After the World War I Armistice, the British Foreign Office refused Zaghlul and two colleagues entry to London to represent Egypt. He then formed the Egyptian delegation, the Wafd ('delegation' in Arabic), to the Paris Peace Conference. The British again opposed him, leading to the 1919 Revolution. Zaghlul was exiled to Malta, though he was permitted to attend the conference. His return to Egypt inspired further riots, and he was again exiled – to Aden, the Seychelles and Gibraltar, returning finally to Egypt in 1923. The Wafd Party under his leadership won a sweeping majority in the ensuing parliamentary elections and in 1924 Zaghlul became premier. In November that year his government fell. The Wafd again won the 1925 and 1926 elections, and Zaghlul was appointed Speaker of Parliament, after refusing to form a government.
44. The British occupation of Egypt extended from September 1882 (when the British defeated the forces led by Urabi) until June 1956 (when the last British troops left the Suez Canal). In the first years Egypt was directly ruled by a British representative (first the consul-general and then the high commissioner). In 1914 Britain officially proclaimed a protectorate regime in Egypt, which was annulled in 1922, when Britain unilaterally declared Egypt's independence, retaining much of its control over the country. A series of Anglo–Egyptian negotiations failed, until 1936 when a treaty was signed, recognizing many of the Egyptian demands and reducing the size of the British army in Egypt during peacetime, but conserving British interests in the Suez Canal. After World War II the British bases in the main Egyptian towns were evacuated. Successive Egyptian governments tried to negotiate total evacuation, but failed. Growing popular dissent and unrest caused by the British presence led

to the eruption of anti-British actions in 1952. The new military government, established after the 1952 Revolution, finally reached an agreement over the total evacuation of British troops from the Suez Canal in 1954. During the 1956 Suez War British forces briefly reoccupied parts of the Canal, but were forced to withdraw.

45. Muhammad Husni Mubarak (b. 1928), Egypt's President since 1981. In 1967–69 he was the commander of the Air Force Academy, then chief of staff of the Air Force. In 1972 he became commander-in-chief of the Egyptian Air Force, heading its preparations for the 1973 war and leading it to an impressive performance. In 1975 President Sadat named him vice-president. Following Sadat's assassination in 1981, Mubarak assumed the country's top post, winning unanimous approval in a popular referendum (and he has continued to win since). In 1995 he narrowly escaped an attempt on his life in Addis Ababa by Egyptians and Sudanese Islamic elements, against whom he has been waging a war since coming to power. His other policies include keeping close ties with the USA, re-establishing Egypt in the leading role in the Arab world (the culmination of which was the return of the Arab League headquarters to Cairo) while maintaining Egypt's peace agreement with Israel. In recent years he has acted as mediator and key player in the Middle East peace process. On the home front Mubarak has tried to carry out economic reforms by which he hoped to elevate the Egyptian citizen's standard of living and to create a more modern and competitive Egyptian economy. To date, these reforms have yielded only moderate success.

46. Arabic version appeared in *Al-Akhbar* in four excerpts in 1987 and later in *The Four Idols* (Cairo, 1988).

47. Cairo University: founded in 1908, by the Egyptian royal family, as the National University, it was Egypt's first secular university. The institution first offered courses in history, philosophy and literature, taught by European professors, mainly Italians and French. With the passage of time new courses were added in law, criminology and other social sciences. Because of high admission fees many Egyptians could not attend. After World War I grave financial problems caused its reorganization by the government as the Faculty of Arts in the Cairo University, named the Egyptian University. As Egyptians gradually replaced European deans and professors in some departments instruction shifted from European languages to Arabic, although English remained the main language of instruction. Before and after the 1952 Revolution the university suffered from continuous government and political interference, with constant dismissals and appointments of deans and rectors. After the revolution the atmosphere in the university became more oppressive. With the tuition fees abolished in 1962 by Nasser the number of students rose sharply, bringing down educational standards. Cairo University's graduates have enjoyed the acceptance of the different Egyptian regimes and have served in different Egyptian governments. As a consequence of its problems, and the foundation of new universities and institutions in Egypt and around the Arab world, Cairo University has seen its status gradually diminished over the years.

48. Arabic version appeared in *Al-Akhbar* daily on 1–2 November 1989 and later in *Trinity of Destruction* (Cairo, 1990).

49. The Socialist Labour Party (SLP) was created by Sadat in November 1978 as a loyal and constructive opposition party to the ruling National Democratic Party. Its founding leader was former agriculture minister, Ibrahim Mahmud Shukri, a former member of Misr al-Fatat. The SLP's founding members were mainly educated people of the upper and middle classes. It initially called for a democratic regime with more political freedom and freedom of speech. It also preached for a balanced distribution of wealth, especially between urban and rural areas. Gradually the party became more critical of the regime's foreign and economic policies. Its leaders were jailed during Sadat's crackdown on the opposition in September 1981. In the 1980s the party grew closer to the Muslim Brotherhood, preaching the need for a bigger role for Islamic-oriented legislation and policy. The alliance with the

Brotherhood peaked in the 1987 parliamentary election, when it formed a coalition with the Liberal Socialist Party and the independent candidates of the Muslim Brotherhood (since when the movement still remains officially banned), winning 1.1 million votes and 60 seats. The party slammed the regime's alignment with the US-led coalition during the Iraq–Kuwait crisis in 1990–91.

50. Misr al-Fatat was the Egyptian nationalist movement. It developed from a youth movement founded in October 1933 by Ahmad Husayn and Fathi Radwan, espousing ultra-nationalistic views and perceived as pro-fascist. The movement preached the foundation of an empire composed of Egypt and Sudan and for a leadership role for Egypt in the Arab world. In 1936 the movement became a political party. From 1937 it became involved in violent acts (clashes with Wafd supporters and other political opponents, campaigns against prostitution, alcohol, etc.). In 1940 it was renamed the Islamic National Party and in 1944 it readopted the name Misr al-Fatat. In 1946 the party was again renamed the Egyptian Socialist Party. Misr al-Fatat was disbanded with all other political parties by the Free Officers' regime in 1953. In 1990 a party bearing the same name was founded.

51. The Wafd, or Egyptian national political party, dominated the Egyptian political scene between 1923 and 1952. It was formed out of the Wafd (delegation) of Saad Zaghlul to the Paris Peace Conference. Zaghlul was also its first president until his death in 1927, when he was succeeded by Mustafa al-Nahas. The party leadership was formed by landowners and members of the urban middle class. Its constituency was composed of small and medium landowners, workers, peasants and members of the urban middle and high classes. The Wafd preached the total independence of Egypt, the development and encouragement of Egyptian industry and agriculture and also labour unions. The party won the 1923 elections and formed a short-lived government; it also won the 1925 election with overwhelming popular support but was not permitted to form a government by the monarchy and the British. The clashes with the monarchy characterized much of its activity. In 1929 the party won again and formed another short-lived government. After a long struggle, sometimes resorting to violent acts, the party returned to power in 1936, reaching the successful 1936 agreement with the British. Internal fighting led to formation of the offshoot Saadist Party in 1938. The king seized this opportunity to dissolve the government. During the same period a violent youth movement called the Blue Shirts was formed. It engaged in violent clashes with other political movements and their organs, such as the Green Shirts of Misr al-Fatat. The party's demise began in 1942, when it returned to power with British support, after the king was coerced to appoint Nahas as premier. In that year the party's secretary-general and finance minister, Makram Ubayd, published his Black Book, which exposed the party leaders' corruption. After the Second World War the party was deposed, returning to power in 1950. The Wafd-led cabinet tried to institute significant social reforms, but was not able to settle its disagreements with the British, which led to the unilateral abrogation of the 1936 agreement by Nahas in October 1951. A violent outbreak of unprecedented dimensions ensued and as a result the Wafd government fell, never to return again to power. The party was dissolved with all other political parties after the 1952 Revolution. The Wafd epitomized in the eyes of the Egyptian masses the opposition to the British and foreign presence in Egypt, but its governments were not successful in implementing its policies and reforms. The New Wafd Party (NWP) was created by former Wafd member Fuad Siraj al-Din in February 1978, only to be disbanded the following June by Sadat. Its leader was arrested in 1981 during Sadat's purge of the opposition. The party was legalized again in 1983 and took part in the 1984 elections in a coalition with the Muslim Brotherhood, winning 58 seats and 15 per cent of the popular vote. In 1987 it won independently 35 seats. It boycotted the 1990 elections, but its members who ran independently won an estimated 14 seats. The New Wafd supports

economic liberalism. It stood by the government during the Iraq–Kuwait crisis and in its struggle against religious extremism.

52. Some 1,800 workers at the Hilwan Iron and Steel Works, just south of Cairo, went on strike after two of their colleagues had demanded better annual bonuses and were immediately suspended. The following day government forces raided the plant, killing one person, injuring several others and arresting about 600. In the ensuing days the government agreed to workers' bonuses, but it also claimed it had uncovered an illegal communist organization, which was responsible for the strike, and arrested 52 alleged members, most of whom were released shortly after.

53. Arabic version appeared in *Al-Akhbar* daily on 5 January 1987 and later in *The Four Idols* (Cairo, 1988).

54. Arabic version appeared in *Al-Akhbar* daily on 13 January 1987 and later in *Trinity of Destruction* (Cairo, 1990).

55. Arabic version appeared in *Al-Akhbar* daily on 17 December 1987 and later in *Trinity of Destruction* (Cairo, 1990).

56. Mass demonstrations broke out in Cairo and other Egyptian cities on 18 January 1977, in response to the decision by Sadat's regime to reduce subsidies on essential foodstuffs, especially bread. The decision was in compliance with terms set by the International Monetary Fund as conditions for further loans. Labourers, slum dwellers, housewives, students and other elements of the lower strata of Egyptian society participated in the riots. The army was called in to quell them, and the result was 79 dead, some 900 injured and 1,500 arrested. The riots were used by leftist elements to incite the protesting crowds against the regime's economic reforms. Muslim elements used them against what they perceived as immoral and Western institutions. Sadat's prestige was damaged by the riots and he became more hostile towards opposition groups. The government was forced to reinstate the food subsidies.

57. The leftist Tajamu Party, or National Progressive Unionist Party (NPUP), originated in Nasser's Arab Socialist Union. Its founding leader is Khalid Muhyi al-Din. The party was formed in 1976, and survived government attempts in 1978 to dissolve it. The government-sponsored formation of the Socialist Labour Party was an attempt to weaken the NPUP's power. In 1976 it won five parliamentary seats, but failed to retain them in subsequent elections. In 1990 it refused to join other opposition parties in boycotting the election, capturing 1.8 of the total votes and six seats in parliament. The Tajamu is often portrayed as Nasserite and socialist, thus appealing to the hard core of the leftist, even communist, elements in Egyptian society.

58. The February 1986 riots erupted among the illiterate conscripts of this special security force created after the 1977 Food Riots in order to assist the police and other internal security forces in times of need. The riots were sparked by a rumour that the government intended to add a year to the conscripts' three-year-long service. In the four days of strife 60 people died and hundreds were injured. Subsequently, 20,000 conscripts were dismissed, but the force was not dismantled and the authorities even augmented it. It continues to aid the police, fight Islamic extremists and perform other tasks.

59. Arabic version appeared in *Al-Akhbar* daily on 16 March 1987 and later in *The Four Idols* (2nd edn, Cairo, 1989).

60. Arabic version appeared in two excerpts in the Cairo daily *Al-Wafd* in 1985 and later in *What is to be Done?* (Cairo, 1986).

61. Ismail (1830–95) became the Egyptian viceroy in 1863. During his tenure he tried to reform and modernize Egypt, and he expanded Egypt's rule in the Sudan. Many cultural institutions such as the National Library and the Cairo Opera House were founded during his rule. He succeeded in obtaining the hereditary title of Khedive (considered of a higher rank in the Ottoman system than that in Muhammad Ali's dynasty) for himself and his heirs from the Ottoman Sultan, thus consolidating control for Muhammad Ali's dynasty over Egypt. Following the end of the American Civil

War demand for Egyptian cotton decreased, causing grave financial problems, which Ismail tried to solve by taking loans from European countries. When Egypt could not repay the loans, he was forced to accept European financial control over Egypt's affairs and eventually a European-controlled government. After the 1879 officers' riots and the resignation of that government the European powers suspected Ismail of orchestrating the riots in order to regain absolute power. They convinced the Sultan to depose him and to appoint his son Tawfiq instead. Ismail went into exile in Naples. He is remembered as a talented viceroy and a capable reformer, but also as the person who, due to his actions and financial mismanagement, was the catalyst for the onset of British rule over Egypt.

62. Arabic version appeared in *Al-Wafd* in three excerpts in 1985 and later in *What is to be Done?* (Cairo, 1986).

63. Arabic version appeared in *Al-Akhbar* daily on 9 December 1987 and later in *The Four Idols* (Cairo, 1988).

64. Original is a speech delivered on 3 June 1992 to the 'Reading for All' Conference.

65. Arabic version appeared in *Al-Wafd* on 2 January 1986 and later in *What is to be Done?* (Cairo, 1986).

66. Arabic version appeared in *Al-Akhbar* on 19 February 1987 and later in *The Four Idols* (Cairo, 1988).

67. The Quran consists of 114 sections called *suras*, with each *sura* composed of verses of varying length (from three to 287).

68. The *hadith* is the narrative containing the saying and deeds (the *suna*) of the Prophet Muhammad and his companions, and also deeds or sayings that were done or uttered in the presence of the Prophet and were sanctioned by him. The *hadith* has a legally binding standing on its own, as it contains most of the basis for Muslim religious law. It is often used to clarify dark passages of the Quran.

69. This chapter presents some of the perspectives of modern management techniques conceptually, as well as commenting on their nature, function and component elements. It also explores the role management can play in reforming a society like Egypt, as it seeks a way of overcoming a multitude of problems considered by some to be economic in nature, by others (including the author) to be social and political and by others still as general crises that can be solved only through effective management. The chapter also sums up the main factors impeding the viability of modern management in Egypt.

70. This chapter was written in November 1997 as a comment on the massacre of 17 November 1997 in Luxor and published in the *Civil Society* newsletter of the Ibn Khaldun Centre, December 1997.

71. A chapter from the author's book *Marxist Ideas in the Balance*, 4th edn (Cairo, 1989).

72. Some Marxists resented the expressions in the first edition, though both are borrowed from Marx and, indeed, do not go as far as Engels did in describing the ideas of Saint Simon, Charles Fourrier and Robert Owen, when he said 'they too should be thrown in the garbage' – *Utopian Socialism and Scientific Socialism, Volume IV, Marx and Engels Selected Works*, Moscow (no date), p. 81.

73. It seems that by 'cannibals' he meant communists. It is the same term used by Karl Marx to describe the enemies of the communards who led the Paris Commune in 1871. For reference see Karl Marx, *The Civil War in France*, Progress Publications, Tashkent, 1976, p. 82.

74. Had Lenin not adopted the ideas of Marx and Engels, had he not taken over power in Russia, establishing a regime based on those ideas, the works of Marx and Engels would have commanded no more attention than those of Hegel, Feuerbach, Saint Simon and other intellectuals of the nineteenth century.

75. Most youth movements have been led by older men such as Herbert Marcuse. When he became the guru of the young, Marcuse was 70. Sartre was 50 when he advocated existentialism!

76. See our article on 'Islam and Conformism in Arab Reality', published in the Moroccan *Green March* on 3 July 1977.

77. See Pierre and Monique Favre, *Le Marxisme après Marx*, trans. Nessim Nasr, Owaidat Publications, Beirut, 1st edn, October 1974, pp. 29, 30, 38.

78. A chapter from the author's book *Marxist Ideas in the Balance*, 4th edn (Cairo, 1989).

79. For the main tasks of the dictatorship of the proletariat during the period of transition to socialism, see: Lenin, *The Main Tasks of the Dictatorship of the Russian Proletariat*, pp. 179 ff.; Lenin, *Economy and Politics Under the Dictatorship of the Proletariat*, pp. 218, 219. See the two studies referred to above in his selected works published under the title, *Socialism: Utopian and Scientific*, Progress Publications, Moscow, 1975.

80. For the full text of the letter, see: Marx and Engels, *Selected Works*, Volume II, p. 452.

81. Karl Marx, *Critique of the Gotha Programme*, ibid., p. 261.

82. Kim Il Sung, *On the Two Questions of the Period of Transition from Capitalism to Socialism, and the Dictatorship of the Proletariat*, pp. 8, 9.

83. See Chapter 3 in this part entitled 'Eurocommunism'. See also *'Eurocommunism' and the State* by Santiago Carillo, translated into Arabic by Samir Karam, Dar El Taliaa, Beirut, pp. 121–48.

84. In the 1920s and '30s, for example, French Marxists believed implicitly in the Soviet experience as a role model and considered any departure from the official Soviet line to be a betrayal of proletarian internationalism. As a result, propagandists were favoured over theoreticians, and the French Communist Party suppressed any discussion of the role and line of the Russian Communist Party. See Pierre and Monique Favre, *Le Marxisme après Marx*, p. 129.

85. Stalin eliminated the Marxist leaders one after another. Between 1928 and 1936 (the year of the notorious Moscow trials where he purged a large number of Communist Party leaders), Stalin used his political police to murder all his opponents, such as Trotsky, Zinoviev, Kamanev, Bukharin, Tomsky, Rykov and Radek.

86. The English historian Herbert Fisher said it was not surprising that the Bolshevik regime had lasted in Russia, for the Russian people had long been accustomed to tyranny and Stalin's rule had not been more cruel and violent than that of Ivan the Terrible or Peter the Great. See Herbert Fisher, *The History of Europe in the Modern Age*, p. 631.

87. See David Thompson, *Europe Since Napoleon*, Penguin Books, London, 1972, p. 843.

88. The Third World has also had its painful experiences with the Soviets. Perhaps the most notable were those of Egypt and Somalia. Both ended with the expulsion of the Soviets (from Egypt in 1971 and from Somalia in 1977) amid popular celebrations. See Walter Laqueur, *The Struggle for the Middle East – the Soviet Union and the Middle East 1958–1970*, Penguin Books, London, 1972, pp. 83–106.

89. See Barraclough, *An Introduction to Contemporary History*, p. 212. See also Georges Sorel, *Three Hundred Days in the Russian Revolution: Observations and Documents*, Egyptian General Book Organization, Cairo, 1972, p. 365.

90. See J. Plamenatz, *German Marxism and Russian Communism*, London, 1954, p. 262.

91. See Pierre and Monique Favre, *Le Marxisme après Marx*, p. 127.

92. It was also the expectation of Karl Marx himself. See the reasons given by Kim Il Sung to justify the non-materialization of Marx's prophecies, op. cit., pp. 5, 6.

93. See Santiago Carillo, *Eurocommunism and the State*, p. 35.

94. See Alec Nove, *An Economic History of the U.S.S.R.*, Pelican, London, 1976, p. 236.

95. See Walter Laqueur, *Europe Since Hitler*, p. 69.

96. Ibid.

97. Ibid.
98. Ibid.
99. Ibid.
100. The European provinces annexed to the Soviet Union during and after World War II are: the Baltic provinces of Lithuania (24,000 square miles); Latvia (20,000 square miles); Estonia (18,000 square miles); the eastern Polish province of Estonia (68,000 square miles); Bessarabia and Bukovina, from Romania (19,000 square miles); Moldavia (13,000 square miles); provinces from eastern Prussia (3,500 square miles); the Czech Subcarpathian region (3,500 square miles); Karelia (16,000 square miles); Petsamo (4,000 square miles); Tannu Tuva (64,000 square miles); Kurile Islands (4,000 square miles); South Sakhalin (14,000 square miles). The total land area of these provinces amounts to 272,500 square miles. See Walter Laqueur, *Europe Since Hitler*, p. 71.
101. See Valéry Giscard d'Estaing, *French Democracy*, translated into Arabic by Abdallah Noman, Tunisian Distribution Co. (Tunis) and Awaidat Publications (Beirut), 1st edn, April 1977, pp. 28, 29, 102, 114.
102. Eduard Bernstein, German Social Democrat, was the first to note the error of Marx's assertion that the middle class would decline to the level of the proletariat. He wrote extensively on the subject, using statistics to show that reality in the industrialized countries proved the exact opposite, and that it is, rather, the middle class that expands as its ranks are swelled by many groups formerly considered proletariat. See Eduard Bernstein, *Evolutionary Socialism*.
103. Marx always said that the proletariat was a product of capitalism, and considered this to be a confirmation of one of the most important laws of dialectics, 'the negation of the negation', an idea formulated by the German philosopher Hegel. Somehow, Marxists do not apply the law of dialectics to themselves. If everything creates its opposite, if capitalism created the proletariat, why does the same principle not apply in the opposite direction? Why would the proletariat not produce its opposite, which would then replace it? Why should communism be considered the ultimate stage of economic and political evolution? Are they exempt from the laws of dialectics, or is it a tacit return to the absolute?
104. A chapter from the author's book *Marxist Ideas in the Balance*, 4th edn (Cairo, 1989).
105. *Marxist Ideas in the Balance*, 1st edn, 1978.
106. Although Japan is in Asia, the political line of its communist party comes under the designation of Eurocommunism, since the significance of the term has spread beyond the confines of Europe.
107. Santiago Carillo, *'Eurocommunism' and the State*, p. 154.
108. Georgi Dimitrov (1882–1949), the Bulgarian Marxist leader who founded the Communist Party of Bulgaria and became head of state after World War II.
109. Carillo, *'Eurocommunism' and the State*, p. 154.
110. Ibid., p. 133.
111. Ibid., p. 134.
112. The idea of revolutionary violence is central to Marxist thinking and has figured scores of times in the works of Marx, Engels, Kautsky (when he was still a Marxist), Lenin, Trotsky and Stalin. The main reference, however, is the study devoted to the subject by Engels; see Friedrich Engels, *The Theory of Violence*.
113. An article by Mohamed Sid Ahmed published in issue No. 14 of *Al-Ahali* on 3 May 1978, under the title, 'A Communist Party Abandons Leninism', is a clear example of the failure by an Egyptian Marxist to understand the indissoluble link between the idea of revolutionary violence – or the transition to socialism through violent proletarian revolution – and the essence of the Marxist ideology. Though it is obvious that the writer considers parliamentary transition to socialism to be the means by which communists can come to power in order to

impose their monopoly over all other forces, in his own words: 'It is no longer conceivable to attain socialism through a sudden transformation, a revolution; rather, the transition to socialism will take the form of a revolutionary transformation achieved gradually, and the domination of society and the state by the working class will come about in stages.'

114. Carillo, *'Eurocommunism' and the State*, p. 80.
115. Ibid.
116. To assimilate this scenario to Eurocommunism is unnecessary, since this is the case in a number of capitalist societies, such as Britain, which apply a mixed system of public and private ownership.
117. Carillo, *'Eurocommunism' and the State*, p. 80.
118. Ibid.
119. Ibid., p. 81.
120. Ibid., p. 89.
121. Ibid.
122. Ibid., p. 12.
123. The Russian tsars exercised weird forms of tyranny, torture and terror. An exhaustive account would require an entire volume, not a footnote, so we shall content ourselves with a few examples: Ivan the Terrible killed one of his sons by his own hand; Peter the Great married the serf of one of the princes; she betrayed him with her servant and Peter cut off his head and kept it pickled in vinegar by his wife's bed; Anne, the daughter of Ivan, had two dwarfs as court jesters. As a joke, she put them in ice where, not surprisingly, they froze to death; Catherine II had the leader of the Peasants' Revolt publicly executed in a cage. Later, she killed her husband when she grew bored with him.
124. After the defeat of the coalition of the Left in the French legislative elections of 1978, the main attack against the lack of democracy inside the communist organizations appeared in four articles by Louis Althusser which were published in *Le Monde*, April 1978, under the title, 'What Should be Changed in the French Communist Party?'
125. Carillo, *'Eurocommunism' and the State*, p. 33.
126. Ibid.
127. Ibid., p. 6.
128. Ibid., p. 40.
129. Palmiro Togliatti, 1892–1964.
130. The human rights movement began with literary works being distributed secretly in the Soviet Union. The first author to launch such works was Alexander Solzhenitsyn, with *One Day in the Life of Ivan Denisovich*, for which he received the Nobel Prize for Literature after spending eleven years in labour camps and exile. He was followed by Abram Tertz, who wrote under the alias, Andrey Siniavsky; Yuli Daniel, alias Nicolai Arzhak; Alexander Ginzburg, who, after writing a white book on Siniavsky's trial, was arrested and sentenced in 1967, along with Yuri Galanskov, editor of the underground magazine, *Phoenix*, the voice of human rights activists in the Soviet Union. Paval Litvinov, grandson of a foreign minister of the USSR – not of Tsarist Russia – wrote *Appeal to Public Opinion* jointly with Larissa Bogorz-Daniel; they also led demonstrations condemning the Soviet invasion of Czechoslovakia in August 1968, and were sentenced to long prison terms. The movement spread in the Soviet Union, especially after world public opinion forced the government to sign the Helsinki Agreement on Human Rights in 1974. Thanks to the strong international pressure that was brought to bear on the Soviet government from many quarters, including the European communist parties, a number of the movement's leaders were allowed to leave the Soviet Union for the West, where they continued to write of the tragic absence of freedoms in the USSR.
131. Carillo, *'Eurocommunism' and the State*, p. 157.

132. Ibid.
133. Ibid.
134. Ibid.
135. Ibid., p. 160.
136. Ibid., p. 35.
137. Ibid., p. 37, where Carillo says, 'Even Althusser who sometimes can be blamed for behaving like a jealous guardian of the scriptures ...'
138. Towards the end of 1978, the Lebanese Communist Party adopted the Eurocommunist line, probably as a result of their experience during the Lebanese civil war and the consequences of the Syrian position that was backed by the Soviet Union.
139. A chapter from the author's *My Experience with Marxism*, 3rd edn (Cairo, 1989).
140. An Egyptian Copt who was one of the leaders of Hadeto', an Egyptian communist organization. He was arrested in 1959 and remained in prison for years. After his release in 1964, he was given an important post in the leftist review, *Al-Taliaa*. In the early 1970s he moved to Paris, where he is now publishing a communist paper in Arabic.
141. A professor of Islamic history at the Faculty of Arts of Ain Shams University.
142. A professor of law at Ain Shams University.
143. A former professor of law at Cairo University who is now living in Iraq.
144. See Dr Abdel Azeem Ramadan's penetrating analysis of the reasons behind the 1967 defeat, which this leftist historian attributes to the collapse of the political regime.
145. Lenin, *The State and Revolution*, Chapter 3: 'Abolition of Parliamentarism', p. 246.
146. Ibid.
147. Ibid., p. 247.
148. Ibid., p. 246.
149. Lenin is referring to the period between the liberal bourgeois revolution of March 1917, and the Bolshevik takeover of November (October in the old Russian calendar) of the same year, when Kerensky's provisional government ruled the country for a few months after deposing Tsar Nicholas II (who was executed by the Bolsheviks in 1918).
150. Lenin, *The State and Revolution*, pp. 246–7.
151. See Engels' letter to A. Bebel, 18–28 March 1875, in *Critique of the Gotha Programme, Marx Engels Selected Works*, Volume II, p. 38.
152. Lenin, *The State and Revolution*, p. 283.
153. Ibid., p. 284.
154. Ibid., p. 290.
155. Ibid.
156. Lenin wrote this book in Zurich in 1916 and it was first published in St Petersburg (Leningrad) in April 1917.
157. Lenin later turned on Rosa Luxemburg, attacking her violently in his book on nationhood, *On the Right of Nations to Self-Determination*, which we discussed in Chapter 4 of our book, *Marxist Ideas in the Balance*.
158. Lenin, *The Proletarian Revolution and the Renegade Kautsky*, Chapter 2: 'Bourgeois and Proletarian Democracy', p. 48.
159. Ibid., pp. 51–2.
160. Mao Tse-tung, *The Role of the Chinese Communist Party in the Nationalist War*.
161. See *Excerpts from the Sayings of Chairman Mao*, 4th edn, Cairo, 1968, pp. 39–44.
162. Mao Tse-tung, *The Role of the Chinese Communist Party in the Nationalist War*.
163. Lenin, *The State and Revolution*, p. 291.
164. Ibid.
165. Ibid.

166. See the article entitled 'The Communist Party', by Rosenthal, the *Soviet Encyclopaedia*, Volume I, p. 48, published by the Novosty Press Agency, 1962.
167. For readers interested in the writings of dissident Soviet authors and in the dissident movement itself, the following works are highly recommended. Fiction: Alexander Solzhenitsyn's novels: *One Day in the Life of Ivan Denisovich*; *Cancer Ward*; *The First Circle*; *August 1914*, and *Lenin in Zurich*; his play, *The Love-Girl and the Innocent*; his short stories, *Matryona's House and Other Stories*; and an anthology of his works, *Published Stories and Poems*. Mikhail Bulgakov, *Black Ice*; Mikhail Sholokhov, *The Don Flows into the Sea* and *And Quiet Flows the Don*. For a brilliant description of life in the prisons and camps of the Soviet Union, see Anatoly Marchenko, *My Testimony*. Non-Fiction: Roy Medvedev, *Let History Judge*, considered one of the finest portrayals of the crimes of the Stalinist era, the other being Solzhenitsyn's *The Gulag Archipelago*. See also Roy Medvedev's *Socialist Democracy*; Roy and Zhores Medvedev, *A Question of Madness*; Andrei Sakharov, *Progress, Peaceful Coexistence and Intellectual Freedom* (1968). In addition to the above-mentioned books, see Solzhenitsyn's letter to Sakharov, his open letter to Nicolai Shchelokov, his interview in the *London Times* of 22 January 1974, his article, *Live without Lies* written on 12 February 1974, as well as the appeal to world public opinion signed by a group of Soviet authors on 13 February 1974, in support of Solzhenitsyn. See also the letter dated 15 January 1968, from Aleksandr Nevardovesky to Kostanti, General-Secretary of the Writers' Union, which we consider a literary masterpiece; the telegram sent by 81 members of the Soviet Writers' Union in May 1967 to the Fourth All-Russia Congress of the Union of Writers in support of Solzhenitsyn. All these texts have been compiled and translated into English by Professor Leopold Labedz of Stanford and Columbia Universities in *Solzhenitsyn: A Documentary Record*, published in a first edition in 1970 and updated several times after that to cover the period between 1970 and 1974 when Solzhenitsyn was expelled from the Soviet Union (Penguin Books, London). See also the chapter entitled 'New Techniques of Oppression' in Hedrik Smith's book, *The Russians*, as well as *Dissent in the USSR*, published by Johns Hopkins University, which includes a wonderful collection of uncensored poems by dissident poets.
168. Mao Tse-tung told a visiting American journalist that sacrificing fifty million human beings was not too high a price to pay for the proletarian revolution!
169. Marx and Engels, *Selected Works*, p. 234.
170. Lenin, *'Left-Wing' Communism, an Infantile Disorder*, Chapter 8: 'Should We Participate in Bourgeois Parliaments?', p. 395.
171. Apparently Nasser was reluctant to go to Khartoum because he thought Feisal would gloat over his defeat. According to eyewitness accounts, he was so moved when Feisal greeted him warmly and without a word of reproach, that he wept openly in gratitude and shame.
172. Konigsberg was renamed Kaliningrad in 1946 after Mikhail Ivanovich Kalinin, President of the Praesidium of the Supreme Soviet from 1938 to 1945, when he was poisoned by Stalin over some difference of opinion.
173. Leopold Lapedz, *Solzhenitsyn: A Documentary Record*, Penguin Books, London, 1970, pp. 156–7.
174. Ibid.
175. He was later expelled from the Academy.
176. Another system generated by Western democracy for the protection of individual freedoms is that of the 'Omsbudsman' in Sweden, which is described in detail by Dr Mohamed Anes Kassem Gaafar in his book of the same name.
177. The persecutions reached a peak when Sakharov received the Nobel Peace Prize in 1975.
178. A chapter from the author's book *My Experience with Marxism*, 3rd edn (Cairo, 1989).

179. Despite the fact that the Eurocommunists repudiate the theory of revolutionary violence which holds that the transition to socialism must be effected through violent revolutionary action, as Bernstein did in his book *Evolutionary Socialism* 80 years earlier and as Kautsky did in his book *Dictatorship of the Proletariat* 60 years earlier, this is not the official Marxist position, which condemns such revisionism. It is closer to Social Democracy. For the orthodox Marxist view on violence, see *Revolutionary Violence* by Engels as well as numerous works of Mao Tse-tung. For example, in *On Contradiction*, Mao says: 'Revolutions and revolutionary wars are inevitable in a class society; without them no social evolution is possible nor can the reactionary ruling classes be overthrown.' Mao also says: 'It is from the muzzles of guns that political power is born.'

180. See my critique of the dictatorship of the proletariat in *Marxist Ideas in the Balance*, 1st edn, Nasr Publishers, Fez, Morocco, 1978, pp. 79–95; 2nd edn, Dar El Maaref, Egypt, 1980, pp. 87–110; 3rd edn, International Federation of Islamic Banks Publications, 1980, pp. 75–102.

181. Karl Marx wrote that book with Engels in 1845/1846. It was first published 80 years later in the Soviet Union.

182. The comments in Volume III of *Marx and Engels, Selected Works*, published in Moscow, clearly state that socialism became a science thanks to Marx's materialist concept of history and his theory of surplus value. Marxists insist on claiming that Marx discovered the concept of historical materialism. Yet serious researches reject that claim, for the concept is as old as Aristotle; it was formulated by intellectuals such as Harrington and Madison, years before Karl Marx. The same goes for the theory of class struggle, which goes back to the French Revolution, and can be traced to the *Manifesto des Egaux* published in 1796 by Baeuf; yet Marx never referred to that book when he wrote of utopian socialists. I. Blanqui, the first to use the term 'dictatorship of the proletariat', also confirmed the theory of class struggle in 1832. Saint Simon knew the theory of class struggle, so did the German socialist Karl Braun, who wrote about it explicitly in 1844. The proper reference is *Communism*, a study written in 1927 by H. Lasky, a fervent admirer of the Russian Revolution.

183. Marx and Engels, *Selected Works*, Volume III, pp. 135–8.

184. Doctoral thesis by Marx, written in 1841–42. Doctorate, according to the German academic system at the time, was a BA.

185. Translated into Arabic by Elis Marcos (*Selections from the Early Writings of Karl Marx: 1842–1846*), Damascus Publications.

186. In a footnote to *Wages, Price and Profit*, Volume III, *Marx–Engels Selected Works*, Foreign Languages Publishing House, Moscow, 1962, p. 447.

187. It is described as 'the scientific treasure of communism', ibid., p. 317.

188. Engels, *The Role of Labour*, pp. 5–24.

189. The chapters of this book were all revised by Marx in *Capital*.

190. Karl Marx, *Wages, Prices and Profit*, p. 447.

191. Karl Marx, *Capital*, pp. 1–6.

192. Ibid., pp. 36–8.

193. Dr Ahmed Game, *Socialist Doctrines*, 1st edn, p. 243.

194. Karl Marx, *Capital*, p. 151.

195. Dr Galal Amin, *Marxism*, p. 160.

196. Sweezy published Bawerk's critique of Marx's theory of value along with Hiferding's reply and his own comments, all in one book.

197. Karl Marx, *Wages, Price and Profit*, pp. 63–4.

198. Ibid.

199. Edward Bernstein, *Evolutionary Socialism*, English edn, 1909, p. 270.

200. R. N. Carew Hunt, *The Theory and Practice of Communism*, Chapter 5, on Marxian Economy.

201. R. Meek, *Studies in the Labour Theory of Value*, Lawrence and Wishart edn, London, 1958, p. 172.
202. Indirect, or dead labour, according to Marx, is labour accumulated in the form of a machine or raw material.
203. Benefiting from training is different from the training *per se*; the former is subjective, the latter objective.
204. Engels, *Marx–Engels Selected Works*.
205. Despite the official slogans, the socialist countries could not cancel the system of inheritance. See Chapter VII of the bases of civil legislation in the USSR, which became applicable as of 1/5/1965 (translation of Dr Sarwat Anis Al Assiouti of the *Laws of Inheritance* published by Progress Publication, Moscow, 1974).
206. In the automobile industry in France, Renault is a public sector project that exists side by side with the private sector Citroën.
207. On the faculties of both Ain Shams University and the American University in Cairo, Dr Amin is one of Egypt's most prominent economists and the son of the renowned scholar Ahmed Amin.
208. Dr Galal Amin, *Marxism*, pp. 172–3.
209. Marx explains what he calls the general law of capitalist accumulation on p. 612 of *Marx–Engels Selected Works*, Volume I.
210. Hedrick Smith, *The Russians*, p. 107.
211. A chapter from *My Experience with Marxism*, 3rd edn (Cairo, 1989).
212. Abbas Al Aqad, *Communism and Mankind*, 2nd edn, Dar Al Hilal, May 1963, p. 173.
213. In his book, *Achievements in the Countryside*, 1941, Mao Tse-tung says: 'The true heroes are the masses; as for us, we often appear naive and ridiculous.'
214. See Viktor Vilatoff, *The Historical Experience of the CPSU*, which proves that without the role of Lenin the enormous tranformation in Russian history, indeed, in the history of the world, following the establishment of the first state ruled by a communist party, would not have taken place.
215. See Galal Kishk, *The Saudis*, London, 1981.
216. See 'Karl Marx', an article written by Engels in Marx's lifetime, in June 1877, and published in *Volkskalender*, an almanac which appeared in Brunswick in 1878, *Marx–Engels Selected Works*, Volume II, p. 156. See also the Preface to the German edition of the Communist Manifesto, written by Engels after Marx's death, on 28 June 1883, in which Engels notes that 'the basic thought running through the Manifesto belongs solely and exclusively to Marx'.
217. That is what Mao Tse-tung said in his book, *On Contradiction*, written in 1937: 'While recognizing that, in the general course of history material things determine spiritual things, that social conditions determine social consciousness, yet we also must admit the effect of things spiritual on things material. By so doing, we avoid mechanical materialism and firmly uphold dialectical materialism.'
218. Engels died on 5 August 1895.
219. *Marx–Engels Selected Works*, Volume II, pp. 504–5. See also Engels' letter to J. Bloch, dated 21–22 September 1980, ibid., p. 488.
220. The Marxist theory of Basis and Superstructure was subjected to a strong philosophical critique by Sartre, who described it as misleading in Chapter 1 of *Matérialisme et Révolution*, which was originally published as an essay in *Temps Modernes*.
221. See Chapter 5 of *Marxist Ideas in the Balance*.
222. We refer those who oppose the argument to *Egypt, a Military Society* by the Egyptian Marxist, Anwar Abdel Malek.
223. A chapter from *Communism and Religions*, 3rd edn (Cairo, 1980).
224. A chapter from *Communism and Religions*, 3rd edn (Cairo, 1980).

Index